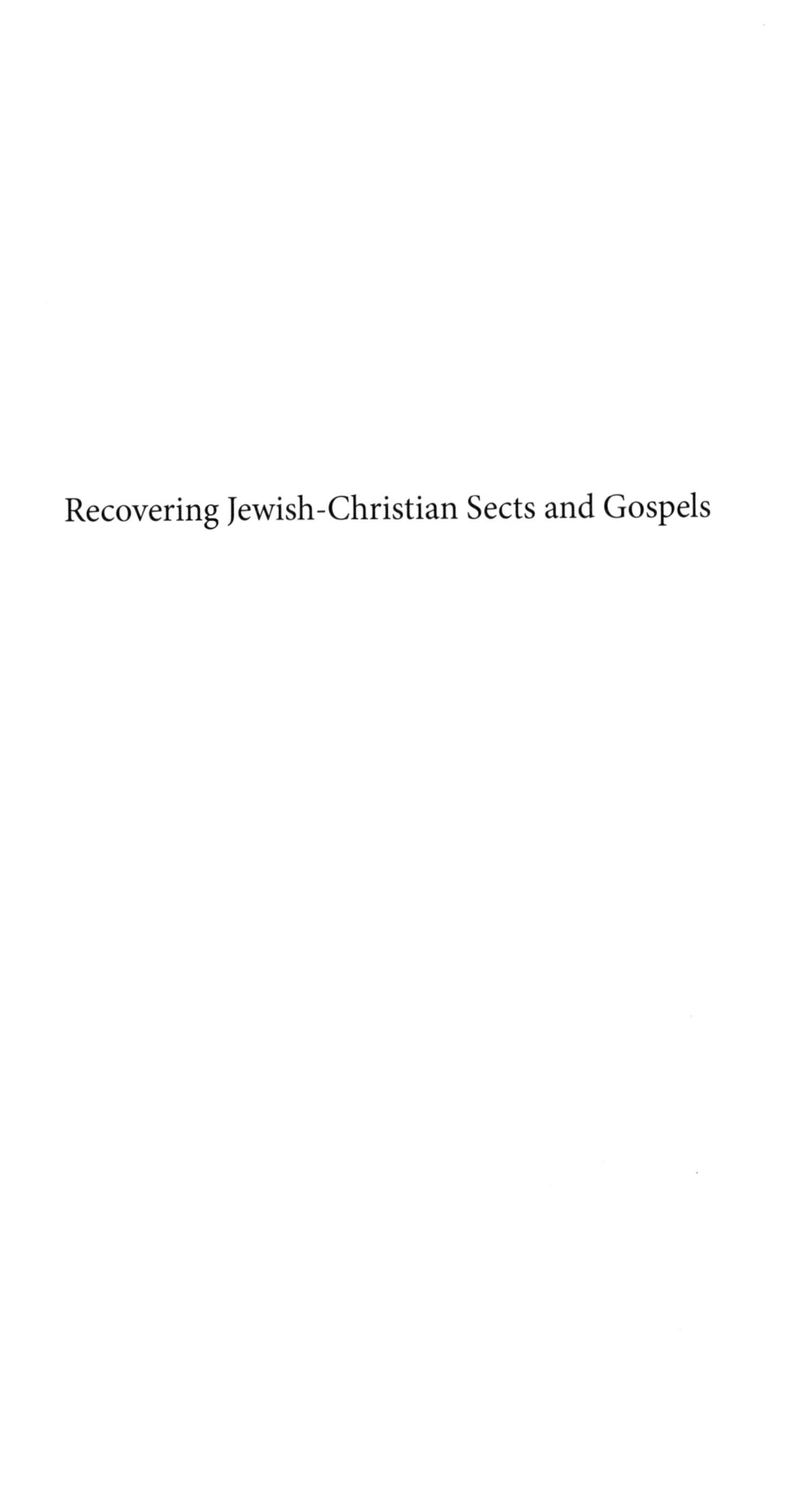

Recovering Jewish-Christian Sects and Gospels

Supplements to Vigiliae Christianae

Texts and Studies of
Early Christian Life and Language

Editors
J. den Boeft – B.D. Ehrman – J. van Oort
D.T. Runia – C. Scholten – J.C.M. van Winden

VOLUME 110

The titles published in this series are listed at brill.nl/vcs

Recovering Jewish-Christian Sects and Gospels

By
Petri Luomanen

BRILL

LEIDEN • BOSTON
2012

This book is printed on acid-free paper.

Library of Congress Cataloging-in-Publication Data

Luomanen, Petri, 1961-
  Recovering Jewish-Christian sects and gospels / by Petri Luomanen.
    p. cm. – (Supplements to Vigiliae Christianae, ISSN 0920-623X ; v. 110)
  Includes bibliographical references (p.) and indexes.
  ISBN 978-90-04-20971-8 (hardcover : alk. paper)
  1. Jewish Christians–History–Early church, ca. 30-600. I. Title.

BR195.J8L86 2012
270.1–dc23

2011036939

ISSN 0920-623X
ISBN 978 90 04 20971 8 (hardback)
ISBN 978 90 04 21743 0 (e-book)

Copyright 2012 by Koninklijke Brill NV, Leiden, The Netherlands.
Koninklijke Brill NV incorporates the imprints Brill, Global Oriental, Hotei Publishing, IDC Publishers, Martinus Nijhoff Publishers and VSP.

All rights reserved. No part of this publication may be reproduced, translated, stored in a retrieval system, or transmitted in any form or by any means, electronic, mechanical, photocopying, recording or otherwise, without prior written permission from the publisher.

Authorization to photocopy items for internal or personal use is granted by Koninklijke Brill NV provided that the appropriate fees are paid directly to The Copyright Clearance Center, 222 Rosewood Drive, Suite 910, Danvers, MA 01923, USA.
Fees are subject to change.

PRINTED BY DRUKKERIJ WILCO B.V. - AMERSFOORT, THE NETHERLANDS

CONTENTS

Preface IX

1. Introduction 1
   1.1. Early Jewish Christians and Their Gospels 1
   1.2. The Contents of the Volume 3
   1.3. How to Define Jewish Christianity: Indicators of
        Jewish-Christian Profiles... 8
   1.4. Gospel Harmonies and Harmonizing Gospels 14

2. Patristic Testimonies Reconsidered 17
   2.1. The Profiles of the Ebionites 18
      2.1.1. Irenaeus' Ebionites 18
      2.1.2. Origen's Ebionites 24
      2.1.3. Eusebius' Ebionites 29
      2.1.4. Epiphanius' Ebionites 30
      2.1.5. From Irenaeus' Ebionites to Epiphanius' Ebionites? ... 45
   2.2. The Nazarenes 49
      2.2.1. Introduction 49
      2.2.2. Who Were Called Nazarenes? 51
      2.2.3. The Profile of Epiphanius' Nazarenes 53
      2.2.4. The Profile of Jerome's Nazarenes 66
      2.2.5. Conclusion: Who Were the Nazarenes? 77

3. Jewish-Christian Gospels Recovered 83
   3.1. Farewell to the Three Gospel Hypothesis (the 3GH) 83
   3.2. Jerome's Life and Quotations from Jewish-Christian Gospels 89
      3.2.1. The Setting of the Quotations in Jerome's Biography .. 89
      3.2.2. An Illustrious Translator 100
      3.2.3. A Greek Translation? 101
      3.2.4. Jerome and the Nazarenes' Gospel Traditions 102
   3.3. A New Reconstruction of the Gospel Used by the Nazarenes 103
   3.4. Reconstructing the *Gospel of the Hebrews* 120
      3.4.1. Eusebius' Testimony: The *Gospel of the Hebrews* on
             the Fringes of Canon 120

3.4.2. A Reconstruction of the *Gospel of the Hebrews*......... 137
3.4.3. Q and the *Gospel of the Hebrews* 139

4. Passion Traditions Reinterpreted 145
    4.1. The Last Supper in the *Gospel of the Ebionites* and Luke
         (Codex Bezae)... 145
        4.1.1. Introduction 145
        4.1.2. Arguments for and against the Shorter Reading 147
        4.1.3. Reconstructing the Passion Narrative in the *Gospel of
               the Ebionites* 150
        4.1.4. The *Gospel of the Ebionites* and Luke (D, Old Latin
               and Old Syriac)................................ 155
        4.1.5. The Dating of the Shorter Reading and the *Gospel of
               the Ebionites* 157
        4.1.6. Eucharistic Tradition Preceding Luke? 159
        4.1.7. Ebionites—An Offshoot of the Hellenists? 161
    4.2. Passion Fragments in Jerome's *Commentary on Matthew* 165
    4.3. Jesus' Appearance to James the Just 168
    4.4. Conclusion: Passion Traditions in Jewish-Christian Gospels 173

5. Jewish-Christian Gospels and Syriac Gospel Traditions 175
    5.1. Three Rich Men in the *Gospel of the Hebrews* and the
         Diatessaron 175
        5.1.1. Introduction 175
        5.1.2. The Rich Man in Origen's Commentary on Matthew .. 177
        5.1.3. Comparison with Parallel Passages 178
        5.1.4. Comparison with Variant Readings and
               Diatessaronic Witnesses............................. 183
        5.1.5. The Influence of the Diatessaronic Context 187
        5.1.6. Summary and Conclusions of the Text- and Source
               Critical Analysis.................................. 190
        5.1.7. Mapping Jewish-Christian Profiles 193
        5.1.8. The Jewish-Christian Profile of Origen's Story 195
        5.1.9. Conclusion: Where Did the Men Come From? 199
    5.2. The *Gospel of Thomas* and Jewish-Christian Gospel
         Fragments 200
        5.2.1. Introduction: *Thomas* and Jewish Christians.......... 200
        5.2.2. The Provenance of the *Gospel of the Hebrews* and the
               Gospel of Thomas 202
        5.2.3. Let Him Who Seeks Continue Seeking................. 204

5.2.4. Your Brothers and Mother Are Standing Outside 206
5.2.5. Wise As Serpents 213
5.2.6. "O Man" and "He Turned To" 218
5.2.7. Jewish-Christian Gospel Fragments and the *Gospel of Thomas*: A Summary of Literary Relationships 223
5.2.8. Jesus As Wisdom Incarnate and the Spirit As Jesus' Mother 225
5.2.9. Conclusion: Common Roots in Harmonized Synoptic Tradition 231

6. Conclusion: Towards the History of Early Jewish Christianity 233
   6.1. The Ebionites and the Nazarenes 233
   6.2. Jewish-Christian Gospels 235
   6.3. Summary and Conclusion 241

Abbreviations and Appendices 245
   Abbreviations 245
   Appendix 1: The New Two Gospel Hypothesis 245
   Appendix 2: Parallel Sayings and Common Harmonizing Readings in Jewish-Christian Gospel Fragments and the *Gospel of Thomas* 253
   Appendix 3: Development and Testimonies of Jewish-Christian Gospel Traditions 255

References 257

Index of Ancient Authors and Texts 277
General Index 286
Index of Modern Authors 294

PREFACE

I launched the research on which this book is based at the end of the 1990s as my post-doctoral project at the Department of Biblical Studies of the University of Helsinki. Having published my doctoral thesis on the Gospel of Matthew, I had become intrigued by the question of the history of Jewish Christianity after the completion of the synoptic gospels. Originally, my plan was to write a book which would trace the history of Jewish Christianity from pre-synoptic times through Matthew and other New Testament material to post-synoptic apocryphal sources and references by the church fathers. Because I had wrestled with the New Testament material for my doctoral thesis for some time, I wanted get my hands on some other sources and decided to start with the analysis of the church fathers and their references.

I soon realized that the topic I had chosen was well worthy of Hans Waitz's often cited charaterization of being the most difficult which the apocryphal literature presents: "*Das Problem, um das es sich handelt, ist eines der schwierigsten der apokryphen Literatur, schwierig wegen der Dürftigkeit und Unstimmigkeit der patristischen Zeugnisse, schwierig auch wegen der sich vielfach widersprechenden Ergebnisse der wissenschaftlichen Forschung*" (Waitz 1924a, 10). Moreover, after Waitz's time, scholars had further complicated the problem by becoming more aware of the problems connected with the definition of Jewish Christianity which was not so much an issue at the beginning of the 20th century.

In the beginning, I was relatively happy with the conventional story about the Nazarenes and the Ebionites and the three gospels that were attributed to early Jewish Christians (the Three Gospel Hypothesis=the 3GH). However, a closer look at the sources started to reveal problems of the kind that had given Waitz the reason for his statement. How is it possible that a relatively late writer like Epiphanius has the most detailed knowledge of the earliest phases of the sect of the Nazarenes? How is it possible that scholars can be so sure about the Matthean character of the "Gospel of the Nazarenes" even though the fragments themselves are not so obviously Matthean? How can they be so sure that "Gnostic" materials cannot stand together with synoptic-type gospel materials, even though the *Gospel of Thomas* clearly includes both types of material? These and other observations led me to think that there are some serious problems in the conventional reconstructions and that detailed historical study is needed to resolve them.

The overall picture presented in this book emerged slowly over the course of historical-critical research. Initially, I became aware of some of the problems in the traditional Vielhauer–Strecker–Klijn reconstruction of three apocryphal Jewish-Christian gospels in late 1990s when I wrote my contribution to the Finnish article that was intended to launch a project on early Jewish Christianity at the University of Helsinki (Myllykoski & Luomanen 1999). When I presented my first critical review of the earlier research at the SBL Annual Meeting in 2001 ("What is the Gospel of the Nazoreans?"; Denver, 2001), I had not yet any clear ideas how to solve the problems I had found up to that time. The artificial nature of Epiphanius' description of the Nazarenes dawned on me two years later, in 2002, when I was preparing an article on the Nazarenes for the Finnish Journal of Theology (Luomanen 2002a). In 2005, I was preparing an enlarged version of a paper delivered at the SBL International meeting for publication (Groningen, 2004). At that point, I started to play with Jerome's references to the "Gospel of the Nazarenes" in order to see if it was possible to reconstruct a gospel used by the Nazarenes on the basis of more neutral criteria than what was applied in the 3GH. This experimenting led me to recovering the Nazarenes' collection of anti-rabbinic Matthew passages. The fact that this collection cohered with the Nazarenes' anti-rabbinic Isaiah collection convinced me that I might be on the right track. Even more so, when I realized that my attempts to reconstruct the "Gospel of the Nazarenes" had actually made a distinct gospel with that name disappear from the scene—a result that joined neatly with my earlier analysis of Epiphanius' Nazarenes. Because the reconstruction of the "Gospel of the Nazarenes" was originally treated as a problem of its own, the arguments presented were in no way dependant on my earlier analysis of Epiphanius' Nazarenes, which had shown the artificial, stereotyped character of Epiphanius' description. Because the basic ideas and arguments of this book have been developed in conference papers and articles that were originally written in view of a monograph, I have been able to make use of much of their contents, although with modifications and additions. I have listed the earlier articles used in this volume in Chapter 1.2.

Over the years, I have become indebted to several persons who have helped me with various academic and practical issues connected to this research undertaking. In the beginning, a valuable framework was

Heikki Räisänen's *Research Unit for the Formation of Early Jewish and Christian Ideology* (Centre of Excellence of the Academy of Finland) at the Department of Biblical Studies of the University of Helsinki. It provided a context for a *Project on Early Jewish Christianity* where I was able delve into problems of studying the patristic sources, together with two colleagues, Matti Myllykoski and Sakari Häkkinen. Cooperation with Matti and Sakari was most helpful in laying the grounds for my approach to the topic of this volume.

Three-year post-doctoral research funding from the Academy of Finland and an invitation from the Institute for Antiquity and Christianity, Claremont Graduate University, enabled me to spend the academic year 1999–2000 as a visiting scholar in the friendly Californian atmosphere, together with my wife Tiina and our three children Laura, Eveliina and Juhana. We all feel very grateful for the warm and helpful reception both in the academic community as well as in the neighborhood. Jon Ma. Asgeirsson, the associate director of the IAC, gave generously of his time—his last weeks in Claremont before leaving for Iceland in order to take up his chair as the Professor of New Testament Studies and Early Christianity there—helping us with the practical arrangements, including finding an appropriate house for the family of five. Our landlord, Donald Wang, and his exciting house as well as our most friendly and helpful neighbors, the Gaetes and the Sears, will always have their special place in our hearts and collective memories. Dennis MacDonald, then newly appointed director of the IAC, and Karen Jo Torjesen, the Dean of the School of Religion at CGU, were equally generous in their academic hospitality. The library of the IAC, with its "Tune room" provided an appropriate context for finalizing a Finnish translation of the Apocryphon of James and my initial studies of the patristic sources of early Jewish Christianity.

In Claremont, we were also privileged to enjoy the hospitality of James and Gesine Robinson. We discussed the relationship between the Nazarenes, the Ebionites and Q, but, for a long time, I could not fit these considerations into the picture that was emerging from my own analysis. The short chapter I have included in the present volume suggests some connections, but it is clear that the topic deserves a more elaborate analysis, to which the conclusions of this book, if accepted, provides some new starting points.

The year in Claremont also launched my cooperation with F. Stanley Jones, the director of the IAC's project *Jewish Christianity: The Pseudo-Clementines*. Stan's research on *Pseudo-Clementines* has been most helpful for my own study of the Ebionites and their gospel. Stan Jones and Matt Jackson-McCabe (also a Claremont alumnus), were among the driving forces when we started a new Jewish Christianity consultation at the SBL Annual Meeting (2005–2007; chaired by Matt), followed by a Jewish Christian/Christian Judaism section (2008–2013) that I have been co-chairing, first with Matt in 2008–2010 and with Stan from 2011 onwards. Discussion with Matt and the sessions that we have organized in the context of the SBL have greatly assisted my own research.

The late William L. Petersen was an invaluable guide through the jungles of textual criticism and Diatessaronic witnesses. Despite his severe illness, he was able to maintain his sense of humor and cheerful support for a younger scholar to the very end. I wish this volume could, at least partly, fulfill his overtly optimistic prophecy—an encouraging farewell a couple of weeks before his death—that I will have something to give to the study of Jewish Christianity.

Jörg Frey's comments on my article on Eusebius were most helpful and he has been very generous in sharing his forthcoming publications, for which I am deeply grateful. Along with this project, I have also had the privilege of cooperating with several other (originally) European colleagues, always in a congenial and supporting atmosphere: Andrew Gregory, Gerard P. Luttikhuizen, Tobias Nicklas, Pierluigi Piovanelli, Christopher Tuckett and Joseph Verheyden deserve to be mentioned—without forgetting many other European and American colleagues whose comments on my papers and articles have helped me to develop my argumentation.

The Department of Biblical Studies and the Helsinki Collegium of Advanced studies (2003–2005) at the University of Helsinki have been the most inspiring frameworks for the present project. I have been able to enjoy cooperation with several colleagues in a congenial, innovative and broadly learned context. The number of people in my "home department" who have given me useful comments and tips over the years is too great to be listed in detail here—in any case, my memory would fail if I tried. Nevertheless, some names cannot be left unmentioned since without these people, this work would probably not exist, or it would at least be much poorer. Risto Uro's contacts with Claremont and his practical advice as an experienced "Claremonter" paved my way to California and to the new contacts and networks that are vital when a post-doc starts with a new research topic. Antti Marjanen has always been a helpful colleague who has the admirable ability to plunge into a deep discussion of another persons' research topic—with the same curiosity and involvement as if it were his own. Foundations for my understanding of the overall history of the Ebionites and the Nazarenes were laid by the time I co-edited the book on second-century Christian "heretics" with Antti. The expertise of Risto and Antti, as well as of Ismo Dunderberg, in the study of Gnosticism have been most vital for my research on the relationship between Jewish-Christian gospel fragments and the *Gospel of Thomas*.

During the past few years, I have also benefited from Risto Uro's curiosity and keen interest in teamwork in a new research area that is not directly related to the present volume: a socio-cognitive approach to early Judaism and early Christianity. As a matter of fact, it will be the task of a preface to another forthcoming book to credit the people who have helped me with these new socio-cognitive explorations but I feel the need to also list some key persons in this context. The main reason for this is that although my new interest in the cognitive science of religion and social psychology have clearly delayed the completion of this volume, the cooperation within this socio-cognitive team of biblical scholars has been a source of inspiration and joy from which the present volume has also benefited. Therefore, many thanks—in addition to Risto—to Raimo Hakola, Jutta Jokiranta, Nina Pehkonen and Minna Shkul, for keeping alive the innovative atmosphere!

The very final editing of this volume has taken place alongside my visit to the University of Eastern Finland, where I have acted as the Professor of Biblical Studies for the academic year 2010–2011. Thanks to the research friendly organizing of the teaching schedule at the UEF's theological department, the last quarter of the academic year has been reserved for research which has smoothed and eased the otherwise rough and time-consuming final technical editing. Many thanks also to colleagues at the UEF, both academic and administrative, who have been most helpful in running the everyday businesses with congenial and supportive attitude.

The responsibility for revising my English was painstakingly borne by Margot Stout Whiting. The flaws, if there remain such, are only due to my negligence.

I also wish to express my gratitude to the always so friendly and professional staff at Brill: Louise Schouten for the patience with which she has followed the progress of this project and Mattie Kuiper for taking care of the correspondence and practical issues in the final stages of the editorial process. Last but not least, I wish to express my gratitude to the editors of the Supplements to the Vigiliae Christianae series, for accepting this book in the series and especially for their comments and observations that helped me to clean up the discrepancies that tend to creep in when results from several articles, written over several years, are wrapped together in one volume.

I dedicate this book to the memory of my grandparents Sulo Villiam Kauppi (1911–1988) and Helvi Maria Kauppi (1912–2008). Having been born in poor working-class homes they had opportunities only for elementary schooling but they were always supportive of the education of their children and grandchildren. I have on the wall of my study a modest painting of a tiny two-room cottage in the midst of birches and blossoming apple trees, the birth place of my grandmother. It reminds me of the fact that the ultimate poverty is not the poverty of the dispossessed but the poverty of mind and spirit.

In Nummi-Pusula, on the traditional Midsummer's Eve, June 23, 2011—the 77th anniversary of Sulo's and Helvi's engagement day.

Petri Luomanen

CHAPTER ONE

INTRODUCTION

1.1. Early Jewish Christians and Their Gospels

The Ebionites' and the Nazarenes' possible relation to the early Jerusalem community has often been debated. Over the history of research, both have been assessed as genuine successors of the early Jerusalem community. Ferdinand Christian Baur argued that the Ebionites were not originally a heretical sect but successors of the very first Jewish Christians in Jerusalem. The Nazarenes, for their part, represented a later phase of Jewish Christianity, which had developed from its strictly anti-Pauline stance to a more lenient attitude towards the gentiles.[1] Among contemporary scholars, Gerd Lüdemann[2] and Michael D. Goulder[3] have supported similar views. On the other hand, Albrecht Ritschl[4] already argued, against Baur, that strict Jewish Christianity with its anti-Paulinism can not be considered the dominant current in first-century Christianity. In his view, the Nazarenes, who accepted the apostle Paul, were the successors of the early Jerusalem community. Ray A. Pritz[5] has presented a similar interpretation.[6] According to him, the history of the Nazarenes can be traced back to the early Jerusalem community, while the Ebionites came out of a split among the Nazarene ranks around the turn of the first century.

Although the church fathers referred to gospels that were used by the Ebionites and the Nazarenes, no manuscripts have survived that could be identified with these references. This is also the case with the *Gospel of the Hebrews* from which the church fathers also present some quotations. The *Gospel of the Hebrews* is the only explicit title that appears in the ancient

---

[1] Baur 1966 (1860), 174, 174 n. 1.
[2] Lüdemann 1996, 52–56.
[3] Goulder 1994, 107–113.
[4] Ritschl 1857, 152–154.
[5] Pritz 1988, 28, 82, 108–110.
[6] Pritz is followed by Mimouni 1998, 82–86; Blanchetière 2001, 145, 183, 238–239, 521; Bauckham 2003, 162.

sources. Although the evidence about early Jewish-Christian gospels is fragmentary, it is often regarded important because of its possible connections to the early Jesus movement. Therefore, modern scholars have spent both time and energy in order to recover these lost gospels from the church fathers' quotations and references.

The publication of the third edition of Edgar Hennecke's Neutestamentliche Apocrypha in 1959 (edited by Wilhelm Schneemelcher)[7] and its English translation in 1963 more or less created a consensus in the German and English-speaking scholarly world about the number and character of the long lost early Jewish-Christian gospels. Several textbooks and general articles on apocryphal gospels have repeated the view according to which there were originally three Jewish-Christian gospels: the *Gospel of the Hebrews*, the *Gospel of the Ebionites* and the "Gospel of the Nazarenes."[8] In the following, I shall call this the Three Gospel Hypothesis (the 3GH). An alternative reconstruction, favored mainly by some French scholars, has counted two gospels: the *Gospel of the Ebionites* and the *Gospel of the Hebrews/Nazarenes*.[9]

During the past decade, more and more critical voices—including mine—have been raised against different aspects of the threefold distinction that was presented in the third edition of Hennecke's collection by Philipp Vielhauer and Georg Strecker. Scholars who have become more aware of the weaknesses of the 3GH, are now either refraining from making any firm conclusions about the number and contents of the gospels—organizing their presentation according to the available sources, the church fathers[10]—or making adjustments to the threefold[11] or to the twofold distinction.

---

[7] Hennecke & Schneemelcher 1959³ (1904¹).

[8] Vielhauer & Strecker 1991² (1963¹). A.F.J. Klijn (Klijn 1992) also argues for three Jewish-Christian gospels. In the first edition of Hennecke's collection, A. Meyer still assumed there were only two Jewish-Christian Gospels. Foundations for the distinction of three gospels were laid in Hennecke's second edition by H. Waitz, and the theory was developed further in the third edition by Vielhauer and Strecker. See, Meyer 1904b; 1904a; Waitz 1924a; 1924b; 1924c; 1924d.

[9] For instance, Mimouni 1998, 209–211, 215–216. Some scholars have also argued for only one Jewish-Christian gospel. W.L. Petersen has drawn attention to Diatessaronic readings in many of the quotations suggesting that all the fragments could as well be rooted in one and the same gospel that is somehow related to Tatian's *Diatessaron*. See, for instance, Petersen 1994, 29–31, 39–41; Only one Jewish-Christian gospel is also presupposed by Pritz 1988, 83–86; Schmidt 1998.

[10] Thus, for instance, Evans 2007, 245–246.

[11] J. Frey, who is writing on Jewish-Christian Gospels in the "new Hennecke" (= Markschies & Schröter Forthcoming) is critical of the close connection that has been

In this volume, I shall argue for a theory that assumes only two Jewish-Christian gospels: The *Gospel of the Hebrews* and the *Gospel of the Ebionites*. Because this theory also assumes a specific Nazarene collection of passages from the Gospel of Matthew, it differs from the earlier theories that have assumed only two Jewish-Christian gospels. Therefore, I shall call it the New Two Gospel Hypothesis (N2GH). Consequently, because I have not found evidence of the existence of the "Gospel of the Nazarenes," the name appears in quotation marks in this volume.

1.2. The Contents of the Volume

This volume focuses on *early* Jewish Christians and their gospels. Therefore, it mainly deals with evidence from the second to the beginning of the fifth century, the last patristic sources being Epiphanius' and Jerome's writings.[12] The evidence deals with the Nazarenes and the Ebionites, the gospels they used, and the *Gospel of the Hebrews*. I concur with A.F.J. Klijn who thinks that, after Jerome, Greek and Latin writers usually depend on earlier sources.[13] In some chapters, I also discuss canonical material but use it mainly as a point of comparison. This does not imply that I find the discussion of Jewish Christianity within the New Testament somehow

---

assumed between the Gospel of Matthew and the "Gospel of the Nazarenes." He is also revising Vielhauer and Strecker's reconstruction by bracketing the so-called "To Ioudaikon" fragments from the "Gospel of the Nazarenes." See, Frey 2003a.

[12] In addition to patristic references, there are two later translations of Matthew's gospel that have sometimes been presented as important sources of early Jewish-Christian gospel traditions: Shem Tob's Hebrew Matthew and the Coptic text of Matthew in the Schøyen Collection. G. Howard (Howard 1995; the first edition 1987), published the text and translation of Shem Tob's Matthew suggesting an early date for the text. Howard's interpretation was opposed—convincingly, in my view—by W.L. Petersen (Petersen 1989; 1998). Petersen argues for a later date of the text of the Hebrew Matthew, showing its connections to Diatessaronic readings and Old Latin translations. Another possible source for Shem Tob's Diatessaronic readings is a Catalan version of Matthew. Thus, Niclós 1999, Joosten 2002, 73–96, 80 n. 31. H.M. Schenke published the Coptic text of Matthew (Schenke 2001). He tries to show the primitive character of the version, suggesting that both the Coptic Matthew and the canonical Matthew must depend on an earlier Hebrew version of Matthew which is also behind the Jewish-Christian gospels. Schenke clearly overestimates the value of the Coptic version as testifying to an earlier version of the Gospel of Matthew. Nevertheless, the study of the Coptic Matthew is still in its infancy and more detailed, text-critical research is needed. For an overview and further bibliography of Shem Tob's Matthew and the Coptic Matthew in the Schøyen Collection, see Evans 2007, 267–276.

[13] Klijn 1992, 20.

irrelevant for the study of early Jewish Christianity. On the contrary, the New Testament is our best source for the earliest Jewish Christianity. However, during the past decades, there has been an extensive re-evaluation of the Jewish and Jewish-Christian character of most of the New Testament writings and I see no reason to recapitulate this discussion in this volume.[14] Instead, my intention is to update the discussion of the non-canonical sources for the earliest Jewish Christianity since this has not received so much attention.

My goal is twofold. On the one hand, my intention is to provide a critical assessment of the hypothesis—often presented by those who have focused on non-canonical sources of Jewish Christianity—that the fragments of Jewish-Christian gospels contain old traditions even dating back to pre-synoptic times. On the other hand, the goal is to see how traditions about Jewish Christians developed and how Jewish Christians themselves developed their traditions after the completion of the writings that are now contained in the canonical New Testament.

Although one of the main intentions of Chapter 2 is to discuss the Jewish-Christian profile of the Ebionites and the Nazarenes from the second century onwards, it will become clear in the course of the discussion that I find the Ebionites better candidates for being the successors of the Jerusalem community than the Nazarenes. In fact, I show in Chapter 2 that the distinctive sect of the Nazarenes was Epiphanius' own invention, a stereotyped picture of the earliest form of the Jewish-Christian heresy, which he developed on the basis of the literary sources available to him: Acts of the Apostles and Eusebius' *Ecclesiastical History*. Jerome also speaks of the Nazarenes but his references are best understood as reflecting the fact that "Nazarenes" was a common name for Christians in the Syriac language. Because Epiphanius' description of the Ebionites is closely tied with the Pseudo-Clementine sources and a religious movement known as the Elchasites, Chapter 2 also includes a short discussion of these movements and their relation to the Ebionites.

In Chapter 3, I argue for a theory that assumes only two Jewish-Christian apocryphal gospels: the *Gospel of the Ebionites* and the *Gospel of the Hebrews*. However, the theory deviates from the previous hypotheses that have assumed only two gospels because, in my view, the evidence indicates that, in addition to two actual gospels, there was also

---

[14] My own contribution to this discussion has taken place especially within Matthean studies. See Luomanen 1998; Luomanen 2002b.

a collection of anti-rabbinic testimonies that Jerome acquired from the Nazarenes. This collection was prepared by making minor adjustments to the wording of an Aramaic translation of the canonical Matthew.[15] Consequently, in this reconstruction, the contents and the character of the *Gospel of the Hebrews* becomes different from what has been previously assumed in the twofold or in the threefold distinction. Five anti-rabbinic passages, transmitted by Jerome, are excluded from the apocryphal Jewish-Christian gospels, but all the rest—excluding the ones that are presented by Epiphanius and commonly attributed to the *Gospel of the Ebionites*—are assumed to be from the *Gospel of the Hebrews*. According to the new reconstruction, the *Gospel of the Hebrews* would have included passages that attest to the influence of Wisdom speculations combined with features familiar from the synoptic gospels. Since these features also characterize Q, Chapter 3 includes a discussion of Q's possible connections with Jewish-Christian gospel fragments.

Chapter 4 deals with passion and resurrection stories, a theme that has not received much attention in the study of Jewish-Christian gospels. The evidence is fragmentary but upon closer examination it reveals some interesting features characteristic of early Jewish-Christian interpretations of Jesus' death and resurrection.

Chapter 5 deals with two topics that have been central to the discussion about early Jewish-Christian gospel traditions: the fragments' relation to the *Diatessaron* and to the *Gospel of Thomas*. The analysis shows, in contrast to A.F.J. Klijn's interpretation, that the passage in the Latin translation of Origen's Matthew commentary is post-synoptic. Second, a comparison with Old Syriac translations shows a connection to Diatessaronic traditions but locates the points of contact to a pre-Diatessaronic level. April de Conick has revived Gilles Quispel's old hypothesis about a Jewish-Christian gospel as a kernel of traditions evolving in the *Gospel of Thomas*. My analysis shows some points of contact between Jewish-Christian fragments and the *Gospel of Thomas* but the common denominators are all too meager to justify an assumption about a Jewish-Christian kernel of the *Gospel of Thomas*. Furthermore, the most natural explanation for the common features is that the Jewish-Christian gospel fragments and the *Gospel of Thomas* both draw on related, post-synoptic, harmonizing gospel traditions.

---

[15] In the Three Gospel Hypothesis, these passages are usually attributed to the "Gospel of the Nazarenes."

Although the volume as a whole creates a new overall picture of the early Jewish Christians and their gospels, it is still possible to take the four main sections of the book—Chapters 2, 3, 4 and 5—as independent studies. One does not have to accept my characterization of the Ebionites and the Nazarenes in Chapter 2 in order to accept the new reconstruction of the *Gospel of the Hebrews* in Chapter 3—or vice versa. Furthermore, the two thematic chapters, Chapters 4 and 5, are written so that their basic arguments do not necessarily presuppose the reconstructions presented in the earlier chapters, even though I have updated these sections in order to show how they fit the overall theory.

The contents of the present volume link up with my earlier articles and conference papers as follows. The study of *indicators of early Jewish Christianity*, described in Chapter 1.3, has been introduced in two earlier articles in 2003 and 2007: "Where Did Another Rich Man Come From?: The Jewish-Christian Profile of the Story About a Rich Man in the 'Gospel of the Hebrews' (Origen, Comm. in Matth. 15.14)." *Vigiliae Christianae* 57, 243–275; and "Ebionites and Nazarenes." *Jewish Christianity Reconsidered: Rethinking Ancient Groups and Texts.* Ed. Matt Jackson-McCabe. Minneapolis, Minn.: Fortress Press, 81–118. However, the first version of the approach was already drafted in 1999, in a Finnish article I wrote jointly with Matti Myllykoski: "Varhaisen juutalaiskristillisyyden jäljillä." *Teologinen Aikakauskirja* ("On the Trail of Early Jewish Christianity"; *Finnish Journal of Theology*) 104, 327–348.

Chapters 2.1 and 2.2 combine and elaborate two earlier articles: the article that was published in the volume edited by Matt Jackson-McCabe (see above) and "Nazarenes." *A Companion to Second-Century Christian "Heretics".* Ed. Antti Marjanen & Petri Luomanen. Supplements to Vigiliae Christianae 76. Leiden: Brill, 279–314.

Chapter 3.4.1 is an elaboration of "On the Fringes of Canon: Eusebius' View of the 'Gospel of the Hebrews.'" *The Formation of the Early Church.* Ed. Jostein Ådna. Wissenschaftliche Untersuchungen zum Neuen Testament 183. Tübingen: Mohr Siebeck, 265–281. Other parts of Chapter 3 combine arguments presented in several earlier articles and also include some previously unpublished sections.

Chapter 4.1 is based on "Sacrifices Abolished: The Last Supper in Luke (Codex Bezae) and in the *Gospel of the Ebionites.*" *Lux Humana, Lux Aeterna: Essays on Biblical and Related Themes in Honour of Lars Aejmelaeus.* Ed. Antti Mustakallio in collaboration with Heikki Leppä and Heikki Räisänen. Publications of Finnish Exegetical Society 89. Helsinki/Göttingen: Finnish Exegetical Society/Vandenhoeck &

Ruprecht, 186–208. Chapter 4.3 makes use of a section in "Passion and Resurrection Traditions in Early Jewish-Christian Gospels." *Gelitten, Gestorben, Auferstanden: Passions- und Ostertraditionen im antiken Christentum*. Ed. Tobias Nicklas, et al. Wissenschaftliche Untersuchungen zum Neuen Testament II/273. Tübingen: Mohr Siebeck, 187–208.

Chapter 5.1 also uses the article published in *Vigiliae Christianae* 57 (see above), and Chapter 5.2 is an elaborated version of "'Let Him Who Seeks Continue Seeking': The Relationship Between Jewish-Christian Gospels and the Gospel of Thomas." *Thomasine Traditions in Antiquity: The Social and Cultural World of the Gospel of Thomas*. Ed. Jon Ma. Asgeirsson, et al. Nag Hammadi and Manichean Studies 59. Leiden: Brill, 119–153.

Over the years, I have criticized the 3GH on several issues but I have not wanted to burden the reader of this volume by repeating the same arguments all over again. Therefore, the main arguments against the 3GH are presented in Chapter 3.1, and corresponding sections have been removed from the other sections. The same holds true as regards other recurring themes and overlapping sections that had to be presented in the individual articles for the sake of the argument but need not be repeated here. Earlier articles also left some questions undecided but I have now revised these sections in the light of the overall theory that is presented in this volume.

Chapters 3.2 and 3.3.3 draw on previously unpublished papers that were presented at the SBL Annual Meetings: "What is the Gospel of the Nazoreans?" (Denver, 2001), and "Q and other Jewish-Christian Gospels." (Boston, 2008).

Finally, the overall picture of the development of the Jewish-Christian gospel traditions and their relation to the quotations presented by the church fathers is presented in full for the first time at the conclusion of this volume (with the Appendix 3).

It would be foolhardy to assume that one can provide the last word on early Jewish-Christian gospels. The evidence available is simply too fragmentary to allow that. Nonetheless, I dare to suggest that this volume succeeds in showing some critical flaws in earlier research. It also presents some observations that shed new light on the riddle of early Jewish Christians and their gospels and perhaps even offers something to think about for those who have found their interest in the study of the *Diatessaron* or the *Gospel of Thomas*.

1.3. How to Define Jewish Christianity: Indicators of Jewish-Christian Profiles

The problematic nature of the term "Jewish Christianity" is well known in present scholarship but no consensus has emerged on how to deal with it.[16] Some scholars have questioned the generalized use of the term as obscuring historical realities[17] or considered the term useless because scholars have applied it in so many ways.[18] Many have experimented with different variations of the term, such as Jewish Christianity (with and without a hyphen), Judaeo-Christianity, Judaic Christianity, Judaistic Christianity, Christian Judaism, Hebrew Christianity, etc., in order to make distinctions between relevant subcategories of the phenomenon.[19]

An overview of the latest attempts to define the term allows only one conclusion: There is no generally accepted and accurately definable meaning for the term "Jewish-Christianity" (or for all its variations as cited above). Need there be?[20]

During the past decades scholars have become increasingly aware of the multifaceted character of both Judaism and Christianity during the first centuries CE. In scholarly discourse, this is often indicated by the plurals "Christianities" and "Judaisms." Consequently, it is likely that there was not just one Jewish Christianity but *several Jewish Christianities*. Acknowledging this possibility, I have not tried to give any narrow, conclusive definition to the term "Jewish Christianity" in this volume. Rather, I approach Jewish Christianity from an analytical point of view, looking for *indicators of Jewish Christian profiles*.[21] The main idea

---

[16] The problems connected with defining Jewish Christianity have been dealt by Strecker 1988; Kraft 1972, 82–92; Klijn 1974, 419–431; Simon 1975, 53–76; Malina 1976, 46–57; Riegel 1978, 410–415; Murray 1974, 303–310; Murray 1982, 194–208; Brown 1983, 74–79; Taylor 1990, 313–334; Visotzky 1995, 129–149. Recent overviews of the discussion are provided by Jackson-McCabe 2007 and Paget 2007.

[17] Thus, Taylor 1990, 313–334.

[18] Paget 2007, 50–52.

[19] For distinctive terms see, Malina 1976, 46–57; Riegel 1978, 410–415; Murray 1974, 303–310; Murray 1982, 194–208; Brown 1983, 74–79.

[20] The problem does not concern only the study of Jewish Christianity. The concept of Gnosticism has become equally problematic, especially after Michael Williams' (Williams 1995) critique. A good overview of the discussion and a reasonable definition is provided by Marjanen 2005a; 2008. For the discussion on Valentinians, see Dunderberg 2008, 14–31.

[21] I have used the approach in a number of earlier articles: Luomanen 2003, 265–269; Luomanen 2007a; Luomanen 2010. Recently, it has been cited approvingly by Verheyden 2008, 127–128.

of this approach is to list and analyze the "Jewish" and "Christian" components of a particular text or a community, paying special attention to the question of how its conceptions and practices create, maintain and cross boundaries between insiders and outsiders.

Thus, a reader who wishes to find a list of necessary and sufficient traits that would constitute the category of Jewish Christianity will be disappointed when reading the following pages. No such definition will be provided. Instead, the basic tenet of the approach is the same as Jonathan Z. Smith's "self-consciously *polythetic* mode of classification" which Matt Jackson-McCabe suggests as a good starting point for the study of Jewish Christianity (or Christian Judaism). Jackson-McCabe, however, only presents the general idea of polythetic classification but does not proceed to discuss the specific "array of traits" that would constitute the basis of classification.[22] In this respect, the analysis of indicators goes further. The analysis of indicators is also compatible with the principles of classification that Daniel Boyarin has brought from linguistic and cultural studies. These approaches imagine members of classes as points on a continuum, not as defined through one single definitive trait.[23]

In my view, both Smith and Boyarin have correctly noticed that the classic Aristotelian idea about classification on the basis of sufficient and necessary traits is problematic for historians whose data seldom meet the criteria of pure categories. The idea about categorization through fixed definitive traits is also incompatible with the way the human brain works. Therefore, it fails to capture social categorizations from the emic point of view. In the human mind, categories are formed through exemplars and prototypes, for which there are separate but parallel running cognitive systems in the brain. Our brains continuously abstract prototypes from the available exemplars.[24] This results in flexibility and continuously

---

[22] Cf. Jackson-McCabe 2007, 36–37.

[23] Boyarin 2003, 78–79, 83–84.

[24] Ground-breaking experiments in this area were conducted by Eleanor Rosch (Rosch 1975). Social psychologists and cognitive scientists have disputed the role of prototypes and their relation to exemplars in (social) categorizations. Some have argued for prototypes as picture-like images of ideal category members (for instance, Brewer 1988) but self-categorization theorists like Turner and his colleagues (Oakes, et al. 1998, 76) have emphasized (drawing on Medin 1989) the dynamic character of prototypes as contextual variables. They also prefer to speak about prototypicality instead of fixed prototypes. For a more detailed discussion, see Luomanen 2007b, 210–215, 217–224, esp. 223–224.

revised categories which are necessary in changing social situations. However, these categorizations cannot be captured through the analysis of necessary and sufficient traits. Thus, it follows that an approach which allows degrees of "Jewishness" and degrees of "Christianness" and which focuses on several aspects that are determinative in social relations—such as ideology, practice, identity and group formation—is likely to do better justice to ancient Jewish Christian groups than the attempts to find one clear definition or a set of definitions for Jewish Christianity.

A number of Jewish and Christian scholars have, during the past decades, emphasized that the parting of ways between Judaism and Christianity took much longer than was assumed earlier and that we can start speaking of two separate religions only after the Constantine turn. A notable proponent of this view, which can be termed as "ways that never parted"-paradigm, has been Daniel Boyarin.[25] I agree with this overall characterization although it is also clear that the ways started to separate much earlier locally. I gladly admit that the concept of Jewish Christianity is anachronistic. It does not appear in ancient sources but I think that it still provides the best starting point for historical analysis. It is useful because it directs attention to the way our modern categories "Judaism" and "Christianity" overlapped in some ancient communities.

The following list of *indicators of Jewish Christianity* includes the most common meanings given to the term "Jewish Christianity." Instead of calling these subcategories as competing "definitions," I have called them "indicators." The term "indicator" acknowledges the value of different "definitions" as appropriate viewpoints in the discussion about Jewish Christianity but keeps reminding that none of them can be taken as the definitive characterization of Jewish Christianity or conclusive proof of the Jewish Christianity of a document or a group. In each case, the type of Jewish Christianity under examination can only be determined in a critical discussion that brings together several of these indicators *forming a Jewish-Christian profile* of a text or a group.

The study of the indicators of Jewish Christianity concentrates on the following questions:

---

[25] Boyarin 1999, 2004. This position is emphatically argued for in a collection of articles edited by Adam Becker and Annette Yoshiko Reed (Becker & Reed 2007; Mohr Siebeck edition in 2003). See also Skarsaune 2007, 747–753.

1. *Are characteristically Jewish practices such as (Jewish) circumcision, the Sabbath and purity laws observed?*
Often these indicators are, together with the second indicator, considered as the most clear evidence of Jewishness.[26]

2. *Are characteristically Jewish ideas such as Yahweh as the only God, the temple as Yahweh's abode, or the Torah, maintained?*

3. *What is the pedigree of the group/person? Jewish or not?*
This indicator of Jewish Christianity can be characterized as the most "natural." At the same time, it is the least revealing since there were contradictory practices and ideas present among Christians of Jewish descendant. Nevertheless, in some cases, knowledge about people's kin, the frame of their primary socialization, may help to understand some aspects of behavior and thinking. For instance, in the light of the first two indicators, Paul hardly meets the standards of a Jewish Christian but the fact that he was a Jew by birth helps to understand why he got tangled with the *theological* problem of the law in the first place and why, although he *practiced* a law-free mission to the gentiles he nevertheless wanted to pay tribute to "the poor" in the law observant Jerusalem community.

4. *What is the role of Jesus in the worship and ideology of the community? Is Jesus considered as a Jewish prophet or is he more a divine being, worshipped as Kyrios ("Lord"), an equal to God?*
The fourth indicator turns the focus on the "Christian" part of Jewish Christianity. Together with the first two indicators, this forms the core of a classic profile of Jewish Christianity as it is determined by Strecker, for instance.[27]

5. *Is baptism in the name of Jesus (or the triune God) an entrance rite to the community?*
This indicator turns attention to the point where daily purifications and baptisms known from many Jewish groups are replaced or

---

[26] Taylor 1990, 314: "For it [Jewish-Christianity] to have any real meaning, the term must refer not only to ethnic Jews but those who, with their Gentile converts, upheld the praxis of Judaism." Strecker 1988, 311: "Anderseits hält das Judenchristentum an der überkommenen jüdischen Struktur von Theologie und Lebenshaltung; insbesondere praktiziert es die Forderungen des Gesetzes Moses mit seinen wesentlichen, auch ritualgesetzlichen Weisungen bis hin zu Beschneidung."

[27] See, Strecker 1988, 311.

complemented with a once-and-for-all rite that marks a person's transition into a Christian community.[28] In *Pseudo-Clementines*, Peter bathes before eating or prayer (*Hom.* 10.1; 11.1; *Rec.* 4.3; 8.1). This would well fit in with Judaism but marks him off as a special kind of Christian. However, a separate baptism is also known. It replaces the sacrifices (*Rec.* 1.32) and is necessary before a person is pure enough to eat with other Christians (*Rec.* 2.72; *Hom.* 9.26–27; 13.4–12).

6. *To what extent are these or other issues important for inter- or intra-group relations? What roles do they play in defining the borders and identity of the group in question?*

A discussion of the above *indicators* will yield a *Jewish-Christian profile* which will show to what extent a group has characteristics which are today associated either with Judaism or Christianity. The above list is not an exhaustive collection of the questions that may help to sketch a Jewish-Christian profile of a community. Obviously, subcategories could be added to every indicator and a number of other indicators might be detected as well. However, in my view, the above list contains the core of the questions that deserve to be discussed before phenomena are labeled Jewish Christian.

The last point in the list also enables one to make a distinction between simple Jewish-Christian inclinations, which might characterize several Jewish and Christian communities, and independent Jewish-Christian movements that stick so devoutly to some of their own border-marking practices and ideas that they become socially distinguishable from other Jewish and Christian movements. These questions that tap into the border-marking of communities are particularly significant in the case of the Ebionites and Nazarenes, who are described as distinct groups by the church fathers, Epiphanius in particular.

---

[28] In rabbinic Judaism, circumcision, baptism and sacrifices were requirements set for proselytes. It is a matter of contention whether baptism was understood as an initiation rite in the Second Temple period or only later on. In any case, "Christian" baptism differs from the rabbinic one in two respects. First, rabbinic sources do not indicate that immersion—which was closely connected with the idea of washing away the impure gentile life—was practiced in someone's name. Second, rabbinic baptism supplemented, but did not replace, circumcision and commitment to the Torah as the real "indicators" of one's conversion. The earliest description of a rabbinic conversion ceremony is to be found in *b. Yebam.* 47a–b. For the analysis of this passage (and a later description in *Gerim* 1:1), see Cohen 1999, 198–238.

Overall, the study of indicators of Jewish-Christian profiles is an analytical approach where the "profile," the summary of "Jewish" and "Christian" components, is the main thing. The terms that are used to characterize this profile are secondary. In the following, I occasionally use various terms—general terms such as "Christian Jews" (emphasizing the "Jewish" core to which "Christian" components are added) or "Jewish Christians" (emphasizing the "Christian" core to which "Jewish" components are added), or more exact terms like "Samaritan-Elchasite Christians," etc.—in order to characterize the overall profile which is being discussed. Notably, these terms are of secondary importance; other terms could be used as well—as long as there is agreement on the actual *Jewish-Christian profile*.

Indicators of Jewish-Christian Gospels?
Andrew Gregory has questioned whether it is justified to speak of *Jewish-Christian gospels* as a category that is somehow set apart from other canonical and apocryphal gospels.[29] Given our meager knowledge about the complete Jewish-Christian gospels, Gregory's point is well taken; as long as we do not have entire gospels available, it is hazardous to characterize the gospels *per se* as Jewish Christian. It might, indeed, be more preferable to speak of apocryphal—these gospels are truly apocryphal!—gospels used by early Jewish Christians. This would leave open the precise nature of the gospels. It is also problematic that the Jewish-Christian character of the *Gospel of the Ebionites* and the *Gospel of the Hebrews* and/or the "Gospel of the Nazarenes" is usually taken more or less as granted. In my opinion, this has often led into eisegesis as regards the social setting of the Jewish Christian gospels: "Jewish" and "Christian" traits are selectively picked from the texts to line up with a scholar's overall theory of the history of Jewish Christianity.[30]

---

[29] Cf. Gregory 2006.

[30] In addition to Klijn's reconstruction of the social setting of the Rich Man's Question in Origen's commentary on Matthew (see below, Chapter 5.1), I provide two other examples that demonstrate how this has happened in the case of Origen's passage. Resch, who thought that the "Gospel of the Nazarenes" and the *Gospel of the Ebionites* were later editions of the *Gospel of the Hebrews* (Resch 1906, 364), assumed that the miserable conditions of the Jews in the quotation (which he thought was from the *Gospel of the Hebrews*) suggest that it originated among Jewish refugees in eastern Jordan and southern parts of Syria after the destruction of Jerusalem (Resch 1906, 218). Handmann—for whom the *Gospel of the Hebrews* (which had nothing to do with Epiphanius' "mutilated" *Gospel of the Ebionites*) was different from the Hebrew original of Matthew but was equal to it as regards age and importance—explained that the story about the rich man in the

14 CHAPTER ONE

The study of indicators of Jewish Christianity also helps to deal with the Jewish-Christian gospel fragments in a more analytical and nuanced manner. Although Gregory's points are healthy reminders of how little we actually know about these gospels, his criterion of what count as Jewish-Christian texts—the ones that deal with law observance—appears quite rigorous and not sensitive enough to the variety of ways Judaism essentially affected the identities of Christ believers during the first centuries CE[31] Although law observance was the bone of contention in many cases, in some other circumstances, other *indicators of Judaism* may have stamped the identities and border-marking of the Christ believers, also leaving their mark on the gospels that were used by them to such a degree that it is justified to speak of Jewish Christians transmitting and reinterpreting *their own* gospel traditions.

In the following chapters, the discussion about the Nazarenes anti-rabbinic collection—which seems to have culminated in Jesus' passion—suitably illustrates this point. Although these pro-Pauline Christians were probably not conservative in their interpretation of the law, there were still strong Jewish components in their religious profile. Whether these were strong enough to grant them—or their version of Matthew's gospel—the label of Jewish Christian will be discussed in more detail below (Chapter 3.3).

1.4. Gospel Harmonies and Harmonizing Gospels

In this work, I have used the term *harmonizing* (gospel) in a broad sense. It simply refers to the fact that readings, phrases or passages that were originally in different gospels have come together in the passage (or gospel) under consideration. Thus, when using the term "harmonizing," I have not made any distinction whether the harmonizing aims at creating one narrative out of two or more earlier versions or whether it is simply a question about some phrases jumping from one passage to another. This is mostly because of the fragmentary nature of the evidence. In many cases, we do not have the whole gospel passages available which makes it difficult to judge whether it is a question about a minor mixture of

---

Gospel of the Hebrews was clearly earlier and more authentic because it was still free from Jewish legalism and a detailed listing of individual commandments (cf. the synoptic versions of the story) and concentrated only on the commandment of love, exactly the way Christ himself must have taught (Handmann 1888, 45, 89–92, 141).

[31] Gregory 2006, 390.

phrases or a case of a more profound reediting which seeks to harmonize entire stories with each other. Another reason for this generalized use of the term "harmonizing" is that my central concern is to determine whether a certain passage precedes or follows the synoptic gospels. For this purpose, it is not necessary to create very detailed taxonomies for the ways different traditions become mixed. It suffices to show that a new composition includes a mixture of smaller or larger elements that originally belonged to different gospels.

However, when I use the term *gospel harmony*, I refer to a work which programmatically seeks to conflate parallel stories with each other. In the *Gospel of the Ebionites*, there are traces of gospel harmony but the best example of a gospel harmony is Tatian's *Diatessaron*. Nevertheless, most of the cases to be discussed in the following fall into the broad category of harmonizing readings or passages.

CHAPTER TWO

PATRISTIC TESTIMONIES RECONSIDERED

Early Christian heresiologists painted stereotyped pictures of the Ebionites and the Nazarenes as Christians who erroneously followed Jewish laws and customs. Therefore, these two groups have frequently served as the best examples of ancient Jewish Christianity.

The Ebionites and the Nazarenes are known only from the writings of the church fathers who present short summaries of their teachings and quotations from their writings, usually in order to confute what they considered to be heretical ideas. The Ebionites appear for the first time in Irenaeus' *Adversus haereses*, written around 180 CE In order to find the first description of the "heresy" of the Nazarenes, we must turn to a work authored some two hundred years later, Epiphanius' *Panarion* (ca. 386 CE). The *Panarion* also contains the richest ancient description of the Ebionites. Because Epiphanius was writing at the end of the fourth century, he was able to use all the information about the Ebionites collected by his predecessors (Irenaeus, Hippolytus, Tertullian, Pseudo-Tertullian, Origen and Eusebius), which he supplemented with many details obtained from his contemporaries.

My treatment of the Ebionites in this chapter will focus especially on Irenaeus and Epiphanius since these two provide the most important information about the Ebionites. The church fathers who followed Irenaeus relied heavily on the information he provided, adding only some details to the picture. I shall briefly discuss this additional information on the basis of Origen's and Eusebius' works but my discussion focuses on comparing Epiphanius' information with the earliest information available, namely Irenaeus' *Adversus haereses*. This makes it possible to sketch an overall view of how the information about the Ebionites developed from the second to the fourth century CE and reflect upon the question whether this development in the descriptions might mirror factual changes in the Jewish-Christian profile of the Ebionite movement.

In the case of the Nazarenes, there are only two church fathers whose information provides a practical starting point for a discussion about the history of the Nazarenes: Epiphanius and Jerome. These two church fathers were contemporaries and knew each other very well. Furthermore, they both lived for a long time in Palestine, which makes their information about Jewish Christianity especially interesting. Although we have good grounds for believing that they both had some personal contacts with Jewish Christians, it is also clear that their information is heavily biased. Therefore, it needs to be assessed in the light of their personal history and their position as representatives of "mainstream" Christianity.

The church fathers' descriptions of the Ebionites and the Nazarenes often differ considerably and we cannot always be sure if they are really describing the same historical group. Therefore, in the course of the following discussion, I shall always specify whose Ebionites and Nazarenes I am discussing.

2.1. The Profiles of the Ebionites

2.1.1. *Irenaeus' Ebionites*

Irenaeus' *Adversus haereses* (*Haer.* 1.26.2; around 180 CE) includes the following description of the Ebionites:

> Those who are called Ebionites agree that the world was made by God; but their opinions with respect to the Lord are similar to those of Cerinthus and Carpocrates. They use the Gospel according to Matthew only, and repudiate the Apostle Paul, maintaining that he was an apostate from the law. As to the prophetical writings, they endeavour to expound them in a somewhat singular manner: they practise circumcision, persevere in the observance of those customs which are enjoined by the law, and are so Judaic in their style of life, that they even adore Jerusalem as if it were the house of God. (trans. *ANF*).

Irenaeus wrote his treatise when he was bishop of Lyons but nothing in his work suggests the Ebionites were a special problem in the environs of Lyons. It is generally assumed that Irenaeus drew on Justin the Martyr's lost *Syntagma*. However, this probably did not include a section on the Ebionites because Justin's other works indicate that he did not regard Ebionite views as clearly heretical (see *Dial.* 46–48). Thus, Irenaeus must either himself have added the information about the Ebionites on his own or he received his information about the Ebionites from another source. Whatever the source was, we may assume that the Ebionites described by it were located in the Eastern parts of the Roman Empire, Asia Minor, Syria or Palestine, where Ebionites are explicitly located in later sources and where Judaism had more influence on Christianity in general.

All the key indicators of Judaism are clearly observable in Irenaeus' description. The Ebionites practiced circumcision and observed other Jewish laws and customs. As regards ideology, they represented monotheism which excluded the idea of a demiurge. Jerusalem also played a central role in their ideology and practice. What Irenaeus describes as the adoring of Jerusalem may reflect the Ebionites' practice of saying their prayers while facing the Holy City. If so, this hardly was only a superficial rite that was carried on even after "the house of God" in Jerusalem was destroyed in 70 CE Rather, the fact that Jerusalem was able to retain its central position even after the destruction of the temple characterizes the perseverance of Jewish ideas in the religion of the Ebionites and suggests that Jerusalem may also have had central role in their end-time expectations.

Because the Ebionites considered Paul as an apostate, it is to be assumed that they were preponderantly of Jewish origin. Active anti-Paulinism also implies that circumcision and observance of Jewish laws was required of those religionists that were of non-Jewish origin.

According to Irenaeus, the Ebionites' views "with respect to the Lord are *similar* to those of Cerinthus and Carpocrates." This does not reveal very much about the Christology of the Ebionites but it provides some clues for its reconstruction. However, before moving on to discuss the implications of this statement, two related problems need to be noted.

First, the fact that Irenaeus presented the Ebionites immediately after Cerinthus and Carpocrates and compared the Ebionites' views with their doctrines had far-reaching consequences. This inspired later heresiologists to enrich their descriptions of the Ebionites by reasoning the necessary details of the Christology of the Ebionites on the basis of the Cerinthian and Carpocratian doctrines, which Irenaeus described as partly compatible and party incompatible with the Ebionite views.

Second, the word "similar" is problematic from a text-critical point of view. The available Latin translation of Irenaeus' *Against Heresies* (the original Greek is lost) reads *non similiter*, which would mean that the Ebionites' Christology was *not similar* to Cerinthus and Carpocrates. In practice, this would suggest that *the Ebionites believed in the virgin birth, did not separate Christ and Jesus*, etc. However, Hippolytus' *Refutation* includes an almost verbatim parallel of this passage in Greek and it reads without the negative ὁμοίως, "similarly" (Hippolytus, *Haer.* 7.34.1). Because this reading also suits the context better, it is usually considered as the original reading derived from Irenaeus. Thus, Irenaeus' Greek *Against Heresies* originally stated that the Ebionites *did not believe in the virgin birth* and *separated Christ and Jesus*.

The exact date of the Latin translation is unknown but it is usually considered very early (and literal). It is important to note that once the Latin translation was made—or the negative was added to the Greek manuscript which the translator used—a possibility for two contradicting interpretations about the Ebionites' Christology was also created. (1) On the one hand, those who read Latin (or the corrupt Greek version) would conclude that the Ebionites did not agree with the Cerinthians and Carpocratians and so *must have accepted the virgin birth*. (2) On the other hand, those who read Hippolytus or Irenaeus' uncorrupted Greek would conclude that they *did not accept the virgin birth*. In Origen and Eusebius, we will find precisely these two options in the religious profile of the Ebionites.

Nevertheless, according to Irenaeus' original version, the Christology of the Ebionites was *similar* to that of Cerinthus and Carpocrates. What does this mean in practice? It is clear that Irenaeus' Ebionites hardly shared all the Cerinthian views about Christ. The Cerinthian Christology, as described by Irenaeus, included the views that Jesus was born in the same way as all other men, that he was more versed in righteousness, and he received Christ from above at his baptism. In Irenaeus' opinion, Cerinthians also claimed that after receiving Christ, Jesus started to proclaim the unknown God and that Christ remained impassive because he flew away from Jesus before his crucifixion. The mere fact that the Ebionites were monotheists makes it improbable that the Christ of the Ebionites would have proclaimed the "unknown God."

The idea of Christ ascending from above also resembles the role of Christ in Gnostic cosmogonies that Irenaeus described in the beginning of his *Against Heresies*. Irenaeus may have exaggerated the Gnostic outlook of Cerinthus' doctrine and described him as believing in the demiurge.[1] Nevertheless, it is probable that Cerinthus' teaching included speculations about a pre-existent Christ who entered Jesus at baptism and for this very reason, he was easily connected to Gnosticism. Most likely, Irenaeus' Ebionites already shared these ideas because in later sources these kinds of speculations are explicitly connected to the Ebionites (see Epiphanius below).

---

[1] For this, see Myllykoski 2005.

Overall, we can only say that the Ebionites' Christology must have been "something like" the Cerinthian Christology as it is characterized by Irenaeus but it is impossible to give any detailed description of it. Only thing we can be relative sure about is that Irenaeus' Ebionites did not accept the virgin birth because Irenaeus criticizes the Ebionites for this elsewhere in *Against Heresies* (for instance, *Haer.* 3.21.1).

According to Irenaeus, the Ebionites were using only the Gospel of Matthew. Because the canonical Matthew announces Jesus' virgin birth, the information seems to be in contradiction with Irenaeus' own statement that the Ebionites denied the virgin birth. There is no doubt that Irenaeus really has in mind the canonical Matthew which he connects to the Ebionites since one of his points is to show that the Ebionites can be confuted by the same gospel they use.

Irenaeus was the defender of the canon of four gospels and he leveled charges against the heretics for their use of only one gospel. These gospels, however, also demonstrated their errors: Marcion was confuted by Luke, those who separate Christ and Jesus (this would apply to the Cerinthians) were confuted by Mark, Valentinus was confuted by John and the Ebionites by Matthew (*Haer.* 3.11.7–8). Because Irenaeus also believed that Matthew had written his gospel for the Hebrews in their own dialect (*Haer.* 3.1.1), it is quite possible that he himself invented the idea that the Ebionites must be using the Gospel of Matthew—not least because this gospel could also be used against them. Another possibility is that the Ebionites really were using a gospel that was entitled the Gospel of Matthew but in reality it was not identical with the canonical one. We will come back to this issue below.

It seems clear that Irenaeus' Ebionites viewed themselves first and foremost as Jews. Most likely they were of Jewish pedigree. The borders and identity of their religious community was defined by traditional Jewish customs and practices. How much Christian there was on top of that is difficult to say because Irenaeus focuses on criticizing the Jewish side of their religion.

Did the Ebionites practice baptism in addition to circumcision? It is most likely they did because if they had not done so, this surely would have been recorded and condemned by Irenaeus (and his sources).

Irenaeus does not explicitly deal with the Ebionites' Eucharistic practices but at one point he formulates his criticism of the Ebionites' Christology in a way which suggests that the Ebionites' chalice contained only water instead of a mixture of wine and water: "Therefore do these men reject the commixture of the heavenly wine and wish it to be water

of the world only, not receiving God as to have union with Him ..."
(Irenaeus, *Haer.* 5.1.3; trans. Klijn & Reinink 1973). Irenaeus' main
point is to criticize the Ebionites because they do not believe that God
was united with man in Jesus. Nevertheless, his argument carries conviction only if the Ebionites' chalice really contained only water. Later
on, Epiphanius explicitly attributes this practice to the Ebionites (*Pan.*
30.16.1).

The Ebionites' anti-Paulinism, which probably also meant that they
wanted the Gentile believers to be circumcised and observe the law,
must have resulted in the separation of the Ebionites from the formative
Catholic Christianity, at least in the form that was developing in Rome
and the Western parts of the Empire. Even Justin, who was more lenient
in his attitude towards Jewish Christians than Irenaeus, accepted the
Jewish believers as part of Christian communities only as far as they did
not try to impose the law and Jewish customs on gentile believers (see
Dial. 46–48).

Another question is how close relations the Ebionites were able to
retain with (other) Jewish communities. Because the Ebionites seem
to have represented a rather low Christology, their Jesus belief alone
might not have prevented them from living on positive terms with
Jewish congregations. Even their baptism might not have aroused fierce
criticism, especially if it was interpreted in the light of Jewish purification
rites (cf. *Dial* 46.2). Nevertheless, very much depends on what kinds
of practical forms their Jesus cult took. In any case, it is clear that the
Ebionites saw something special in Jesus and if that something was
not his divine preexistence or his virgin birth then it must have been
something connected to his prophetic message. This, in turn, may also
have had some practical consequences as regards the way the Jewish laws
were interpreted and practiced by the Ebionites, and possibly also what
kind of eschatological expectations they entertained.

The fact that Irenaeus reports that the Ebionites expounded the prophets "diligently" or "singular manner" (lat. *curiosius*)—whatever that
means exactly—suggests that their interpretation of the prophets was
somewhat singular, evidently not in line with Irenaeus' (or his sources')
own view. Nevertheless, it may still have been acceptable within (other)
Jewish communities. Thus, the Ebionites may not have been regarded as
outward heretics by (other) Jews. According to Epiphanius, the Ebionites
had their own synagogues (*Pan.* 30.18.2–3) but this probably applies only
to the more syncretistic branch of the Ebionites that Epiphanius knew in
Cyprus (see below).

The assumption that the Ebionites formed separate factions or communities—within Judaism but separated from other Christian communities—is also attested by their name. Irenaeus' introduction suggests that his audience was familiar with the name Ebionites. They are simply termed "those who are called Ebionites." Irenaeus' designation does not even add any derogatory explanations to their name. Since in Hebrew אביונימ (pl.) means poor, later heresiologists explained the name as signaling the Ebionites' poor intellect. They also derived the name of the Ebionites from Ebion, the putative founder of this branch of heresy (see below). Apparently, these derogatory explanations are later attempts to cover the pious Jewish and Christian connotations of the name: the poor as the traditional Hebrew Bible designation of the humble servants of God and as the term that was used to characterize an esteemed group of Christians in Jerusalem. Because the name is accepted as an appropriate designation of these people by outsiders, it must also have matched their lifestyle to some extent. If they only claimed to be "poor" but were not in practice, their opponents would surely have picked up on that. Because of the positive connotations—that the later heresiologists tried to suppress—it is unlikely that hostile outsiders would have originally given them the name. Instead, it must be based on their self-designation or be a name originally given to a subgroup by friendly coreligionists (as Acts suggest).

Four facts make an assumption about the Ebionites' connection to the earliest Jerusalem community reasonable:[2]

1. The title Ebionites, the "poor," which matches the title of the earliest Jerusalem community (or at least its subgroup). Cf. Rom 15:26; Gal 2:10.
2. Anti-Paulinism especially characterizes the groups that come from Jerusalem before 70 CE
3. The same groups also emphasize the observance of the law and the need to circumcise the gentile Christians as well.
4. Directing prayers towards Jerusalem testifies to the centrality of Jerusalem in the Ebionites' ideology and possibly in their end-time expectations. The earliest Jerusalem community stayed in the Holy City for the same reasons. There is also evidence of the importance of the temple for the early Jerusalem community and its leader, James the Just (Acts 2:46; 21:17–26; Eusebius, *Hist. eccl.* 2.23.3–18;

---

[2] Cf. Lüdemann 1996, 52–53.

see also Painter, 2001 49–50) which fits well with the Ebionites' reported—and ridiculed—interest in Jerusalem "as if it were the House of God" (Irenaeus, see above).

The evidence is not conclusive but there are enough points of contact to show that the Ebionites as they are described by Irenaeus may very well have been an offshoot of the earliest Jerusalem community. Judaism also seems to have been such integral part of their identity that in their case the term *Christian Jews* might best characterize their religious position.

Although the origin of Irenaeus' information about the Ebionites remains somewhat obscure, its significance for later authors can be easily demonstrated since practically all heresiologists from the second to the fourth century were more or less influenced by the Irenaean tradition. Hippolytus follows Irenaeus almost word for word and Tertullian and Pseudo-Tertullian also drew on the same tradition.[3] Therefore, their descriptions do not offer much new material for the present discussion, except the name of the founder of the heresy, Ebion, which they all use. The situation is different with Origen and Eusebius who lived in the East and who offer some new information about the Ebionites.

2.1.2. *Origen's Ebionites*

Origen was born (ca. 185) and raised in a Christian family in Alexandria.[4] He lost his father when he was in his teens in the persecutions during the reign of Septimus Severus (193–211). Nevertheless, he was able to complete his studies with the support of a wealthy patroness and he became a teacher of Greek literature. Origen soon became familiar with the variety of religious and philosophical traditions circulating in Alexandria. The patroness supported a Gnostic whose teaching he followed and he also studied under the Platonist Ammonius Saccas and probably with Clement of Alexandria. During the second persecution of Severus, Origen gained fame for his courageous teaching while Demetrius, the bishop of Alexandria and other church leaders fled or hid. Soon after that, Origen abandoned the study of pagan literature, probably underwent voluntary castration and devoted himself to Christian teaching.

---

[3] See Häkkinen 2005, 251–253.
[4] For an overview of Origen's life, see Trigg 1992.

Ambrosius, a wealthy Alexandrian whom Origen had converted from Gnosticism, became his patron and lifelong friend. Ambrosius provided Origen with scribes and means which enabled him to become one of the most prolific authors of Antiquity, esteemed both by his Christian and non-Christian contemporaries. After 233, Origen settled in Palestine, in Caesarea, but before that he had already made several trips to Rome and Greece, and he had been called to an audience by the empress Julia Mammaea at Antioch in 231. Origen's survived literary production dates mostly to the time he lived in Caesarea. He died during the Decian persecutions (ca. 253).

As regards Origen's understanding of the Ebionites, it should be, first of all, noted that Origen understood the name Ebionites as a general title for all Jews who accepted Jesus but were not willing to forsake their Jewish heritage (*Cels.* 2.1.; *Comm. Matt.* 11.12). Origen comments are also very polemical because he often refers to the Ebionites—whose name he takes as a reference to their poor intellect—in order to provide examples of "poor" literal interpretation of scriptures. In his view, the Ebionites are primary examples of interpreters who do not understand the deeper spiritual meaning of the text. Thus, his comments are often more like generalizations concerning certain theological position, than observations of the beliefs and practices of historical Ebionite communities.

Because Origen did not write any heresiology, his view of the Ebionites has to be reconstructed from short remarks scattered throughout his literary production. Because of this, it is also difficult to conclude if he was familiar with the heresiologies that already existed by his time (Justin's, Irenaeus' and Hippolytus'). Nevertheless, it is clear that he attributes to the Ebionites the same basic beliefs and practices that can also be found in Irenaeus' and Hippolytus' works. There are some verbal similarities (see below) and the contents of his information coheres—with some enlargements—so well with the Irenaean tradition that I am inclined to assume Origen's dependence on the earlier heresiologists, Hippolytus in particular.

Origen shares with the Irenaean tradition the notions that Ebionites require circumcision (*Hom. Gen.* 3.5), follow Jewish customs (food laws; *Comm. Matt.* 11.12), do not believe in the virgin birth (*Comm. Matt.* 16.12), and are anti-Pauline (*Hom. Jer.* 19.12). Origen also knows that the Ebionites assumed Jesus to have been sent primarily to the Israelites (*Princ.* 4.3.8). This agrees with the profile of Irenaeus' Ebionites whose religion was also centered on traditional Jewish identity markers, circumcision, Jewish laws and Jerusalem, and who must have thought that the salvation of the Gentiles was possible only if they were integrated into Judaism.

Origen does not give any information about the writings that the Ebionites used but he adds some new details to their profile. According to Origen, the assumption that Easter should be celebrated in the way of the Jews, is characteristic of the Ebionite heresy (*in Matth comm. ser.* 79). Origen's comments seem to be connected to the so-called "Quartodeciman controversy," which concerned the timing of Passover/Easter. The Quartodecimans deemed it appropriate to celebrate Passover/Easter on the 14th of Nisan, like the Jews did, irrespective of which day of the week that might be. Others thought that Easter should always be celebrated on Sunday. The Quartodeciman timing was common in Asian churches. Thus, it was not restricted only to the Ebionite churches and Origen is also well aware of that because he states: "somebody with no experience perhaps does some investigating and falls into the Ebionite heresy ..." Obviously, these inexperienced "somebodies" were the Quartodecimans whose position thereby is labeled as Ebionite heresy. What does this say about the Ebionites themselves? If the Ebionites followed Jewish law, it is natural that they sided with the Quartodecimans. Thus, although the evidence is indirect, it is safe to assume that the Ebionites also followed the same timing of Passover/Easter as the Quartodecimans.

The most significant new feature Origen adds to the profile of the Ebionites is that there were two factions among them which had different views about Jesus' virgin birth.

> These are the two kinds of Ebionites, some confessing that Jesus was born of a virgin as we do and others who deny this but say that he was born like the other people. (*Cels.* 5.61; trans. Klijn & Reinink 1973).

This distinction has often played a central role in the attempts to reconstruct the history of Jewish Christianity. For those scholars who argue that the "nearly orthodox" Nazarenes were the real offshoot of the earliest Jerusalem community, this passage works as one stepping stone, which helps them to connect Jerome's and Epiphanius' fourth century descriptions of the Nazarenes to the "Nazarenes" described in Acts. The assumption is that the Nazarenes were there all the time but were erroneously called Ebionites by Origen.[5] However, this theory is problematic in many respects. It is doubtful in my opinion if the kind of separate group of the Nazarenes that Epiphanius describes in *Panarion* 29 ever existed—

---

[5] See Pritz 1988, 28, 82, 108–110.

"Nazarenes" was instead a common name for Syriac Christians. Since this question will be discussed in more detail below, we may for a moment—for the sake of argument—assume that a "sect of the Nazarenes" existed at the end of the fourth century. Even in this case, it would be hard to see a reference to this kind of group in Origen's passage, for two reasons.

First, the distinctive feature of the first group of Origen's Ebionites is their belief in the virgin birth. However, this belief does not play any role in the religious profile of Epiphanius' Nazarenes who are depicted as the successors of Origen's Ebionites in this theory. Epiphanius explicitly states that he does not know what the Nazarenes thought about Jesus' birth (see below). Thus, if we presume that Origen's first group of the Ebionites was in fact Epiphanius' Nazarenes we would also have to assume that the dispute about Jesus' birth—which originally could have caused a split among the Ebionites—had become a matter of indifference by the end of the fourth century. Given the increasing interest in Christological speculation among Christians in the third and fourth centuries, this kind of development is unbelievable.

Second, the reference is also incompatible with Jerome's descriptions of Christians he called Nazarenes. To the extent that Jerome provides historical evidence about the beliefs of Christians called Nazarenes (which cannot be identified with Epiphanius' Nazarenes; see below), their religious profile differed from Origen's and his predecessors' Ebionites in many respects, most notably in their relation to Paul whose message they heeded (see below). This means that the religious outlook of Jerome's Nazarenes was totally different from the profile of the Ebionites as it is described by Origen. Notably, Origen explicitly states that both groups of the Ebionites were against Paul (*Cels.* 5.65). Therefore, it should be clear that neither the first nor the second of Origen's two types of Ebionites can be identified with Jerome's Nazarenes.

In one of Jerome's letters to Augustine, there is a reference which some scholars have taken as proof that Jerome's Nazarenes believed in the virgin birth. This reference, however, is of little value as a historical description of the Nazarenes' doctrine because it quotes early creeds and only aims at reinforcing Jerome's arguments. In this connection, Jerome also uses the terms "Nazarenes," "Ebionites" and *minim* interchangeably, which makes it difficult to argue that Jerome was referring to characteristically Nazarene ideas.[6]

---

[6] Jerome's letter to Augustine is discussed in more detail below. See Chapter 2.2.

If Origen's second group of the Ebionites are not camouflaged Nazarenes, how are we to interpret Origen's distinction? Of course, it is possible that Origen had received historically reliable information about the Ebionites' different views concerning Jesus' virgin birth.[7] However, I find it unlikely that—other things being equal—this doctrinal difference would have triggered a severe crisis within the Ebionite community/communities and resulted in the formation of two separate groups (or sets of communities), as is often assumed. If the Ebionites agreed on the importance of circumcision, on the interpretation of the law, and about their relation to Gentiles, had similar views about Jesus' message, entertained similar end-time expectations, interpreted the prophets similarly, used the same gospel, and understood themselves as אביונים, devout, pious, humble Jews, would it have made great difference if they thought that Jesus was divine from the very beginning of his life, or if they understood him to have become coupled with divine reality only at his baptism? In the last analysis, Origen's distinction may say more about Origen's own tendency to group people on the basis of their Christological views than about differences in belief that the Ebionites themselves would have found significant.

Although it cannot be excluded that Origen's distinction is based on reliable information that he had received about the Ebionites' Christology, I am more inclined to believe that Origen drew his conclusions about the Ebionites' Christological doctrine from earlier heresiologies. As was noted above, there were two versions of Irenaeus' passage on the Ebionites available. One version suggested that the Ebionites believed in the virgin birth (Irenaeus' corrupted text) while the other one was open to the opposite interpretation (Hippolytus and uncorrupted Irenaeus). Origen may have come across these two traditions and concluded that there must be two kinds of Ebionites. This assumption is corroborated by the fact that the passage in *Contra Celsum* where Origen describes the two kinds of Ebionites has clear verbal connections to Hippolytus' *Refutation*.[8] However, Origen must also have been familiar with the Irenaean

---

[7] Origen wrote his *Against Celsus*—where he referred to the two groups of the Ebionites—after he had moved to Caesarea. There he may very well have met with or heard about different kinds of "Ebionites" since he refers to Jewish-Christian missionaries in his sermon on Psalm 82 (Eusebius, *Hist. eccl.* 6.38). More on these missionaries below (the section *Possibly Ebionite Information II: The Book of Elchasai and Elchasaite Missionaries*).

[8] Origen, *Cels.* 5.61, and Hippolytus, *Haer.* 7.34.1, share the verb ὁμολογέω and the adverb ὁμοίως. Hippolytus' reference to becoming justified (δικαιοῦσθαι) indicates that

tradition while he was writing *Contra Celsum* because later on he refers to the Ebionites' anti-Paulinism (*Cels.* 5.65), which Hippolytus' *Refutation* does not mention. If this Irenaean text was in its corrupted form, then it suggested that some Ebionites accepted the virgin birth.

On the whole, Origen does not add very much substantially new and historically reliable information to the religious profile of the Ebionites. He refers to the Ebionites' timing of Passover/Easter but he is not concerned with characterizing the Ebionite practices on their own in this connection. He only aims at labeling the Quartodeciman practice as based on "poor," Ebionite, literal interpretation of the law. His distinction between the two kinds of Ebionites is the most notable new feature in the Ebionites' profile but if the above considerations have been on the right track, the distinction reveals more about Origen's careful reading of his sources and about the categories that he himself found distinctive, than about the Ebionites themselves and the factions among them.

2.1.3. *Eusebius' Ebionites*

Eusebius was elected the bishop of Caesarea in 313. Eusebius admired Origen and he had also carefully studied Origen's writings which were readily available to him in the library of Caesarea. He was also familiar with Irenaeus' heresiology (see, for instance, *Hist. eccl.* 3.28.6). All this is reflected in his references to the Ebionites. His *Ecclesiastical History* has one overall description of the Ebionites which repeats the basics of Irenaean tradition in the framework of Origen's distinction between two kinds of Ebionites and is decorated with Origen's derogatory interpretation of the name of the Ebionites as a reference to the Ebionites' poor intellect.

Eusebius also adds two interesting details to the profile of the Ebionites. First, he notes in his *Onomasticon* that the Hebrews who believed in Christ, the Ebionites, were living in the region of the village of Choba

---

he already enriched the description of the Ebionites by picking out some details from Irenaeus' description of Cerinthus' and Carpocrates' teaching (cf. Irenaeus, *Haer.* 1.25.1; 1.26.1). Because it was Hippolytus' version that identified the Ebionites' teaching with that of Cerinthus and Carpocrates (ὁμοίως), it is natural that Origen also checked with what Hippolytus' *Refutation* had to say about these teachers and described the *similar* teaching of the Ebionites accordingly. Therefore, Origen's *Cels.* 5.61 shares expressions with Hippolytus, *Haer.* 7.33.1: ἐκ παρθένου, γεγεννῆσθαι, ὡς/ὁμοίως, τοὺς λοιποὺς ἀνθρώπους/ τοῖς λοιποῖς ἀνρώποις. Thus, it is clear Origen made use at least Hippolytus' *Refutation*.

(*Onom.* ed. Lagarde 1966 [1887], p. 301,28–34). Unfortunately, the exact location of this village remains open. It may have been a village near Nazareth or located somewhere in Syria, perhaps to the north of Damascus. Second, Eusebius notes that the Ebionites observed the Sabbath but also celebrated the Lord's Day. If this information is historically correct, it would strengthen the picture of the Ebionites as people who wanted to be both Jews and Christians at the same time.

As was noted in connection with Irenaeus' Ebionites, it is likely that the Ebionites practiced baptism. We also know that they had Eucharistic meals, albeit not with wine but water. Although we cannot be sure if Eusebius had much personal contact with the Ebionites, the information about the Ebionites' celebration of the Lord's Day is unlikely to be based on Eusebius' own imagination. It is less certain, though, if we can add this detail to the profile of Irenaeus' Ebionites since it is also possible that Eusebius' note reflects the practice of some Jewish Christians that did not necessarily share all the ideas of Irenaeus' Ebionites. Eusebius may refer here to the problem that is also addressed in the *Didascalia Apostolorum* (*DA*) which exhorts the Jewish converts to stop observing the Sabbath (*DA* XXVI/ed. Lagarde 1911 [1854], pp. 112–115). John Chrysostom was also faced with the same problem in his *Discourses against Judaizing Christians*.[9] The intensity of these admonitions—and other related exhortations—suggests that double attendance was an acute problem which the writer(s) sought to overcome.

Whether Eusebius' reference to those who kept both the Sabbath and the Lord's Day applies to a specific group of Ebionites or only to some converts that did not stop attending synagogues on the Sabbath, it shows in any case, that by Eusebius' time there were people who tried to practice both Judaism and Christianity. This presented a serious challenge to representatives of the formative Catholic tradition. In the following, we will take a closer look at some of the strategies that were developed in order to tackle this problem.

2.1.4. *Epiphanius' Ebionites*

Epiphanius was born in Palestine near modern Gaza around 315. He probably had Christian parents, and was first educated in local monasteries. He later moved to Egypt to complete his education but came back to Palestine in his twenties and founded a new monastery in Eleuthero-

---

[9] For discussion and the collection of passages, see Skarsaune 2007, 749–753.

polis. He was the head of that monastery for about thirty years until he was elected the bishop of Salamis in Cyprus in 367. About ten years later, he completed a major work on heresies, the *Panarion*, in which he describes and confutes eighty Jewish and Christian heresies. The name of the work, *Medicine Chest* in English, characterizes its main intent: In Epiphanius' view, the heresies represented poisonous doctrines that threatened the Christians of his day, and his intention was to provide the antidotes.

Although Epiphanius may have believed that there once was a person called Ebion, who founded the "heresy" of the Ebionites, modern scholars generally agree that the person is fictive. Ebion was introduced by Tertullian and Hippolytus but, by Epiphanius' time, his existence seems to have been taken for granted. Because heresies were usually thought to have been introduced by actual persons, the genesis of the Ebionites was made to conform by being traced back to the activity of a person called Ebion.

Epiphanius' description and refutation of the Ebionites (*Panarion* 30) is the richest ancient source on the Ebionites available. Together with the passage on the Nazarenes (*Panarion* 29), it amounts to a full-blown history of the Jewish-Christian "heresy" from the times of the early Jerusalem community to Epiphanius' day. Earlier heresiologists had described the heresies of Cerinthus[10] and the Ebionites successively, but Epiphanius placed the Nazarenes between these two, claiming that Ebion whom he identifies as the originator of the Ebionite heresy, was originally one of the Nazarenes. As we shall see below, this whole history mainly serves Epiphanius' polemical interests and has little or nothing to do with the actual course of events.

In the *Panarion*, Epiphanius was able to use all the information provided by his predecessors, especially by Irenaeus, Hippolytus, Origen and Eusebius. In addition, he had some knowledge about Ebionites who were his contemporaries, and was able to quote passages from their literature.[11] Epiphanius presents quotations from a gospel they used, and

---

[10] Scholars have debated whether the historical Cerinthus was a Gnostic or a Jewish-Christian teacher. Irenaeus' heresiology (*Haer.* 1.26.1) depicts him more like a Gnostic but Epiphanius (*Pan.* 28) counts him among the conservative Jewish Christians who opposed Paul. For discussion, see above and Myllykoski 2005.

[11] When Epiphanius lists the dwelling places of the Ebionites, he also remarks that there are Ebionites in Cyprus where he himself was bishop (*Pan.* 30.2.7–8; 30.18.1). The Ebionite literature he used was probably derived from them.

refers to their Acts of the Apostles as being different from the canonical one. Epiphanius also states that the Ebionites used "Clement's so-called *Circuits of Peter*" (*Periodoi Petrou*; *Pan 30.15.1*), "though they corrupt the contents and leave a few genuine items," as well as the "*Ascents of James*" (*Anabathmoi Iakobou*; *Pan. 30.16.7*) which is "full of nonsense." Modern scholars connect these writings to sources that stand behind the present Pseudo-Clementine *Recognitions* and *Homilies*.[12] At some points, Epiphanius obviously quotes the *Book of Elchasai* as well. (I will deal with the *Pseudo-Clementines* and the *Book of Elchasai* in more detail below).

Much of what Epiphanius reports about the Ebionites is consistent with the accounts of his predecessors, Irenaeus, Hippolytus, Origen and Eusebius:[13]

1. Christ was the seed of man, Joseph (*Pan.* 30.2.2).
2. The Ebionites adhere to the law, circumcision, the Sabbath and other Jewish (and Samaritan) practices (*Pan.* 30.2.2, 30.26.1–2).
3. The Ebionites use the Gospel of Matthew, calling it "according to the Hebrews" (*Pan.* 30.3.7, 30.13.2).
4. The Ebionites are anti-Pauline (*Pan.* 30.16.8–9).

At the same time, the profile of Epiphanius' Ebionites clearly differs from those of the earlier reports due to all the new information Epiphanius provides. He presents a number new details about the Ebionite beliefs and practices that are not found in the earlier sources:

1. Ebion, the alleged founder of the movement, was originally a Samaritan (*Pan.* 30.1.3,5, 30.2.3).
2. They are careful not to touch a heathen (*Pan.* 30.2.3).
3. They had to purify themselves after having intercourse with a woman (*Pan.* 30.2.4).
4. They also practiced other lustrations several times a day, fully clothed (*Pan.* 30.2.5, 30.15.3, 30.16.1).
5. They forbade virginity and chastity even though they had earlier boasted of virginity (*Pan.* 30.2.6; cf. below #16).

---

[12] If compared with the earlier evidence about the Ebionites, there is nothing in the contents of the *Pseudo-Clementines* that would necessitate their classification as Ebionite writings. Therefore, the reason why Epiphanius connected the *Ascents of James* and the *Circuits of Peter* to the Ebionites must be that they were in use in communities that were understood to be Ebionite in Epiphanius' time.

[13] Cf. Irenaeus, *Haer.* 1.26.2, 3.11.7; Hippolytus, *Haer.* 7.34.1–2, 10.22; Origen, *Cels.* 5.65, *Hom. Gen.* 3.5, *Hom. Jer.* 19.12.2; Eusebius, *Hist. eccl.* 3.27.1–6, 6.17.

6. In Epiphanius' view, they maintain contradictory views of Christ: Some of them say that (a) Adam is Christ (*Pan.* 30.3.3) while others claim that (b) Christ is eternal and has appeared several times in history—to Abraham and others—in the guise of Adam's body, and that he was finally crucified, raised and returned to heaven (*Pan.* 30.3.4–6). Some of them may also say that (c) Christ went into Jesus (*Pan.* 30.3.6; see also *Pan.* 30.16.4).
7. Epiphanius presents quotations from the Ebionites' gospel, arguing that the Ebionites have mutilated the Gospel of Matthew (*Pan.* 30.13.2, etc.).
8. They detest Isaiah, Jeremiah, Ezekiel, Daniel, Elijah, Elisha, Samson, Samuel, David, Salomon and all the prophets (*Pan.* 30.15.2, 30.18.4–5, 30.18.9).
9. They abstain from meat (*Pan.* 30.13.5, 30.15.3, 30.18.7, 30.22.3–5).
10. They accept baptism in addition to their daily purifications (*Pan.* 30.16.1).
11. They celebrate the Eucharist annually with unleavened bread and water only (*Pan.* 30.16.1).
12. They believe that Christ came to abolish the sacrifices (*Pan.* 30.16.5) and James, the brother of Jesus, preached against the temple and the sacrifices (*Pan.* 30.16.7).
13. They claim to have received their name, Ebionites ("poor", from the Hebrew word אביונים), when their ancestors had given up their property to the Apostles (*Pan.* 30.17.1–3; cf. Acts 4:32–37).
14. They have invocations and lustrations to help those stricken by sickness or bitten by a snake (*Pan.* 30.17.4–5; also in the *Book of Elchasai*).
15. Like Elchasai, they picture Christ as a huge invisible figure, 96 miles long and 24 miles wide (*Pan.* 30.17.5–7; also in the *Book of Elchasai*).
16. Young Ebionite men are obliged to marry, coerced by their teachers (*Pan.* 30.18.2; cf. above #5).
17. The Ebionites have synagogues, governed by archisynagogues and elders (*Pan.* 30.18.2–3).
18. They do not accept the entire Pentateuch (*Pan.* 30.18.7–9).

In addition, Epiphanius transmits some new (fictitious) stories that illustrate the Ebionites' anti-Paulinism. For instance, the Ebionites explained that Paul's antipathy toward the law and circumcision was caused by his unfortunate love affairs. According to this account, Paul was originally of Greek parentage. He went to Jerusalem and fell in love with the daughter of the high priest. In order to get the girl, he became a proselyte and had himself circumcised. However, because he still could not get the girl after all his trouble, he became angry and wrote against circumcision, the Sabbath and the Jewish law (*Pan.* 30.16.8–9).[14]

Because many of the new ideas and practices attributed to the Ebionites are paralleled in the literature that Epiphanius was using as his sources, it is not clear at the outset how many of these ideas can be attributed to Epiphanius' contemporary Ebionites.[15] Thus, a critical assessment of Epiphanius' sources and information is necessary before it is possible to sketch a picture of the religious profile of Epiphanius' Ebionites. I shall do this by proceeding from "clearly Ebionite" evidence and sources to "possibly Ebionite" ones. The information Epiphanius received from his contemporaries and the fragments he quoted from the *Gospel of the Ebionites* will provide the basic "clearly Ebionite" information. A critical assessment of Epiphanius' "possibly Ebionite" information—his references to Pseudo-Clementine and Elchasaite sources—will add some important details to the profile.

Since the resulting overall profile of Epiphanius' Ebionites will be clearly different from the profile of Irenaeus' Ebionites, I shall discuss in the following subsection (2.1.5) if it is possible to regard Epiphanius' and Irenaeus' Ebionites as representatives of the same Ebionite movement which might have considerably changed its character in two hundred years.

Clearly Ebionite Information I: Contemporary Reports
There are four ideas in Epiphanius' description that are not easily attributable to literature but seem to be based on his own knowledge of contemporary Ebionite practices. First, the Ebionites claimed (falsely, in

---

[14] Epiphanius also tells a story about the apostle John meeting Ebion in a bathhouse (*Pan.* 30.24.1–6). Irenaeus had presented the same legend but with Cerinthus and John as the main characters (cf. Irenaeus, *Haer.* 3.3.4).

[15] Many scholars think that Epiphanius mistakenly read Ebionite doctrines from the Pseudo-Clementine sources. I do not agree. It would have been much easier for Epiphanius to write his confutation of the Ebionites only on the basis of the Irenaean information which was heretical enough. Why would he have wanted to make things more complicated for himself by inventing the idea that the Pseudo-Clementine writings are Ebionite? It is much more believable the Ebionites, who were Epiphanius' contemporaries, really used Pseudo-Clementine sources. That is a historical fact that Epiphanius cannot escape. The only thing he was able to do was to try to rewrite the Ebionites' prehistory so that it would explain his present reality.

Epiphanius' view) to have received their name when their ancestors had given their property to the Apostles (*Pan.* 30.17.1–3; cf. Acts 4:32–37). This claim is not found in earlier reports or in the extant fragments of Ebionite literature, so it would seem that Epiphanius received this information from the Ebionites themselves.[16] Because Epiphanius is forced to deny the validity of the Ebionites' own etymology of their name, it is also clear that the name was a self-designation and not merely one used by outsiders. Second, the way Epiphanius describes the Ebionites' therapeutic lustrations suggests that he was informed about their practices (more on this below). Third, information about Ebionite synagogues and leaders has an authentic ring since Epiphanius describes their practices in the manner an eyewitness provides additional background information for his less knowledgeable readers. The same applies, finally, to the report about their teachers coercing young males to marry.

Moreover, while the Ebionites' abstinence from meat and their critical attitude towards the prophets can be found in their literature (the *Gospel of the Ebionites* and the *Pseudo-Clementines* in particular), Epiphanius also reports contemporary disputes between him (or his fellow Christians) and the Ebionites concerning these particular issues:

> When you ask one of them why they do not eat meat they have nothing to say, and foolishly answer, "Since it is produced by the congress and intercourse of bodies, we do not eat it." Thus, according to their own foolish regurgitations, they are wholly abominable themselves, since they are results of the intercourse of a man and a woman.   (*Pan.* 30.15.4).

> Nor do they accept Moses' Pentateuch in its entirety; certain sayings they reject. When you say to them, of eating meat, "Why did Abraham serve the angels the calf and the milk? Why did Noah eat meat, and why was he told to by God, who said, 'Slay and eat?' Why did Isaac and Jacob sacrifice to God—Moses too, in the wilderness?" he will not believe that and will say, "Why do I need to read what is in the Law, when the Gospel has come?" "Well, where did you hear about Moses and Abraham? I know you admit their existence, and put them down as righteous, and your own ancestors." Then he will answer, "Christ has revealed this to me," and will blaspheme most of the legislation, and Samson, David, Elijah, Samuel, Elisha and the rest.   (*Pan.* 30.18.7–9; translations from Williams 1987b).

The answer given in the first quotation would seem to imply a very ascetic lifestyle because it suggests that all sexual intercourse is prohibited. However, if the information about the Ebionites' obligation to marry is

---

[16] It is possible that the claim was supported by the Ebionites' own Acts of Apostles.

correct, as it seems, then the Ebionites' abstinence concerned only food and wine. Nevertheless, their rejection of meat was more fundamental than that described in the Pseudo-Clementine sources, which prohibited only the foods listed in the Apostolic Decree (Acts 15:19–20, 29; cf. *Rec.* 4.36.4; *Hom.* 7.8.1).[17]

The second quotation, which seems to question the validity of all Mosaic law, is very problematic in the light of the traditional information about the Ebionites' strict observance of Jewish law. Nevertheless, Epiphanius' reference to the Ebionites' selective use of the Pentateuch and their rejection of the prophets after Moses is in harmony with the fact that he also connects Ebion to the Samaritans, who were famous for accepting only their own version of the Pentateuch as their religious literature.[18] In the beginning of *Pan.* 30, Epiphanius claims that Ebion was originally a Samaritan (*Pan.* 30.1.3; 30.2.2–3) before he came in contact with the Nazarenes (*Pan.* 29.7–8; 30.2.7). He also describes the Ebionites' relations to the gentiles and their purifications after sexual intercourse in terms similar to which he had earlier used for describing the Samaritans. Furthermore, when he refers to the Ebionites' observance of the Sabbath, circumcision and the law—practices traditionally attributed to the Ebionites in the heresiologies—he is careful to record that the Ebionites also observed other things, just like the Jews and the Samaritans. Thus, it seems clear that, in Epiphanius' view, the Ebionites accepted only the Pentateuch and excluded the prophets from their canon—just like the Samaritans. The second quotation also suggests that the law is not studied in its own right because it is clearly overshadowed by Christ's revelation (cf. *Rec.* 1.58.2–6). In this regard, they differed from the Samaritans. The

---

[17] The passage is attributed to the Pseudo-Clementine *Basic Writing* by Jones 2005, 321. For the *Basic Writing*, see below.

[18] For the Samaritans and their Pentateuch, see Kartveit 2009, 259–312, 313–349, esp. 280–288, 290–191, 299, 315–317. The Samaritan Pentateuch includes thousands of minor differences when compared with the Masoretic text. Mostly these are textual variants but there are also significant transpositions and additions, the most famous of which is the Samaritans' own tenth commandment which orders them to build a temple on Mount Gerizim. Theologically, these modifications aim at emphasizing the prophetic role of Moses. Samaritans also expect a future prophet like Moses. Consequently, the Samaritans excluded the prophetic books from their canon (which consisted only of the Pentateuch). These ideas also appear in Pseudo-Clementine texts which supports the idea that the Ebionites—who used some versions of the Pseudo-Clementine sources—were connected to the Samaritans. The Ebionites went further in their criticism of the law than the Samaritans but their starting point was obviously in the Samaritan ideas about Moses as the true prophet. See below.

Ebionites found Christ the expected prophet like Moses and therefore he even had the authority to modify the Mosaic law. As compared with the earlier tradition about the Ebionites, this kind of attitude results in a significantly different Jewish-Christian profile, but it accords so well with Epiphanius' overall view of the contemporary Ebionites that we have no reason to doubt its historicity.

Clearly Ebionite Information II: The Gospel of the Ebionites
Epiphanius presents quotations from the *Gospel of the Ebionites* that are not known from other sources, mostly in order to illustrate ideas that he considered typically Ebionite. They are therefore just as important as the contemporary reports as a source of ideas typical of Epiphanius' Ebionites. The translations of the surviving passages are in Appendix 1.

According to Epiphanius, the Ebionites dropped the genealogies at the beginning of Matthew's gospel because they did not accept the virgin birth. He quotes the beginning of the gospel, which indicates that it opened with the description of Jesus' baptism by John (*Pan.* 30.1.5, 30.14.3). In Epiphanius' view, the Ebionites thought that Christ came into Jesus in the form of a dove at his baptism. This, indeed, accords with the wording of their gospel, which states that the "Holy Spirit in the form of a dove descending and *entering into* him." (*Pan.* 30.13.7, 30.14.4).

On the other hand, Epiphanius claims that the Ebionites denied Jesus' being man on the basis of his saying: "These are my brothers and my mother and my sisters who do the will of my Father" (*Pan.* 30.14.5). The passage harmonizes the wordings of corresponding canonical passages (cf. Matt 12:47–50 and pars.) but, in practice, its contents do not differ from them.[19] Thus, the key question is how the Ebionites themselves interpreted the passage. To my mind, the Ebionites probably did not find any contradiction between this passage and their own ideas about Jesus' natural birth. Rather, it was Epiphanius, who had found the passage in the *Gospel of the Ebionites* and saw his opportunity to turn the tables on the Ebionites by pointing out that even their own gospel indicates that Jesus did not have human brothers or sisters.

Epiphanius also finds examples of the Ebionites' abstinence from meat in their gospel. They have changed John the Baptist's diet from *locusts* to *honey cakes* (*Pan.* 30.13.4–5) and they have made Jesus say that he does "*not* earnestly desire to eat meat" with the disciples at Passover

---

[19] For a detailed analysis of this passage, see Chapter 5.1.4 and Luomanen 2006.

(*Pan.* 30.22.4–5). One passage also indicates that Jesus chose the twelve apostles for the testimony of Israel (*Pan.* 30.13.2–3).

The most significant information about the contents of the gospel, however, is a statement by Jesus that is unparalleled in the synoptic gospels: "I have come to abolish the sacrifices, and if you do not stop sacrificing the wrath will not cease from you." (*Pan.* 30.16.5). The idea that Jesus, the True Prophet, came to abolish the sacrifices is central to the *Pseudo-Clementines*. In this respect, it is clear that the *Gospel of the Ebionites* agreed with them.

Possibly Ebionite Information I: The Pseudo-Clementine Sources
It is generally assumed that Epiphanius had access to Pseudo-Clementine sources underlying the present *Homilies*, *Recognitions* and the introductory letters attached to these. Scholars have been able to reconstruct Pseudo-Clementine sources partially, but we cannot be sure about the relation of these modern reconstructions to the sources that were available to Epiphanius (*Circuits of Peter* and *Ascents of James*, see above). Therefore, we can only compare the modern reconstructions with the information Epiphanius probably derived from his own Pseudo-Clementine sources—keeping in mind that inconsistencies may either (a) indicate that Epiphanius' sources were not identical with the modern reconstructions or (b) that Epiphanius' Ebionites simply interpreted their own Pseudo-Clementine sources freely. Nevertheless, the similarities we will find between the modern reconstructions and Epiphanius' evidence will help us to refine the picture of Epiphanius' Ebionites and make understandable why Pseudo-Clementine literature was in use in the Ebionite community/communities.

In their present state, the Pseudo-Clementine *Homilies* and *Recognitions* are two reeditions of an earlier source that is usually called the *Basic Writing*. A general outline of the *Basic Writing* can be deduced from parallel passages contained in the *Recognitions* and the *Homilies*. Scholars also largely agree that one section in the *Recognitions*, *Rec.* 1.27–71, is based on an independent source, but there is no consensus about the possible original title of the text. Some think that this section of the *Recognitions* (*Rec.* 1.27–71) may indeed have preserved the *Ascents of James*, which Epiphanius ascribes to the Ebionites in *Pan.* 30.16.7.[20] On the other hand, it has been pointed out that the content of *Rec.* 1.27–71 does

---

[20] Van Voorst 1989.

not fit with Epiphanius' characterization of the *Ascents*.[21] For instance, Epiphanius attributes to James much more severe and outspoken criticism of the temple and sacrifices than what is found in James' speeches in *Rec.* 1.27–71. For the sake of convenience, I will simply refer to this section of the *Recognitions* as *Rec.* 1.27–71.[22] Though *Rec.* 1.27–71 clearly forms an entity of it own, scholars think that it had become integrated into the *Basic Writing* before the *Basic Writing* was used by the editors of the *Recognitions* and the *Homilies*.[23]

The similarities between ideas attributed to Epiphanius' Ebionites and the *Basic Writing* (including *Rec.* 1.27–71) include speculations on Christ's position over the angels (*Pan.* 30.3.4, 30.16.4; cf. *Rec.* 2.42.5, 1.45.1–2),[24] his pre-Christian appearances to Abraham and the patriarchs (*Pan.* 30.3.3, 30.3.5; *Rec.* 1.32.4–33.2; cf. *Hom.* 8.10), and speculations about Adam as a prophet and one that was anointed (*Pan.* 30.3.3,5; *Rec.* 4.9, par. *Hom.* 8.10; *Rec.* 1.47.1–4).[25] The Pseudo-Clementine *Basic Writing* also discusses food regulations and lustrations, and forbids sharing meals with unbaptized gentiles because of their impurity (*Rec.* 1.19.5 par. *Hom.* 1.22.5; *Rec.* 7.29.3–5 par. *Hom.* 13.4.3–5; *Rec.* 7.36.4 par. *Hom.* 13.11.4; cf. *Rec.* 2.71.2). According to Epiphanius, the Ebionites shared the same concerns but their policy was even more stringent. They forbade the eating of meat altogether and did not want any physical contact with gentiles under any circumstances. The *Basic Writing* also prohibits sexual intercourse during menstruation. In this regard, Epiphanius' Ebionites may have been more lenient since they refer only to the obligation to wash after intercourse. The fact Epiphanius explicitly mentions baptism, in addition to the daily lustrations, as the Ebionite practice also finds a parallel in *Rec.* 1.39.2.

Theologically, the most significant similarities between the Ebionite ideas and the *Basic Writing* are Christ's criticism of the sacrificial cult and the rejection of the prophets. In this regard, the Ebionites' position

---

[21] Jones 1995, 146–148.

[22] I agree with Jones (Jones 1995, 3, 118–138), however, that it is to be located more specifically in *Rec.* 1.27–44.1 and 53.4–71.6. I rely on Jones' (1995) translation of *Rec.* 1.27–71 from the Syriac in what follows.

[23] Jones 1995, 118–125.

[24] Jones (1995, 122), along with several others, attributes *Rec.* 2.42.5 to the *Basic Writing*. *Rec.* 1.45.1–2, for its part, belongs to the section (*Rec.* 1.44.2–53.3) that has been inserted in *Rec.* 1.27–71. However, Jones (1995, 135) argues that this was done by the editor of the *Basic Writing*.

[25] *Rec.* 1.47.1–4 was probably in the *Basic Writing*. See above.

especially resemble the views presented in *Rec.* 1.27–71. Epiphanius quotes the list of the Patriarchs that the Ebionites accepted in *Pan.* 30.18.4: "They acknowledge Abraham, Isaac and Jacob, Moses and Aaron—and Joshua the son of Nun simply as Moses' successor, not as of any importance. But after these they acknowledge no more of the prophets …" This corresponds to the salvation-historical storyline depicted in *Rec.* 1.27–71. The positive part of the history from creation to Moses' death is closed with a reference to Joshua who was nominated as the commander of the people by Moses (*Rec.* 1.38.1). A decline follows the death of Joshua, resulting in the building of the temple in the place of the house of prayer (1.38.4). In this salvation-historical scheme, there is no need for the prophets because the coming of the True Prophet was sufficiently anticipated by Moses himself. The history continues by referring to the coming of the appropriate time when the True Prophet announced by Moses appeared (*Rec.* 1.39.1). Epiphanius undoubtedly found the "from Moses to the True Prophet" scheme in his Pseudo-Clementine sources which must have been closely related to *Rec.* 1.27–71. Moreover, as we saw above, Epiphanius' Ebionites had also actively resorted to this scheme in debates about the validity of the law and the prophets.

The Ebionites' emphasis on the superiority of the gospel and Christ's revelation over Mosaic law also find parallels in *Rec.* 1.27–71 where one of the apostles, Bartholomew, argues for the superiority of Christ as follows: "For what Moses was, a prophet, Jesus is, too; but what Jesus is, the Christ, Moses is not. Thus, what Moses is, Jesus is, too, but what Jesus is, Moses was not (*Rec.* 1.59.3)." According to Bartholomew, there is no need of prophetic witness for Christ either: "For it is not right for one to receive faith in the greater and more excellent one through the witness of lesser ones. Rather, through the witness of the greater and more excellent one, one will know the lesser ones" (*Rec.* 1.59.6). The Ebionites' comments in the above quoted dispute ("Why do I need to read what is in the law when the Gospel has come?" and "Christ has revealed this to me"; see above) are in full accord with these ideas.

Nevertheless, *Rec.* 1.27–71 also records ideas that are more conservative in regard to the prophets. In particular, James the archbishop (Jesus' brother) points out that the prophets are in agreement with the law. Furthermore, he recommends the Books of Kings and lists many proofs which show that Jesus was Christ and that he fulfilled everything predicted about him (*Rec.* 1.69.1–3). This view is clearly more irenic than the Ebionite interpretation of the history of salvation which rejects the prophets, focuses only on Moses and submits even him to Christ.

At the same time, despite their arrogance towards the Pentateuchal stories, the Ebionites seem to have been more outspoken regarding some indicators of Judaism than the community where *Rec.* 1.27–71 was produced. According to Epiphanius, for example, the Ebionites did not want to touch the gentiles under any circumstances. In addition, the Ebionites called their meeting places "synagogues" and their leaders had the same titles as among other Jews. They also observed the Sabbath and practiced circumcision. These practices are not explicitly attested in *Rec.* 1.27–71, but it seem likely that circumcision was practiced in the community of the *Basic Writing*.[26] These features also indicate that *Rec.* 1.27–71, in its present form as part of the *Recognitions*, does not totally cohere with the views of Epiphanius' Ebionites.[27]

Despite the difference, there is such fundamental agreement among the Pseudo-Clementine sources (especially *Rec.* 1.27–71), the *Gospel of the Ebionites*, and Epiphanius' description of the Ebionites, that there has to be a connection. The idea that Jesus came to abolish the sacrifices and the temple was destroyed because people were reluctant to cease sacrificing is unique within the early Christian tradition, making its appearance in both *Rec.* 1.27–71 and the *Gospel of the Ebionites* an unlikely coincidence.[28] Epiphanius' Ebionites and *Rec.* 1.27–71 also share marked anti-Paulinism.

Possibly Ebionite Information II: The Book of Elchasai and Elchasaite Missionaries

Epiphanius' description of the Ebionites' beliefs has similarities with the *Book of Elchasai* and there is one point where he brings forth clear evidence for the Ebionites' actual use of the book:

---

[26] Circumcision is not clearly documented in the parallel passages of *Rec.* and *Hom.* However, in the *Adjuration*, an introductory letter to the *Homilies*, it is stated that only the circumcised are qualified to receive Peter's sermons, and in *Rec.* 1.33.5, circumcision is depicted in a positive light. On the basis of these references, it can be assumed that circumcision was practiced in the community of the *Basic Writing* (Jones 2005, 323).

[27] As we have seen above, there are grounds for assuming that the version of *Rec.* 1.27–71 (or/and the *Basic Writing*) that was used by Epiphanius' Ebionites was even more critical of temple worship and the prophets than the version that is now available as part of *Recognitions*. My hypothesis is that Epiphanius' Ebionites had available a version of the *Basic Writing* of the *Pseudo-Clementines*, which Epiphanius called the *Circuits of Peter*, and a separate, earlier and more critical version of *Rec.* 1.27–71, entitled the *Ascents of James*. When the *Ascents* was incorporated into the *Basic Writing* (or into the *Recognitions*), it was partly rewritten to better comply with a more positive evaluation of the Prophets and the Mosaic law.

[28] Bauckham 2003, 168.

> When one of them falls ill or is bitten by a snake, he gets into water and invokes the names in Elxai—heaven and earth, salt and water, winds and "angels of righteousness" as they say, bread and oil—and begins to say, "Help me, and rid me of my pain!"
> (*Pan.* 30.17.4, trans. Klijn & Reinink 1973).

The *Book of Elchasai* has not survived but its basic contents can be deduced from Hippolytus', Eusebius' and Epiphanius' references.[29] It was originally Jewish, probably written by a Mesopotamian Jew around 116 CE, during Trajan's Parthian war. The book predicted an apocalyptic war in the near future, "when three years of the reign of the emperor Trajan are again completed," and it promised that those who took an oath in front of seven witnesses not to sin any more would be saved at the Last Judgment. The protection was provided by a huge angel whose measurements were given in detail. The angel was connected to, or perhaps even named, the "Hidden Power" (*Pan.* 19.2.2; Aramaic: *hayil kesai* → Elchasai). The huge angel-like figure was also known as Christ and "Great King"—at least in the version that was available to Epiphanius—but Epiphanius was not able to say if the author was referring to "our Lord Jesus Christ" or to someone else (*Pan.* 19.3.4). This comment also indicates that there was nothing specifically Christian in the contents of the book.

Gerard Luttikhuizen, who has studied the *Book of Elchasai* extensively,[30] argues that the book was later used by Transjordanian and West-Syrian Jewish Christians who applied the oaths and witnesses of the book to their purification rites and baptism(s). We learn from Hippolytus that one representative of this branch of Jewish Christianity was Alcibiades, from Apamea in Syria, who preached in Rome around 230 CE Similar "Elchasaite" Jewish-Christian missionaries were also known in Caesarea some ten to twenty years later when Origen referred to them in his sermon on Psalm 82 (Eusebius, *Hist. eccl.* 6.38). Hippolytus' report on Alcibiades' activities suggests that the rites prescribed for those afflicted by diseases and animal bites were not described in the *Book of Elchasai* itself, although the oaths of these rites were sworn in the form—and in front of the witnesses—described in the book. Obviously, their intention was to call forth the protection of the "Hidden Power"/Christ. Alcibiades is said to have written instructions on how to use the oaths, incantations

---

[29] For an overview of the book, see Luttikhuizen 2005.
[30] See Luttikhuizen 1985, 2005.

and lustrations of the book as remedies for major sins, animal bites and sicknesses (Hippolytus, *Haer.* 10.14.3–15.1).[31]

Epiphanius connects the *Book of Elchasai* to both the Transjordanian area and the area south and east of the Dead Sea since this is where he locates the Ossaeans (*Pan.* 19), the Ebionites (*Pan.* 30), the Nazarenes (*Pan.* 29) and the Sampsaeans/Elkeseans (*Pan.* 53)—all of whom are said to have used the *Book of Elchasai*. Since Epiphanius was born in Palestine and had headed a monastery there for three decades, it is not unwarranted to assume that he had some knowledge of the basic tenets of the Transjordanian religious movements. It is likely that some ideas derived from the *Book of Elchasai* were also circulating there among different syncretistic Jewish and Jewish-Christian (Ebionite) movements.[32]

Furthermore, because the activity of Elchasaite Jewish-Christian missionaries is attested in Rome, Apamea (Alcibiades' hometown) and Caesarea, it seems natural that, at some point, the Ebionites in Cyprus also became familiar with these practices. Ships regularly sailed from Cyprus to both Caesarea and Seleucia, the city from which the Apamean Alcibiades probably embarked when he headed to Rome (cf. Acts 13:4–12; I will come back to this hypothesis at the conclusion of this section). Thus, the most plausible explanation for Epiphanius' use of the *Book of Elchasai* in his description of the Ebionites is that he acquired the book from the Ebionites in Cyprus, along with the Pseudo-Clementine sources (which he called the *Circuits of Peter* and the *Ascents of James*), the Ebionites' Acts of the Apostles and (excerpts from) the gospel used by the Ebionites.

Several pieces of data indicate that the Elchasaite missionaries resembled the traditional Irenaean picture of the Ebionites more than Epiphanius' Ebionites did. According to Origen (apud Eusebius, *Hist. eccl.* 6.38), the Elchasaites were anti-Pauline and made *selective* use of every part the Old Testament and the Gospels. Irenaeus' Ebionites were also famous for their anti-Paulinism, and such "selective use" of the Old Testament might go a way towards explaining his characterization of their interpretation of the prophets as "careful/curious" (cf. Irenaeus, *Haer.* 1.26.2). Selective

---

[31] It is possible that the Ebionites also possessed such companions to the *Book of Elchasai*. If worked into the text of the book itself, these additions would make a new edition; a sort of manual for purification and repentance. Cf. Jones' thesis (Jones 1996), according to which the *Book of Elchasai* should be classified as a primitive church order.

[32] In contrast to Luttikhuizen (Luttikhuizen 2005, 355–356), who denies the use of the *Book of Elchasai* among these movements.

use of the gospels may also indicate that the Elchasaites were using a gospel harmony comparable to the *Gospel of the Ebionites*. Hippolytus, for his part, states that Alcibiades, the Elchasaite missionary in Rome, required men to be circumcised and to live according to the law. He also taught that Christ was born like all the other men (in conjunction with his Adam-Christology; Hippolytus, *Haer.* 9.14.1). Undoubtedly, on the basis of these beliefs alone—if Alcibiades had not made use of the *Book of Elchasai*—he would have been as easily called an Ebionite. We also learn from Epiphanius that the *Book of Elchasai* ordered all people to turn their faces to Jerusalem while praying (*Pan.* 19.3.5). This practice was already connected to the Ebionites by Irenaeus.

While none of these descriptions matches Irenaeus' description of the Ebionites in every detail, it is possible to see in them the central Ebionite ideas dispersed among the various representatives of the Elchasaite missionary movement. This justifies the hypothesis that the Jewish *Book of Elchasai* was received by some "traditional Ebionites" who adopted some new ideas from it and initiated relatively extensive missionary activities, traces of which can be found both in Rome and in Caesarea. In these cities they had no success—apparently because other forms of Christianity had the upper hand—but they were welcomed by other Jewish-Christian communities which had "heretical" views about the Jewish canon of scriptures, that is Epiphanius' Ebionites.

The Profile of Epiphanius' Ebionites
In the last analysis, the extent to which the Ebionites really agreed with all that was written in the literature Epiphanius received from them remains an open question. Nonetheless, the substantial agreement between Epiphanius' contemporary information about the Ebionites and the information paralleled in their literature enables us to draw an overall picture of the Ebionites' religious profile.

On the one hand, the Jewish Christianity of Epiphanius' Ebionites is characterized by adherence to customs that traditionally have been boundary markers between Jews and gentiles: circumcision, purity laws and Jewish institutions (synagogue, leadership, marriage). On the other hand, their ideology and interpretation of scriptures had features that were more Samaritan than Judaean in nature, and they had adopted rites and incantations based on the revelation of a "Hidden Power," who they probably interpreted as the Christian Christ, but who is not attested in the scriptures that "mainstream" Judaism and Christianity had begun to regard as authoritative by the end of the fourth century.

The profound character of the break with Jewish (Judaean) traditions represented by the Ebionites' attitude toward the temple and sacrificial cult has perhaps not always been fully recognized by scholars. Epiphanius' Ebionites did not simply criticize the performers or performance of the temple cult but considered the cult itself only a temporary arrangement made because Moses was not able to root out the people's inclination towards sacrifices all at once. For this reason, Moses announced the coming of a prophet who would complete the task. If, as Epiphanius reports, the Ebionites portrayed James as attacking the temple cult, this also surely implies a radical reinterpretation of traditions connected to him: James "the Just" is usually depicted as one who frequently visited the temple, and who was held in high esteem among his Jewish compatriots (Eusebius, *Hist. eccl.* 2.23).

A clear indicator of the Christian character of the Ebionites' doctrine is the central role attributed to the "eternal Christ" (*Rec.* 1.43.1). Indeed Adam, the patriarchs and Moses have earned their place in history only through his authority and his presence with them. Christian baptism also had a key role in their religious system since it was instituted to replace sacrifices. At the same time, the Ebionites' rejection of sacrifices probably also had larger implications for their Christology and their interpretation of the Eucharist. This kind of theology would seem to exclude any reference to Jesus' sacrificial death in the Eucharist.[33] This is very much in line with the fact that they only used water in their Eucharistic meals: since the Ebionites found blood abhorrent, they paid more attention to purifications with water in their religious rites. The Ebionites' Christ, in sum, was a preexistent divine being, but he did not come to the world to sacrifice himself or to give his life for the ransom for many. Instead, he had a prophetic task.[34]

2.1.5. *From Irenaeus' Ebionites to Epiphanius' Ebionites?*

The name "Ebionites" as an obvious self-designation, anti-Paulinism, and reverence of Jerusalem are the three features that most clearly connect Epiphanius' Ebionites to the earlier Irenaean tradition about the Ebionites. There also seems to be a significant point of contact with respect

---

[33] For the Ebionites' interpretation of the Eucharist, see Chapter 4.1 below and Luomanen 2005a.

[34] Although the term "True Prophet" in the *Pseudo-Clementines* is more typical of the *Basic Writing* than *Rec.* 1.27–71, there is no doubt that the Christ of *Rec.* 1.27–71 fulfills a prophetic task as the prophet announced by Moses.

to specific ritual practice. Because sacrifices were abhorrent to Epiphanius' Ebionites, we have every reason to accept his report that they celebrated the Eucharist with unleavened bread and water only. This practice is not unique within early Christianity, but it certainly is distinctive, and accords with Irenaeus' report that the Ebionites "reject the commixture of the heavenly wine and wish it to be water of the world only" (Irenaeus, *Haer.* 5.1.3).[35]

There are also, however, a number of features in the religious profile of Epiphanius' Ebionites that are not included in the earlier reports. Were such features simply not mentioned by earlier heresiologists, or were they in fact peculiar to the form of the Ebionite movement known to Epiphanius? To what extent do they suggest significant development in Ebionite belief and practice in the centuries between Irenaeus and Epiphanius?

Among the new features found in Epiphanius' account, for example, are speculations about Christ's preexistence (*Pan.* 30.16.3), his being created and set over the angels (*Pan.* 30.3.4, 30.16.4), and his pre-Christian appearances in and to Adam and the patriarchs (*Pan.* 30.3.3, 30.3.5). Although these kinds of ideas are not explicitly attested in earlier descriptions of the Ebionites, they do have a certain consistency with the basic tenets of the Christology of the Irenaean Ebionites. Irenaeus' description implied that the Ebionites' view of Christ was *similar to* that of Cerinthus and Carpocrates.[36] That would mean that, in the Ebionite view, Christ entered Jesus at (or after) his baptism. It is precisely these beliefs we meet in Epiphanius' Ebionites, only in a more elaborate form: Christ took on Jesus' body, but this was not the first time he had done such a thing; he had in fact done the same thing several times in the course of history.

A number of differences, however, seem much more significant. The oaths and magical incantations attested in the *Book of Elchasai* and in the rites that the Ebionites themselves performed together with the Christological speculations lend Epiphanius' Ebionites a more syncretistic outlook when compared to the earlier heresiologists' views. Moreover, Epiphanius' Ebionites' rejection of the temple and sacrifices as well as the prophets represents not only, as noted above, a clear break with Jewish

---

[35] Irenaeus' main point is to criticize the Ebionites because they do not believe that God was united with man in Jesus. Nevertheless, his argument carries conviction only if the Ebionites' Chalice contained no wine.

[36] See above Chapter 2.1.1.

(Judaean) traditions, but it is also the most significant feature that does not agree with the Irenaean tradition about the Ebionites. The key question here is if, in spite of this break, the Epiphanian Ebionites could still be regarded as representatives of the same movement that Irenaeus attacked two centuries earlier. It is hard to believe that all the similarities could be incidental results from the judaizing tendencies of two unrelated Christian groups. Are we then to assume a development from Irenaeus' Ebionites to Epiphanius' Ebionites?

In general, religious movements are rather conservative in their attitude towards scriptures honored in their tradition. If necessary, new scriptures may be adopted and old ones updated, reedited and reinterpreted but they are seldom discarded if they have, at some point, held a highly valued position. This kind of patching characterizes human cognition in general: rather than starting all over from scratch, new information is integrated into the existing cognitive structures and old structures are modified only to the extent that is necessary.[37] Therefore, it is hard to believe that a community that had interpreted the prophets "carefully" or "curiously"—as Irenaeus' Ebionites did (*curiosius exponere*; Irenaeus, *Haer.* 1.26.2)—would suddenly have dropped them and resorted only to the use of the Pentateuch.

Another type of development is more believable. The Jewish-Christian profile of Epiphanius' Ebionites would be a predictable result of the reception of Christian missionaries by Jews (or Samaritans) whose religious canon consisted mainly (or only) of the Pentateuch. If inclined towards the Christian message, they might accept Christ as the prophet predicted by Moses but would probably be less willing to enlarge their collection of scriptures if the understanding of the new message did not require it.

According to Acts, the Hellenists of the early Jerusalem community commenced missionary activity among the Samaritans after the execution of Stephen (Acts 8:4–7; 11:19–20). If this activity really resulted in conversions among the Samaritans—as is indicated in Acts—then the religious profile of these "Samaritan-Hellenistic" Christians would be likely to resemble the profile of Epiphanius' Ebionites.[38] This possibility

---

[37] Bless, et al. 2004, 67–68; Wilkes 1997, 57–62, 209–210, 294–296.

[38] According to Acts, Philip headed to Samaria after Stephen's execution and had success there (Acts 8:4–7). Acts also refers to Cyprus as the target of the missionary work that followed Stephen's execution (Acts 11:19–20). Furthermore, in Luke's view, the religiosity of both Samaria and Cyprus was characterized by false prophets and magicians (Acts 8:4–25; Acts 13:4–12; cf. the Ebionites' use of the *Book of Elchasai*).

will be discussed in more detail below (Chapter 4.1.7), but—anticipating that discussion—we may note here that the connection between Epiphanius' Ebionites and the "Samaritan-Hellenistic" Christians would have been even more clear if these Hellenists also understood themselves as "poor"[39] and hated Paul not only because of his liberal interpretation of the law but also because he had been involved with the execution of Stephen (Acts 7:57–8:1).

Thus, we may have to reckon with the possibility that, from very early on, there may have been at least two types of Ebionites: (1) Hebrew/Aramaic-speaking Ebionites (= Irenaeus' Ebionites?) who shared James the Just's positive attitude towards the temple and accepted all the prophets, and (2) Hellenistic-Samaritan Ebionites (= the predecessors of Epiphanius' Ebionites) who totally rejected the worship in the temple, used only the Pentateuch and, carrying with them the memory of Stephen's execution, perceived Paul as one of their major opponents.

In the last analysis, Epiphanius—the great *doctor confusus* of early church history—may have been on the right track when he concluded that the Ebionites of his day had adopted their ideas from the Samaritans and from a certain Elchasai. Whatever the real history of Epiphanius' Ebionites, it is perfectly clear that, in Epiphanius' view, they had adopted ideas which showed them to have strayed away not only from correct Christian doctrine but also from what he considered genuinely Jewish traditions.

Epiphanius' Ebionites had such a clear and independent Jewish-Christian profile that they must have distanced themselves from other Christian as well as from other Jewish communities. They thus represent an

---

Thus, it is possible that some Hellenists found refuge among the Samaritans or closely related groups after the execution of Stephen. In any case, it seems clear that Epiphanius' Ebionites and *Rec.* 1.27–71 found something to build on in the traditions connected to Stephen. Stephen's "proclamation," as it is described in Acts, probably found acceptance among Hellenistic Jewish Christians who criticized the temple and sacrifices and saw Jesus mainly as a prophet predicted by Moses. For this hypothesis, see also Luomanen 2005a.

[39] Not only Epiphanius' Ebionites but also modern scholars have suggested that "poor" as the self-designation might go back to the Jerusalem community (see above Chapter 2.1.1). If such is the case, there is no need to restrict this term only to the "Hebrews" of the early Church. Even the Hellenists of the Jerusalem community were surely bilingual enough to understand the meaning of the Hebrew word *ebyon*. Moreover, we know that Epiphanius' Ebionites did perceive of themselves as "Ebionites" although they spoke Greek and used Greek scriptures.

independent branch of *Jewish Christianity*. At the same time, their Jewish-Christian profile appears to be so unique that it raises the question whether they should also be given a name of their own. Because they seem to have called themselves Ebionites, it would be natural to simply call them Epiphanius' Ebionites in order to keep in mind that they differed considerably from the Ebionites known to earlier church fathers. Another possibility would be to call them Samaritan-Elchasaite Christians. In any case, it seems that to label these Ebionites as simply Jewish Christians would not do justice to some of the very distinctive beliefs they had developed when they did not accept the prophets and adopted the *Book of Elchasai*.

2.2. The Nazarenes

2.2.1. Introduction

The Jewish-Christian "heresy" of the Nazarenes was first discussed by Epiphanius, the fourth-century bishop of Salamis. Although Epiphanius dates the origin of the heresy back to the first century, it is striking that none of his predecessors refers to a heretical sect called Nazarenes whereas the Ebionites are often described by earlier heresiologists, starting with Irenaeus. By the end of the fourth century, the only other father who knows something about the Nazarenes, is his contemporary and friend Jerome.

Scholars have explained this gap in the recorded history of the Nazarenes in various ways. The explanations can be roughly divided into three categories, each connected to a particular concept of the overall development of early Christianity.

1. *The Nazarenes were later, more tolerant Jewish Christians.* Ferdinand Christian Baur argued—in contrast to early heresiologists—that the Ebionites were not originally a heretical sect but successors of the very first Jewish Christians in Jerusalem. The Nazarenes, for their part, represented a later phase of Jewish Christianity, which had developed from its strictly anti-Pauline stance to a more lenient attitude towards the gentiles.[40]

---

[40] Baur thought that the teaching and the practices of the Ebionites were so close to the very first Jewish Christianity that, in general, one could call the early Jewish Christianity Ebionism. However, he also notes that it is more common to restrict the name Ebionites

2. *The Nazarenes were early "orthodox" Jewish Christians.* Albrecht Ritschl argued—in contrast to Baur—that strict Jewish Christianity with its anti-Paulinism cannot be considered as the dominant current in first-century Christianity because the Nazarenes, who accepted the apostle Paul, were the successors of the early Jerusalem community.[41] Ray A. Pritz presents a similar interpretation in his 1988 monograph. According to Pritz, the history of the Nazarenes can be traced back to the early Jerusalem community and the Ebionites came out of a split among the Nazarene ranks around the turn of the first century. The split was possibly caused by disputes concerning Christology. The doctrine of the Nazarenes was "orthodox" although they still followed Jewish law. Thus, the Nazarene Jewish Christians existed from the first century onwards but they were mistakenly called Ebionites by such church fathers as Origen and Eusebius. Justin, who wrote in the middle of the second century, possibly also had knowledge of the Nazarenes although he did not explicitly name them. The earliest heresiologists may have failed to mention the Nazarenes simply because they were not heretical enough.[42]

3. *The Nazarenes were later, local "Catholic" Jewish Christians.* Alfred Schmidtke argued in the beginning of the 20th century that the Nazarenes in Beroea were a purely local phenomenon who had no connection to the early Jerusalem community. The Catholic Church in Beroea had originally consisted of members that were of both Gentile and Jewish pedigree. During the first half of the second century, the Jewish members had formed a community of their own in order to be better able to follow

---

to those Jewish Christians who excluded themselves from the Catholic Church because they were not able to keep up with the development of the Christian consciousness ("Bewusstsein") that moved from Jewish Christianity towards Catholicism. See, Baur 1966 (1860), 174, 174 n. 1. Among contemporary scholars, for instance, G. Lüdemann and M.D. Goulder have argued that the Jewish Christians described as Ebionites by Irenaeus were an offshoot of the earliest Jerusalem community. See, Lüdemann 1996, 52–56; Goulder 1994, 107–113.

[41] Ritschl 1857, 152–154. Ritschl also argued that Origen and Eusebius erroneously identified the Nazarenes with the more heretical Ebionites (p. 156) and that the separation of Gentile and Jewish Christians was caused by both the growing intolerance of the strict Jewish Christians toward the Gentile Christians and by the Bar Kochba war (pp. 250, 252–258, 266). Although Ritschl originally belonged to the Tübingen school, he wrote the second edition (1857) of *Die Entstehung*, where he rejects Baur's construction, after the breakdown of his relationship with Baur. For the Tübingen school see, for instance, Morgan 1994, 710–713.

[42] Pritz 1988, 108–110. Similarly Mimouni 1998, 82–86; Blanchetière 2001, 145, 183, 238–239, 521; Bauckham 2003, 162–181, esp. 162.

their national customs. Nevertheless, the Nazarenes still felt themselves part of the worldwide *ekklesia*.[43] Hans J. Schoeps followed Schmidtke, emphasizing that Epiphanius was responsible for the heretical reputation of the Nazarenes because he connected these "Catholic" Jewish Christians with the heretical sect of the Ebionites, the real offshoot of the early Jerusalem church.[44]

All the above interpretations agree that, although Epiphanius' description of the genesis of the Nazarenes cannot be trusted as such, it is clear that by the second half of the second century, at the latest, the Nazarenes had formed a community of their own with its own peculiar theology. Opinions differ, however, as regards the question of how closely the Nazarenes were integrated with the other forms of Christianity and whether the Nazarenes represented the theology and practice of the early Jerusalem church or were a group that had only later on broken away from Gentile Christians.

Because the ancient writers that explicitly deal with the Nazarenes, Epiphanius and Jerome, are from the fourth century and are known for often allowing their polemical interests and personal ambitions to dictate the contents of their presentations, it is no wonder that the role of the Nazarenes in second-century Christianity has been open to various interpretations. The aim of this chapter is to introduce the evidence provided by Epiphanius and Jerome and to assess its character and reliability. Critical analysis of Epiphanius' and Jerome's presentations leaves us with very little material that could be connected to the heresy of the Nazarenes—if the Nazarenes are understood as a separate, historically definable group or movement. Therefore, instead of being a description of a concrete "heresy" that once existed, the following presentation reads more like a pathology of heresiological writing, a story of how Christian identity is created and supported by cultivating stereotypes of others.

2.2.2. Who Were Called Nazarenes?

Epiphanius discusses the correct spelling of the word Nazarene (Ναζωραῖος) in *Pan*. 29.5.6–29.6.1, emphasizing that the name does not refer to nazirites or to the pre-Christian heresy of the Nasarenes (cf. *Pan*. 18) but is derived from the name of Jesus' hometown. In the New Testament,

---
[43] Schmidtke 1911, 41–42, 105, 124–125, 301–302.
[44] Schoeps 1949, 19–20.

Jesus is called Nazarene using the Greek words Ναζωραῖος (in Matt, Luke, John and Acts) and Ναζαρηνός (in Mark and Luke) which are rendered in English translations either as Nazorean or Nazarene. Accordingly, the present "heretics" are known in English either as the Nazoreans or the Nazarenes.[45]

In addition to the fact that Jesus himself is called Nazarene several times in the canonical gospels and Acts, Paul is accused in Acts of being a leader of the "sect of the Nazarenes" by the high priest Ananias' attorney, Tertullus: "We have, in fact, found this man a pestilent fellow, an agitator among all the Jews throughout the world, and a ringleader of the sect of the Nazarenes." (Acts 24:5; trans. NRSV).

Obviously, the early followers of Jesus were named after their leader, Jesus of Nazareth.[46] Two of Epiphanius' predecessors in the formative Catholic tradition still used the term "Nazarenes" in this general sense. Tertullian noted in his *Against Marcion*: "Christ had to be called Nazarene according to the prophesy of the Creator. Therefore also by this very name the Jews call us Nazarenes because of Him." (*Marc.* 4.8; trans. Klijn & Reinink 1973).[47] Furthermore, Eusebius' *Onomasticon* has the following description: "Nazareth. From this name Christ was called Nazarene and we being now called Christians received in the past the name Nazarenes." (*Onom.* ed. Lagarde 1966 [1887], p. 138,24–25).

Eusebius' information that the term Nazarenes was used of Christians in the past is correct only concerning Greek and Latin literature since Syrians, Arabs, Persians and Armenians used the cognates of the term Nazarenes to designate Christians in general, even after Eusebius' time.[48]

---

[45] For the term Nazarene in general, see Goranson 1994, 1049–1050; Schaeder 1967, 874–879.

[46] Certainly, other hypotheses about the origin of the term have also been discussed in connection with the interpretation of Matt 2:23 or based on speculations about Jesus' being a nazirite or a former member of the allegedly pre-Christian sect of the Nasarenes, the "observants." See, Schaeder 1967, 874–875. Pritz argues that the very first Christians used the term Nazarenes as a self-designation on the basis of a messianic interpretation of Isa 11:1, which refers to the shoot (*netser* in Hebrew) of Jesse. See, Pritz 1988, 12–14. Although Isa 11:1 may be the passage that the writer of Matthew's gospel had in mind when writing Matt 2:23—but which he did not explicate (!)—the interpretation is too speculative to constitute a basis for the naming of the first Christians in general.

[47] If not otherwise indicated, in this chapter the translations of patristic passages are based on Klijn & Reinink 1973. However, minor corrections and modifications, like the spelling of the name Nazarenes, have been made. My own translations are indicated by the initials PL.

[48] See, Schaeder 1967, 874–875; Goranson 1994, 1049. In Syriac, a Christian is *natsraya* (ܢܨܪܝܐ).

In addition, Talmudic tradition includes some references to *notsrim* (נוצרימ)[49] and some versions of the Jewish *Eighteen Benedictions* include a curse against the *notsrim*, which seems to refer to Christians in general.[50]

The assumption that *notsrim* in the *Eighteen Benedictions* refers to Christians in general is in harmony with Jerome's references. In his *Commentary on Amos*, Jerome writes: "Until today they blaspheme the Christian people under the name of Nazarenes." (*Comm. Am.* 1.11–12). Epiphanius also knows about the versions of the *Eighteen Benedictions* that refer to *notsrim* but he connects the curse only to the heretical sect of the Nazarenes he is describing in *Panarion* 29.

Overall, among early Christian and Jewish writers, there are only two men, Epiphanius and Jerome, and some later writers who depend on them, who clearly used the term Nazarenes to designate a specific Jewish-Christian group. Furthermore, of these two writers, it is mainly Epiphanius who condemns the Nazarenes as heretics. For Jerome, the Nazarenes provided useful information from Hebrew writings. For the majority of writers before and after Epiphanius and Jerome, the term Nazarenes referred to (Jewish) Christians in general.

2.2.3. *The Profile of Epiphanius' Nazarenes*

An Overview of the Main Sources and Composition of Pan. 29
Eusebius' *Ecclesiastical History* and Acts provided the background for the information Epiphanius collected in *Panarion* 29. Most of the information that Epiphanius used from Eusebius' *Ecclesiastical History* can be found between *Hist. eccl.* 2.16 and 3.5, which covers the time from Mark's alleged preaching in Egypt to the disciples' flight from Jerusalem, as is shown by the following table:

Mark's preaching in Egypt,	*Hist. eccl.* 2.16	*Pan.* 29.5.4
Philo's description of Therapeutae	*Hist. eccl.* 2.17	*Pan.* 29.5.1–3
James as the first bishop	*Hist. eccl.* 2.23	*Pan.* 29.4.1–4
The disciples' flight from Jerusalem	*Hist. eccl.* 3.5.3	*Pan.* 29.7.8

---

[49] b. 'Abod. Zar. 6a; b. Ta'an. 27b.
[50] Thus, for instance, Horbury 1982, 19–61, esp. 59–61, in contrast to Kimelman 1975, 226–244, and de Boer 1998, 250. The different versions are discussed by Schäfer 1975, 54–64, 116–124, esp. 57–61 who suggests that *notsrim* were included in the prayer in localities where the "Nazarenes" had become a problem. In most cases, the "benediction" refers only to the *minim*.

Epiphanius explicitly refers to Acts concerning the following points:

Jesus was called a Nazarene	Acts 2:22	*Pan.* 29.5.6
		Pan. 29.6.7
Quote from the Apostolic decree	Acts 15:28–29	*Pan.* 29.8.6
Paul as the "leader" of the Nazarenes	Acts 24:5	*Pan.* 29.6.2
Paul's "Nazarene confession"	Acts 24:12–14	*Pan.* 29.6.4

In addition, the wording of Acts influenced Epiphanius' diction in several places and he drew on Galatians and several other New and Old Testament passages in his refutation of the Nazarenes, as will be shown in the course of the following discussion.

The Genesis of the Heresy of the Nazarenes: Epiphanius' Three Explanations

When Epiphanius lists the heresies in *Panarion*, one of his main concerns is to show how they developed from each other. Therefore, the opening lines of each chapter usually link the heresy to be treated with the one that has been refuted in the previous chapter. A model for this composition was already provided by Irenaeus who traced the heresies he discussed back to the activity of Simon Magus. Heresiologists who preceded Epiphanius—Irenaeus, Hippolytus and Pseudo-Tertullian—had presented the heresies of Cerinthus and Ebion in that order. Epiphanius inserts the Nazarenes between these two, arguing that the Nazarenes came after, or were contemporary with, the Cerinthians and that the Ebionites were founded by a certain Ebion who came from the Nazarenes' school.

In the beginning of *Panarion* 29, Epiphanius still admits that he is not sure whether the Nazarenes followed the Cerinthians or vice versa. This does not prevent him from trying to locate stories in his sources that would tell about the genesis of the Nazarenes with the result that *Panarion* 29 now contains three different and—partly incompatible—explanations of the genesis of the Nazarenes.

First, in the beginning of *Panarion* 29, Epiphanius states that he does not know when the Nazarene heresy began. According to Epiphanius, after the Cerinthians

> come Nazoreans, who originated at the same time or even before, or in conjunction with them or after them. In any case they were contemporaries. I cannot say more precisely who succeeded whom. For, as I said, these were contemporaries with each other, and had similar notions.
> (*Pan.* 29.1.1; trans. Williams 1987b).

If the Nazarenes originated at the same time or even before the Cerinthians, they must—using Epiphanius' timeline—have been a pre-70 movement since Epiphanius states that Cerinthus was among those conservative Jewish Christians who, according to Acts, had gone from Jerusalem to Antioch and caused confusion there (Acts 15:24), and who also had opposed Peter (Acts 11:2–3).

Second, Epiphanius makes an attempt to determine the beginning of the heresy more exactly. He states that in the period of time when Christians

> were called Jessaeans,[51] for a short time after the Savior's ascension and after Mark had preached in Egypt, some again seceded (τινὲς ἐξεληλύθασι πάλιν). They were called the followers of the apostles, indeed, but I think that they were the Nazarenes who I am describing here. They are Jews by birth and they dedicate themselves to the law and submit to circumcision.
> (*Pan.* 29.5.4; trans. PL).

Epiphanius is clearly using here a source (or sources) that refer to "some people" who "went out" (ἐξεληλύθασι) and were called the followers of the apostles, and draws a conclusion of his own that these must have been the Nazarenes. What is Epiphanius' source and how does he date this event?

The timing, "a short time after the Savior's ascension and after Mark preached in Egypt," shows that Epiphanius still has in mind Eusebius' account. There the conversion of Egyptian Therapeutae, who Eusebius falsely identifies with Christians, is said to be caused by Mark's preaching in Alexandria (*Hist. eccl.* 2.13,16).[52] Epiphanius has quoted this

---

[51] Jessaeans as the title of the first Christians is not discussed by other church fathers. However, in Syriac, Christians are called not only *natsraye* (ܢܨܪܝܐ), as was indicated above, but also *yeshuaye* (ܝܫܘܥܝܐ), and a cognate title is to be found in Arabic as well (I owe this observation to Prof. Heikki Räisänen; see also Blanchetière 2001, 144). Therefore, it is possible that these titles were in fact known to Epiphanius from Syriac traditions but he connected them—or better, their appropriate use—only to the very first followers of Jesus. According to Jerome (*Ruf.* 2.22, 3.6), Epiphanius was versed in Syriac and Hebrew (in addition to Egyptian, Latin and Greek) but because Jerome listed Epiphanius' language skills in order to ridicule Rufinus, who knew only two languages, he may have been slightly exaggerating. In any case, Epiphanius was trained in Egypt and wrote mainly in Greek. If his knowledge of Semitic languages was limited and he did not converse with orthodox Syriac-speaking Christians, that would explain why he thought that the terms Nazarenes and Jessaeans belonged only to the past in the history of "orthodox" Christianity.

[52] The expression "after the Savior's ascension" seems to be based on *Hist. eccl.* 2.13 where Eusebius quotes Justin's *First Apology* (1 *Apol.* 26). Epiphanius' wording follows Eusebius (μετὰ τὴν ἀνάληψιν) instead of Justin (μετὰ τὴν ἀνέλευσιν).

description in the preceding lines of *Panarion* 29 where he discusses the Jessaeans (= Eusebius' Therapeutae). Eusebius does not say anything about "some people" who "again went out/seceded." Therefore, it is clear that Epiphanius either is using here an additional source that has not survived[53] or is drawing his own inferences from Eusebius' account and the New Testament writings.[54]

Be that as it may, it is clear that Epiphanius describes the appearance of these "some" in terms similar to Acts 15:24 where the "*apostles*" and presbyters write: "Since we have heard that some (τινές) of us have come (ἐξελθόντες, literally "went out"; the same Greek term as in the *Panarion*!) and confused you ..." Notably, the majority of Greek manuscripts also include a summary of the message of these envoys. They came "saying that one has to be circumcised and keep the law." Thus, the content of the message of these envoys is the same as the "doctrine" of the Nazarenes that Epiphanius quotes in this connection: "They are Jews by birth and they dedicate themselves to the law and submit to circumcision" (*Pan.* 29.5.4). Furthermore, the description of Simon's conversion in Acts has clearly inspired Epiphanius' description of the Nazarenes' "conversion:"

> When they heard Jesus' name and *saw the* divine *signs that happened through the hands of the apostles they* also *believed* in Jesus.
> (*Pan.* 29.5.6; trans. PL).

> *Simon* also *believed* and was baptized ... and when *he saw the signs* and great miracles *that happened* he was amazed ... and when he saw that *through* the laying on *the hands of the apostles* ...
> (Acts 8:13,18; trans. PL).

It is clear that Eusebius' reference to the genesis of the Nazarenes draws heavily on Acts. Even if Epiphanius made use of a traditional descrip-

---

[53] For instance, Williams 1987a, xx suggests that Epiphanius may have known Justin's lost Syntagma.

[54] The description in Acts 15 of the envoys that come from Jerusalem and cause problems in Antioch is not entirely compatible with Paul's description of similar events in Gal 2. Therefore, Epiphanius—or the writer of the source he is using—may have concluded that the church in Antioch must have been attacked twice by Jerusalem conservatives: first before the Apostolic council (described in Acts 15) and then again after it (as suggested by Gal 2). As was shown above, Epiphanius claims in *Pan.* 28 that Cerinthus was among those men who came from Jerusalem, and in this connection, he explicitly quotes Acts 15. If he counted two invasions from Jerusalem, it is natural to assume that he made the Nazarenes responsible for the second one because the Nazarenes are refuted after the Cerinthians in the *Panarion*. In any case, Epiphanius consulted both Acts and Gal for *Pan.* 29 since he quotes Acts 15:28–19 and Gal 3:10, 5:2, 4 when he later moves on to refute the Nazarenes (*Pan.* 29.8.1, 6–7).

tion of the activities of early Jewish Christians, it is clear that he was himself responsible for identifying these with the Nazarenes. When he made this identification, he was mainly concerned with criticizing the Nazarenes and he did not pay much attention to the timing of the incidents described. In Eusebius' timeline, which Epiphanius basically follows, Mark's preaching in Egypt happened well before 70, whereas Epiphanius' third reference to the genesis of the sect, which will be discussed next, is clearly a post-70 event.

> This heresy of the Nazarenes exists in Beroea in the neighbourhood of Coele Syria and the Decapolis in the region of Pella and in Bashan in the so-called Kokaba [ἐν τῇ Κωκάβῃ], Chochabe in Hebrew. For from there it took its beginning after the exodus from Jerusalem when all the disciples went to live in Pella because Christ had told them to leave Jerusalem and to go away since it would undergo a siege. Because of this advice they lived in Perea after having moved to that place, as I said. There the Nazarene heresy had its beginning. (*Pan.* 29.7.7–8; trans. Klijn & Reinink 1973).

Epiphanius' source for the story about the exodus from Jerusalem is again Eusebius (*Hist. eccl.* 3.5) but, in contrast to the two earlier descriptions, he now dates the genesis of the Nazarene heresy after the fall of Jerusalem. There are two obvious reasons for this. First, in this connection, Epiphanius presents a list of villages where the Nazarenes supposedly lived in his time and the list also includes Pella, which connects it with the tradition about the disciples' flight from Jerusalem. Second, the timing after the fall of Jerusalem provides a very good starting point for the following refutation of the Nazarenes where Epiphanius argues that it is impossible to fulfill the law because access to Jerusalem and its temple worship is denied.

Overall, Epiphanius' remark in the beginning of *Panarion* 29 that he does not really know when the Nazarene heresy begun, accords with his contradictory descriptions about its beginning. Epiphanius ends up locating the genesis of the heresy after the fall of Jerusalem because it provides a good starting point for his refutation but he has no historical data about the origins of this movement.

The Summary of the Nazarenes' Practices and Doctrine: Pan. 29.7.2–8, 29.9.2,4

In Williams' English translation, *Panarion* 29 covers approximately seven and half pages but a relatively small number of lines describe the beliefs and practices of the Nazarenes. On the first five pages, Epiphanius discusses the reasons why all Christians were, for a short while, called

Jessaeans and Nazarenes before they began to be called Christians in Antioch. In practice, this long "introduction"—which contains several digressions typical of Epiphanius' style—does not reveal anything more about the Nazarenes except that, in Epiphanius' opinion, these "heretics" adopted the name that once was common to all Christians. The actual description of the Nazarenes' practices and doctrines is to be found in Pan. 29.7.2–8:

> *Pan.* 29.7.2:
> (1) They used not only the New but also the Old Testament confessing everything
> (2) as the law proclaims it.
>
> *Pan.* 29.7.3: They "acknowledge both
> (3) the resurrection of the dead, and
> (4) the divine creation of all things, and declare that
> (5) God is one, and that
> (6) his Son/servant (παῖς) is Jesus Christ."
>
> *Pan.* 29.7.4:
> (7) They read the law, the prophets and the writings in Hebrew
>
> *Pan.* 29.7.5:
> The position of the Nazarenes is summarized: They disagree with the Jews only because of their belief in Christ and they are not in accord with Christians only because they are still fettered by the law.
>
> *Pan.* 29.7.6:
> Epiphanius "confesses" that he does not know whether or not the Nazarenes believed in the virgin birth
>
> *Pan.* 29.7.7–8:
> (8) List of the locations of the Nazarenes and their connection to the Pella tradition

This concise description of the Nazarenes is followed by the refutation which begins in *Pan.* 29.8.1. Epiphanius quotes several passages from the Old and New Testament, including Acts and Galatians, in order to show that the Jewish law no longer binds the Christians. The refutation culminates in a description which also gives more information about the Nazarenes' relation to Jews. Epiphanius' point is that the Nazarenes who try to be Jews are also cursed by the Jews themselves:

> *Pan.* 29.9.2:
> (9) The Jews "stand up at dawn, at midday, and toward evening, three times a day when they recite their prayers in the synagogues, and curse and anathematize them. Three times a day they say, 'God curse the Nazarenes.'"
> (trans. Williams 1987b, modified).

Finally, before moving on to deal with the next sect, the Ebionites, Epiphanius reveals one more detail about the Nazarenes.

Pan. 29.9.4:
(10) The Nazarenes have Matthew's gospel in its entirety in Hebrew.

However, Epiphanius does not know whether or not they have removed the genealogies from Abraham to Christ.

The Locations of the Nazarenes
As already noted, Epiphanius locates the Nazarenes in Syrian Beroea, as well as the areas of Bashan (Kokaba/Chochaba) and Decapolis (Pella). Because Jerome, who spent some time near Beroea,[55] also locates the Nazarenes there, it is clear that, by the time of Epiphanius and Jerome, Beroea had some Christian inhabitants who were called Nazarenes.

Because Epiphanius had himself lived in Palestine, in Eleutheropolis (Beth Guvrin), one can also assume that he had some knowledge about the areas where Jewish Christians were living in his time. Epiphanius locates his Kokaba/Chochaba in the area of Bashan, near Karnaim and Ashtaroth (*Pan.* 29.7.7 and *Pan.* 30.2.8–9). Kokaba/Chochaba has been identified with the remains of a town some twenty-seven kilometers east of the Sea of Galilee.[56] In the nearby village of Farj, some archaeological evidence has also been found which may suggest the presence of a Jewish-Christian community: inscriptions including both menorahs and Christian symbols. The inscriptions are dated between the latter part of the fourth century and the early fifth, which makes them roughly contemporary with Epiphanius.[57] Eusebius has also located Ebionites in a village called Choba (Χωβά),[58] which might be the same village as Epiphanius' Kokaba/Chochaba.[59] In any case, it seems that Epiphanius indentified these villages with each other because he locates the genesis of the sect of the Ebionites in his Kokaba/Chochaba (*Pan.* 30.2.8–9).

---

[55] Jerome first tried to fulfill his ascetic goals around 374–377 CE in Syria, near Chalcis, which was located 88 km east-southeast of Antioch and 27 km southwest of Beroea. Kelly 1975, 46.

[56] Taylor 1993, 37.

[57] Taylor 1993, 39–41.

[58] Eusebius, *Onomasticon*, ed. Lagarde 1966 [1887], p. 172,1–3; See Klijn & Reinink 1973, 150–151.

[59] Thus Klijn & Reinink 1973, 27 and Taylor 1993, 38. If the village is not the same, Eusebius' Choba must have been closer to Damascus because the biblical Hobah (Gen 14:15)—in connection with which Eusebius mentions the Choba of the Ebionites—is located to the north of Damascus.

The tradition about the disciples' flight to Pella before the conquest of Jerusalem, as transmitted by Eusebius in his *Ecclesiastical History* (*Hist. eccl.* 3.5), is hardly historical as such. G. Lüdemann has shown that the story can be understood as a foundation legend of a Jewish-Christian community that was living in Pella.[60] If the Pella-tradition was transmitted by Aristo of Pella, as Lüdemann suggests, then it is clear that the Jewish-Christian community had settled in Pella in 135 CE, at the latest.[61] In any case, it is clear that, by the time of Epiphanius, Pella was known as a local center of Jewish Christians who claimed to be the successors of the early Jerusalem community.

Another question is whether or not the Jewish Christians living in Kokaba/Chochaba and Pella were called Nazarenes. At least Epiphanius' predecessors in the formative Catholic tradition presumably called the Jewish Christians of Pella, who understood themselves to be the successors of Jerusalem community, Ebionites. Irenaeus already knew that the Ebionites were "adoring Jerusalem as if it were the house of God." Epiphanius himself also testifies that the Ebionites traced their name—*ebion* means "poor" in Hebrew—back to the time of the Apostles by claiming that they sold their properties and laid the money at the Apostles' feet (*Pan.* 30.17.2). Epiphanius' own interpretation of the prehistory of the Ebionites is in sharp contrast with this explanation since he traces the genesis of the Ebionites back to the activity of Ebion, a former member of the sect of the Nazarenes.

Although one cannot exclude the possibility that there were Jewish Christians who were generally called Nazarenes in Pella and Kokaba/Chochaba in Epiphanius' time, it is more likely that Epiphanius is responsible for connecting the Nazarenes to these environs. Because Epiphanius' *Panarion* depicts the Nazarenes as the first representatives of heretical Jewish Christianity, they had to be connected to the places where Jewish Christians were traditionally thought to be living.

---

[60] Lüdemann 1980, 161–173, 245–254, esp. 165.

[61] Lüdemann 1980, 248 n. 19 argues that the emigration must have happened before 135. I agree with Lüdemann that, if the Pella tradition was transmitted by Aristo of Pella, who wrote around 140–150, the Bar Kokhba War (in 135) cannot have been the disaster that gave rise to the legend. However, in contrast to Lüdemann, I cannot see any apparent reason why the legend could not be rooted in the flight of some members of the Jerusalem community to Pella in the wake of the execution of James the Just. This happened a couple of years before the disaster of 70, and if there were only a few members from Jerusalem, it is perfectly possible that they survived when the Jews raided the town in revenge for the killing of their compatriots in Caesarea (Josephus, *Bell.* 2.458).

The Nazarenes' Use of the Scriptures

Because Jewish Christians were generally thought to be competent in the Hebrew language[62] and obedient to Jewish law, there is no need to assume that Epiphanius must have used a source where it was stated that the Nazarenes used both the New and the Old Testament. On the contrary, the context where Epiphanius presents this information indicates that the reference to the Nazarenes' use of the scriptures only serves to exemplify his accusation that Nazarenes are "complete" Jews. Unlike the representatives of the Jewish sects that Epiphanius has discussed in the beginning of his work, the Nazarenes did not repudiate any parts of the Old Testament but were representatives of "orthodox" Judaism since they accepted the law, the prophets and the Writings. In Epiphanius' view, the Nazarenes were blameless as regards Judaism—except for their belief in Christ.

The Nazarenes' use of the Gospel of Matthew in Hebrew is referred to at the very end of *Panarion* 29, as if it were a sort of appendix to the discussion. Obviously, Epiphanius has added this note in view of his following treatment of the Ebionites.

In the next chapter of his heresiology (*Pan.* 30), Epiphanius presents several quotations from a gospel that was used by the Ebionites saying that the Ebionites call their writing the "Gospel according to the Hebrews." Epiphanius admits that Matthew, indeed, wrote his gospel in Hebrew (*Pan.* 30.3.7). However, it is clear that the gospel used by the Ebionites was a Greek document since the quotations that Epiphanius presents are in Greek and they include wordplays that are understandable only in Greek.[63] According to Epiphanius, the gospel that the Ebionites used was "corrupt and mutilated" (*Pan.* 30.13.1) and a quotation from the beginning of their gospel shows that it opened with the description of the baptism of John. Thus, it did not include the birth narratives (*Pan.* 30.13.6, 30.14.3).

With this kind of evidence about the writings of the Ebionites in his hands, Epiphanius must have been faced with the dilemma of how to explain the information he found in his sources which stated that the Ebionites used only Matthew's Gospel (Irenaeus, *Haer.* 1.26.2) or the "Gospel according to the Hebrews" (Eusebius, *Hist. eccl.* 2.27.4). An easy

---

[62] See Eusebius, *Hist. eccl.* 3.25.5, 3.39.16–17, 5.8.2.
[63] For instance, the Ebionites, who were vegetarians, had introduced changes to John the Baptist's diet by replacing locusts with honey cakes (see Chapter 2.1.4).

solution was that the Gospel of Matthew in Hebrew was used by the Nazarenes who preceded the Ebionites. However, Epiphanius was not able to decide if the birth narratives were already cut from the version that was used by the Nazarenes, or only from the Greek version that was used by their successors, the Ebionites. In reality, Epiphanius had no first-hand information at all about the character of the gospel that was allegedly used by the Nazarenes. Everything he says about their gospel is based on his own deductions.

The Ebionite gospel (or some passages of it) that Epiphanius had in his hands was not the only information that was at odds with the characterization of the Ebionites that Epiphanius found in his sources. Epiphanius reports that the Ebionites were using *Circuits of Peter* and *Ascents of James* (30.15.1, 30.16.6), that obviously were sources for Pseudo-Clementine writings,[64] and "other Acts of the Apostles." Furthermore, Epiphanius seems to have ascribed to the Ebionites views that were typical of the *Book of Elchasai*.[65]

Because the documents were used by Epiphanius' Ebionites and they gave a picture of Ebionite practices and doctrine that differed remarkably from the earlier information about the Ebionites, Epiphanius was faced with the problem of how to deal with the "traditional" picture of the Ebionites. Furthermore, had Epiphanius dealt only with the "Pseudo-Clementine" and "Elchasaite" Ebionites, he would have left open the possibility that Jewish Christianity in its more traditional, "pure" form was not so corrupt after all. My hypothesis is that, because this is not what he wanted to say, he created a picture of an earlier Nazarene heresy which made it possible for him to refute all attempts to try to be both a Jew and a Christian at the same time.

The Doctrines of the Nazarenes
As regards the Christology of the Nazarenes, Epiphanius confesses that he does not know whether or not the Nazarenes followed the Cerinthians in regarding Christ as a mere man (*Pan.* 19.7.6). This statement is revealing in two respects. First, since Epiphanius did not know the Nazarenes' stance on such a burning Christological issue, it is unlikely that he had any personal contact with a sect known as the Nazarenes. Second,

---

[64] For the sources of the Pseudo-Clementine writings, see the discussion above, Chapter 2.1.4; Jones 2005.

[65] For the *Book of Elchasai*, see Chapter 2.1.4.

Epiphanius' ignorance also shows that, by his time, the Nazarenes were not generally known as "those believing Jews who do believe in the virgin birth."

In the light of Epiphanius' ignorance, it is surprising that modern scholars usually characterize the Nazarenes' theology by highlighting their belief in the virgin birth. One argument presented in favor of this view is that, although the Nazarenes were not mentioned by Epiphanius' predecessors, they were already known to Origen (*Contra Celsum* 5.61) and Eusebius (*Hist. eccl.* 3.27.1–3), who make a distinction between two groups of Ebionites: some Ebionites did believe in the virgin birth (= "Nazarenes"), while others did not (= the "real" Ebionites).[66] However, as was shown above[67] this distinction may itself be based on an early textual corruption of Irenaeus' heresiology. In any case, it is clear that Epiphanius, the "inventor" of the Nazarenes, did not identify the Nazarenes with these "more orthodox" Ebionites. Further evidence of the Nazarenes' belief in the virgin birth has been found in Jerome's letter to Augustine (*Epist.* 112) but, as will be shown below (2.2.4), the reference to the Nazarenes in this letter is extremely problematic from a historical point of view.

If Epiphanius' did not know the stance of the Nazarenes on the virgin birth, how is it possible that he was able to present some other details about their doctrines? Where did he get his information?

Everything that Epiphanius does reveal about the doctrines of the Nazarenes can be read in *Pan.* 29.7.3. Therefore, the passage will be repeated here, with the numbering of the information about the Nazarenes' doctrines that was used above:

> They acknowledge both (3) the resurrection of the dead, and (4) the divine creation of all things, and (5) declare that God is one, and that (6) his Son/servant (παῖς) is Jesus Christ.

According to Pritz, one indication of the fact that the Nazarenes were the successors of the earliest Jerusalem church is that Epiphanius' information in *Pan.* 29.7.3 about the doctrines of the Nazarenes accords with Acts' information about the early Jerusalem church:

> One need make only a quick comparison with the opening chapters of Acts to see that these basic doctrines had a place in the teaching of the earliest Jerusalem church: the resurrection of the dead (Acts 2:24,32; 3:15;

---

[66] See, Pritz 1988, 28, 108–109; Wilson 1995, 155–157; Mimouni 1998, 82, 86; Bauckham 2003, 162–163.
[67] See above, Chapter 2.1.2.

4:10); God is the creator of all things (4:24); and belief in one God and his child (παῖς) Jesus Christ (3:13,26; 4:27,30). To this point we do not have anything that would differentiate the Nazarene church from the primitive church.[68]

Pritz finds here substantial evidence for his thesis, according to which the Nazarenes were successors of the early Jerusalem community and that their doctrine was "orthodox" from the very beginning. However, this line of thought is problematic in two respects. First, from a historical point of view, it is clear that Acts presents Luke's interpretation of the life and doctrines of the early Jerusalem community. Therefore, if there is a perfect match between *Pan.* 29.7.3 and Acts, it is questionable how much this reveals about the Nazarenes' relation to the early Jerusalem community. It only accords with Luke's picture of the early Jerusalem community. Second, as was shown above, at least some connections between *Panarion* 29 and Acts can be traced back to Epiphanius' use of Acts as a source in *Panarion* 29, which raises the question if that is also the case in *Pan.* 29.7.3.

Because the *belief in resurrection* does not play any role in other parts of Epiphanius' discussion of the Nazarenes, it is somewhat surprising to find it listed among the Nazarene doctrines. This reference becomes understandable in the light of Epiphanius' use of Acts since the resurrection is one of the main points of contention between Paul and his Jewish accusers in Acts.[69] For the sake of his own rhetoric, Paul—who is accused of being the leader of the Nazarene heresy—"confesses" the main points of the "Nazarene doctrine" in Acts 24:14–15:

> However, I admit that I worship the God of our fathers as a follower of the Way, which they call a heresy (αἵρεσις). I believe everything that agrees with the law and that is written in the prophets, and I have the same hope in God as these men, that there will be a resurrection of both the righteous and the wicked. (trans. NIV).

A few verses later, Paul's defense culminates in his recalling of the earlier events in Jerusalem:

> Or these who are here should state what crime they found in me when I stood before the Sanhedrin—unless it was this one thing I shouted as I stood in their presence: "It is concerning *the resurrection of the dead* that I am on trial before you today." (Acts 24:20–21; trans. NIV).

---

[68] Pritz 1988, 44. Similarly, de Boer 1998, 246.
[69] Cf. Schmidtke 1911, 122–123.

Pritz correctly notes that Acts often connects resurrection with Jesus' position as *God's servant*. Notably, Epiphanius uses here the same Greek word (παῖς) that is also used in Acts 3:13-15, 26.[70] Because Epiphanius argued that the Nazarenes were mimicking the early Jerusalem church, it is easy to understand why he spiced up his description of the Nazarenes by borrowing these details from Acts.

However, Epiphanius did not need to consult Acts in order to state that the Nazarenes believed in the *divine creation of all things*—though one can find this belief in Acts 4:24—or that the Nazarenes declared *belief in one God*. These characteristics were traditionally connected to Jewish Christians ever since Irenaeus' heresiology, which emphasized that, in contrast to the Cerinthians, the Jewish Christians (Ebionites) did not believe that the world was created by a power (demiurge) that was separate from the supreme God (Irenaeus, *Haer.* 1.26.1-2).

Conclusion: The Profile of Epiphanius' Nazarenes
Besides Eusebius' *Ecclesiastical History* and Acts, Epiphanius seems to have had no sources from which he could have derived information about the Nazarenes. His intention was to provide a prehistory for the Ebionites who were his contemporaries, and he accomplished this by tracing evidence of the activities and beliefs of conservative Jewish Christians in Acts and *Ecclesiastical History*.

The Jewish-Christian profile Epiphanius created for the Nazarenes is perfect in the sense that it combines exemplary Jewish features with exemplary Christian characteristics, derived directly from the early Jerusalem community. In contrast to the Ebionites, who rejected the prophets and part of the Pentateuch, the Nazarenes

> use not only the New Testament but the Old Testament as well, as the Jews do. For unlike the previous sectarians [Jewish sects in the *Panarion*], they do not repudiate the legislation, the prophets, and the books Jews call "Writings." (*Pan.* 29.7.2; trans. Williams 1987b).

He summarizes their position as follows:

> They are different from Jews, and different from Christians, only in the following. They disagree with Jews because they have come to faith in Christ; but since they are still fettered by the law—circumcision, the Sabbath, and the rest—they are not in accord with Christians.
> (*Pan.* 29.7.5; trans. Williams 1987b).

---

[70] παῖς appears 24 times in the NT: Matt 8, Luke 9, John 1, Acts 6.

This short characterization could function as a simple definition of Jewish Christianity for modern scholars as well. It is no wonder because this is what Epiphanius was aiming at: a description of Jewish Christianity in its simplest, stereotypic form. With a picture like this, it was easy to condemn all attempts to mix Christianity with characteristically Jewish practices and ideas: "In this section, too, my brief discussion will be enough. People like these are refutable at once and easy to cure—or rather, they are nothing but Jews themselves." (*Pan*. 29.9.1; trans. Klijn & Reinink 1973).

Social psychologists have known for a long time the importance of stereotypes in the creation and maintenance of social identities. The so-called *social identity approach*[71] has also been successfully applied in Biblical studies to cast light on group phenomena where strong stereotypes and boundaries are created.[72] Heresiologies are also perfect objects for such socio-cognitive analyses since they were written and used precisely for the kinds of purposes that the social identity approach is designed to expose: categorization of outgroups, accentuation of differences between the ingroup and the outgroups and the search for subjective cognitive coherence.[73] Epiphanius' Nazarenes are a prime example of an identity-building stereotype which has very little to do with reality but which perfectly serves border marking and the building of a positive group identity.

2.2.4. *The Profile of Jerome's Nazarenes*

In *Pan*. 29, Epiphanius devotes an enormous amount of energy and space to a discussion of what kinds of names were applied to the first Christians; how the heretical Nazarenes differed from the "orthodox" Nazarenes; how the term Nazarene is not to be confused with the nazirites or with the pre-Christian sect of the Nasoreans; and that, besides Nazarenes, the Christians were for a short while also called Jessaeans.[74] These termino-

---

[71] The term *social identity approach* is an umbrella term that refers to Henri Tajfel and John Turner's *social identity theory*, mainly developed in the 1970s in Bristol, to Turner's *self-categorization theory* developed in the mid-1980s, as well as to later adaptations of these theories. For an introduction, see Tajfel 1981; Hogg & Abrams 1988 and Hogg & Abrams 1999.

[72] For instance, Esler 1998, 2003; 2007; Hakola 2007; Jokiranta 2007.

[73] Luomanen 2007b, 220–224.

[74] Jessaeans as the title of the first Christians is not discussed by other church fathers. However, in Syriac, Christians are called not only *natsraye* (ܢܨܪܝܐ), as was indicated above, but also *yeshuaye* (ܝܫܘܥܝܐ) and a cognate title is to be found in Arabic as well. Therefore, it is possible that Epiphanius knew these titles from Syriac traditions

logical clarifications indicate that the term "Nazarenes" was not commonly used as a title for "heretical" Jewish Christians before Epiphanius wrote his *Panarion*. However, once the point of reference for the term "Nazarenes" was fixed in the *Panarion*, it worked very well among Greek and Latin-speaking Christians because no contemporary, "orthodox" Christian group bore that name in Latin or Greek. After Epiphanius, several authors in the West used the term, but usually referring to Jewish Christians in general, so that it became synonymous with "Ebionites." Yet we know that before and after Epiphanius in the East, the cognates of the term Nazarenes were commonly used to denote Christians in general among Syrians, Arabs, Persians and Armenians.[75] It follows that, once we move over to sphere of Semitic Christianity in the East, we have to reckon with the possibility that the term "Nazarenes" was used to denote Christians whose beliefs and practices were not clearly "heretical." As a matter of fact, it seems that Jerome's Nazarenes provides an example of one such group.

Before a discussion of Jerome's references to the Nazarenes, a short overview of Jerome's biography is needed in order to determine how his references are related to Epiphanius' information about the Nazarenes. A more detailed account of Jerome's life with special emphasis on his literary activity follows in Chapter 3.2.

Jerome was born in Stridon in 347 or 348.[76] He had Christian parents and he received his education in Rome. He made his first trip to the East in 372. Originally he had planned to go to Jerusalem but illness prolonged his stay in Antioch and finally made him give up the plan. Instead, he tried the life of a monk in Beroea (374/375–377). Most scholars assume that if Jerome really met Nazarenes, whose gospel he started to quote ten years later, it must have happened here. Jerome returned to Rome in 382 in the company of bishops Paulinus and Epiphanius, with whom he stayed in regular contact afterwards. After the death of Pope Damasus in 384, Jerome entertained hopes of becoming his successor. However, he was not elected and he headed again to Jerusalem where he arrived in 385. After a short trip to Alexandria, Jerome settled in Bethlehem in

---

and connected them to the first Christians because, being Semitic, they had a ring of authenticity. See above footnote 83.

[75] For the term Nazarene in general, see Chapter 2.2.2.

[76] Kelly 1975, 337–339 has argued for an earlier date of birth, 331. However, this is not convincing since that would make Jerome 32 years old when starting grammar school. Thus, Nautin 1986, 304–306.

386. He founded a monastery and spent the rest of his life there. Because Jerome spent long periods of time in the East, it is reasonable to assume that he had some reliable information about Christians who were called Nazarenes there.

Jerome's information about the Nazarenes can be classified into three main categories: 1) occasional references to Nazarene beliefs and practices in connection with the treatment of other topics, 2) explicit descriptions of the Nazarene biblical exegesis in Jerome's *Commentary on Isaiah*, and 3) quotations from a gospel used by them. In this chapter, I focus on the first two categories. The Nazarenes' gospel tradition is treated in more detail in Chapter 3.3.

Jerome's Occasional References and His Letter to Augustine
When assessing Jerome's references to the Nazarenes, it should be kept in mind that he wrote after Epiphanius' *Panarion* was composed and after he had been in contact with Epiphanius several times, especially during their common journey to Rome in 382. Although Jerome does not explicitly quote the *Panarion*, it is probable that, when he moved to Palestine and started to refer to the Nazarenes, he was already influenced by Epiphanius' interpretation of the Nazarenes as "heretics."

Most of Jerome's references to the Nazarenes are to be found in contexts where he refers to or quotes writings that were used by the Nazarenes: a gospel that they used and a commentary on Isaiah. However, occasional references to Nazarenes are also scattered around Jerome's large literary production. According to Jerome, Christians were called Nazarenes because of Jesus' home village (*Sit.* 143). The Nazarenes are cursed in the synagogues of the Jews (*Comm. Am.* 1.11–12; *Comm. Isa.* 5.18–19, 49.7, 52.4–6). The Nazarenes use the Gospel of Matthew in Hebrew (*Vir. ill.* 3). Jerome also tells how he has met Nazarenes and received their writings (*De vir. ill.* 3, *Comm. Matt.* 27.9–10) and he refers to the Nazarenes' beliefs in his letter to Augustine (*Epist.* 112.13).

As compared to Epiphanius, Jerome's attitude towards Christians called Nazarenes is much more positive. Jerome's critical comments are usually aimed at Ebion and the Ebionites but on one occasion he also criticizes the Nazarenes. This is in his letter to Augustine in 404, where Jerome defends his interpretation of Paul's and Peter's conflict in Antioch (cf. Gal 2).

As regards the scholarly discussion about the Nazarenes' doctrine, the letter to Augustine has played a central role since this quotation is the only place where one might see an explicit reference to the Nazarenes' belief in the virgin birth.[77] However, scholars who draw such conclusions about the Nazarenes on the basis of this passage seldom pay attention to its overall context and, more specifically, to the way Jerome develops his case against Augustine. Jerome's overriding interest is to confute Augustine's interpretation of the Antioch incident. Jerome's and Augustine's disputation had a long and complicated prehistory and Jerome's reputation as a biblical scholar was at stake. Therefore, Jerome's critical reference to the Nazarenes cannot be understood correctly without knowing the background of the letter.

Almost two decades earlier (386/7), Jerome had stated in his *Commentary on Galatians*—following Origen and other Greek commentators—that in reality Paul and Peter did not have any disagreement concerning the Christians' obedience to the law. The conflict in Antioch (cf. Gal 2:11–14) was staged only for didactical purposes: Peter pretended to obey the law in order to win Jews to his side and Paul pretended to reprimand him in order to make it clear that the gentile Christians were not obliged to obey the law. Augustine was offended by this interpretation because it seemed to indicate that the Bible was not trustworthy. He sent his own interpretation of the incident followed by some critical remarks and questions to Jerome. Jerome did not get Augustine's first letter and Augustine had to resend his inquiries. The original of the second letter also failed to reach Jerome and when Jerome was finally informed of Augustine's critical remarks through an abbreviated copy of the letter that was circulated around, he refused to answer. However, the dispute had become widely known and in 404 Jerome could no longer postpone his answer.[78] Jerome pushes Augustine's case to the extreme, claiming that Augustine obviously wants all the Jews who have become Christians to continue to obey the law. This would lead into the heresy of Cerinthus and Ebion:

> If this [i.e., Augustine's interpretation] is true, we shall fall into the heresy of Cerinthus and Hebion, who believe in Christ and for this only have been anathematized by the fathers, because they mixed the ceremonies of the law with the Gospel of Christ and in this way they confess new things while they did not cut loose from the old. What shall I say of the Ebionites who claim to be Christians? Until now a heresy is to be found in all parts of the East where Jews have their synagogues; it is called "of the Minaeans" and

---

[77] See for instance, Pritz 1988, 53–55.
[78] For the conflict between Augustine and Jerome, see Kelly 1975, 217–220, 263–272; Hennings 1994, 274–291.

> cursed by Pharisees up to now. Usually they are named Nazoreans. They believe in Christ, the Son of God born of Mary the virgin, and they say about him that he suffered and rose again under Pontius Pilate, in whom also we believe, but since they want to be both Jews and Christians, they are neither Jews nor Christians.
>
> (Jerome, *Epist.* 112.13; trans. Klijn & Reinink 1973).

Jerome comes back to the same argument a bit later (112.16) but then he refers only to the Ebionites. Clearly, Jerome is not giving here an objective account of the Nazarenes' doctrines. The name of the Nazarenes is mentioned only in passing, as a synonym for the Ebionites whose heresy Augustine is propagating, in Jerome's opinion. Jerome is making exactly the same point here as Epiphanius does at the end of *Panarion* 29: If you try to be both a Jew and a Christian at the same time, you end up being neither Jewish nor Christian and you will be anathematized. I think it is not too far-fetched to assume that Jerome owed this argument to Epiphanius.

The reason why the name of the Nazarenes is taken up in this context is that the Pharisees were not known for cursing the Ebionites in their synagogues but the "Minaeans" and the "Nazarenes"—obviously corresponding to the two forms of the *Eighteen Benedictions* that were in use in Jewish synagogues. Since no curse of the Ebionites was known, Jerome had to bring in the "Minaeans" and the "Nazarenes" in order to show that Augustine's position was anathematized both by Jewish and Christian "fathers." Furthermore, Epiphanius' description of the Nazarenes'/Ebionites' beliefs is all but a quotation from early Christian creeds: "They believe in Christ, the Son of God born of Mary the virgin, and they say about him that he suffered and rose again under Pontius Pilate, in whom also we believe ..." The "fact"[79] that some of the Ebionites believed in the virgin birth was certainly known to Jerome from Origen's and Eusebius' writings. By reciting an early Christian creed, Jerome demonstrates that correct doctrine does not help if one still adheres to Jewish law.

This passage does not necessarily have anything to do with specifically Nazarene doctrine (if there even was one—which I doubt). Jerome only quotes the creed in order to make clear that even if a person has the correct doctrine but tries to combine Christianity with Judaism (like

---

[79] As was noted above (Chapter 2.1.1), the distinction between two kinds of Ebionites is historically unreliable.

·Augustine does, in Jerome's view), that person is cursed. Therefore, one should not build any concept of the character of the Nazarenes on this passage.

The Nazarenes and the Rabbis
A much more reliable source for information about the Nazarenes is the Nazarenes' explanation of Isaiah, quoted by Jerome in his *Commentary on Isaiah*, written around 408/410. Jerome's commentary contains five quotations from the Nazarenes' explanation. Three of these are to be found in one block, at the end of Isaiah 8 and in the beginning of Isaiah 9. The remaining two are in Isa 29:17–21 and 31:6–9. All these quotations exemplify the Nazarenes' highly critical attitude towards the early rabbis and their tradition. Because Jerome does not draw on the Nazarenes' commentary in any other connection or even refer to the work in any of his writings, he probably did not have the entire explanation available. More likely, he was only using a Nazarene collection of prophetic testimonies against the "scribes and the Pharisees" that he had either received from the "Nazarenes" or that was connected to them for some other reason.[80]

The Nazarenes' Interpretation of Isa 8:14: The "Scatterer" and the "Unholy"
At the beginning of the first quotation, Jerome introduces the Nazarenes as the ones "who accept Christ in such a way that they do not cease to observe the old law." The quoted explanation itself concerns the two houses mentioned in Isaiah 8:14.[81]

According to Jerome,

> the Nazarenes … explain the two houses as the two families, viz. of Shammai and Hillel, from whom originated the Scribes and the Pharisees. Akiba who took over their school is called the master of Aquila the proselyte and after him came Meir who has been succeeded by Joannes the son of Zakkai and after him Eliezer and further Telphon, and next Ioseph Galilaeus and Josua up to the capture of Jerusalem. Shammai then and Hillel were born not long before the Lord, they originated in Judea.

---

[80] Schmidtke 1911, 63–90 assumed that Jerome had received the information about the Nazarenes' Isaiah exegesis from his teacher Apollinaris. The assumption is a part of Schmidtke's—generally dismissed—hypothesis that both Jerome and Epiphanius (in *Pan.* 29) derived their information about the Nazarenes from Apollinaris.

[81] Isaiah 8:14: "… but for both houses of Israel he will be a stone that causes men to stumble and a rock that makes them fall. And for the people of Jerusalem he will be a trap and a snare."

The name of the first means scatterer and of the second unholy, because he scattered and defiled the precepts of the law by his traditions and δευτερώσεις. And these are the two houses who did not accept the Saviour who has become to them destruction and shame. (*Comm. Isa.* 8.11–15 [interpretation of Isaiah 8:11–15]; trans. Klijn & Reinink 1973).

The interpretation of the name of Hillel indicates that the one who was responsible for it was working with the Hebrew script since Hillel becomes "unholy" if one reads the root as הלל instead of חלל. Pritz has also pointed out that Telphon in Jerome's quotation most likely refers to Tarphon, who was one of Akiva's students. This mistake is also understandable only in an unpointed Hebrew text where vowels are not indicated and a defective ל may resemble ר. A third indication of Hebrew/Aramaic being the original language of the exposition is to be found in the passage that is quoted below. There it is stated that the "preaching became more dominant, that means the preaching was multiplied" (*ingrauata est, id est multiplicata praedicatio*). However, neither "becoming more dominant" or "multiplied" fits the context very well. Obviously, Jerome has here had difficulties in translating the Hebrew root כבד which can mean (in Hiphil) both "make heavy" and "make honored." Jerome's Vulgate opted for the first meaning in Isa 8:23 and that was also his starting point when he was translating the Nazarene's exposition. However, the original meaning in the context of the Nazarenes' expositions must have been "made honored," which Jerome did not realize. Klijn has also pointed out several connections between the Nazarenes' expositions and Targumic traditions,[82] which is a further indication of the fact that the passages Jerome quoted were derived from Aramaic-speaking Christians.

The trick with the explanation of the name Shammai (שמאי) is that it is interpreted as being derived from the root שמם so that it becomes "scatterer." As a matter of fact, this pun has a clear connection to Jerome's Latin translation of the Old Testament. In the Vulgate, *dissipare* ("to scatter") is often used to translate the Hebrew root שמם. Thus, it is possible that Jerome himself was responsible for this interpretation. Furthermore, the sequence of the rabbis is incorrect since Meir should be the last one on the list. This may indicate that the list was later enlarged with

---

[82] Klijn 1972, 241–255. In addition to connections that Klijn has pointed out, it is to be noted that the translation *vectigales* (see below *Comm. Isa.* 31:6–9) reflects the later Hebrew meaning of the root מס and the language of the Targums. See, BDB, מס (pp. 586–587).

Yohanan ben Zakkai and his students and the reviser did not know the real sequence of the rabbis, or that the one who added the reference to the rabbis was not too well-versed in the rabbinic tradition in the first place.[83]

In addition to the interpretation of the name Shammai the quoted passages also have other connections to the wording of the Vulgate.[84] Because the exposition often paraphrases Isaiah's passages, it is natural that Jerome drew on his own Latin translation instead of preparing an independent, direct translation from the Nazarenes' exposition.

Nevertheless, even if the passage was enlarged with some critical notes later on (by Jerome), the mere fact that Shammai's and Hillel's schools are identified with the two houses of Israel, which are to face the judgment, indicates that the Nazarenes' own explanation must already have been directed against the rabbinic tradition.

The Nazarenes' Interpretation of Isa 9:1: Did They Still Observe the Old Law?

The criticism of the Scribes and the Pharisees is so obvious in the Nazarenes' expositions that there is no doubt that the Nazarenes totally rejected the early rabbis and their teaching. However, at some points the criticism goes so far that it becomes questionable if the excerpts really were derived from people "who accept Christ in such a way that they do not cease to observe the old Law," as Jerome claimed in the introduction to the first quotation.

> The Nazarenes whose opinion I have set forth above, try to explain this passage [Isaiah 9:1] in the following way: When Christ came and his preaching shone out, the land of Zebulon and the land of Naphtali first of all were freed from the errors of the Scribes and the Pharisees and he shook off their shoulders the very heavy yoke of the Jewish traditions. Later, however, the preaching became more dominant, that means the preaching was multiplied, through the Gospel of the apostle Paul who was the last of all the apostles. And the Gospel of Christ shone to the most distant tribes and the way of the whole sea. Finally the whole world which earlier walked or sat in darkness and was imprisoned in the bonds of idolatry and death, has seen the clear light of the gospel.
> (*Comm. Isa.* 9.1; trans. Klijn & Reinink 1973, modified).

---

[83] See Pritz 1988, 59,61; Schmidtke 1911, 123.

[84] For instance, the following expressions are paralleled in the Vulgate: *stridunt in incantationibus suis* (Isa 8:19), *qui peccare faciebant homines in verbo* (Isa 29:21).

According to this quotation, the Nazarenes fully accepted Paul's mission to the Gentiles. Thus, their stance was totally different from the Ebionites and from the Jewish-Christianity of the *Pseudo-Clementines*.[85]

Even though it might be possible to interpret the clause "were freed from the errors of the Scribes and the Pharisees" so that only the rabbinic tradition was dismissed by Christ, in the following sentence the "heavy yoke of Jewish traditions" (*grauissimum traditionum Iudaicarum iugum*) is discarded altogether. Notably, the image of the "yoke"—which in Judaism is often connected to covenant loyalty in general—cannot be found in those verses of Isaiah that the passage paraphrases (Isa 8:23, 9:1). It is deliberately brought into the exposition in order to make it clear that Jesus' preaching did not comply with the "Jewish traditions."

The Nazarenes' Interpretation of Isa 8:19–22: Idol Worship

The total rejection of Jewish traditions can also be seen in the following passage which equates the following of the traditions with a nation's worship of idols:

> For the rest the Nazarenes explain the passage [Isaiah 8:19–22] in this way: When the Scribes and the Pharisees tell you to listen to them, men who do everything for the love of the belly and who hiss during their incantations in the way of the magicians in order to deceive you, you must answer them like this. It is no wonder if you follow your traditions since every nation consults its own idols. We must not, therefore, consult your dead about the living ones. On the contrary God has given us the Law and the testimonies of the scriptures. If you are not willing to follow them you shall not have light, and darkness will always oppress you.
> (*Comm. Isa.* 8.19–22; trans. Klijn & Reinink 1973).

The last passage that Jerome quotes also targets the Israelites as whole, not just the Scribes and the Pharisees as their leaders:[86]

> The Nazarenes understand this passage [Isaiah 31:6–9] in this way: O sons of Israel who deny the Son of God with the most vicious opinion, turn to him and his apostles. For if you will do this, you will reject all idols which to you were a cause of sin in the past and the devil will fall before you, not because of your powers, but because of the compassion of God. And his young men who a certain time earlier fought for him, will be the

---

[85] Cf. Häkkinen 2005 and Jones 2005.
[86] Klijn 1972, 253–254 thinks that the Nazarenes' exposition only attacks the Jewish leaders but it is hard to find such a distinction in the texts.

> tributaries of the Church and any of its power and stone will pass. Also the philosophers and every perverse dogma will turn their backs to the sign of the cross. Because this is the meaning of the Lord that his will take place, whose fire or light is in Sion and his oven in Jerusalem.
> (*Comm. Isa.* 31.6-9; trans. Klijn & Reinink 1973).

The passage reveals a viewpoint that is nothing short of the formative Catholic view: The Jews are expected to convert and accept the apostolic faith. In order to do so, they will have to abandon their worship of idols, which—as was shown above—is the same as following Jewish traditions. Consequently, the young men of Israel, who earlier had fought with the devil against the Christians, will become the tributaries of the Church. Finally, the conclusion of the passage also indicates that, despite its sharp criticism of the Scribes and the Pharisees, the Nazarenes' exposition was also attacking the "philosophers" and other "perverse dogmas." Thus the Nazarenes guarded their dogmatic frontiers much like the church fathers themselves.

The Nazarenes' Interpretation of Isa 29:17-21: The Dating of the Exposition
On the basis of the rabbis named in the quotations, the passages cannot be dated earlier than the mid-second century. However, the quotation that deals with Isaiah 29:17-21 may give us further evidence about the time of the composition of the Nazarene's commentary.

> What we understood to have been written about the devil and his angels, the Nazoreans believe to have been said against the Scribes and the Pharisees, because the δευτερωταί passed away, who earlier deceived the people with very vicious traditions. And they watch night and day to deceive the simple ones who made men sin against the Word of God in order that they should deny that Christ was the Son of God.
> (*Comm. Isa.* 29.17-21; trans. Klijn & Reinink 1973).

Since the exposition also indicates that the δευτερωταί—the church fathers' standard expression for early rabbis—have passed away and states that these dead teachers should not be consulted, it is to be assumed that the writer(s) of the exposition were confronted with Jewish teachers who already had the Mishnah in their hands, and that the Mishnah had also been established as authoritative teaching. If this is correct, then the most likely time of composition for the expositions would be the late third or early fourth century. Because the comments were written in Hebrew script and the writer was acquainted with Targumic traditions, the writer must have been a Jewish convert.

Second Legislation in the Didascalia Apostolorum
A remarkable parallel to the Nazarenes' position can be found in the *Didascalia Apostolorum* (*DA*), which confirms that the Nazarenes' interpretation exemplified a typically Syrian attitude towards the early rabbis. The *Didascalia Apostolorum* makes a clear distinction between the First law that binds the Christians (Moses' Ten Commandments) and the Second Legislation (δευτέρωσις; cf. δευτερώσεις in Jerome, *Comm. Isa.* 8.11–15) with which the Jews were bound after they had fallen into idol worship (Exod 32). Consequently, obedience to this Second Legislation is equated with *idol worship* and described as a *heavy burden* and a *hard yoke* in contrast to the First law, which is described as a *light yoke* and equated with the "*law and the prophets*" that Jesus has come to fulfill according to Matt 5:17.[87] Obviously, Jerome's Nazarenes and the *Didascalia Apostolorum* had a similar view of the Second Legislation. The *Didascalia Apostolorum* is usually dated to the third century but it was still used in Syria in the latter half of the fourth century since Epiphanius found it in the hands of the Audians who were Syrian Christians and "heretics" to Epiphanius (*Pan.* 70.10.1–4; cf. *DA* XXI; Lagarde, pp. 91–92).

Conclusion: The Profile of Jerome's Nazarenes
In the light of Jerome's passages and similar views presented in the *Didascalia Apostolorum*, it is difficult to picture Jerome's Nazarenes as a strict, law-observant sect separated from the formative Catholic Church. The Christians from whom Jerome received the expositions unreservedly accepted Paul and his mission to the gentiles. They also leveled criticism at the Jewish nation and people as a whole. The Jews were required to repent/convert, and this did not presuppose the maintenance of a particular Jewish identity or aim at the reestablishment of a traditional Jewish covenantal relationship, as one would expect if a person who still had a Jewish self-understanding repented. Instead, the Jews were expected to adopt a Christian identity by becoming subjects of the Apostles.

---

[87] See, *DA* II/ed. Lagarde 1911 [1854], pp. 4–5; *DA* IV/ed. Lagarde 1911 [1854], p. 12; *DA* XIX/ed. Lagarde 1911 [1854], p. 79 and *DA* XXVI/ed. Lagarde 1911 [1854], pp. 107–109, 111–112, 115. For *DA*'s use of the term δευτέρωσις, see Fonrobert 2001, 495–499.

[33] Irenaeus' heresiology is probably based on Justin Martyr's (lost) *Syntagma* (written before 150 CE). However, most scholars think that Justin's heresiology did not mention Ebionites because Justin's other works show that he did not regard them as clearly heretical. See Häkkinen 2005, 248–249.

Overall, Jerome's Nazarenes—as far as their beliefs can be reconstructed from their Isaiah exegesis—exemplify such clear Christian self-understanding that I would not label them Jewish Christian. The sole basis for doing so would be the fact that they were versed in Semitic languages and might have been ethnic Jews. Jerome's Nazarenes clearly sided with Catholic Christianity and nothing of the idea of *tertium quid* between Jews and (other believing) Christians, which seems to characterize the ideology of the Pseudo-Clementine *Basic Writing*, can be found in Jerome's Nazarenes.[88] These Nazarenes may simply have been *Syriac Christians*, who were of Jewish pedigree—enough to render them suspicious in the eyes of the overtly anti-Jewish Jerome and his compatriots—but who no doubt felt themselves Christian and would have been classified as such by most modern critics.

2.2.5. Conclusion: Who Were the Nazarenes?

Epiphanius' description of the "heresy" of the Nazarenes in *Panarion* 29 is first and foremost a refutation of an idealized, stereotyped picture of people who try to be both Jews and Christians at the same time. The refutation of this standard type of Jewish Christianity needed to be included in the *Panarion* because—as it seemed from Epiphanius' point of view—the Ebionites who were known to him had adopted all kinds of strange ideas from Elchasite and Pseudo-Clementine writings. Epiphanius did not have any Nazarene texts or any sources describing the Nazarenes available, but on the basis of Eusebius' *Ecclesiastical History*, Acts and his own conclusions, he was able to create a picture of the genesis, doctrines and practices of the heresy of the Nazarenes that was easy for him and his fellow Christians to refute. The heresy of the Nazarenes as it is depicted in *Panarion* 29 is pure fiction.[89]

---

[88] cf. Jones 2005, 329–332.

[89] If the "heresy" of the Nazarenes is fictional, as is argued in this volume, it probably is not the only fictional group in Epiphanius' long list of heresies. An interesting point of comparison is the Alogi, who Epiphanius discusses in *Pan.* 51. In the case of the Alogi, Epiphanius explicitly states that he himself invented the term to be used for those who reject the Gospel of John and Revelation. For Alogi, see Marjanen 2005b, 249–252. According to Williams 1987a, xvii, "We cannot assume that, because Epiphanius refers to a given group as a 'sect' and gives it a name, it was necessarily an organized body ... Epiphanius says that he himself coined the names, 'Alogi', 'Antidicomarians', and 'Collyridians', and he may have done the same in other cases. Certainly some of his 'sects' are simply persons who take a particular position; ... An Epiphanian 'sect', then, may represent anything from an organized church to a school of thought, or a tendency manifested by some exegetes."

Nevertheless, three pieces of information with some historical credibility can be inferred from Epiphanius' story. First, by Epiphanius' time in some Jewish synagogues in Palestine and Syria, the prayer of *Eighteen Benedictions* included a curse on the Nazarenes, that is Aramaic/Syriac-speaking Christians. Second, areas to the east and north-east of the Jordan River and especially the villages of Kokaba and Beroea were known as places where Christians adhered to Jewish law. Third, "Nazarenes" was a common title for all Christians in Syriac and it seems that, in the Latin/Greek-speaking Christian communities of Antioch, the term Nazarenes was especially used for some Christians who lived in Beroea. This, together with the fact that for the Latin and Greek fathers, Syriac-speaking Christians, the "Nazarenes," had a reputation for being heretical,[90] may have been a good enough reason for Epiphanius to call the "standard" Jewish Christians, who were not yet influenced by Ebion's and Elchasai's weird doctrines, Nazarenes.

In principle, Jerome shared Epiphanius' view of the Nazarenes as Jewish-Christian heretics but in practice, except for some general references, he did not polemicize against them. Obviously, some Christians who were called Nazarenes had provided Jerome useful information about the Hebrew scriptures which he was able to use to back up his program of *Hebraica veritas*. As will become clear below, Jerome may also have been reluctant to criticize the Nazarenes because the excerpts from the Nazarenes' writings he had received did not evince heretical ideas or practices. Instead, they provided him with a powerful weapon to be used in his anti-rabbinic polemics. As a matter of fact, the fragments in Jerome's writings that are likely to be derived from some Christians called Nazarenes—instead of testifying to the existence of a group of heretics—indicate that the term Nazarenes was also connected to Syriac/Aramaic-speaking Christians whose views barely differed from mainstream Catholicism.

Overall, there is no historically reliable evidence which would justify an assumption that, among Syriac/Aramaic-speaking Christians, there might have been a more or less organized faction with borders defined by characteristically "Nazarene" doctrines, practices or self-understanding, distinct from other Syriac/Aramaic-speaking Christians. Even for the church fathers who lived in Palestine, Syriac/Aramaic-speaking Chris-

---

[90] This is especially reflected in their earlier history up to the time of Ephrem and the bishop Rabbula. See, Segal 2001 [1970], 87–93.

tianity was by and large an unmapped territory of which they had gained knowledge more by hearsay than through personal experience.

Christian Identity in the Making: The "Genesis" of the Heresy of the Nazarenes

Why did Epiphanius create the picture of the Nazarene heresy practically out of nothing? I have suggested above that this was because the sources that Epiphanius had in his hands, and which he connected to the Ebionites, did not match the traditional information about the Ebionites and because Epiphanius still wanted to refute Jewish Christianity even in its "pure form." Thus, in line with his basic conviction that heresies sprung from each other, he painted a picture of the development of Jewish-Christian heresies where the Nazarenes, placed between the Cerinthians and the Ebionites, played the role of imitators of the early Jerusalem church, pure in their "Christian doctrine" as the early Jerusalem community was pure in Epiphanius' mind, and erring only in their adherence to Jewish law. With such a clear picture, it was easy to refute all the attempts to connect Christianity with the practicing of Jewish law. Epiphanius' comment at the end of *Panarion* 29 is revealing: "People like these are easy to catch and refute—they are nothing but Jews" (*Pan.* 29.9.1).

Stereotypes are very powerful tools in creating and maintaining boundaries. According to social identity theory, stereotyping often accompanies ingroup/outgroup categorization.[91] Fredrick Barth has modeled the formation of (ethnic) identity on three levels: 1) the micro level which focuses on personal and interpersonal interaction, 2) the median level which focuses on the formation of collectives, and 3) the macro level which is connected to the apparatus of the state. According to Barth, the

> median level is needed to depict the processes that create collectivities and mobilize groups ... This is the field of entrepreneurship, leadership and rhetoric; here stereotypes are established and collectives are set in motion ... Processes on this level intervene to constrain and compel people's expression and action on the micro level; package deals and either-or choices are imposed, and many aspects of the boundaries and dichotomies of ethnicity are fashioned.[92]

---

[91] See, for instance, Hogg & Abrams 1988, 77–78; Esler 2003, 21–22.
[92] Barth 1994, 20–22. For a summary of Barth's approach, see Esler 2003, 42–49. According to Esler, the median level of Barth's modeling "corresponds to what Paul is attempting to achieve in Romans."

Although Barth is mainly interested in the formation of ethnic identity, it is clear that the median level of his analysis can also be applied to illuminate the role of heresiologies in the formation of Christian identity, especially as far as this identity is formed in relation to an ethnic group such as the Jews. Epiphanius—and other heresiologists—can be seen as social entrepreneurs who create stereotypes and collectives in order to control the actions of individual Christians and their relation to outsiders.

One central aspect in the formation of social identities is the patterning of time by highlighting significant events in the history and future of the people whose collective identity is being created. The concept of "social time" refers to the recording of events of social change which a group finds significant. Those who have the power to impose their interpretation of the significance of events on others, largely determine which events will become significant within a group. Consequently, when power relations change within the group or when new events call forth restructuring of the social time, the history of the community needs to be rewritten. Philip Esler has aptly described this process: "Thus, as power relations in society at large or within a particular group change, modifications are made to the patterning of social time. Those in power rewrite the meaning of some events, erase some, and invent others."[93]

In the case of early Christian heresiologies, one can clearly see that the heresiologists not only aimed at refuting undesirable doctrines and practices but also imposed their interpretation of the history of the "heresies" they were discussing. The history of the early Catholic Church was purified and all ties to "heretic" groups cut by claiming that the heresies were sprouting from one single root separate from the Church. The heresiologists, who were writing mainly for their own community, had full power to create a prehistory for the groups and doctrines they were refuting. At some points, where the writers were involved with polemics, glimpses of the way in which their opponents themselves viewed their own earlier history come to the surface, as can be seen in Epiphanius' note about the Ebionites who traced their origins back to Apostolic times. Yet it was easy for Epiphanius to place the Ebionites in the history created for the heretics by claiming that the Ebionites originated with a certain Ebion—who had already been invented by

---

[93] Esler 2003, 24.

Epiphanius' predecessors[94]—and that Ebion got his "poor" name from his parents by prophecy. All this is nonsense from the viewpoint of present standards of critical history but its value for building up the sense of the doctrinal purity of the church cannot be underestimated.

The parallel story of the heresies was already there when Epiphanius started to write his *Panarion*.[95] He only needed to update the story to incorporate more recent heresies as well. In the case of Jewish Christians, he was able to anchor the genesis of this branch of heresy more firmly in history when he came up with the idea that the Nazarenes started to imitate the Christians who had escaped to Pella. By doing this, Epiphanius argued that people who mixed Jewish practices with their Christian way of life were not descendants of the early Jerusalem community. Instead, they were people who had misunderstood the true character of Christianity from the very beginning.

The stereotyped picture of the Nazarenes that was created by Epiphanius has proved to be very pervasive. In the light of the above assessment, this persistence is hardly based on the weight of historical evidence about their existence. However, even present critical scholarship usually takes it for granted that there once existed a group of Christians who were not just called Nazarenes (as all Christians were in Syriac) but who were also distinguishable from other Christians in respect of their doctrine, practices and the literature that they used.[96] One reason for this might be that once a very clear picture of a historical entity is created, it may be easier for the human mind to try to define its "true" character and place it in history rather than to discard the idea altogether. There may be other explanatory factors as well. One cannot help asking if the image of the Nazarenes has been so pervasive in scholarly discourse because it still has a positive role in legitimizing the present Christian identity. For instance, by showing that to the extent that Christians continued to regard the Jewish law binding, this was done in full accord with the earliest community in Jerusalem by Christians whose Christology was "orthodox" in character.

---

[94] The name Ebion probably appeared for the first time in Hippolytus' *Syntagma*. See, Häkkinen 2005.

[95] Irenaeus had traced the heresies back to Simon Magus, and Hippolytus back to Greek philosophies.

[96] Cf. Taylor 1990, 326; Bauckham 2003, 162; de Boer 1998, 239.

CHAPTER THREE

JEWISH-CHRISTIAN GOSPELS RECOVERED

3.1. Farewell to the Three Gospel Hypothesis (the 3GH)

The riddle of Jewish-Christian gospels is tied to the question of how to sort out the original sources of Jerome's quotations. According to a widely accepted hypothesis, Jerome had two sources: the actual "Gospel of the Nazarenes"[1] and Origen (possibly with other Greek authors) whose quotations were originally derived from the *Gospel of the Hebrews*. In this volume, this hypothesis is called the Three Gospel Hypothesis (the 3GH). It assumes that there were altogether three different Jewish-Christian Gospels: (1) The *Gospel of the Hebrews* written in Greek, used only by Christians in Egypt and originally quoted by Origen, Clement of Alexandria and Didymus the Blind. In addition, the supporters of this theory ascribe some passages quoted by Jerome to this gospel, assuming that Jerome must have found the passages in the writings of Origen. (2) The *Gospel of the Ebionites*, a Greek harmonistic gospel quoted only by Epiphanius in his *Panarion*, (3) The "Gospel of the Nazarenes," used by Aramaic-speaking Nazarenes near Beroea in Syria, and quoted several times by Jerome.[2] Scholars usually agree that the *Gospel of the Ebionites*, quoted by Epiphanius, is an entity of it own. Therefore, the discussion

---

[1] The "Gospel of the Nazarenes" appears in quotation marks in this volume because I argue that it is a purely scholarly reconstruction.

[2] See, Klijn 1992, 27–32, 38. With minor differences, Klijn's reconstruction is the same as the one presented in Vielhauer & Strecker 1991² (1963¹), 160–165, 169–171; Funk 1985, 365–370, 372–389. The Three Gospel Hypothesis has a prominent position because it is presented in widely used handbooks. Nevertheless, there are scholars who do not want to make a distinction between the *Gospel of the Hebrews* and the "Gospel of the Nazoreans." See, for instance, Mimouni 1998, 209–211, 215–216; Pritz 1988, 85. Furthermore, from the viewpoint of Diatessaronic studies, W.L. Petersen has raised the question whether the fragments usually thought to derive from two (or three) different gospels could as well be rooted in one and the same gospel related to the Diatessaronic tradition because there are Diatessaronic readings in both the reconstructed "Gospel of the Nazoreans" and in the "Gospel of the Ebionites." See, Petersen 1994, 29–31, 39–41. For the earliest history of research, see Handmann 1888, 1–25.

focuses on the question whether it is justified to make a distinction between the "Gospel of the Nazarenes" and the *Gospel of the Hebrews*.

Foundations for the reconstruction of three Jewish-Christian gospels were laid by Hans Waitz who wrote chapters on the Jewish-Christian gospels in the second edition of Edgar Hennecke's *Neutestamentliche Apokryphen*.[3] In contrast to Hennecke's first edition, where A. Meyer had still assumed only two Jewish-Christian gospels,[4] Waitz argued that a distinction should be made between the clearly apocryphal *Gospel of the Hebrews* and the synoptic type "Gospel of the Nazarenes" that closely resembles the Gospel of Matthew.[5] Philipp Vielhauer and Georg Strecker, who contributed to the third edition of Hennecke's collection (revised by W. Schneemelcher), adopted the same principle but made some changes to the actual reconstructions.[6] Several text editions and collections of Christian apocrypha have followed Vielhauer and Strecker's reconstruction, and A.F.J. Klijn has adopted the same solution in his monograph on Jewish-Christian gospels.[7]

Vielhauer and Strecker took over Waitz' view of the Matthean character of the "Gospel of the Nazarenes" and explicitly made it one central criterion for assigning passages either to the *Gospel of the Hebrews* or to the "Gospel of the Nazarenes:"

> Criteria for derivation from the Aramaic GN must be: (a) indications that the text has a semitic basis and (b) the synoptic character of the text or its affinity in particular with Mt., since the GH, according to all that we know of it, diverged very much from the synoptic type.[8]

These criteria and the resulting reconstruction of the 3GH has four main problems.

First, the starting point of Waitz' reconstruction was an untenable assumption that the Jewish-Christian gospel fragments must come from

---

[3] Waitz 1924a, 10–17; Waitz 1924c, 17–32; Waitz 1924b, 32–48 and Waitz 1924d, 48–55.

[4] See, Meyer 1904b, 11–21 and Meyer 1904a, 24–27.

[5] It is true that Waitz' reconstruction was inspired by Schmidtke who introduced the idea that Jerome's fragments were derived from a Greek gospel and an Aramaic gospel but he also argued that the Greek one is to be identified with the *Gospel of the Ebionites* thereby assuming only two Jewish-Christian gospels. See, Schmidtke 1911, 242–246.

[6] Vielhauer & Strecker 1991² (1963¹), 1:134–177. The most important change was that Vielhauer and Strecker no longer regarded the gospel quotations in the *Pseudo-Clementine Recognitions* and *Homilies* as part of the *Gospel of the Ebionites*.

[7] Klijn 1992. For different views, see Mimouni 1998, 209–211, 215–216; Petersen 1994, 29–31, 39–41; Luomanen 2003, 245–246, 262–265.

[8] Vielhauer & Strecker 1991² (1963¹), 148.

two totally different types of gospels: from the synoptic type (the "Gospel of the Nazarenes" and the *Gospel of the Ebionites*) and from an apocryphal gospel with more philosophic and Gnostic orientation.[9] Waitz' criteria were understandable at the time because when he wrote, the *Gospel of Thomas* was not yet found and the only parallel for Clement's quotation from the *Gospel of the Hebrews* ("He who has become astonished will become king and he who has become king will rest"; Clement of Alexandria, *Strom.* II IX 45.5; par. *Strom.* V XIV 96.3) was known from an Oxyrhynchus papyrus (P.Oxy. 654). Waitz even went so far as to include all the sayings preserved in P.Oxy 654 in his reconstruction of the *Gospel of the Hebrews*.[10]

However, after the entire *Gospel of Thomas* was found, it has become clear that the sayings in P.Oxy. 654 are from a Greek edition of *Thomas* and subsequent reconstructions have taken this into account, assigning only Clement's fragment to the *Gospel of the Hebrews*. Nevertheless, Waitz' original assumption about two totally different types of gospels has been retained despite the fact that the *Gospel of Thomas* itself is a prime example of a gospel which includes both Gnostic types and synoptic types of sayings and parables. The *Gospel of Thomas* being now available, no reconstruction of Jewish-Christian gospels should start with the assumption that Clement's fragment must be from a gospel that did not include parallels to synoptic passages. The fact that Eusebius lists the *Gospel of the Hebrews* as one of the "disputed" writings but not among those that were used by the heretics (like the *Gospel of Thomas*), also suggests that the *Gospel of the Hebrews* did not deviate too much from the canonical gospels.[11]

Second, Vielhauer and Strecker back up their criteria for classification by pointing out that "according to all that we know" the *Gospel of the Hebrews* "diverged very much from the synoptic type." On closer examination, this criterion proves to be based on a circular argument.

---

[9] Waitz 1924a, 12; Waitz 1924d, 52.

[10] See, Waitz 1924d, 54–55.

[11] Eusebius (*Hist. eccl.* 3.25.3) has three main categories: (1) Generally accepted books (ὁμολογούμενα) that are true, genuine, and accepted in the tradition of the church. (2) Disputed (ἀντιλεγομένα) writings that are not canonical but familiar to most church writers. (3) The writings used by the heretics. The *Gospel of the Hebrews* is placed in the second category but as a kind of addition: "Among those some have placed also the Gospel according to the Hebrews with which those of the Hebrews that have accepted Christ are especially pleased." Of course, the value of Eusebius' statement depends on the question of how well Eusebius' himself, or the "some" he is referring to, really knew the "*Gospel of the Hebrews*." For a more detailed discussion, see Chapter 3.4.1.

How much do we actually "know"—according to the 3GH—about the contents of an Egyptian "*Gospel of the Hebrews*?" Only three authors cited that gospel in Egypt and of these, Didymus the Blind's quotation (*Comm. Ps.*) deals only with the problem of a disciple's double name (Matthew = Levi or Matthias = Levi). Therefore, we are left with only two pertinent sayings: Clement's saying about finding rest (*Strom.* II IX 45.5 and V XIV 96.3),[12] and Origen's saying about the Spirit as Jesus' mother (*Comm. Jo.* 2.12). However, precisely these sayings are most clearly paralleled in the *Gospel of Thomas* and the *Acts of Thomas*. Since scholars usually assign the composition of these writings to Syria,[13] the existing evidence suggests a Syrian rather than an Egyptian origin also for the *Gospel of the Hebrews*.[14]

The third main problem is that Waitz emphasized the close relationship between the "Gospel of the Nazarenes" and the Gospel of Matthew[15] but many of the fragments that Waitz and other proponents of the 3GH have assigned to the "Gospel of the Nazarenes" are not particularly close to Matthew's versions of the synoptic stories or they do not have a clear parallel in Matthew at all. Furthermore, several of the fragments that are assigned to the "Gospel of the Nazarenes" and which do have some Matthean expressions also share readings with the Gospel of Luke.[16] Thus, it is clear that there are fragments which were not derived from

---

[12] *Strom.* II IX 45.5: "He who has become astonished will become king and he who has become king will rest." *Strom.* V XIV 96.3: "He who seeks will not cease until he finds and having found he will marvel and having marvelled he will become king and having become king, he will rest." Origen, *Comm. Jo.* 2.12: "A moment ago my Mother the Holy Spirit, took me by one of my hairs and brought me to the great hill, the Tabor." Trans. Klijn 1992.

[13] See below Chapter 5.2.

[14] In the *Acts of Thomas*, the Holy Spirit is often called "Mother" (*Acts Thom.* cc. 7, 27, 39, 50). Vielhauer & Strecker 1991² (1963¹), 174 contend that in Egypt the *Apocryphon of James* (6.19–20) also refers to Jesus as the Son of the Holy Ghost. However, the translation of the passage is difficult. F.E. Willams translates: "Become better than I; make yourselves like the Son of the Holy Spirit." See, Williams 1985, 13–53. According to Klijn 1992, 55, the idea about the Spirit as mother "may go back to pre-Christian Syriac or Mesopotamian sources." Nevertheless, Klijn also refers to Philo (*Ebr.* 30) and to the idea about the sons of Wisdom in *Sir.* 4.11 and Luke 7:35, concluding that the fragment must be understood "against the background of Jewish Hellenistic traditions." This hypothesis makes it possible for him to locate the *Gospel of the Hebrews* in Egypt.

[15] Waitz 1924a, 16–17; Waitz 1924c, 18.

[16] See, for instance, τὸ ἰουδαϊκόν in Matt 7:5; Origen, *Comm. Matt.* 15.14; Eusebius, *Theophania*, 4.22 (PG 24, 685–688); *Theophania Syriaca* 4.12; Jerome, *Comm. Matt.* 12.13; *Pelag.* 3.2a. See Vielhauer and Strecker's reconstruction (Vielhauer & Strecker 1991² (1963¹), 160–162). Frey 2003a, 135–136 has correctly noted the differences between the canonical Matthew and the "Gospel of the Nazarenes" of the 3GH.

a gospel that was a sort of new (Aramaic) edition of Matthew or from a clearly apocryphal gospel but from a gospel that creatively used materials from several synoptic gospels (Matthew and Luke in particular) combining it with passages that do not have parallels in the canonical gospels.

The fourth major flaw of the 3GH is that it uncritically assigns a group of variant readings entitled τὸ ἰουδαϊκόν to the "Gospel of the Nazarenes." These variants that are attributed to a "Jewish gospel", appear in the margins of some manuscripts of the Gospel of Matthew. The framers of the 3GH took it for granted that these references in the margins of manuscripts 566, 899 and 1424[17] were from the "Gospel of the Nazarenes." However, this view has been recently questioned,[18] and with good reason.

There are thirteen of these τὸ ἰουδαϊκόν readings.[19] Tischendorf had already published four of these in 1860 (cod. 566; to Matt 4:5; 16:17; 18:22; 26:74).[20] Schmidtke found two of Tischendorf's readings (in Matt 18:22; 26:74) and an additional one (in Matt 12:40) in manuscript 899. He found the rest of the thirteen readings in manuscript 1424 (9th/10th

---

[17] In addition, in Matt 26:74, manuscripts 4 and 273 share a τὸ ἰουδαϊκόν reading with 566, 899 and 1424 but the reading appears in the text itself. Thus, Schmidtke 1911, 21.

[18] See Frey 2003a, 126–129. According to Frey, the 7th edition of Hennecke's collection will list these variants separately—excluding them from the reconstruction of the "Gospel of the Nazarenes." See also Lührmann 2004, 252–253. Petersen 1992, 1098.

[19] Vielhauer & Strecker 1991² (1963¹), 149, state erroneously: "in the *subscriptiones* of thirty-six Gospel manuscripts dating from the 9th to the 13th centuries there is a reference to a gospel described as τὸ ἰουδαϊκόν, and two of these manuscripts (codices 566 and 899) adduce readings of the Judaikon as marginal notes to Matthew." The same mistake is to be found in the German edition as well (see Vielhauer & Strecker 1987, 126–127). In reality, τὸ ἰουδαϊκόν references have been found in only five manuscripts (4, 273, 566, 899, 1424) and always in the margins (or in the actual text) of the Gospel of Matthew. Thirty-eight (thirty-six according to Schmidtke 1911, 21–22) manuscripts have subscriptions referring to a manuscript on Mount Zion (= so-called "Zion Gospel Edition"), and two of these (566 and 899) also have references to τὸ ἰουδαϊκόν in the margins of Matthew. It seems that Vielhauer and Strecker have not made clear the distinction between the Zion Gospel Edition and τὸ ἰουδαϊκόν references. The Zion Gospel Edition and τὸ ἰουδαϊκόν references overlap in only two manuscripts which together cover five variants (two in common) of all thirteen of τὸ ἰουδαϊκόν references. For correct information, see Petersen 1992, 1097–1098; Klijn 1992, 25, 34–35.

[20] Tischendorf 1860, 58. For some reason, Edwards 2009, 40–42, 291 claims that there would be four τὸ ἰουδαϊκόν readings in the Codex Sinaiticus. Possibly Edwards, who only refers to Harnack (Harnack 1893, 10), has mistaken Harnack's reference to Tischendorf to mean that Tischendorf is describing the Codex Sinaiticus (!). However, Tischendorf, in his work from the year 1860 (see above), describes manuscript 566. Harnack's short title for this work of Tischendorf's is "Notit. edit. cod. Sin." which may have led Edwards astray. Today, when the Codex Sinaiticus is available on the internet, it is easy to check this out in the original manuscript and to see there are no τὸ ἰουδαϊκόν readings.

century), which is the sole witness for eight of these variants (to Matt 5:22; 7:5; 10:16; 11:12; 11:25; 15:5; 16:2–3; 27:65; in addition 1424 shares a τὸ ἰουδαϊκόν in 16:17 with 566, and in 26:74 with 566 and 899).[21] Jerome provides a connecting link between the variants and the "Gospel of the Nazarenes" in *Pelag.* 3.2 where he assigns to the "Gospel of the Nazarenes" a passage that is found among the τὸ ἰουδαϊκόν variants as well.

It is clear that the references to a "Jewish gospel" were not produced by a systematic comparison of the Greek Gospel of Matthew with a Jewish gospel. Schmidtke himself already concluded that the readings were collected from a lost Greek commentary on the Gospel of Matthew. Although Schmidtke's assumption about a commentary of Apollinaris of Laodicea as the source of the notes is generally discarded as too speculative,[22] it is reasonable to assume that the notes were based on second-hand information, presumably derived from a commentary/commentaries on the Gospel of Matthew.[23] If this is correct, how can one know that the source of the marginal notes must have been a gospel closely resembling the Gospel of Matthew? It is clear that the writers of the commentaries on the Gospel of Matthew were by no means bound to cite only texts that were closely related to Matthew. It must have been enough for them that the passage in a "Jewish gospel" was somehow connected to the theme they were dealing with in their exposition. Because Matthew's gospel was considered relatively early on to have been written in Hebrew, it is understandable that a copyist who came across these comments about the variants in a "Jewish gospel" was likely to consider it especially important for Matthew and therefore noted it in the margins. Thus, the mere fact that a variant was added in the margins of Matthew does not say very much about the character of its source. All conclusions about the nature of the original source of τὸ ἰουδαϊκόν variants must be drawn from the variant readings themselves and solved case by case.[24] To argue on the basis of τὸ ἰουδαϊκόν variants that the "Gospel of Nazarenes" must have been particularly closely connected to the Gospel of Matthew is to take a hypothesis for evidence.[25]

---

[21] Schmidtke 1911, 21–22.
[22] Schmidtke 1911, 31, 70–74. For the criticism of Schmidtke's position, see Frey 2003a, 127.
[23] Klijn 1992, 35.
[24] Cf. below Chapter 5.2.5 where τὸ ἰουδαϊκόν to Matt 10:16 is discussed.
[25] See Vielhauer & Strecker 1991² (1963¹), 154: "in content and compass the GN was closely related to Mt. That is shown first and foremost by the readings of the Judaikon, but also by the other fragments that have been preserved."

Admittedly, the 3GH's assumption that a Semitic basis would suggest a connection to the "Gospel of the Nazarenes" seems to be partly valid since it coheres with observations about the language of the fragments that Jerome derived from the Nazarenes' *Commentary on Isaiah* (see above). In spite of this, traces of Semitic language in the fragments cannot prove that Jerome must have received the passage in question from the Nazarenes, as the 3GH suggests, since there may also have been other Semitic gospels around.[26] Nevertheless, the criterion can be applied the other way around: *if there are indications that the fragment was excerpted from a Greek writing, it is unlikely that Jerome got it from the Nazarenes.* This observation will be used as the starting point in the following new reconstruction but, before moving on to the reconstruction itself, a short overview of Jerome and his literary activity is needed.

3.2. Jerome's Life and Quotations from Jewish-Christian Gospels

3.2.1. *The Setting of the Quotations in Jerome's Biography*

The Three Gospel Hypothesis' (the 3GH) use of Jerome's testimony is quite arbitrary. Jerome is sometimes trusted and sometimes not. The decision whether or not Jerome is trustworthy is made on the basis of hypothesized gospel categories, not on the basis of the study of Jerome's own situation and motives. The categories of "canonical" and "non-canonical" determine the origin of the passages and the quality of Jerome's attributions.

Although Jerome made extensive use of Origen in many of his writings, Origen was not his only source because Jerome also used many other commentators. Therefore, the simple sorting out of materials into two categories of "Origenistic" and "Nazarene" in accordance with the 3GH, will also lead to the wrong conclusion.

In the following, Jerome's citations will be discussed in chronological order and with special emphasis on the situation in which they were presented. This should help finding answers to some of the questions the Three Gospel Hypothesis has left unanswered. Although Jerome might be an unreliable witness, he probably had his reasons for doing what he did.

---

[26] See below Chapter 5.1.

90   CHAPTER THREE

Without knowing these reasons and the situation where he worked, it is hazardous to assess the information he provided about Jewish-Christian gospels.

Letter to Damasus (Epist. 20)
Jerome's first quotation is in his epistle to the pope Damasus, usually dated 383 CE. By that time, Jerome was back in Rome after his trip to the East, where he had headed in 372 in order to fulfill the ascetic ideals he and his friends had adopted. Jerome's original plan was to go to Jerusalem but sudden illness struck him while he was staying in Antioch with Evagrius, a presbyter of a small, Old Nicene church. Illness prolonged Jerome's stay in Antioch and finally made him give up the plan of going to Jerusalem. Instead, he tried the life of a monk in the desert in the neighborhood of Chalcis (374/375–377). Despite the ascetic ideals—that he never gave up in his later life—the life of a solitary was not for him. He came back to Antioch (377–379) where he continued his studies and writing. During a visit to Constantinople (380–382), he was able to attend the famous assembly, the Council of Constantinople. There he met Gregory of Nazianzus who made a lasting impression on him.[27] During the years in Antioch and Constantinople, Jerome studied Greek and became acquainted with Origen's and Eusebius' works.[28] He also said that he had listened to Apollinaris' lectures.[29] He started to study Hebrew, and from Syriac monks with whom he was living near Chalcis, he must have picked up some Syriac.[30] Most scholars assume that if Jerome really met Nazarenes, whose gospel he started to quote ten years later, it must have happened here.

Jerome came to Rome in the company of the bishops Paulinus and Epiphanius. Originally, Jerome was an interpreter for the bishops, but—thanks to Jerome's language skills and the knowledge of church life in the East—the pope Damasus found his assistance so useful that when Paulinus and Epiphanius headed back to their home cities, Jerome decided to stay in Rome. Jerome had also made friends with wealthy Roman ladies

---

[27] The exact chronology of the time Jerome spent in the East is obscure. The approximate dates given above are based on Kelly 1975, 46–80. Although one cannot be sure about the dates, the main outline of Jerome's activities is well known.

[28] Jerome translated (and elaborated) Eusebius' *Chronicle*, probably in Constantinople, and Origen's homilies on Jeremiah, Ezekiel and Isaiah. See, Kelly 1975, 72–77.

[29] Schmidtke's hypothesis of Apollinaris as the other source for Jerome's quotations (see above Chapter 3.1), is based on this short note.

[30] Kelly 1975, 49–50.

and become their spiritual tutor. One of them, Paula, was to become his lifelong companion.

Jerome's letter answers the pope's question about the meaning of the Hebrew acclamation "Hosanna," with which Jesus is welcomed by people in Jerusalem:

> Finally Matthew, who wrote the Gospel in the Hebrew language, put it in the following way 'osianna barrama' which means 'ossanna in excelsis.'
> (*Epist.* 20.5; trans. Klijn 1992).

The source of this citation has been contested. Vielhauer argues, on the basis of chronology, that the citation cannot be from a Jewish-Christian gospel. According to him, Jerome's letter to the pope was composed in 383, and Jerome mentions a Jewish-Christian gospel for the first time in 386–387 and speaks of a Hebrew Jewish-Christian gospel first in 390–393.[31] He also suggests that Jerome's "retranslation" presents an incorrect form "for 'height of heaven' is *rama* neither in Hebrew nor in Aramaic, but in Hebrew *marom* or *meromim* and in Aramaic *marom* or *meroma* and therefore the information that passage gives about the original language of the "Gospel of the Nazarenes," is useless.[32] However, as Vielhauer himself notes, the Hebrew/Syriac word *rama* (רמה) which usually means "high" or "higher place" is documented in Ephrem's Syriac in the sense of "heaven."[33] Ephrem was Jerome's contemporary[34] and he was held in high regard among the Christians of Edessa. Even Jerome knew that in some churches Ephrem's Syriac writings were publicly read after the Scriptures (*Vir. ill.* 116), and his hymns were used in the liturgy.[35] Thus, it is likely that by the time of Jerome, the word *rama* was also used

---

[31] In my opinion, Vielhauer's reasoning would be valid only if Jerome really possessed an entire Jewish-Christian gospel. But this is not what Vielhauer suggests. If Jerome was only working with fragments, then the question must be: When and why Jerome started to claim that he had the entire gospel in his hands and that he had translated it? This did not happen when he was still in Rome. However, there are things which make claims like this understandable later, when Jerome was in Jerusalem (cf. below). Thus, Jerome may quite well have already possessed some fragments in Rome but he did not find it necessary to claim that he had the entire gospel available.

[32] Vielhauer & Strecker 1991² (1963¹), 155. Similarly, Nautin 1986, 309, argues that when Jerome is not following Origen, he presents a totally wild ("völlig abenteuerliche") orthography.

[33] Vielhauer points to this in an endnote (Vielhauer & Strecker 1991² (1963¹), 164 n. 1). See, Brockelmann 1928, 720b. Klijn 1992, 31, 120–121, also thinks that *Epist.* 20.5 was not from a Jewish-Christian gospel.

[34] According to Jerome, Ephrem died during the reign of the emperor Valens (364–378). See *Vir. ill.* 116.

[35] Halton 1999, 149, n. 3.

to denote "heaven" by Syriac-speaking Christians. This would mean that Jerome's explanation was drawing on Syriac tradition.

Where did Jerome get the explanation? If he was writing to the pope in 383, he had already spent at least seven years in the East and had had several chances to come across the explanation for the word Hosanna. Because Jerome obviously believes that "osianna barrama" was in the original "Hebrew" copy of Matthew, it is quite possible that the reading was derived from a gospel used by Syriac-speaking Christians. Whether he had at the same time also obtained some other information from the same gospel and if this was the same gospel that he claimed to have translated from 392 onwards, will be discussed below.

The above considerations have been based on the traditional dating of *Epistle* 20 (383 CE), which results in the 8–10 year time gap between the explanation of Hosanna and Jerome's other quotations from Jewish-Christian gospels. However, if one accepts Nautin's alternative date of 392 for Jerome's epistle to the pope, then the letter would have been composed approximately at the same time as Jerome started to quote from the gospel that he said was used by the Nazarenes. According to Nautin, Jerome fabricated the letters later on in Jerusalem. This was after pope's death and the tragic events in Rome (see below), and the publication of the letters Jerome and the pope had allegedly sent to each other would have aimed at showing Jerome's exegetical skills to the Romans and showing what close relations Jerome had with the former pope.[36] Thus, Nautin's chronology would make the reference in Jerome's letter roughly contemporary with quotations from the "Gospel of the Nazarenes." Although it would be tempting to follow Nautin, his theory is highly speculative and not very much can be built on it.

Nevertheless, even if we trust more the traditional dating, it seems that it is perfectly understandable as information that Jerome had received from some Syriac-speaking Christians who may have had this phrase in their Syriac translation of Matthew's gospel. There is no evidence that it would have come from a pre-Matthean Hebrew gospel although Jerome presents it as such.

Commentary on Ephesians

Jerome left Rome in 385. After the death of Damasus in 384, he had entertained hopes of becoming his successor but Siricius was elected

---

[36] See Nautin 1986, 306 and Nautin 1983, 331–344.

as the new pope. Jerome also became entangled with scandalous events which involved rumors about the character of his relationship with Paula. The details of the conflict Jerome experienced in Rome are not known but the hatred and resentment he expressed towards "Babylon," make it clear that for him there was no other option but to leave. Paula also left Rome later on and joined Jerome for a pilgrimage to the Holy Land. They visited the holy sites of Palestine and concluded their journey with a trip to Alexandria where they visited monasteries and Jerome studied with Didymus the Blind. They were already back in Palestine in 386 and settled down there in Bethlehem which was to be the place of their monasteries.

Jerome commenced feverish literary activity. Several translations, studies and commentaries were published within a couple of years. Among these were the commentaries on Paul's letters to Philemon, Galatians, Ephesians and Titus. The writing of these commentaries was completed within a few months, in 387/8. Especially in the commentary on the Ephesians, Jerome made extensive use of Origen. Even Jerome himself acknowledges this in his preface but he also says that he had the expositions of Didymus, Apollinaris and others stored in his mind when he was dictating the commentary.[37] In view of the hasty writing and all the acknowledgments, it is quite possible that the citation from the Hebrew gospel was derived from another Christian author:

> ... as we read in the Hebrew Gospel that the Lord said to the disciples: And never rejoice, he said, unless when you look at your brother in love.
> (*Comm. Eph.* 5.4; trans. Klijn 1992).

The source of the citation may have been Origen, but could have been some of the other authors he had stored in his mind as well. Given that Jerome was just starting a monastery with "brothers" and that he had visited several monastic communities in Egypt, it is no wonder that he had the saying in his mind. But whether he had recently picked it up in Egypt or remembered it from the times he himself had tried monastic life or from the lectures of Apollinaris that he had listened to in Antioch, cannot be known. All these options are equally possible.

Commentary on Micah and All Those "Illustrious Men"
The years 389–391 mark a turning point in Jerome's career as a writer. By that time, he started to devote more and more time to the study of the Hebrew Bible in its original language. In his commentary on

---

[37] See, Kelly 1975, 144–149.

Ecclesiastes (389), he makes extensive use of rabbinical exegesis which he probably picked up from a Jew with whom he was reading the book. His translation also made use of the Hebrew original but the wording was still adjusted to the more familiar text of the Septuagint. Nevertheless, the trilogy of books he published next, *Hebrew Names*, the *Book of Places* and *Hebrew Questions*, were dealing with the etymology of Biblical names, sacred places—some of which he had personally visited—and the interpretation of problematic texts in Genesis. Eusebius' *Onomasticon* was an invaluable aid for Jerome, but he also worked with several name lists of unknown origin, and for the *Hebrew Questions*, he consulted Josephus and rabbinic exegesis. As a matter of fact, Jerome's preface to *Hebrew Questions* contains a defense and unveiling of his program which finds the ultimate truth of the Bible in the Hebrew language (*hebraica veritas*). For instance, he points out that the evangelists, Paul and Christ himself, when they were referring to the Old Testament, used texts that differed from the one used in the church. He also noted that Origen, in his scholarly studies, preferred the Hebrew original.[38] Interestingly, these same ideas soon appear in his *On Illustrious Men*.

Jerome's *On Illustrious Men* contains a list of his own publications. The last items on the list are commentaries on the minor prophets: Micah, Nahum, Habakkuk, Zephaniah and Haggai, which must have appeared just before *On Illustrious Men*. In practice, Jerome must have been working with them approximately at the same time he was preparing *On Illustrious Men*.

The commentary on Micah contains Jerome's first reference to his translation of the Gospel according to the Hebrews:

> ... and who should believe the Gospel which is edited according to the Hebrews and which we translated not so long ago, in which it is said of the person of the Saviour: A moment ago my Mother the Holy Spirit took me by one of my hairs. (*Comm. Mich.* 7.5-7; trans. Klijn 1992).

There are good reasons for believing that precisely this passage depends on Origen's wording: Jerome quotes this passage several times (*Comm. Mich.* 7.5-7; *Comm. Isa.* 40.9-11; *Comm. Ezech.* 16.13) and it is also found in Origen's writings (*Comm. Jo.* 2.12; *Hom. Jer.* 15.4).

Jerome wrote *On Illustrious Men* in order to provide a Christian counterpart to the chronicles of secular authors. Jerome's inspiration for writing becomes clear in the last paragraph of his introduction to the book:

---

[38] Kelly 1975, 153-157.

> Let Celsus, then, learn, and Porphyri and Julian, those rabid dogs barking against Christ; let their followers learn—those who think that the church has had no philosophers, no orators, no men of learning; let them learn the number and quality of the men who founded, built and adorned the church, and let them stop accusing our faith of such rustic simplicity, and recognize their own ignorance. (trans. Halton 1999).

At the end of this list of illustrious, noble men there is—Jerome. Nevertheless, the reader of the book does not have to wait until the last lines of this collection before he/she gets a glimpse of the linguistic skills of its author. Second in the row, after Peter, is James, the brother of the Lord. Some information about him is also to be found in the Gospel according to the Hebrews,

> which I have recently translated into Greek and Latin of which also Origen often makes use. (*Vir. ill.* 2; trans. Klijn 1992).

After James follows Matthew who, according to Jerome, composed a gospel in Hebrew, which was later translated into Greek by an unknown author.[39] However,

> The Hebrew itself has been preserved until the present day in the library at Caesarea which Pamphilus the martyr so diligently collected. From the Nazarenes who use this book in Beroia, a city of Syria, I also received the opportunity to copy it. (*Vir. ill.* 3; trans. Klijn & Reinink 1973).

Jerome continues explaining how it is to be noted that in this volume, the scriptures are not quoted according to the Septuagint but according to the Hebrew original. The view is exactly the same that he had expressed a bit earlier in his preface to *Hebrew Questions*. Thus it seems that Jerome's campaign for using the Hebrew original gets further support because the Nazarenes had provided him with access to the original "Hebrew" text of Matthew.

The third reference to a Jewish-Christian gospel in *On Illustrious Men* is in connection with Ignatius. After having presented the list of Ignatius' letters which is concluded by the letter to the Polycarp, Jerome relates (*Vir. ill.* 16):

> In this he bore witness also to the gospel which I have recently translated, in respect of the person of Christ stating ...
> (*Vir. ill.* 16; trans. Klijn & Reinink 1973).

---

[39] This information is obviously derived from Eusebius *Hist. eccl.* 3.24.6, 3.39.16, 5.8.2.

Jerome is here using Eusebius' *Ecclesiastical History* (3.36.11). Eusebius discusses the passage in connection with Ignatius of Antioch who seems to cite an unknown gospel in his *Letter to the Smyrnaeans* (Ign. *Smyrn.* 3) but Eusebius does not know Ignatius' source. Although Jerome claims that the same passage is in the "Gospel of the Hebrews that the Nazarenes use," it is clear that he knows the passage only through Eusebius' *Ecclesiastical History*. Jerome quotes Ignatius' passage as it is recorded by Eusebius but he does not realize that the beginning of Eusebius' quotation repeats Ignatius' own words in his *Letter to the Smyrnaeans*. Thus, Jerome ends up attributing Ignatius' own words to the apocryphal source that Ignatius was quoting. Furthermore, Jerome erroneously attributes the passages to Ignatius' *Letter to Polycarp* because Eusebius discusses Polycarp immediately above the quoted passage.[40]

Commentary on Matthew

Jerome refers once more to his translation work in his *Commentary on Matthew* which he wrote six years later (398). He wrote the commentary after a serious illness which had confined him to bed for three months. According to Jerome, the exposition was prepared in haste, in only two weeks in March, because the commentary was meant to be reading for Eusebius of Cremona's trip to Italy. Probably Jerome does not exaggerate very much—the book is filled with minor historical errors and the commentary is quite short. It is quite believable that it was finished in haste. Jerome gives a long list of previous commentaries that he had read earlier but which he had not had time to consult afresh. However, a comparison

---

[40] The validity of the passage as a witness to a Jewish-Christian gospel is denied by Vielhauer & Strecker 1991² (1963¹), 143–145, 147–148, and Klijn 1992, 123. Schmidtke 1911, 62, 257, and Waitz 1937, 64–65, already thought that Jerome derived his information from Eusebius but they still assumed that Ignatius' original source was one of the Jewish-Christian gospels. Vielhauer also contends (p. 144) that the passage cannot be based on a Semitic original because the word "bodyless" is impossible in Semitic language. However, Vielhauer records, in an endnote (153, n. 4) that in Syriac the expression is a Greek loan word, and that it is attested for the first time by Ephrem. Thus, just as in the case of Hosanna (see above), it is possible that by the time of Jerome, there may have been a Syriac gospel that did include the saying about a "bodyless" demon. In this connection, we may also note that the saying has parallels in Diatessaronic witnesses and that it has played a major role in discussions about the possible relationship between the *Diatessaron* and Jewish-Christian gospels. Be that as may, the fact that Origen knows the saying from the *Teaching of Peter* (*de Princ.* I, praef. 8) shows that by Jerome's time, it already had established its status as a saying of Jesus and that it was circulating around. Nevertheless, Jerome clearly seems to have received it from Eusebius.

with Origen's commentary and the surviving fragments of Apollinarius and Theodore of Heraclea show that at least these were consulted.[41]

The commentary includes a total of six quotations from a Jewish-Christian gospel. These are central for the reconstruction of the materials that Jerome received from the Nazarenes and they will be discussed in detail in the following chapter.

Commentary on Isaiah, Commentary on Ezechiel and Dialogue Against Pelagius

After the *Commentary on Matthew* Jerome refers to a Jewish-Christian gospel in three of his writings: *Commentary on Isaiah, Commentary on Ezekiel* and his polemical writing *Dialogue Against Pelagius*. Since the *Commentary on Isaiah* was written between 408 and 410, there is almost a ten-year gap in Jerome's references to Jewish-Christian gospels. However, the writings produced meanwhile are not totally without significance for the study of the early Jewish Christianity since Jerome's letter to Augustine where he refers to the doctrines of the Nazarenes—discussed above in Chapter 2.2.4 (*Epist.* 112)—was written towards the end of the year 404.

When Jerome exchanged letters with Augustine he was also distressed by Paula's prolonged illness. In his first reply to Augustine (*Epist.* 102; 402 CE)—where Jerome did not yet answer Augustine but complained that Augustine's letter had been so widely circulated in Rome without Jerome knowing anything about it—Jerome excused himself for not answering earlier because of the time he had been sitting at Paula's sick bed.[42]

Paula died in January 404 and for some months after that Jerome was unable do any literary work. However, towards the end of the year 404, Jerome was working again effectively. After having translated Pachomius' monastic rule into Latin, he was also able to finish two projects. He finally sent his answer to Augustine in a letter which he rhetorically labeled as a hasty draft but which in truth was very carefully crafted. In late 404 or early 405, he also finally completed his translation/revision of the Old Testament on the basis of the Hebrew original.[43] As regards exegesis, commentaries on four minor prophets—Zechariah, Malachi,

---

[41] Kelly 1975, 222–225.
[42] Kelly 1975, 265, 277.
[43] Kelly 1975, 269, 283–285.

Hosea and Amos completed in 406—were followed by the writing of the *Commentary on Isaiah* between 408 and 410.

The *Commentary on Isaiah* is the largest one of Jerome's commentaries. Its writing was accompanied by several misfortunes that delayed the work: Jerome's own frequent illnesses, shortage of professional stenographers, etc. The tone of the commentary is even more anti-Jewish than usual. Jerome made extensive use of Origen's and Eusebius' works, often borrowing sections from them verbatim. He also used many other sources, such as Didymus, Apollinaris and Victorinus of Pettau, and the acknowledgments in the preface to the commentary are exceptionally long.[44] The commentary also included a mass of Jewish exegesis—which was usually cited in order to be refuted—and interpretations that Jerome had received from the Nazarenes (see above, Chapter 2.2.4). In the *Commentary on Isaiah* there are three quotations from a Jewish-Christian gospel, two of which Jerome had presented earlier in other contexts (*Comm. Isa.* 40.9–11 = *Comm. Mich.* 7.6; *Comm. Isa.* Pro. 65 = *Vir. ill.* 16). In addition to these, there is description of Jesus' baptism:

> ... but according to the Gospel which was written in the Hebrew language and read by the Nazarenes: The whole fountain of the Holy Spirit came upon him.
>
> Further in the Gospel which we mentioned above we find that the following is written: It happened when the Lord ascended from the water, that the whole fountain of the Holy Spirit descended and rested upon him and said to him: My son, I expected you among all the prophets that you should come and that I should rest upon you: For you are my rest, you are my firstborn son, who shall reign in eternity.
>
> (Jerome, *Comm. Isa.* 11.1–3; trans. Klijn 1992).

After finishing the *Commentary on Isaiah*, Jerome started to work on Ezekiel. The work, however, was disturbed and halted by dreadful news from the West: Rome had been seized by Alaric and many of Jerome's Christian friends had been killed. Jerome resumed the work in the winter of 411 but it was repeatedly interrupted by refugees from the West who were swarming to the Holy Land. The commentary was not finished until 414. Jerome again made extensive use of Origen, often word for word, but he also describes how he had had "commentaries by Greeks" read to him. By the time of writing the *Commentary on Ezekiel*, Jerome's eyesight also became worse. He complained that because he had to take care of the refugees by day, he had to try to work by night but this was difficult

---

[44] Kelly 1975, 298–302.

because he was no longer able to read Hebrew by lamplight. As regards the Greek commentators, he had to rely on the brothers of the monastery who read them aloud to him.[45]

The *Commentary on Ezekiel* contains two references to Jewish-Christian gospels. The first one (*Comm. Ezech.* 16.13) repeats again the tradition about the Holy Spirit lifting Jesus by one of his hairs, which he had already presented in his commentaries on Micah and Isaiah. The other one (*Comm. Ezech.* 18.5-9) refers to the distressing of one's brother:

> And in the Gospel which is according to the Hebrews which the Nazarenes are accustomed to read, among the worst crimes is set he who has distressed the spirit of his brother.
> (Jerome, *Comm. Ezech.* 18.5-9; trans. Klijn 1992).

The last years of Jerome's life were overshadowed not only by the fall of Rome but also by a heretic who had joined other refugees and settled in the Holy Land in 411, namely Pelagius. Some twenty years earlier, Jerome had disputed with Pelagius about Christian marriage. When Pelagius came to Palestine, Jerome was still working on his *Commentary on Ezekiel*. From then on, he dealt with Pelagius' teachings in several of his letters and finally completed a fuller treatise against him at the end of 415: *A Dialogue Against Pelagius*.[46] This work contains Jerome's last reference to Jewish-Christian gospels. The reference also exhibits the most extensive collection of epithets:

> In the Gospel according to the Hebrews which was written in the Chaldaic and Syriac language but with Hebrew letters, and is used up to the present day by the Nazarenes, I mean that according to the Apostles, or, as many maintain, according to Matthew, which Gospel is also available in the Library of Caesarea, the story runs: ... (*Pelag.* 3.2; trans. Klijn 1992).

The next year, 416, the monasteries in Bethlehem were attacked and destroyed by a mob that was rumored to have consisted of Pelagius' supporters. Jerome managed to escape and save his life. He died four years later, in 420, seventy-two or seventy-three years old and was buried in one of the grottoes under the Church of Nativity.[47]

---

[45] Kelly 1975, 304-308.
[46] Kelly 1975, 309-321.
[47] Kelly 1975, 322,331. According to Kelly, Jerome would have been 90 or 91 years old when he died. However, I have followed the majority view, dating Jerome's birth to 347 or 348. See above 2.2.4.

3.2.2. *An Illustrious Translator*

The last quotation from the year 416 decidedly proves that Jerome did not manage to get a clear picture of the number of "Jewish-Christian" gospels and their relations to each other. According to this quotation, the Gospel of the Hebrews = a gospel written in the Syriac language (but with Hebrew letters) = the gospel which the Nazarenes used = the Gospel of the Apostles = the Gospel of Matthew.

Although Jerome claimed several times that he had translated the gospel used by the Nazarenes, modern scholars usually think that he cannot have had a full copy of the gospel available and that he did not translate it. The main argument is that had Jerome really possessed the gospel, its differences to the Gospel of Matthew could not have escaped his attention, and he certainly would have cited it more often than he does.[48] Even Jerome's *Commentary on Matthew* contains only six references.

The reason why Jerome started to speak about having translated the Gospel according to the Hebrews must be connected to the fact that in *On Illustrious Men*, his own list of publications includes the entire New and Old Testaments, although he never completed the translation of the New Testament and the translation of the Old Testament was to be completed only about a decade later. It seems that the fact that he had started the work and was looking forward to completing it gave him reason to include these accomplishments in his list of publications. Jerome must have known the value of his work among the Latin-speaking Christians and he also probably wanted to show off to the Romans who had not realized his true value in the context of the papal election and the following incidents which caused him to leave Rome. Jerome wanted to be remembered as a man who had translated the entire Bible from Greek and Hebrew. Something similar must have happened with the "Gospel according to the Hebrews." Jerome had a plan to do the translation and by the time he was writing *On Illustrious Men*, he also thought that it was possible.

Before Jerome started to translate Bible from the original Hebrew, he prepared translations, or revisions of the Old Latin versions, of some books of the Old Testament (Psalms, Job, Chronicles, Proverbs, Ecclesiastes, Song of Songs). The translations were based on Origen's *Hexapla*,

---

[48] Vielhauer & Strecker 1991² (1963¹), 147.

in which obeli and asterisks were used to indicate the readings from Hebrew as compared to the Septuagint. During the years preceding the writing of *On Illustrious Men*, Jerome prepared several works that required much collating and compiling. In addition to Eusebius' work he collated information from various Christian and rabbinical sources for his *Hebrew Names, Biblical Places* and *Hebrew Questions*. He also prepared a small exegetical work on Psalms (*Commentarioli*). This was based on Origen's *Enchiridion*, which Jerome had supplemented with the remarks that Origen had made on the Psalms in his larger works.[49] Thus, it is quite conceivable that along with these projects, he also planned a translation of the "Gospel according to Hebrews" and was compiling material for that. However, he never managed to get hold of a complete copy of it and he had to rely on various "Jewish" gospel fragments he was able to collect from other authors and some also from Syriac Christians known as Nazarenes.

3.2.3. A Greek Translation?

In *On Illustrious Men*, Jerome says that he has translated the "Gospel according to the Hebrews" into Greek and Latin. If the Greek translation was mentioned only in *On Illustrious Men*, one might think that Greek is there because Jerome wants to compare himself with Origen and point out that he is a man who is able to translate from the original Hebrew into Greek and Latin. However, the Greek translation is also referred to in his *Commentary on Matthew* in a story about a mason with a withered hand, and there without Latin (*Comm. Matt.* 12.13; see below). Had Jerome derived the information directly from a gospel in a Semitic language, he would hardly have spoken only about a Greek translation while he was writing in Latin to Latin audience. In my view, the references indicate that the material Jerome had at hand was at least partly in Greek.[50]

---

[49] See, Kelly 1975, 157–158. *Commentarioli* is not mentioned in Jerome's list of publications in *On Illustrious Men*, but on the basis of Jerome's other remarks, it must have been written earlier.

[50] This suggest that the source of the story about the mason was not necessarily the same as in the cases where Jerome talks about a gospel used by the Nazarenes. Note that in this connection, Jerome also refers to the Ebionites, which he does not do anywhere else in the quotations. More on the classification of this and Jerome's other fragments in the next chapter.

3.2.4. *Jerome and the Nazarenes' Gospel Traditions*

If Jerome did not get a complete copy of a gospel from the Nazarenes, what did he get from them? One possible interpretation has been presented in Thomas P. Halton's translation that was published in the Fathers of the Church series:[51]

> the Hebrew itself has been preserved until the present day in the library at Caesarea which Pamphilus the martyr so diligently gathered. I have also had the opportunity of having the volume *described* to me by the Nazoreans of Beroea, a city of Syria, who use it. (*Vir. ill.* 3; italics added).

If the Nazarenes only described the contents of their gospel to Jerome, that would solve many problems. Is Halton's translation correct? The Latin runs: *Mihi quoque a Nazareis qui in Veria, urbe Syriae hoc uolumine utuntur, describendi facultas fuit*. In Latin "describe" can mean "to copy," "to sketch," and also "to describe." For me, it is difficult to read the Latin so that the Nazarenes would have described the gospel to Jerome. However, I think it is possible to understand that the Nazarenes provided Jerome an opportunity to describe the gospel. This interpretation also suits the context very well, because "describing" is precisely what Jerome does in the next sentences, where he goes on by explaining how it can be seen "in this [gospel]" (*in quo*) that testimonies of the Old Testament are quoted according to the Hebrew text. Had Jerome really wanted to point out that he had transcribed or copied the entire gospel, he could have used verbs like "exscribo", or "transcribo."

If the above interpretation of the Latin text is correct, then the Nazarenes would have provided Jerome with some notes or fragments on the basis of which he was able to "describe" what there was in their gospel. When and from whom did Jerome get the information?[52] Because he only got notes from the gospel, that may have happened almost any time but most likely at the same time he was compiling materials for his other compilations. At any rate, it is believable that the original source of the information was—to Jerome's knowledge—in Beroea in Syria. He often

---

[51] Halton 1999, 10.

[52] If Jerome himself (or his stenographers) had copied the gospel, one possible date would be the time he spent around Antioch. This possibility is usually rejected on the grounds that Jerome would have been unlikely to have kept silent so long had he possessed a copy of Matthew in Aramaic/Syriac. I agree that Jerome's silence indicates that he did not possess a copy of the whole gospel but it is not impossible that he may have had some notes. Nevertheless, in the final analysis, it is more probable that he came across the information from the Nazarenes when he was in Jerusalem.

identifies the gospel as the one "that the Nazarenes" use but never says that he is quoting from the copy that he believed to be in the library of Caesarea, although this is the place where the "original Matthew" would have been most easily available for him. Both times when he refers to the copy in Caesarea, the information is provided in addition to the fact that the gospel was used by the Nazarenes (see above, *Vir. ill.* 3 and *Pelag.* 3.2).

In my view, there is no evidence that Eusebius would have known an entire gospel in a Semitic language,[53] but it is quite possible that Jerome interpreted Eusebius' statements to the effect that the library of Caesarea must have possessed a copy of Matthew's gospel in the original Hebrew. If Jerome believed that it might be possible for him to find such a copy in Caesarea, it would partly explain why he started to see himself as an author of a finished translation.

3.3. A New Reconstruction of the Gospel Used by the Nazarenes

As was noted above, Jerome's own introductions to the passages sometimes suggest that the passages were derived from Greek sources since he claims to have translated them into Greek as well. Introductions may also bear witness to another group of users or to another title that was connected to the fragment in Jerome's source. For instance, one of the fragments (about a mason whose withered hand Jesus healed) is introduced as follows: "In the Gospel which the Nazarenes *and the Ebionites* use which *we* translated recently from Hebrew *into Greek.*" The 1st person plural, the reference to the Ebionites and to the Greek language all indicate that the passage was probably derived from a Greek source where it was ascribed to the Ebionites.[54]

In the ancient world, writing was often a collective undertaking. Jerome also used scribes from the very beginning of his career (Jerome, *Epist.* 5.2), even when he was leading an ascetic life near Chalcis, away

---

[53] See below, Chapter 3.4.1.

[54] Because the term Ebionites was a standard title for Jewish Christians, the passage was not necessarily derived from the same gospel that was known to Epiphanius (= the *Gospel of the Ebionites*). The legendary and elaborate style resembles Origen's Latin passage (Origen, *Comm. Matt.* 15.14; cf. "man scratching his hair"). There is also a similar contrast between *honor and shame* (see the shameful situation of the "brothers" of the rich man who should alleviate their misery and restore their honor). In my own reconstruction, I have attributed both passages to the *Gospel of the Hebrews*.

from all the conveniences and attractions of Rome.[55] When Jerome grew older and was losing his eyesight, he needed more and more help preparing his publications. He used scribes not only to take down his dictation but he also had texts read to him because he was no longer able to read Hebrew and Greek script without effort.[56] Keeping this in mind, it is easy to understand why some of the fragments have double or triple attributions. Jerome was not able—and he had no need—to hide the fact that the fragment in the hands of the assisting scribes was in Greek or had other attributions because he could always claim that he had in fact *also* translated the passage into Latin or that the gospel from which the fragment came was *also* used by the Nazarenes.

Especially when Jerome had much at stake in his argumentation, it weighed in his favor if he was able to trace an apocryphal saying back to the *Gospel of the Hebrews* that had a sort of semi-canonical status (cf. Eusebius, *Hist. eccl.* 3.25)[57] and hint at the possibility that it may even have been in the original Hebrew text of Matthew.

All this is clearly illustrated by an introduction to a fragment in Jerome's *Dialogue Against Pelagius*. Pelagius was Jerome's old enemy who had arrived in Jerusalem and against whom Jerome wrote a treatise in 417. Thus, there was much at stake.

> In the **Gospel according to the Hebrews** which was **written in the Chaldaic and Syriac language but with Hebrew letters**, and is **used** up to present day **by the Nazarenes**, I mean that **according to the Apostles**, or, as many maintain, **according to Matthew**, which is also available in the Library of Caesarea, the story runs. (*Pelag.* 3.2; trans. Klijn 1992).

In this connection, Jerome presents two quotations one after another. The exceptionally high number of attributions (five if the language and script are counted as one) in the first introduction is probably due to the fact that Jerome presents two fragments in the same context and has placed all the relevant titles at the beginning of the first one. The second one is introduced simply with the words: "And in the same volume ..."

After the quotations (which also include a short reference to Psalms), Atticus, who represents Jerome's stance against the Pelagians states: "If you do not allow the authority of this evidence, at least admit its antiquity, and see what has been the opinion of all good churchmen." Thus, it is clear that for Jerome, the reference to the *Gospel of the Hebrews*, the Syriac

---

[55] See, Kelly 1975, 48–49; Grützmacher 1901–1908, 1:157–158.
[56] Kelly 1975, 306–308. See also above 3.2.1.
[57] For Eusebius' canon, see Chapter 3.4.1.

language, the apostles and Matthew function as evidence for the antiquity and the reliability of the transmitted tradition.

In the following, *I shall reconstruct the collection that Jerome received from the Nazarenes by excluding the fragments that Jerome probably did not get from them*. First, I shall exclude a group of fragments on the basis of their introductions that use the 1st person plural or refer to Greek as the target language. After that, I shall discuss other evidence which indicates a non-Nazarene origin of some of the fragments. By applying this method, it is possible to reach back to some key characteristics of Jerome's Nazarene collection.

The following list contains all the introductions to the fragments that have been preserved by Jerome. *The ones whose introductions contain the 1st person plural, references to Greek as the target language or give exceptional titles for the gospel have been marked with an asterisk*. In addition, I have also highlighted (bold + underlined) features that suggest some other source than Nazarenes for the passage in question.[58]

1. *Epist.* 20.5 (383 CE).
   Finally, Matthew, who wrote the *Gospel in the Hebrew language*, put it in the following way "osianna barrama" which means "ossanna in excelsis."

2. *Comm. Eph.* 5.4 (386/7 CE)
   As we read in the *Hebrew Gospel* that the Lord said to the disciples: and never rejoice, he said, unless when you look at your brother in love.

* 3. *Comm. Mich.* 7.6 (391 CE)
   … and who should believe the *Gospel which is edited according to the Hebrews and which __we__ translated not long ago*, in which it is said of the person of the Saviour: A moment ago my Mother, the Holy Spirit took me by one of my hairs.
   Parallels: Origen, *Comm. Jo.*2.12; *Hom. Jer.* 15.4 and Jerome, *Comm. Isa.* 40.9–11 ("gospel written according to the Hebrews"; 408/10 CE) and *Comm. Ezech.* 16.13 ("Gospel which is of the Hebrews and is read by the Nazarenes"; 410/14 CE).

* 4. *Vir. ill.* 2 (392 CE)
   And also the *Gospel which is called according to the Hebrews* and which I have recently translated into __Greek__ and Latin of which *__also__*

---

[58] Translations follow Klijn 1992 with some modifications.

<u>**Origen often makes use**</u>, says after the account of the resurrection of the Lord: but the Lord after he had given the linen cloth to the servant of the priest, went to James and appeared to him ...

5. *Vir. ill.* 16 (392 CE)

   Ignatius ... wrote ... to the Smyrnaeans and separately to Polycarp ... in which he bore witness also to *the Gospel which I have recently translated*, in respect of the person of Christ, stating: I indeed saw him in the flesh ... I am not a demon without a body, and straightaway they touched him and believed.

   <u>Parallels</u>: Origen, *Princ.* 1. praef. 8 and Jerome, *Comm. Isa.* Prol. 65.

6. *Comm. Matt.* 2.5 (398 CE)

   And they said to him: In Bethlehem of Judea. Here there is an error on the part of the copyists; for we believe that the evangelist in his first edition wrote, as we read *in the original Hebrew*: Juda and not Judea.

7. *Comm. Matt.* 6.11 (398 CE)

   In *the Gospel which is called according to the Hebrews*, I found MAAR in place of "which is necessary to support life" which means "for tomorrow."

   <u>Parallels</u>: *Tract. Ps.* 135 ("In the Hebrew Gospel according to Matthew;" after 392 CE)

* 8. *Comm. Matt.* 12.13 (398 CE)

   In the Gospel which the Nazarenes and **the Ebionites** use which **we** translated recently from Hebrew **to Greek** and which is called the authentic text of Matthew by a good many, it is written that the man with the withered hand is a mason ...

9. *Comm. Matt.* 23.35 (398 CE)

   In *the Gospel which the Nazarenes use*, we find that there is written son of Jojada instead of son of Barachia.

10. *Comm. Matt.* 27.16 (398 CE)

    The name of this man is interpreted in the Gospel which is written *according to the Hebrews* as the son of their rabbi.

11. *Comm. Matt.* 27.51 (398 CE)

    In *the Gospel which we have already often mentioned*, we read that a lintel of an enormous size was broken and split.

12. *Comm. Isa.* 11.1–3 (408/10 CE)

    But according to the Gospel which was written in the *Hebrew language and read by the Nazarenes*: The whole fountain of the Holy Spirit came upon him. The Lord is the Spirit and where the Spirit of the Lord is, there is freedom ...

* 13. *Comm. Isa* 40.9–11 (408/10 CE),
   For the text, **see above #3**. Here the fragment is introduced:
   in that Gospel written according to the Hebrews which is read by the Nazarenes

14. *Comm. Isa.* Prol. 65 (408/10 CE),
    For the text, **see above, # 5**. Here the fragment is introduced:
    according to the Gospel which is of the Hebrews and read by the Nazarenes

* 15. *Comm. Ezech.* 16.13 (410/5 CE)
   For the text, **see above #3**. Here the fragment is introduced:
   Gospel which is of the Hebrews and read by the Nazarenes

16. *Comm. Ezech.* 18.5–9 (410/5 CE)
    And in the *Gospel which is according to the Hebrews which the Nazarenes are accustomed to read*, among the worst crimes is set: He who has distressed the spirit of his brother.

* 17. *Pelag.* 3.2 (415 CE)
   In the *Gospel according to the Hebrews which was written in the Chaldaic and Syriac language but with Hebrew letters, and is used up to the present day by the Nazarenes*, I mean that <u>**according to the Apostles**</u>, or, as many maintain, according to Matthew, which is also available in the Library of Caesarea, the story runs:

17a. See, the mother of the Lord and his brothers said him: John the Baptist baptizes for the remission of the sins, let us go to be baptized by him. He said to them, however: What sin have I committed that I should go and be baptized by him? Unless perhaps something which I said is ignorance.

17b. And in the same volume: If your brother, he said, sinned to you with a word and makes amends to you, accept him seven times a day. Simon his disciple said to him: Seven times a day? The Lord answered and said to him: And I say to you until seventy times seven. For even among the prophets after they were anointed with the Holy Spirit there was found a word of sin.

On the basis of the introductions, it is possible to exclude fragments # 3, 4, 8, 13, 15 and 17 a/b from the material that Jerome received from the Nazarenes. Fragment #17 is problematic because it is difficult to conclude whether it was the first or the second quotation to which the titles were originally attributed. Since both passages are suspected of being derived from a gospel that was not attributed to the Nazarenes, they cannot be used as a starting point for the reconstruction of Jerome's Nazarene collection. I will come back to this problem after having delineated the nature of the collection on the basis of other fragments, and then discuss whether it is possible that Jerome received either #17a or #17b from the Nazarenes.

It is often noted that Jerome started to refer to the Nazarenes in 391–392 CE when he wrote his *Commentary on Micah* and his encomium of the Christian teachers, *On Illustrious Men*. In both of these writings, which he probably prepared simultaneously, he claims that he had recently translated the gospel that was used by the Nazarenes.[59] Because fragments #1 and #2 were written before that time and Jerome does not refer to the Nazarenes or his own translation work in them, the fragments are not usually attributed to the Nazarenes. For instance, Klijn lists the first fragment in the category of "spurious and doubtful texts." In his view, Jerome got the explanation from a translation that was in circulation. This is corroborated by the fact that the explanation does not explicitly refer to any gospel but only gives the supposed original Hebrew text of Matthew.[60] Vielhauer and Strecker, followed by Klijn, attribute the second fragment (*Comm. Eph.* 5.4; 386/7 CE) to the *Gospel of the Hebrews* of the 3GH.[61]

The fifth fragment (together with #14) is also considered spurious. As we have seen above, Jerome quotes Ignatius' passage as it is recorded by Eusebius but he does not realize that the beginning of Eusebius' quotation repeats Ignatius' own words in his *Letter to the Smyrnaeans*. Thus, Jerome ends up attributing Ignatius' own words to the apocryphal source that Ignatius was quoting. Furthermore, Jerome erroneously attributes the passages to Ignatius' *Letter to Polycarp* because Eusebius discusses Polycarp immediately above the quoted passage. Thus, Jerome has clearly taken the passage from Eusebius.

When fragments #1–2, 5 and 14 are also excluded from the materials that Jerome received from the Nazarenes, the Nazarene collection can be reconstructed from the following fragments:

---

[59] As was noted above, by that time Jerome had lived in Palestine almost ten years and he had advanced his skills in Hebrew so that he was able to start preparing Latin translations directly from the Hebrew. He was eagerly defending his program of *Hebraica veritas* and therefore pictured himself in *On Illustrious Men* as a man who was very competent in Hebrew. See Kelly 1975, 159–167. This makes it understandable why he exaggerated the work he had done with the Nazarene fragments. The limited number of fragments shows that Jerome did not have an entire gospel available. See above.

[60] Klijn 1992, 120–121. Similarly, Vielhauer & Strecker 1991² (1963¹), 155. However, as was noted above (Chapter 3.2.1), the fragment seems to be based on a Syriac source.

[61] Vielhauer & Strecker 1991² (1963¹), 149; Klijn 1992, 78–79.

6. *Comm. Matt.* 2.5 (398 CE)
7. *Comm. Matt.* 6.11 (398 CE)
9. *Comm. Matt.* 23.35 (398 CE)
10. *Comm. Matt.* 27.16 (398 CE)
11. *Comm. Matt.* 27.51 (398 CE)
12. *Comm. Isa.* 11.1–3 (408/10 CE)
16. *Comm. Ezech.* 18.5–9 (410/5 CE)

At this juncture, it is important to keep in mind that the reconstruction has been accomplished by simply excluding the passages that are extremely unlikely to have been derived from the Nazarenes because of their early date, the wording of their introductions or because it can be proved that Jerome derived his information from other sources. No passages have been excluded on the basis of their content or because they do not cohere with a particular hypothesis about the character of the "Gospel of the Nazarenes." In this regard, the process is totally different from the reconstruction of the 3GH, which starts with a hypothesis and proceeds by sorting out the fragments into three predetermined categories.

Nevertheless, due to the fragmentary character of the evidence, it is clear that at some point one has to resort to arguments based on the contents of the fragments. Anticipating that phase, it can be noted that fragment #12 has, in earlier reconstructions, been attributed to the same gospel as fragment #3,[62] which was excluded from the Nazarene collection on the basis that Jerome was likely to have gleaned it from Origen's writings. In contrast to synoptic descriptions of Jesus' baptism, which imply that God's voice sounds from the heavens, fragment #12 explicitly attributes the voice to the Holy Spirit, who addresses Jesus as her son and—the word Spirit being feminine in Hebrew—proves to be his mother. Thus, it is clear that fragments #12 and #3 exemplify the same understanding of the Holy Spirit as Jesus' mother and are therefore likely to be derived from the same source. If fragment #3 was not from the Nazarene collection, it is likely that neither is fragment #12. These preliminary considerations will be confirmed if fragment #12 does not cohere with the content and focus of the other remaining fragments.

The majority of remaining fragments are to be found in Jerome's *Commentary on Matthew*. This fits very well with the fact that when Jerome started to refer to the gospel that he had "copied" from the Nazarenes,

---

[62] Vielhauer & Strecker 1991² (1963¹), 148–149; Klijn 1992, 52, 98; Klauck 2003, 40–41.

he identified the gospel with the Hebrew original of Matthew and it is natural that he made use of it when he was writing his own commentary to the same book. The number of these relatively certain cases is very limited and raises the question of why precisely these passages were chosen as the points of comparison. Were these the only points where the Nazarene gospel differed from the canonical Matthew? Or had Jerome knowledge of only these passages? Or is there an underlying common denominator that could connect the seemingly random variant readings with each other?

At first glance, there seems to be no apparent connection between the different Matthean fragments and one is tempted to conclude that Jerome made up the whole story about the Nazarenes' gospel. The fragments presented in Jerome's *Commentary on Matthew* give the impression that Jerome had received only a collection of alternative readings from the Nazarenes. These do exemplify a comparison of Matthew's Greek phrases with Semitic expressions but hardy justify Jerome's claims that he had copied and translated the Nazarenes' gospel. A collection like this could have been transmitted in the margins of a manuscript of a Greek gospel as well.[63]

However, a closer look at the Matthean contexts[64] of the fragments reveals a remarkably clear pattern. The fragments are from Matthean passages whose severe criticism of the Jewish people and their leaders closely resembles the anti-rabbinic tone of the Nazarenes' Isaiah expositions. When the variant readings are replaced in their Matthean contexts, it appears that fragments # 6,9,10 and 11 form a unified collection consisting of (1) the initial rejection of the newborn "king of the Jews" by Herod and "all Jerusalem," (2) the words of judgment upon the nation because of its treatment of the prophets, (3) the nation's avowed responsibility for the death of Jesus (who died instead of a "son of their rabbi"), and (4) of the signs following Jesus' death that prove him to have been "the son of God." Even (5) the Matthean version of the Lord's Prayer (fragment # 7) accords very well with this collection because the Lord's Prayer

---

[63] In my paper "What is the Gospel of the Nazoreans?" delivered at the 2001 SBL Annual Meeting in Denver, I suggested that Jerome was using a Greek manuscript with some notes about "original" Hebrew readings.

[64] Because Jerome lists only minor details that are different in the gospel used by the Nazarenes, it is to be assumed that—excluding the differences that Jerome describes in his commentary—the wording of the passages was not too far from the Greek text of Matthew. Thus, the main contents of the collection can be sketched by simply listing the Matthean passages whose wording Jerome discusses.

in Matthew is presented as an alternative to Jewish prayer practices and similar criticisms of Jewish prayers and praying habits also characterize the Nazarenes' relation to the rabbis.

It is impossible to know the exact extent or wording of the quotations but, as the following reconstruction indicates, the phrases that Jerome quoted from the Nazarene collection clearly belong to contexts that exemplify the hostility of the Jewish people and the judgment upon them. The following English reconstruction draws on the wording of the NRSV. <u>*Reconstructed variant readings*</u> in the Nazarene collection <u>*are underlined and italicized*</u>. Phrases that exemplify **the hostility of Jews/rabbis towards God's Son, who was sent to rule them, are written with bold.**

6. *Comm. Matt.* 2.5 (398 CE); Context: Matt 2:1–8 (see also Matt 2:13, 16,20)

> In the time of King Herod, after Jesus was born in Bethlehem of Judea, wise men from the East came to Jerusalem, ²asking, "Where is the child who has been born king of the Jews? For we observed his star at its rising, and have come to pay him homage." ³**When King Herod heard this, he was frightened, and all Jerusalem with him;** ⁴and calling together all the chief priests and scribes of the people, he inquired of them where the Messiah was to be born. ⁵They told him, "In Bethlehem of <u>*Juda*</u>; for so it has been written by the prophet: ⁶ 'And you, Bethlehem, in the land of Judah, are by no means least among the rulers of Judah; **for from you shall come a ruler who is to shepherd my people Israel.**'" ⁷Then Herod secretly called for the wise men and learned from them the exact time when the star had appeared. ⁸Then he sent them to Bethlehem, saying, **"Go and search diligently for the child; and when you have found him, bring me word** so that I may also go and pay him homage."

9. *Comm. Matt.* 23.35 (398 CE). Context: Matt 23:29–38

> ²⁹**Woe to you, scribes and Pharisees, hypocrites!** For you build the tombs of the prophets and decorate the graves of the righteous, ³⁰and you say, "If we had lived in the days of our ancestors, we would not have taken part with them in shedding the blood of the prophets."³¹Thus you testify against yourselves that **you are descendants of those who murdered the prophets.** ³²Fill up, then, the measure of your ancestors. ³³**You snakes, you brood of vipers!** How can you escape being sentenced to hell? ³⁴Therefore I send you prophets, sages, and scribes, some of whom you will kill and crucify, and **some you will flog in your synagogues and pursue from town to town,** ³⁵so that upon you may come all the righteous blood shed on earth, from the blood of righteous Abel to the blood of Zechariah son of <u>*Jojada*</u>, whom you murdered between the sanctuary and the altar. ³⁶Truly I tell you, all this will come upon this generation. ³⁷Jerusalem, Jerusalem,

CHAPTER THREE

the city that kills the prophets and stones those who are sent to it! How often have I desired to gather your children together as a hen gathers her brood under her wings, and you were not willing! ³⁸See, your house is left to you, desolate.

10. *Comm. Matt.* 27.16 (398 CE). Context: Matt 27:15–48.

¹⁵Now at the festival the governor was accustomed to release a prisoner for the crowd, anyone whom they wanted. ¹⁶At that time they had a notorious prisoner, called Jesus *Barrabban*. ¹⁷So after they had gathered, Pilate said to them, "Whom do you want me to release for you, Jesus *Barrabban* or Jesus who is called the Messiah?" ¹⁸For he realized that it was out of jealousy that they had handed him over. ¹⁹While he was sitting on the judgment seat, his wife sent word to him, "Have nothing to do with that innocent man, for today I have suffered a great deal because of a dream about him." **²⁰Now the chief priests and the elders persuaded the crowds to ask for *Barrabban* and to have Jesus killed.** ²¹The governor again said to them, "Which of the two do you want me to release for you?" And they said, "*Bar Rabban*," ["the son of our rabbi"]⁶⁵ ²²Pilate said to them, "Then what should I do with Jesus who is called the Messiah?" All of them said, "**Let him be crucified!**" ²³Then he asked, "Why, what evil has he done?" **But they shouted all the more, "Let him be crucified!"** ²⁴So when Pilate saw that he could do nothing, but rather that a riot was beginning, he took some water and washed his hands before the crowd, saying, "I am innocent of this man's blood; see to it yourselves." ²⁵Then the people as a whole answered, "**His blood be on us and on our children!**" ²⁶ So he released *the son of their rabbi*⁶⁶ for them; and after flogging Jesus, he handed him over to be crucified.

11. *Comm. Matt.* 27.51 (398 CE). Context: Matt 27:45–54

"He saved others; he cannot save himself. He **is the King of Israel; let him come down from the cross now**, and we will believe in him. ⁴³He trusts in God; let God deliver him now, if he wants to; **for he said, 'I am God's Son.'**" ⁴⁴**The bandits who were crucified with him also taunted him in

---

⁶⁵ According to Jerome, "the name of the man is interpreted in the Gospel which is written *according to the Hebrews* as the son of their master." Scholars have found this problematic for two reasons. First, an "interpretation" of a Semitic name would seem unnecessary in a Semitic text. Second, Barrabban means literally "son of *our* master/rabbi," not "son of *their* master/rabbi." However, in this context the "interpretation" does not refer to a translation but to spelling/reading the name in such a way that it comes to mean the "son of our master" instead of the "son of our father." See Chapter 4.2; Lagrange 1922, 3:329; Klijn 1992, 90–93. The form the "son of *our* master/rabbi" is perfect in the mouth of the crowds and Jerome's "interpretation" expresses the same thing from a Christian point of view: the crowds wanted to free the "son of their master/rabbi." The Nazarene version may even have expressed the idea from the same Christian point of view at the end of the passage. See the reconstruction of Matt 27:26.

⁶⁶ See the previous footnote.

the same way. ⁴⁵From noon on, darkness came over the whole land until three in the afternoon. ⁶And about three o'clock Jesus cried with a loud voice, "Eli, Eli, lema sabachthani?" [that is, "My God, my God, why have you forsaken me?"]⁶⁷ ⁴⁷When some of the bystanders heard it, they said, "This man is calling for Elijah." ⁴⁸At once one of them ran and got a sponge, filled it with sour wine, put it on a stick, and gave it to him to drink. ⁴⁹But the others said, "Wait, let us see whether Elijah will come to save him."

⁵⁰ Then Jesus cried again with a loud voice and breathed his last. ⁵¹At that moment *a lintel of an enormous size in the Temple was broken and split*. The earth shook, and the rocks were split. ⁵²The tombs also were opened, and many bodies of the saints who had fallen asleep were raised. ⁵³After his resurrection they came out of the tombs and entered the holy city and appeared to many. Now when the centurion and those with him, who were keeping watch over Jesus, saw the earthquake and what took place, they were terrified and said, **"Truly this man was God's Son!"**

In the Matthean context, the Lord's Prayer is clearly presented as an alternative to Jewish prayers in synagogues. It is clear from Jerome's *Commentary on Amos* and his *Letter to Augustine* that he also had knowledge of anti-Nazarene Jewish prayers. In a context where Jerome accuses Augustine (*Epist.* 112.13) of supporting Ebionite views, he notes that "Until now a heresy is to be found in all parts of the East where Jews have their synagogues; it is called "of the Minaeans" and cursed by Pharisees up to now. Usually they are named Nazarenes." It is generally agreed that Jerome refers here to an addition—known as *Birkat ha-Minim*—that was made to the twelfth "blessing" of the Jewish *Eighteen Benedictions*. Some versions of the "blessing" are also known to have included a reference to *notsrim* that is obviously a Semitic variant of Jerome's Nazarenes.⁶⁸ Jerome refers to the same practice in his *Commentary on Amos* (*Comm. Am.* 1.11–12): "Until today they blaspheme the Christian people under the name of Nazarenes." Jerome refers to the prayer on a general level but a more detailed description of the Jewish practice, to which the Nazarenes may have contrasted Jesus' teaching about prayer, is preserved by Epiphanius (*Pan.* 29.9.2):

---

⁶⁷ The translation of Jesus' words may have been unnecessary in a Semitic version.

⁶⁸ Different versions of the prayer are quoted by Schäfer 1975, 57–61, who suggests that the *notsrim* were included in the prayer in localities where the "Nazarenes" had become a problem. In most cases, the "benediction" refers only to the *minim*. Scholars have discussed whether the term refers to Christians in general or only to the "sect" of the Nazarenes. However, if I have been on the right track in arguing that the kind of separate sect Epiphanius characterizes in his *Panarion* 29 never existed, then the whole discussion may be based on a misconception. For the discussion, see Horbury 1982, 59–61; Kimelman 1975, 226–244; de Boer 1998, 250.

> The Jews "**stand up** at dawn, at midday, and toward evening, three times a day when they recite their prayers **in the synagogues**, and curse and anathematize them. Three times a day they say, 'God curse the Nazarenes.'"

7. *Comm. Matt.* 6.11 (398 CE). Context: Matt 6:5–15

> "**And whenever you pray, do not be like the hypocrites; for they love to stand and pray in the synagogues** and at the street corners, so that they may be seen by others. **Truly I tell you, they have received their reward.** ⁶But whenever you pray, go into your room and shut the door and pray to your Father who is in secret; and your Father who sees in secret will reward you. ⁷When you are praying, do not heap up empty phrases as the Gentiles do; for they think that they will be heard because of their many words. ⁸Do not be like them, for your Father knows what you need before you ask him. ⁹ Pray then in this way: Our Father in heaven, hallowed be your name. ¹⁰Your kingdom come. Your will be done, on earth as it is in heaven. ¹¹Give us this day our <u>bread for tomorrow</u>. ¹²And forgive us our debts, as we also have forgiven our debtors. ¹³And do not bring us to the time of trial, but rescue us from the evil one. ¹⁴For if you forgive others their trespasses, your heavenly Father will also forgive you; ¹⁵but if you do not forgive others, neither will your Father forgive your trespasses."

In addition to its internal coherence, the reconstructed collection of the anti-rabbinic texts from Matthew is also connected to the Nazarenes exposition of Isaiah. These two collections have at least the following points of contact:

> 1. The Nazarenes' Isaiah commentary (Jerome, *Comm. Isa.* 9.1) refers to an Old Testament citation found only in Matthew (Matt 4:15–16), which proves that the Nazarenes used Matthew's gospel in their exegesis.

> 2. The most negative attitude towards the rabbis.

> 3. A similar scribal method that attributes anti-rabbinic meaning to Semitic names. In the *Commentary on Isaiah*, the names of Shammai and Hillel are interpreted as meaning "scatterer" and "unholy." In the Matthean collection, Barrabban is interpreted to mean the "son of their rabbi."

> 4. Both collections are concerned with criticizing the prayer practices of the rabbis. See Jerome, *Comm. Isa.* 8.19–22 and the above reconstruction of the socio-historical context of the Lord's Prayer in the Nazarene collection.

> 5. According to the Isaiah collection, the Israelites *deny the Son of God* with the most vicious opinion (Jerome, *Comm. Isa* 31.6–9) and the scribes and the Pharisees try to deceive people in *denying the Son of God* (Jerome, *Comm. Isa.* 29.17–21). In contrast, the centurion and his companions respond to the miracles following Jesus' death (including the breaking of the lintel) with the confession "*Truly this man was the Son of God.*"

6. Both collections entertain the hope for the Israelites conversion and submission to their ruler. According to Matt 23:38, "your house" (= the Temple or the house of Israel?) will be left desolate but people will finally bless Jesus as the one who "comes in the name of the Lord." According to *Comm. Isa.* 31.6–9, the "sons of Israel" who earlier fought with the devil and denied the Son of God will become tributaries of the church.

There are four fragments whose origin still needs to be discussed (#12, #16, #17a and #17b). Of these four, the 3GH attributes #12 and #16 to the *Gospel of the Hebrews* and #17a and #17b to the "Gospel of the Nazarenes."[69]

It was already noted that fragment #12 (which deals with Jesus' baptism) has a thematic connection to fragment #3 (Jesus taken by one of his hairs) which made it suspect of being derived from another gospel. The fact that there seems to be no connection between fragment #12 and the anti-rabbinic Matthean collection confirms this assumption.

Fragment #16 (Jerome, *Comm. Ezech.* 18.5–9) only paraphrases the wording of the "Gospel according to the Hebrews." It is difficult to say anything definite about the fragment's relation to the synoptic gospels but there is no apparent passage in the synoptic tradition to which it could be connected. Judging on the basis of the Matthean fragments, the Nazarenes were using a Semitic copy of Matthew that did not differ very much from the Greek version. Of course, this may have included some passages that are unknown within the synoptic tradition but because fragment #16 emphasizes the obligation not to distress the spirit of one's brother, it is usually attributed to the same gospel as fragment #2. Since there seems to be no connection to the Matthean anti-rabbinic collection, the fragment #16 probably comes from a different source.

Finally, there is the question about the origin of fragments #17a and #17b that was suspended because earlier it was impossible to decide which one of these two (or both) should be excluded from the Nazarene collection. The method of exclusion resulted in detecting a coherent collection of Nazarene fragments, but there is no apparent connection between the reconstructed Nazarene collection and these two fragments. This suggests that Jerome did not get these passages from the Nazarenes.

---

[69] See, Vielhauer & Strecker 1991² (1963¹), 148–149; Klijn 1992, 98–105.

Some church fathers refer to the *Gospel of the Apostles* by name but nobody quotes it and it is never described as particularly Jewish. Thus, given Jerome had much at stake in his dispute with Pelagius (see above) he may have added the title.[70] However, there are two things in fragment #17b that speak for its Jewish-Christian origin—the name Simon and the fragment's connection to τὸ ἰουδαϊκόν readings.

Is one then to conclude that Jerome received fragment #17b from the Nazarenes? Usually fragment #17b is attributed to the "Gospel of the Nazarenes" and with it all the marginal readings from the Matthean manuscripts that refer to a Jewish gospel (τὸ ἰουδαϊκόν). However, it was already noted above that, in contrast to the assumptions of the supporters of the 3GH, τὸ ἰουδαϊκόν readings do not necessarily constitute a unified collection which could be attributed to a particular Jewish-Christian gospel (see above Chapter 3.1). If the readings were collected from commentaries, they may have their origin in several different gospels that were for some reason or other regarded as "Jewish."[71] Furthermore, some of the readings—including the one paralleled in fragment #17b—have connections to both Matthew and Luke[72] and there is also a reading that does not have any point of reference in Matthew. This indicates that these

---

[70] The *Gospel of the Ebionites* is certainly sometimes identified with the "Gospel of the Apostles" because, in the Ebionite fragments, the disciples appear as storytellers: "There was a man called Jesus. He was about thirty years old and he chose us" (Epiphanius, *Pan.* 30.13.2–3). Thus, for instance, Waitz 1937, 79–81 and Lagrange 1922, 170. For a different view and other literature, see Schmidtke 1911, 170–175. Vielhauer & Strecker 1991² (1963¹), 166, list *Pan.* 30.13.2–3 among the fragments from the *Gospel of the Ebionites* but think that it is questionable if it really was from the *Gospel of the Ebionites*. In contrast to Waitz, it should be noted that Jerome's fragment (#17a in this article) was unlikely from the *Gospel of the Ebionites*—which Waitz identifies with the *Gospel of the Apostles*— because, according to *Pan.* 30.13.6, John "baptized with the baptism of repentance," not "for the remission of sins" as in fragment #17a (Jerome, *Pelag.* 3.2). This shows that at this point, the wording of the *Gospel of the Ebionites* was closer to Matthew's gospel (Matt 3:1–2) whereas the wording of fragment #17a draws on Mark and Luke (Mark 1:4; Luke 3:3).

[71] Frey 2003a, 131–136, correctly emphasizes that τὸ ἰουδαϊκόν variants cannot be connected to the "Gospel of the Nazarenes" as it is reconstructed in the 3GH hypothesis but he seems to attribute the fragments to a fourth, independent Jewish-Christian gospel. I do not believe that the character of the fragments justifies this kind of assumption. The fragments may have been derived from several different "Jewish" gospels but nothing in the preserved fragments indicates that τὸ ἰουδαϊκόν variants were derived from a gospel that was different from other available fragments.

[72] In Matthew (Matt 18:21–22), Peter presents to Jesus the question about the need to forgive and Jesus gives his instructions in a dialogue with Peter. In Luke (Luke 17:3–4) Jesus addresses the disciples directly and there is no dialogue between Jesus and the disciples. τὸ ἰουδαϊκόν (fragment #17b) is a combination of these two forms since it

readings were not derived from a gospel that was almost an exact copy of the Greek Matthew like the one used by the Nazarenes probably was.

Conclusion: The "Gospel of the Nazarenes" and the Nazarenes' Isaiah Exegesis

The above reconstruction shows how the Nazarenes' picked up key passages from Matthew's narrative in order to show that that Jesus was the Son of God who was sent to his own people. From the very beginning, the people mistreated him as they had earlier done with their prophets. The story, which has obvious Deuteronomistic overtones, culminates in Jesus' trial when the people choose "the son of their rabbi" instead of Jesus the Son of God. However, Jesus is proven to be God's Son through the centurion's confession and signs accompanying his death which predict the future punishment: the destruction of the Temple.

If the Nazarenes' collection was based on the canonical Matthew, is it justified to call its fragments Jewish Christian?[73] As far as the question concerns only the text of the Nazarene's collection, the question is closely tied with the question about Matthew's Jewish-Christian character. I agree with scholars who think that the Gospel of Matthew was edited in a community where strict observance of the law was no longer required.[74] However, an understanding of the original audience or the community where the text was edited does not yet solve the question about the Jewish-Christian character of the text as it stands. The mere fact that the degree of Matthew's Judaism remains controversial among scholars shows that the text itself is also open to interpretations that locate it within Judaism. Thus, if applied to the case of the Nazarenes, from a theoretical point of view it is quite possible that, for the Nazarenes, the Gospel of Matthew was more Jewish than it was for its original editor.

Although a discussion of the Jewish Christianity of *a text as it stands* is informative to some extent,[75] it is not fully possible in the case of the

---

opens with Jesus' direct speech to which "Simon" reacts by asking Jesus to confirm if one really has to forgive seven times a day.

[73] Cf. Andrew Gregory's critical comments cited in Chapter 1.3 of this volume.

[74] Applying Stark and Bainbridge's definition of cult and sect movements, I have characterized Matthew's community as a Christian cult movement. See Luomanen 2002b. Cf. Gregory 2006, 405.

[75] In the light of the indicators of Jewish Christianity such a discussion would concern the questions how and to what extent a text propagates, supports, allows or prohibits Jewish and/or Christian ideas and practices. This would give a rough picture of what sort of Jewish-Christian thinking and practice is more likely or possible on the basis of a given text, but this does not yet determine how the text is used and interpreted in actual life.

gospel used by the Nazarenes because of the fragmentary character of the evidence. Furthermore, I find it more interesting to try to describe and understand the social reality where the texts were interpreted and applied, if such information is available. Luckily, we do have some additional information about the Nazarenes, thanks to Jerome who quoted their Isaiah exegesis (see above Chapter 2.2.4).

If observance of the law is made the key criterion, as Andrew Gregory has suggested,[76] the Nazarenes' interpretation of Matthew was not Jewish Christian: the Nazarenes were so clearly pro-Pauline that their interpretation of the law must have been quite liberal.[77]

However, a more nuanced picture of the Nazarenes' Jewish-Christian profile can be achieved with the help of the *indicators of Jewish Christianity*. The Nazarenes' identity, in terms of their language and knowledge of Jewish culture, the rabbinic movement in particular, seems to have been even more pronounced than in the case of the editor of Matthew's gospel.

The Nazarenes' *Commentary on Isaiah* and the gospel that they used were products of Aramaic/Syriac-speaking Christians who probably were converts from Judaism. In many ways, they can be compared to Paul whose work they admired and found this already predicted by Isaiah. They hoped for the conversion of the rest of the House of Israel and had fierce disputes with their contemporary rabbis. The rabbis "cursed" them in their synagogues. The Nazarenes, in turn, twisted the words of the Hebrew Bible against their enemies, trying to show that Isaiah predicted the destruction of Jerusalem and the shameful state of the House of Israel and that the rabbis and their forefathers were the ones to be blamed for this. Isaiah also gave advice on how the fresh converts should answer the rabbis who propagated their own views: the rabbinic tradition is idol worship. Nazarenes (Christians) have no need to listen to the rabbis since they themselves have direct access to the Scriptures, and if the rabbis will not agree with the Christian interpretation of the Scriptures, they will always remain oppressed. Legal debates were obviously fierce but the main bone of contention was Jesus' position as the Son of God.

---

[76] Thus, Gregory 2006, 390. See also Chapter 1.3 above.

[77] The Nazarenes' Isaiah exegesis in Jerome, *Comm. Isa.* 9.1 (trans. Klijn & Reinink 1973, 223): "When Christ came and his preaching shone out, the land of Zebulon and the land of Naphtali first of all were freed from the errors of the Scribes and the Pharisees and he shook off their shoulders the very heavy yoke of the Jewish traditions. Later, however, the preaching became more dominant, that means the preaching was multiplied, through the Gospel of the apostle Paul who was the last of all the apostles …".

The Nazarenes obviously found Jesus' life and Paul's mission predicted in Isaiah. Isaiah had also correctly predicted the actions and destiny of their enemies. But that was not all. The Nazarenes had also compiled a collection of passages from the Gospel of Matthew which showed that everything the Scriptures had predicted about Jesus was indeed fulfilled in the course of his life.

The vigor with which the Nazarenes attacked the rabbis very much gives the impression of a struggle over a common Jewish heritage. The Nazarenes were so closely tied with their Jewish compatriots that the teaching of the rabbis could not simply be ignored. Instead, much effort was put into finding evidence in the Scriptures—we know of Isaiah and Matthew expositions—which would put their opponents in a bad light and justify the Nazarenes' own position. On the other hand, as regards the terms and consequences of being either inside or outside the Nazarene group, it seems that the Nazarenes possessed a clear Christian identity: Jews can be saved only by becoming Christians.[78] Thus, although the Nazarenes overall religious profile was clearly more on the Christian side, it was accompanied by such pronounced Jewish elements that to describe it simply as Christian without any further qualification would certainly give an oversimplified picture of their position and the strong bonds with which they were tied to their Jewish heritage.

The discussion about the Nazarenes' *Commentary on Isaiah* (see Chapter 2.2.4) and the gospel that they used has not revealed anything to support the view that the Nazarenes were a separate heretical sect, wandering somewhere in the no man's land between Judaism and Christianity. The Christians from whom Jerome received these writings had developed a clear Christian identity which, nevertheless, also included some strong Jewish elements. Perhaps "Nazarene Christians" would be a suitable name for these people—"Nazarene" referring to the strong Jewish elements in their identity and "Christians" highlighting the fact that they were not a separate sect but sided with the formative Christianity.

The "Gospel of the Nazarenes" as it is reconstructed in the 3GH is pure fiction. Needless to say, a heresy that did not exist did not need a gospel of its own.

---

[78] Jerome, *Comm. Isa.* 31.6–9 (Trans. Klijn & Reinink 1973, 223–225): "O sons of Israel who deny the Son of God with the most vicious opinion, turn to him and his apostles. If you will do this, you will reject all idols which to you were a cause of sin in the past and the devil will fall before you, not because of your powers but because of the compassion of God. And his young men, who a certain time earlier fought for him, will be tributaries of the Church and any of its power and stone will pass …".

3.4. Reconstructing the *Gospel of the Hebrews*

In the previous chapter, it was argued that there never existed a separate "Gospel of the Nazarenes;" Jerome had only received a collection of anti-rabbinic passages from Syriac speaking Christians who were called Nazarenes in their native tongue. This solution to Jerome's problematic quotations does not yet solve the whole riddle of Jewish-Christian gospels since we do not yet know how to classify the remaining fragments. Should the rest of Jerome's fragments still be attributed to two different "real" Jewish-Christian gospels or is it more likely that they were derived only from one Jewish-Christian gospel? In my view, the latter option is better grounded and I shall support it in detail in the latter part of this chapter. Before that, it is helpful to take a look at Eusebius' understanding of the *Gospel of the Hebrews* since after Jerome (and Origen), he is the third important witness to the *Gospel of the Hebrews*.

3.4.1. *Eusebius' Testimony:*
The Gospel of the Hebrews *on the Fringes of Canon*

Eusebius' Canon
Eusebius introduces the *Gospel of the Hebrews* in the list of canonical and non-canonical writings in the third book of his *Ecclesiastical History* (*Hist. eccl.* 3.25). Eusebius has three main categories:

1. Generally accepted books (ὁμολογούμενα) that are "true, genuine, and accepted in the tradition of the church:"[79] The four Gospels, Paul's epistles, 1 John and 1 Peter.

2. Disputed (ἀντιλεγόμενα) writings that are not canonical but familiar to most church writers: The epistles of James, Jude, 2 Peter, 2 and 3 John. The books that Eusebius characterizes as disputed (νόθα) also belong to this same category: the *Acts of Paul*, the *Shepherd* [*of Hermas*], the *Revelation of Peter*, the *Epistle of Barnabas*, the *Teachings of the Apostles* [*Didache*], and the Revelation of John. In addition, the *Gospel of the Hebrews* is also placed in this category:

---

[79] The English translations from *the Ecclesiastical History* presented in this chapter draw on Maier 1999.

Among those some have placed also the Gospel according to the Hebrews with which those of the Hebrews that have accepted Christ are especially pleased.

3. The writings used by the heretics but not quoted by any church writers: "the Gospels of Peter, Thomas, Matthias and others, the Acts of Andrew, John and other apostles."

The *Gospel of the Hebrews* provides an interesting—but seldom discussed—example of a writing whose canonical status was not perfectly clear. Notably, Eusebius places the *Gospel of the Hebrews* in the same category as the Revelation of John, which was later on able to secure its canonical status. Moreover, many of the other writings named in the same category were well received among mainstream Christians although they were not able to make their way into the core of the canon. However, in addition to Eusebius' list, there are no other early lists of canonical writings that deal with the *Gospel of the Hebrews*.[80]

In this chapter, I will discuss the reasons why Eusebius included the *Gospel of the Hebrews* in the category of the "disputed writings." I will focus on two sets of questions: 1) Was Eusebius merely listing the *Gospel of the Hebrews* among the disputed writings because "some" had done that before him or was he also able to draw his own conclusions about the character of the gospel? What kind of information did Eusebius have about the *Gospel of the Hebrews*? Had he seen it or did he only have second hand information available? 2) What kind of gospel was the *Gospel of the Hebrews* on the basis of Eusebius' references? Do his references reveal something of the character of the *Gospel of the Hebrews* which would explain why it was not able to retain its position in the "second category" of not strictly canonical writings but seems to have sunk into oblivion like the gospels of Peter, Thomas and Matthias of the third category?[81]

---

[80] For instance, Clement of Alexandria, accepts as authoritative (in addition to others) James, 2 and 3 John, 2 Peter, Jude, the *Letter of Barnabas*, and the *Apocalypse of Peter*, that Eusebius lists in his category of disputed writings. The Muratorian Canon also refers to the *Shepherd of Hermas* as worthy of being read. However, Origen only accepts as clearly canonical the same writings that Eusebius lists in his first category. Thus, from Eusebius' second category, only the *Gospel of the Hebrews*, the *Acts of Paul* and the *Teachings of the Apostles* are ignored in these other discussions of canonical writings by Clement, Origen and the Muratorian Canon. For an overview of the contents of the canonical lists, see Kee 1997, 572–573 and Metzger 1988, 305–315.

[81] For instance, Metzger suggests that the *Gospel of the Hebrews* was excluded from the canon because it was written in a Semitic language and because it "differed considerably in substance and in character" from the gospels that were finally regarded as the canonical

In order to answer these questions, two sets of evidence must be investigated. (1) Eusebius' references to the *Gospel of the Hebrews*: In addition to the passage quoted above (*Hist. eccl.* 3.25), Eusebius writes that the *Gospel of the Hebrews* was used by the Ebionites (*Hist. eccl.* 3.27.4.), Papias knew a story from it (*Hist. eccl.* 3.39.17) and finally he relates that it was used by Hegesippus (*Hist. eccl.* 4.2.28). (2) Eusebius' own quotations from a gospel written in Hebrew characters or language: *Theoph.* 4.22 (PG 24, 685–688) and *Theoph. Syriaca* 4.12. For the passages (and my reconstruction of the *Gospel of Hebrews*) see Appendix 1.

Eusebius himself does not make clear whether or not he identifies the gospel written in Hebrew characters with the *Gospel of the Hebrews* and it is impossible to say for sure how he saw the relation. As a matter of fact, I shall suggest below that Eusebius may intentionally have left open whether the passages he himself quoted came from the *Gospel of the Hebrews* or from early "canonical" tradition, perhaps the Gospel of Matthew in Aramaic, in order to give further credence to his quotations. On the other hand, I shall also argue that from historical point of view, there are many common features pointing out that passages quoted by Eusebius came from the same gospel or the same sphere of gospel traditions as the passages quoted by Eusebius' predecessors, Papias in particular.

The Ebionites Use the Gospel of the Hebrews
Eusebius' second reference to the *Gospel of the Hebrews* is in the section where he describes the heresy of the Ebionites (*Hist. Eccl.* 3.27). Following Origen (*Cels.* 5.61), he makes a distinction between two kinds of Ebionites: one group denied the virgin birth, others did not. Although this distinction between the two kinds of Ebionites is hardly historical as such (see above Chapters 2.1.2 and 2.1.3), it is worth considering whether Eusebius' references to the *Gospel of the Hebrews* have some historical value. When describing the latter group, Eusebius notes that despite the fact that they accept the virgin birth, they are still heretics, especially because they are zealous in observing the law and because they reject the letters of the apostle Paul, calling him apostate, and "used only the so-called *Gospel of the Hebrews* and accorded the others little respect."

---

gospels. Metzger 1988, 169–170. Metzger obviously does not make any distinction between the "Gospel of the Nazoreans" and the *Gospel of the Hebrews* for he ascribes both Origen's Greek quotations and Jerome's Semitic quotations to the one and the same gospel.

Irenaeus was the first church father who provided specific information about the Ebionites but according to him, the Ebionites only used the Gospel of Matthew. Irenaeus was the defender of the canon of four gospels and he argued that heretics erred precisely for the reason that they used either more or less than the four gospels.[82] Eusebius' description of the "second" group of the Ebionites is clearly based on Irenaeus (*Haer.* 1.26.2) with the exception that Eusebius replaces Matthew's Gospel with the *Gospel of the Hebrews*. Because Eusebius' description totally relies on the information he derived from his predecessors, Irenaeus, Hippolytus and Origen, it is unlikely that he could have personally known Ebionites who used the *Gospel of the Hebrews*. Instead, he adopted the general description of the Ebionites' doctrine from Irenaeus, elaborating it with two pieces of information that Origen had written about Jewish Christians: (1) There were two different groups of Ebionites and (2) there was a gospel called the *Gospel of the Hebrews*. Eusebius' list of canonical books shows that, in Eusebius' view, the heretics tended to use gospels of their own (see above). By Eusebius' time, the reputation of the Ebionites as stupid heretics was well known—Origen, for instance, thought the Ebionites received their name because of their poor intellect. Thus, it would have been embarrassing had a heretical group based its teaching on the Gospel of Matthew. In the light of Eusebius' categories, it was more appropriate that they based their teaching on the half-canonical *Gospel of the Hebrews*.

A Woman Accused of Many Sins
Eusebius' third reference to the *Gospel of the Hebrews* is in the context where he first discusses the reliability of the writings of Ignatius, Polycarp and Clement. He records by name only those authors whose writings of the teaching of the apostles have survived to his time (*Hist. Eccl.* 3.36–38). After dealing with the writings of Clement, he moves on to Papias (*Hist. Eccl.* 3.39).

First, he corrects Irenaeus by saying that Papias did not himself meet the apostles but learned the basics of faith from those who knew the apostles (3.39.1–2). Then he presents the famous quotation where Papias relates that he relied more on the living word than on the information gained from the books (3.3.3–4). In modern scholarship, Eusebius' quotation of Papias is often referred to in order to show that by Papias' time,

---

[82] Irenaeus, *Haer.* 3.11.8–9.

oral tradition was still highly valued and was even more important than written tradition for Papias. However, this is not the point which Eusebius' wants to make. He obviously presents Papias' lengthy quotation because it seems to make a distinction between two persons called John, making it possible to exclude the Revelation from the collection of the canonical books, if needed (*Hist. Eccl.* 3.39.5-6). Eusebius also summarizes approvingly two stories related by Papias (about Philip's daughter and Justus; *Hist. Eccl.* 3.39) but then moves on to criticize him for accepting "strange parables, teachings, and other mythical traditions." Eusebius especially targets Papias' chiliasm, which in Eusebius' view indicates Papias' very modest intellectual skills.

The last part of Eusebius' discussion of Papias includes quotations of what Papias said about Mark and Matthew. The reference to the *Gospel of the Hebrews* closes the section:

> Papias also used evidence from 1 John and from 1 Peter and provides another story of a woman falsely accused before the Lord of many sins, which is contained in the *Gospel of the Hebrews*. (*Hist. Eccl.* 3.39).

After many sweeping descriptions of traditions and writings that Papias used, why does Eusebius single out the story about a woman accused of many sins as an example of what Papias quoted from the *Gospel of the Hebrews*? Matthew, Mark, 1 John and 1 Peter are regarded as generally accepted books by Eusebius, but the *Gospel of the Hebrews* belongs to de disputed ones. Why is it mentioned?

The supporters of the 3GH emphasize that the information about the origin of the quotation must be from Eusebius. However, given the superfluous character of Eusebius' other references to the *Gospel of the Hebrews*, I find it likely that Papias already indicated the "source" of the quotation.[83] For the supporters of the 3GH, a conclusion like this is inconvenient because it would indicate the presence of a Greek gospel "according to the Hebrews" in Asia Minor in the early second century.[84]

---

[83] In contrast to Schmidtke 1911, 149–152, who thinks that Eusebius reasoned—unjustly—that the passage must be derived from the *Gospel of the Hebrews*. Vielhauer & Strecker 1991² (1963¹), 138 think that Eusebius must have found the passage in the *Gospel of the Hebrews*. Klijn 1992, 11, thinks that Eusebius did not possess the gospel but got his information elsewhere or was merely guessing.

[84] Notably, Didymus the Blind seems to have known a version of the same story (see below) where the woman was not accused of adultery but of "sins," just like in Papias' quotation. According to Didymus, the quotation is in "some gospels." Because Didymus is one of the few authors whose writings have seemed to indicate that the *Gospel of the*

Because Eusebius quotes the *Gospel of the Hebrews* in connection with the canonical writings and not in the context where he lists Papias' "legendary accounts," it seems that the story about the woman who was accused of many sins was not too far from the style of the canonical gospels. Perhaps the contents of his story was one of the reasons why Eusebius was willing to list the *Gospel of the Hebrews* among the disputed and not among the totally heretical writings?

The Origin of the Passage about a Woman Accused of Many Sins
Since Rufinus, the passage referred to by Papias has often been identified with the story about a woman caught in adultery, which is later on added to John 7:53–8:11 (or in some manuscripts after John 7:26; 21:25 or Luke 21:25). John's passage is found for the first time in manuscript D (fifth century). However, the passage is found even earlier in the *Didascalia Apostolorum* where the woman is not called an adulteress but a sinner (*DA* VII/Lagarde, p. 31), as in Papias' fragment ("accused of sins"). Notably, also D and manuscript 1071 refer to the "sin" (sg.) of the woman and not to adultery.[85] Moreover, Didymus the Blind also quotes a story about a woman condemned for a sin:

> We find in certain Gospels. A woman, it says, was condemned by the Jews for a sin and was being sent to be stoned in a place where that was customary to happen. The Savior, it says, when he saw her and observed that they were ready to stone her said to those who were about to cast stones: He who has not sinned let him take a stone and cast it. If anyone is conscious of himself of not having sinned, let him take a stone and smite her. And no one dared. Since they knew in themselves and perceived that they themselves were guilty in some things, they did not dare to strike her.
> (Didymus the Blind, *Comm. Eccl.* 4.223,7–13; trans. Klijn 1992, 118).

The variants in manuscript tradition, the *Didascalia* and Didymus' passage indicate that several versions of the same basic story were circulating among Christians in the late fourth and early fifth century (Didymus died 398). Therefore, it possible that Papias had already cited one version of the story, and that he, as well as Didymus, had found the story in the *Gospel of the Hebrews*.[86]

Furthermore, it is interesting to note that the character of the story as it is presented in the Johannine tradition would quite well fit with

---

Hebrews was known only in Egypt, the similarity with Papias' passage is striking, and raises serious doubts about the correctness of one of the basic assumptions of the 3GH.
[85] Vielhauer & Strecker 1991² (1963¹), 138. Cf. the discussion below, Chapter 3.4.2.
[86] Thus, for instance, Frey 2003b, 203.

other Jewish-Christian gospel fragments. Although the story about the woman caught in adultery is added to the Gospel of John, it is generally acknowledged that its language is not typical of John. Instead, it has many features typical of the synoptic gospels, Luke's gospel in particular. Moreover, if some Markan expressions are not later additions then the passage would also be characterized by harmonization as are many of the Jewish-Christian gospel fragments.[87]

Hegesippus' Gospel of the Hebrews
Eusebius' last reference to the *Gospel of the Hebrews* is to be found in his summary of Hegesippus' work (*Hist. Eccl.* 4.22). According to Eusebius, Hegesippus quotes from

> the Gospel according to the Hebrews and from Syriac and also something from the Hebrew dialect, showing that he was a convert from the Hebrews, and he also mentions other things from unwritten Jewish traditions.
> (trans. PL).

From a grammatical point of view, it is most natural to "fill out" Eusebius' sentence by adding "gospel" after the adjective "Syriac." The expression "Syriac" is unique in Eusebius' writings, which suggests, that he got the information from his sources.[88] According to Klijn, Eusebius' quotation clearly indicates that the *Gospel of the Hebrews* must have been in Greek "since the second gospel is explicitly said to have been written in Aramaic." Although there are some problems with this line of thought, the assumption about Greek as the original language of the *Gospel of the Hebrews* coheres with other evidence about the gospel. Thus, I agree that by the time of Hegesippus, the *Gospel of the Hebrews* was probably known only in Greek.[89]

---

[87] The Lukan character of the language is clearly demonstrated by Becker 1963, 68–74. Mark's language has possibly effected John 8:2 (cf. Mark 2:13). Also κύψας can be found, in addition to this passage, only in Mk 1:7 (omitted by Luke). For harmonizing readings, see Chapters 5.1 and 5.2 in this volume, also Luomanen 2003, 57, 243–275 and Luomanen 2006.

[88] Similarly, Vielhauer & Strecker 1991² (1963¹), 139. Eusebius himself only uses the expression "Hebrew" when he refers to the original language of the Jewish scriptures (several instances in *Dem. ev.* and *Onomasticon*).

[89] There are two main problems. First, Eusebius says nothing about the language of the *Gospel of the Hebrews*. He obviously takes up the title of the gospel only in order to show that Hegesippus was familiar with Jewish(-Christian) traditions. Thus, it must have been enough for Eusebius that he had seen the title of the *Gospel of the Hebrews* in Hegesippus' writings, and it is impossible for us to know for sure the original language of the gospel Hegesippus had used. Second, it is not altogether clear that "Syriac"

Because Eusebius only includes short notes about the Jewish(-Christian) traditions quoted by Hegesippus, it is impossible to say how long the quotations were in Hegesippus' writings and whether or not Eusebius himself was able to draw some conclusions about the character of these writings.

Nevertheless, Eusebius' own view of Hegesippus is very positive; in *Hist. Eccl.* Hegesippus is presented as one of the guarantors of the correct apostolic faith (for instance, *Hist. Eccl.* 2.23, 3.32, 4.22). Thus, the mere fact that Eusebius knew Hegesippus quoted the *Gospel of the Hebrews* would have been enough to convince Eusebius that the *Gospel of the Hebrews* was not a totally heretical writing.

Eusebius' Own Quotations
Eusebius' own quotations from the "Hebrew" gospel are usually read in the light of Jerome's information according to which the gospel that was used by the Nazarenes was also to be found in the library of Caesarea (Jerome, *Vir. ill.* 3). Therefore, it is assumed that Eusebius also must have known this Aramaic gospel.[90] However, as was noted above (see Chapter 3.2.4) Jerome himself does not say that he has seen the gospel in Caesarea. Instead, he relates that the Nazarenes themselves who lived in Beroea let him copy or describe their gospel. Thus, Jerome's information about the gospel in the library of Caesarea was probably based only on the conclusions he was able to draw on the basis of Eusebius' *Ecclesiastical History* and *Theophania* (see below). On the basis of these writings, he concluded that there must have been an Aramaic gospel in the library of Caesarea.

---

must here refer to (West) Aramaic, which would give an archaic slant to Hegesippus' tradition. Because Hegesippus was Tatian's contemporary, he may already have known some (Diatessaronic) gospel traditions in the Syriac alphabet (East Aramaic). In contrast to Klijn 1992, 12 n. 32, Schmidtke 1911, 52, n. 1 also rejects the possibility that the "Syriac (gospel)" might refer to the *Diatessaron* on the grounds that it did not belong to the special literature of Jewish Christians. However, there are many connections between the readings of the *Diatessaron* and the fragments from the Jewish-Christian gospels, which proves that at some point, either the *Diatessaron* was influenced by a Jewish-Christian gospel, or the Jewish-Christian gospel(s) by the *Diatessaron*. Usually it is assumed that the *Diatessaron* was the first gospel in Syriac (writing). I deal with the Diatessaronic traditions in Chapter 5, arguing that the *Gospel of the Hebrews* was translated into Syriac some time during the third or fourth century. Thus, by the time of Hegesippus, it would probably have been known only in Greek.

[90] Klijn 1992, 33; Vielhauer & Strecker 1991² (1963¹), 146.

According to Eusebius, the gospel he uses "has come to us" (*Theophania*). This expression would seem to suggest that Eusebius (as well as Pamphilus?) had the whole gospel at his disposal. However, in connection with the other quotation he says that it is to be found "somewhere in the gospel which exists among the Jews in Hebrew language" (*Theophania Syriaca* 4.12), which makes it more probable that he only had access to some quotations that were derived from a gospel used by the "Jews."

Theophania

In *Theophania*, Eusebius paraphrases a version of the Parable of the Talents (Matt 25:14–30), which has come to him "in Hebrew letters:"

> Since the Gospel that has come to us in Hebrew letters directs it threat not against the one who has hidden (his talent) but against the one who lived in extravagance. For he [the master] possessed three slaves, one spent the fortune of his master with harlots and flute-girls, the second who multiplied his trade and the third who hid his talent. One of them was accepted, one rebuked only, and one thrown into prison. I wonder whether the threat in Matthew, which, according to the letter was spoken against the one who did nothing, applies not to him but to the earlier one who was eating and drinking with the drunkards, by way or resumption.
>
> (*Theoph.* 4.22, trans. Klijn 1992, modified).

Matthew's version of the Parable of the Talents, which is Eusebius' point of comparison, has three servants of whom two double their money (of two and five talents). The gospel in Hebrew letters obviously has replaced one of these traders with a servant who spent his fortune. Consequently, this servant who lived in extravagance is also the one who is thrown into prison, not the one who only hid the talent. This gives Eusebius a reason to wonder if this is also the case in Matthew: The worthless slave "to be thrown into the outer darkness, where there will be *weeping and gnashing of teeth*" (Matt 25:30) is not really referring to the slave who hid the talent. Instead, it is the "wicked servant" whose actions were described a bit earlier in Matthew's Gospel (Matt 24:45–51). The wicked servant had started to beat his fellow servants and "eat and drink with the drunkards," wherefore he was to be put with "the hypocrites where there will be *weeping and gnashing of teeth*." Notably, the destiny of the punished person is described similarly in both cases, which may also have drawn Eusebius' attention to these passages.

Because Eusebius only summarizes the parable, it is not possible to compare it with the synoptic stories in detail. However, Klijn has drawn attention to the fact that the phrase "spent the fortune of his master with harlots and flute-girls" (τὸν μὲν καταφαγόντα τὴν ὕπαρξιν τοῦ δεσπότου μέτα πορνῶν καὶ αὐλητρίδων) closely resembles Luke 15:30 where the prodigal son "spent his fortune with harlots" (καταφαγών σου τὸν βίον μετὰ πορνῶν). Nevertheless, Klijn closes the discussion by noting that the phrase may also be commonplace.[91] This assumption would seem to be confirmed by the fact that the prostitutes and flute-girls appear together in P.Oxy 840, exemplifying extravagant, impure life.[92] However, it may have escaped Klijn's notice that there is another phrase in Eusebius' summary that also agrees with the Parable of the Prodigal Son. Both the prodigal son and the "wicked" servant "lived in extravagance" (Luke 15:13: ζῶν ἀσώτως; Theoph. ἀσώτως ἐζηκότος). Because ἀσώτως is a *hapax legomenon* in the NT, the agreement is hardly coincidental. Given that many of the Jewish-Christian gospel fragments combine phrases from different synoptic gospels, it seems clear that Eusebius also had found a later edition of Matthew's Parable of Talents where the part of one of the servants was rewritten, borrowing phrases from Luke's Prodigal Son. Notably, Eusebius' own interpretation only plays with phrases to be found in Matthew's passages (see above), which makes it unlikely that the connections to Luke derived from Eusebius.

The introduction of the quotation indicates that Eusebius did not have the entire gospel to hand but was relying on a fragment and had only second hand information about its origin. At first glance, the reliability of the information about the Semitic origin of the quotation may seem dubious because there are word for word connections to the Greek Gospel of Luke. However, ἀσώτως is used as a Greek loanword in a Syriac translation of Luke 15:13 (Sy^h). This suggests that the original language of the fragment that Eusebius paraphrased was Syriac, not Hebrew. This observation is in line with the hypothesis, to be developed in more detail in Chapter 5, that the Greek *Gospel of the Hebrews*, which was using synoptic gospels, was later on translated into Syriac.

The Parable of the Talents in Ancient Mediterranean Culture
The version of the parable in the *Gospel of the Hebrews* is interesting because its punishment of the servants is different. Scholars who have approached the Eusebian version from the viewpoint of Matthew's and

---

[91] Klijn 1992, 62, n. 34. Klijn also notes that in Syriac gospel tradition, the same word is used to translate both βίον (Luke 15:12,30) and τα ὑπάρχοντα (Luke 8:3, 12:33, Matt 19:21, 25:14).
[92] I owe this reference to Dr. Thomas Kazen.

Luke's parables have found it difficult to reconstruct the order of servants and their punishments. It is clear that the servant who spent the money for his own entertainment was thrown into prison but what was the destiny of the other two servants? Because Eusebius describes the servants in the order (1.) spent, (2.) multiplied, (3.) hid, and describes the punishment of the first servant last, it would seem that he presents the punishment in the reversed, khiastic order:

The Gospel of the Hebrews		*The Gospel of Matthew*	
Servant	Judgment (Eusebius's order reversed)	Servant	Judgment
1. spent the fortune with flute girls	thrown into prison	1. doubles five talents	was praised
2. multiplied the trade	rebuked	2. doubles two talents	was praised
3. hid the talent	accepted	3. hid the talent	was thrown into darkness

However, the assumption about the khiastic order is difficult because then the servant who hid the talent would have been the one who was accepted, not the one who multiplied his trade as in the synoptic versions. Therefore, Klijn suggests that Eusebius' first listing does not follow the original order. Eusebius focused on the servant who was punished and therefore mentioned him first. According to Klijn, the original order and the corresponding punishments were as follows:[93]

1. multiplied the trade → was accepted
2. hid the talent → was rebuked
3. spent the money → was thrown into prison

However, Malina and Rohrbaugh think that Eusebius did not make a mistake. He described the judgments in the same (reversed) order as they were in the *Gospel of the Hebrews*.[94] This suggestion draws on

---

[93] Klijn 1992, 61.
[94] Malina & Rohrbaugh 1992, 148–150. However, Malina and Rohrbaugh follow the standard 3GH classification and attribute the passage to the "Gospel of the Nazarenes."

Mediterranean anthropology and sets the parable in the context of poor Galilean peasants. The starting point of this suggestion is that in the Mediterranean culture, where Jesus and his first followers lived, the idea of limited good was one of the most important culturally shared values. Since the amount of good was restricted, it followed that everyone who tried to get more for him/herself was inevitably stealing from others. Good persons did not try to become rich at the expense of others. From the viewpoint of the idea of limited good, both the man who spent his money with the flute girls and the servant who multiplied his trade were morally dubious characters.

According to Biblical law (Deut 23:19–20), it was not allowed to charge interest on loans. Interest is not directly mentioned in the Matthean version but it is certainly implied, and in Luke we have a more direct reference to making more money with money. Furthermore, in later rabbinic tradition, burying was considered a perfectly responsible way of taking care of someone else's money.[95]

The version that we have in the *Gospel of the Hebrews* seems to be in accordance with these values. It accepts with joy the servant who simply kept the allotted money in a safe place. The servant who multiplied the money is rebuked and the servant who spent the money of his master with harlots and flute players is cast into prison. Thus, the parable that was recorded in the *Gospel of the Hebrews* would make perfect sense in the context of ancient Mediterranean culture. Should we then perhaps regard it as the version that comes closest to the original parable of Jesus? Consequently, could the *Gospel of the Hebrews* have preserved an earlier version of the parable than Matthew and Luke?

In my view, this is not the case for several reasons. First, it is very difficult to argue for a tradition-historical line of development from "more Mediterranean" to "less Mediterranean" within such a short time span as we would have to presume between the Matthean/Lukan version(s) and the version in the *Gospel of the Hebrews*. Because the overall culture is the same, there have to be some specific reasons for the development. Nevertheless, these cultural considerations show that the Eusebian version of the parable is perfectly possible and that there is no need to presume any mistake on Eusebius' part. The parable in the *Gospel of the Hebrews* probably praised the servant who simply hid his talent.

---

[95] Thus, for instance, Luz 1997, 500–501, referring to BM 42a.

Second, as we have already seen, some linguistic details suggest that text that Eusebius quoted had connections to both Matthew and Luke. This points rather towards a post-synoptic harmonizing tradition.

Third, the characterization in the Matthean and Lukan versions—especially in the light of the idea of limited good—seem to belong to the same group of morally questionable parables as, for instance, the Parable of Dishonest Manager (Luke 16:1–13) and the Parable of the Unjust Judge (Luke 18:1–8).[96] All these parables use morally questionable characters as figures who exemplify something of what God requires of men. Furthermore, in the case of the Parable of the Talents/Mina (in Matthew and Luke), it is not only the praising of the smartest businessman that may have raised the eyebrows of the hearers but also the characterization of the master who obviously stands for God: he is hard and merciless (σκληρός in Matthew; αὐστηρός in Luke) who "reaps where he did not sow and gathers where he did not scatter." These characteristics are hardly ideal for a farmer who wishes to live in peace with his neighbors in a world which presumes the idea of limited good. Because of these morally dubious features, it is easier to understand a tradition-historical development from the Matthean/Lukan version to the parable in the *Gospel of the Hebrews* which is more compatible with the common values of ancient Mediterranean culture.

Fourth, if we attribute to the *Gospel of Hebrews* both the Eusebian version of the Parable of the Talents and the parable about three rich men in Origen's Latin commentary on Matthew (see Chapter 5.1), we can see that both these parables are against being or becoming rich at the expense of others.[97]

---

[96] Thus, Luz 1997, 498, who thinks that these parables may well be derived from historical Jesus.

[97] Interestingly, this line of critique resonates also with the *Gospel of Thomas*. Logion 64 concludes: "Businessmen and merchants [will] not enter the places of my father." I will deal with Thomas' relation to Jewish-Christian gospel more in Chapter 5.2. However, at this point it can already be noted that the passage in Origen's Latin *Commentary on Matthew* is closely connected to *Gos. Thom.* 63, and that *Gos. Thom.* 62 and possibly also the previous saying 61 seem to link up with the passage to be treated next, a quotation in Eusebius' *Theophania Syriaca*, which also comes from the *Gospel of the Hebrews*. Thus, there is a cluster of four sayings in the *Gospel of Thomas* (61–64) which seems to have parallels in Jewish-Christian fragments that this volume attributes to the *Gospel of Hebrews*. As will become clear in the following chapters, the reason for these connections is that both the *Gospel of the Hebrews* and the *Gospel of Thomas* are drawing on similar post-synoptic, pre-Diatessaronic harmonizing gospel traditions, and that these two gospels come from the same cultural sphere where riches and businessmen were criticized.

Theophania Syriaca 4.12
The Syriac version[98] of Eusebius' *Theophania* contains the following passage:

> Then he taught about the divisions of the souls which will come about in the houses, as we have found somewhere in the gospel which exists among the Jews in the Hebrew language, in which it is said: "I choose myself the good ones, the good ones whom my father in heaven has given to me."[99]

Eusebius is dealing with synoptic the story of the Divisions within the Households (Matt 10:34–36/Luke 12:51–53) but it is not certain if this also was the original context of the passage that he quotes. Eusebius' introduction suggests that he found the passage as a floating saying without knowing its exact context in the "gospel which exists among the Jews in Hebrew language." If the quoted passage was explicitly dealing with the "divisions of the souls," as Eusebius suggests, then its context may not have been the passage of the Divisions Within the Households which Eusebius himself is explaining.

Another synoptic story that would come closer to the theme of choosing is the exhortation to watchfulness in Luke 17:33–35/Matt 24:40–43, where "there will be two in one bed; one will be taken and the other left" and "two women grinding meal together, one will be taken and the other left." Notably, in Luke, these stories explicitly deal with the problem of how to save one's "soul" (ψυχή).

Klijn points out—correctly—that it is typical of John to emphasize that Jesus has chosen the ones that the Father has given to him (John 17:2,6,9,24; 18:9).[100] However, the idea that a savior chooses the "worthy ones" that are predestined to salvation by the Father is not restricted to the Gospel of John. Instead, it can be seen as a typical idea in wisdom literature, rooted in the myth of Wisdom seeking a worthy place of rest. In the *Gospel of Thomas*, the idea appears in a slightly gnosticized form which describes the disciples of Jesus as the ones who have "come from the light" and are "elect of the living father" (*Gos. Thom.* 50). It is to these who are worthy of Jesus' mysteries that he tells his mysteries

---

[98] Eusebius' *Theophania* has survived in some Greek fragments (see the previous section) and in a Syriac translation which, however, is considered early and quite accurate (dated to the beginning of the fifth century).

[99] The translation follows Klijn 1992, 62. The translation of the repeated "good ones" (ܗܿܘ ܛܒ̈ܐ ܛܒ̈ܐ ܠܗܘܢ) is problematic but I agree with Klijn's solution. For the discussion, see Klijn 1992, 62–64.

[100] Klijn 1992, 64.

(*Gos. Thom.* 62). These Thomasine ideas are not very far from the idea expressed in the passage quoted by Eusebius ("I choose myself the good ones").

It is hardly a coincidence that Luke's exhortation to watchfulness (Luke 17:33–35/Matt 24:40–43), which is the possible synoptic background for Eusebius' quotation (see above), finds its parallel in the *Gospel of Thomas* in logion 61 that also deals with the problem of being "divided" (cf. Eusebius' "divisions of souls") and states that Jesus was given some of the things of his father (cf. Eusebius' "the ones who my Father in Heaven has given to me"). These considerations are then followed by logion 62, which talks about those who are worthy of being told Jesus' mysteries.

The analysis in Chapter 5.2 indicates that *the Gospel of Thomas* and many Jewish-Christian fragments are rooted in similar harmonizing gospel traditions. This supports the view that Eusebius' fragment and *Gos. Thom.* 61–62 have some kind of tradition-historical connection. Furthermore, one of the Jewish-Christian fragments that Jerome quotes (*Comm. Isa.* 11.1–3) shows that the fundamental Wisdom myth was known in the *Gospel of the Hebrews*:

> But according to the Gospel that was written in Hebrew language and read by the Nazoreans: 'The whole fountain of the Holy Spirit came upon him.' ... Further in the Gospel ...: 'It happened then when the Lord ascended from the water, that the whole fountain of the Holy Spirit descended and rested upon him and said to him: My son, I expected you among all the prophets that you should come and that I should rest upon you. For you are my rest, you are my first-born son, who shall reign in eternity.[101]
>
> (trans. Klijn 1992, 98).

In addition, Clement of Alexandria quotes a saying from the *Gospel of the Hebrews* that has a parallel in *Gos. Thom.* 2. In the light of these fragments, the "good ones" in Eusebius' passage do not refer to "morally superior" Christians[102] but to those "seekers of Wisdom" who prove to be chosen by the father.

However, although in the *Gospel of the Hebrews* the "good ones" probably referred to those who possessed Wisdom, it is clear that Eusebius is able to quote it "approvingly" for his own purposes. The title of the section where Eusebius presents the passage ("Concerning the divisions of the houses and the families which exist until the present day because

---

[101] Because of the close connection to Wisdom theology, the fragment is often ascribed to the *Gospel of the Hebrews* also in the 3GH. See, for instance, Klijn 1992, 98; Frey 2003b, 202, esp. n. 57. The passage is also attributed to the *Gospel of the Hebrews* in this volume.

[102] Suggested by Klijn 1992, 64.

of the doctrine")¹⁰³ suggests that for Eusebius, the "good ones" probably were those who agreed with the correct apostolic faith.

According to *Theophania Syriaca*, the gospel "exists among the Jews in Hebrew language." However, the above analysis of the Greek fragment from the *Theophania* (GHeb's version of the Parable of the Talents), suggested that although Eusebius is referring to a gospel written in "Hebrew letters," the language was actually Syriac. That is most likely also true in this case. Eusebius is paraphrasing the passage on the basis of secondhand information and the information is not quite accurate.

More important is that according to Eusebius, the gospel in question "exists among the Jews" (ܒܐܘܪܝܐ ܕܝܢ ܐܝܬܘܗܝ). Usually scholars have not paid much attention to this detail but their discussion implies that they take "among the Jews" to mean Jewish converts who had abandoned their ancestral religion and become Christians.¹⁰⁴ However, it is natural to take the wording as it stands: the Christ believers who used this gospel were factually living as Jews within Jewish communities (cf. Chapter 1.3).

Summary: Eusebius' View of the Gospel of the Hebrews
In addition to the list of canonical and non-canonical writings, Eusebius refers to the *Gospel of the Hebrews* three times. (1) Eusebius may have connected the *Gospel of the Hebrews* to the Ebionites on the basis of his own reasoning. Although he may have been on the right track, we cannot be sure about the historical value of his statement. (2) Eusebius hints at the contents of the passage about a woman accused of many sins which he knew from Papias' writings but he does not explicitly quote the passage. Papias' fragment was in Greek. If Papias' fragment was connected to John 7:53–8:11, as was argued above, it is clear that Greek was also the language of the "original" *Gospel of the Hebrews* and that the fragment may have included phrases from different synoptic gospels, especially from Luke. (3) Eusebius may have also seen some quotations in Hegesippus' writings but he does not say a word about their contents. Nevertheless, it is possible to conclude that by the time of Hegesippus, the *Gospel of the Hebrews* was still known in Greek.

Eusebius also knows that Hegesippus quoted from a "Syriac gospel." This may have been a gospel written in West or East Aramaic. However,

---
¹⁰³ Klijn 1992, 63.
¹⁰⁴ Cf. Resch 1906, 363–364; Vielhauer & Strecker 1991² (1963¹), 139; Klijn 1992, 62–65.

nothing indicates that this "Syriac gospel" would have been especially Jewish Christian. It is quite possible that it was the *Diatessaron*.

Eusebius says that his own quotations are from a gospel written in Hebrew characters/language. The character of the quotations indicates that Eusebius did not have the entire gospel(s) in hand but was relying on secondhand information. There are also word for word connections to the Greek Gospel of Luke which suggests that the traditions available to Eusebius had originally been in Greek but were later on translated into Syriac (more on this in Chapter 5).

Overall, the passages referred to and quoted by Eusebius fit with other Jewish-Christian gospel fragments. There are clear indications of the influence of harmonizing traditions and the possible influence of Wisdom traditions. Papias testifies to a Greek *Gospel of the Hebrews* in Asia Minor in the early second century, which is much earlier than Origen and Clement of Alexandria start to quote the *Gospel of the Hebrews* in Egypt. This also coheres with the hypothesis, to be discussed in the next chapter, that Jewish-Christian gospels/gospel traditions were only later on transmitted to Egypt and therefore it is no need to postulate a separate Egyptian *Gospel of the Hebrews*.

The main reason why Eusebius placed the *Gospel of the Hebrews* in the second category in his list of canonical writings was that it was referred to by writers he understood to be trustworthy transmitters of apostolic tradition. He also must have seen some quotations from the *Gospel of the Hebrews* which he was able to utilize in his own exposition of the scriptures. However, on the whole, his knowledge about the actual contents of this gospel must have remained limited. This means that although Papias, Hegesippus, Origen and Clement of Alexandria still had Jewish-Christian gospels available in Greek, by Eusebius' time the actual Greek *Gospel of the Hebrews* was no longer available for writers within "mainstream" Christianity. Rather, the way in which Eusebius introduces the *Gospel of the Hebrews* suggests that the Christ believers who used this gospel were living as Jews within Jewish communities.[105]

This is perhaps one of the reasons why the career of the *Gospel of the Hebrews* on the fringes of canon was so short. In Eusebius' time, it was no longer a real option for writers within the "mainstream" but Eusebius, who had carefully reviewed the writings of his predecessors, could not dismiss it out of hand because it was referred to by esteemed teachers of

---

[105] Further evidence for this view in Chapter 5.1.

the apostolic faith. On the other hand, from a historical point of view so many of the surviving fragments seem to combine phrases from different synoptic gospels that had a complete *Gospel of the Hebrews* been in the hands of church writers, it would probably have been considered a gospel harmony just like the *Gospel of the Ebionites*. Thus, from the viewpoint of the "mainstream," the history of Jewish-Christian gospels may go hand in hand with Tatian's *Diatessaron*. Gospel harmonies were dismissed and destroyed as the "doctrine" about the four separate gospels gradually became the standard.[106]

3.4.2. *A Reconstruction of the* Gospel of the Hebrews

The above review of Eusebius' references has added the last pieces to the puzzle and now it is possible to sketch out the character of the *Gospel of the Hebrews* and to create the most likely picture of its history. Before the analysis of Eusebius' passages in the preceding chapter, there were still two arguments that could have been presented in favor of the old 3GH. First, the 3GH emphasizes that the first witnesses of the *Gospel of the Hebrews* are located in Egypt: Clement of Alexandria and Origen. Second, Hans-Joseph Klauck, for instance, thinks that the three descriptions of the baptism of Jesus are so different that they must stem from three different gospels.[107]

As regards Clement and Origen, we are left with only two sayings that are important for this question: Clement's saying about finding rest (*Strom.* II IX 45.5 and V XIV 96.3), and Origen's saying about the Spirit as Jesus' mother (*Comm. Jo.* 2.12).[108] However, in the provisional critique of the 3GH, it was already noted that precisely these sayings are most clearly paralleled in the *Gospel of Thomas* and the *Acts of Thomas*. Since scholars usually assign the composition of these writings to Syria,[109] the existing evidence suggests a Syrian rather than an Egyptian origin for the *Gospel of the Hebrews* as well (see above Chapter 3.1).

---

[106] In contrast to Metzger 1988, 170, who thinks that the *Gospel of the Hebrews* was dismissed because of it Semitic language and character that was totally different from the synoptic gospels.

[107] Klauck 2003, 37.

[108] *Strom.* II IX 45.5: "He who has become astonished will become king and he who has become king will rest." *Strom.* V XIV 96.3: "He who seeks will not cease until he finds and having found he will marvel and having marvelled he will become king and having become king, he will rest." Origen, *Comm. Jo.* 2.12: "A moment ago my Mother the Holy Spirit, took me by one of my hairs and brought me to the great hill, the Tabor."

[109] See below Chapter 5.2 (on Thomas).

The analysis of Eusebius' passages substantiates this argument by revealing that Clement and Origen, at the beginning of the third-century in Egypt, were not the earliest witnesses. Rather, the *Gospel of the Hebrews* was already known to Papias and Hegesippus in the second century (roughly within the time span 100–180). Moreover, it can be shown that both Clement and Origen had good opportunities to acquire knowledge of these fragments from the Syro-Palestinian area.

Clement of Alexandria casts light on his tutors as follows:

> Now this work of mine in writing is ... truly an image and outline of those vigorous and animated discourses which I was privileged to hear, and of blessed and truly remarkable men. Of these the one, in Greece, an Ionic; the other in Magna Graecia: the first of these from Coele-Syria, the second from Egypt, and others in the East. The one was born in the land of Assyria, and the other a Hebrew in Palestine. When I came upon the last (he was the first in power), having tracked him out concealed in Egypt, I found rest. He, the true, the Sicilian bee, gathering the spoil of the flowers of the prophetic and apostolic meadow, engendered in the souls of his hearers a deathless element of knowledge. (*Strom.* I 1; trans. ANF).

Origen, for his part, started writing his *Commentary on John* in Alexandria and continued it after he moved to Caesarea in 232. The section where we find the Jewish-Christian fragment (*Comm. Jo.* 2.12; Klijn's date: "before 228") was written in Alexandria. However, Origen had already visited Rome, Palestine and Antioch between ca. 213–218 and could very well have come across traditions of the *Gospel of the Hebrews* in any of those places.

As regards Klauck's argument concerning the three baptismal stories, it is really hard to see why the discussion about the appropriateness of Jesus' baptism could not be connected to the actual description of the baptism (cf. the reconstruction in the Appendix). Although Jesus presents a critical question concerning the baptism of John, this does not necessarily mean that he would not eventually have gone to be baptized. The fragment that describes the actual baptism shows clearly that baptism was not about forgiveness of sins in Jesus' case. Instead, it was an occasion where an unblemished, unique character was revealed.

There does not seem to be any reasons why the rest of the fragments—after Jerome's anti-rabbinic collection is removed—could not come only from the *Gospel of the Hebrews*. This assumption is the simplest one and it presumes a character for the *Gospel of the Hebrews* which best coheres with Eusebius' understanding about its positions on the fringes of canon.

Thus, it is possible to see the history of the *Gospel of the Hebrews* as follows. The *Gospel of the Hebrews* was originally written based on the canonical gospels in Greek. Papias, Hegesippus, Clement and Origen knew the gospel when it was still in Greek. At some point, the gospel was translated into Syriac. Eusebius received some passages from it in Syriac and the later edition was also known to an anonymous writer who added a passage to the Latin translation of Origen's *Commentary on Matthew* (*Comm. Matt.* 15.14; see below Chapter 5.1). The *Gospel of the Hebrews* was clearly drawing on the synoptic gospels (especially Matthew and Luke) since it contained harmonizing readings but it also contained non-canonical materials. The *Gospel of the Hebrews* was also clearly characterized by Wisdom speculations. This raises the question about its possible relation to Q.

3.4.3. *Q and the* Gospel of the Hebrews

The *Gospel of the Hebrews*' close affinity with Wisdom traditions becomes clear, at least in fragments 2 and 5 (numbered according to the Appendix 1) that are attributed to the *Gospel of the Hebrews* also in the old 3GH.

2. The Holy Spirit takes Jesus to Tabor

[If somebody accepts the Gospel according to the Hebrews, where the Saviour himself says:]

A moment ago my Mother, the Holy Spirit, took me by one of my hairs and brought me to the great hill, the Tabor. (Origen, *Comm. Jo.* 2.12, *Hom. Jer.* 15.4; Jerome, *Comm. Mich.* 7.5–7, *Comm. Isa.* 40.9–11, *Comm. Ezech.* 16.13). before 228 CE; 3GH: GHeb.

5. Attaining rest

[For similar to these the following is possible:]

He who seeks will not cease until he finds and having found he will marvel and having marvelled he will become king and having become king, he will rest. (Clement of Alexandria, *Strom.* V XIV 96.3; *Strom.* II IX 45.5; cf. *Gos. Thom.* 2). 202 / 215 CE; 3GH: GHeb.

These features have not remained unnoticed. Ron Cameron, for instance, thinks that the fragments "presuppose the descent of divine Wisdom, embodying herself definitively in a representative of the human race for the revelation and redemption of humankind."[110] According to Hans-Josef Klauck, the baptism of Jesus in the *Gospel of the Hebrews* (of the

---
[110] Cameron 1982, 84.

3GH) "shows the intersection of the prophetic and sapiental traditions which have their roots in the Old Testament."[111] For A.F.J. Klijn, it "seems hardly necessary to repeat that the theological conception of this Gospel is dominated by Jewish-Christian Wisdom Theology."[112] Philipp Vielhauer and Georg Strecker emphasize the close affinity of the *Gospel of the Hebrews* with gnostic speculations. According to them, the Jewish Christianity of the *Gospel of the Hebrews* contains "syncretistic-gnostic elements," and the baptism pericope of the *Gospel of the Hebrews* belongs to "the circle of such gnostic speculations" that can also be found in Sirach, Wisdom of Solomon and *Pseudo-Clementines*.[113] Today, when scholars have become more aware of the problems with defining Gnosticism, one would probably be more hesitant to label the fragments "Gnostic."[114] However, Vielhauer and Strecker's characterization becomes more understandable when viewed in its historical context and in conjunction with the arguments that were used when the 3GH was originally framed.[115]

Since the *Gospel of the Hebrews* is so closely tied with sapiental traditions even in the 3GH, one may wonder why there has not been more discussion about the relationship between the *Gospel of the Hebrews* and Q. There are probably several reasons for this. First of all, the study of early Jewish-Christian gospels has partly been a playground for alternative solutions to the synoptic problem. For instance, A.F.J. Klijn, in his 1992 monograph, often suggests in the context of his detailed analyses of fragments, that the fragments may go back to pre-synoptic sources. Klijn does not explicitly deal with the synoptic problem or develop any clear alternative theory, but his comments seem to support a sort of proto-Matthew theory.[116]

Several theories which involved an Aramaic "Urgospel" were presented before the Two Document Hypothesis received its present prestige. Ferdinand Christian Baur, for example, assumed that an Aramaic *Gospel of the Hebrews* preceded the present canonical Matthew.[117] If the

---

[111] Klauck 2003, 41.
[112] Klijn 1992, 39.
[113] Vielhauer & Strecker 1991² (1963¹), 173–174.
[114] For an overview of the discussion, see Marjanen 2005a.
[115] See above Chapter 3.1.
[116] Klijn 1992, 37, 59–60.
[117] For an overview of the theories, see Kloppenborg Verbin 2000, 272–309. Baur, of course, was not referring to the *Gospel of the Hebrews* of the 3GH since the 3GH was developed much later. See Chapter 3.1.

study of Jewish-Christian gospel fragments is tied with theories that seek to challenge the Two Document Hypothesis, comparison with Q becomes irrelevant.[118] Second, in the 3GH, it is presumed that the *Gospel of the Hebrews* was totally different from the synoptic gospels. Since Q sits tightly at the core of the synoptic tradition, there does not seem to be very much to be discussed, at least as far literary dependence is concerned, or a sort of trajectory between Q and the *Gospel of the Hebrews*.

Nonetheless, although the relationship between Q and other Jewish-Christian gospels has not been among the most popular topics of scholarly discussion during the past decades, some scholars have occasionally drawn attention to the question. James M. Robinson has, in several connections, referred to the Ebionites or the Nazarenes as holdouts from the Q community who refused to become absorbed into the gentile Christian church through Matthew's gospel. He has also observed similarities between the feminine Wisdom imagery of Q and the *Gospel of the Hebrews* where the Holy Spirit appears as Jesus' mother.[119]

Notably, these observations and suggestions are made on the basis of the widely accepted 3GH which categorically rules out any literary dependence between the *Gospel of the Hebrews* and synoptic materials. Therefore, it is understandable that they have not evoked any further discussion about a possible socio-cultural relationship between the Q people and the Jewish Christians who composed and transmitted the *Gospel of the Hebrews*. The N2GH, for which I am arguing in this volume, changes the situation in some important respects. It attributes to the *Gospel of the Hebrews* not just fragments that have a clear interest in Wisdom traditions but also sayings that are paralleled in synoptic gospels. Some of them can also be located in Q-sections.

In contrast to earlier speculations which connect the *Gospel of the Hebrews* to an Aramaic "Urgospel," I have not found any evidence to suggest that the *Gospel of the Hebrews* might be pre-synoptic. On the contrary, many of the fragments that are attributed to the *Gospel of the Hebrews* in the N2GH clearly depend on synoptic material. Thus, if it is possible to find the same kind of socio-cultural and theological features in the *Gospel of the Hebrews* that we can also see in Q, then the *Gospel of the Hebrews* might represent a case of post-synoptic reediting of the synoptic material from the viewpoint of Q's distinctive theology. Could the *Gospel of the Hebrews* have been composed and edited by

---

[118] A recent example of this approach is Edwards 2002.
[119] Robinson 2007, 80, 85, 158, 200.

Jewish Christians who were successors of the Q people, or at least heavily influenced by Q traditions?

The following fragments in the new reconstruction have affinities with Q traditions. There are passages that are clear parallels as well as more general thematic connections.

Parallel passages:

1. Fragment 1, The baptism of Jesus, is paralleled in Q 3:21–22.
2. Fragment 10, Even anointed prophets sinned, is paralleled in Q 17:3–4.
3. Fragment 12, The parable of the talents, has parallels only in Matthew and Luke; despite the differences, IQP attributes it to Q.
4. Fragment 5 (*Strom.* V XIV 96.3) contains the idea of seeking and finding which is paralleled in Q 11:9–10.
5. Fragment 4, Jesus chooses the good ones. Within the synoptic tradition, one possible parallel is Q 12:49–53, the other one being Q 17:33–35. Thus, possible parallels are in Q material.

Given the limited number of preserved fragments, the number of parallel passages is impressive. In addition, there are also more general thematic connections:

1. The centrality of Wisdom speculations and how that connects with Q was already observed at the beginning of this section.
2. A connection to prophetic traditions can already be observed in the conventional reconstruction of the 3GH, since the Holy Spirit refers to the prophets as Jesus' predecessors in the context of his baptism. In the reconstruction of the N2GH, this becomes even more pronounced because the prophets' position as anointed ones who are in need of forgiveness provides a model for how one should treat a sinning brother.
3. Brotherly love and an admonition not to distress the spirit of one's brother are central in fragments 7 and 8. In the *Gospel of the Hebrews*, brothers receive the prophetic attributes of being chosen ones (fragment 4!), endowed with spirit but still in need of forgiveness. This seems to presuppose the Deuteronomistic scheme—typical of Q—of a series of envoys of God running from the OT prophets, through John and Jesus, up through the disciples. Admonitions to forgive one's brother and not to judge are found not only in Q 17:3–4 but also in Q 6:41–42.

4. Finally, the ideal of giving up one's property and becoming a poor follower of Jesus (fragment 11) coheres with the central ethos of Q as it appears in Q's sermon, Q's mission instructions and Q 12:22–34.

The point of these comparisons is not to claim a direct literary dependence between Q and the *Gospel of the Hebrews*. As I see it, the *Gospel of the Hebrews* was clearly a post-synoptic writing. However, these points of contact suggest that the framers of the *Gospel of the Hebrews* were preoccupied with the same topics as the Q people, and were, therefore, possibly, their post-synoptic successors.

As regards provenance, I have already argued that the Syro-Palestinian area is the most likely region where the *Gospel of the Hebrews* was composed. The observed affinities with the Q-tradition fit with this hypothesis because Q seems to presume Galilee as its social setting.[120]

The above-sketched topics also have clear connections to Matthew's gospel. The Deuteronomistic scheme is further emphasized in Matthew's redaction (parables in Matt 21:28–22:14), and the exhortations to forgive one's brother (Matt 18:23–35) and the passage where Jesus promises rest to his followers (Matt 11:28–30) can be located in Matthew's special tradition. Thus, from the viewpoint of the *Gospel of the Hebrews* reconstructed in this book, it is easy to agree with James Robinson who sees a close relationship between Q, Matthew and later Jewish-Christian groups.[121]

To summarize, if the new reconstruction is on the right track, then the *Gospel of the Hebrews* would exemplify a sort of post-synoptic reclaiming of some of Q's central ideas by successors of the Q people. As compared to the synoptic gospels, the ideology of the framers of the *Gospel of the Hebrews* stayed closer to Semitic Wisdom thinking when they depicted the Holy Spirit as a feminine being and Jesus' mother. The first version was probably edited on the basis of Greek canonical gospels and then translated into Syriac. In this scenario, the Jewish Christianity of Q, was not totally out of the game after its message was partly compromised with gentile Christianity in the Gospel of Matthew. One branch of the successors of the Q people prepared a new gospel where they used the synoptic gospels and their own living Wisdom traditions. When Eusebius prepared his list of canonical writings, this gospel was still hanging around, being relatively highly valued in some early Christian circles.

---

[120] See Kloppenborg Verbin 2000, 214–261.
[121] Robinson 2007, 158, 200.

There are also some interesting points of contact between Q and the *Gospel of the Ebionites* and even between Q and the Nazarenes' anti-rabbinic collection. The Deuteronomistic interpretation of Jesus' commission and passion is apparent in the Nazarenes' collection. However, on the whole, the Nazarenes' communal life and ideology—as it can be reconstructed on the basis of their Isaiah commentary—does not show any closer affinity with Q. The situation is a bit different with the Ebionites whose profile as "poor" followers of Jesus, their non-sacrificial interpretation of Jesus' death[122] and, to some extent, their understanding of Jesus as (the True) prophet[123] may have some resemblance to Q's theology and practice. On the other hand, there are also obvious differences. In Q the Temple appears in positive light (Q 4:9–12) and Q accepts prophets up to John the Baptist (Q 16:16) while the Hellenistic-Samaritan branch of the Ebionites, who used the *Gospel of the Ebionites*, disregarded the prophets between Moses and the True Prophet (see Chapter 2.1.4). Thus, Q and the *Gospel of the Ebionites* seem to share some motifs but less than Q and the *Gospel of the Hebrews*.

The fact that Q was swallowed by Matthew's gospel with its gentile orientation was not—to use Robinson's expression—the "swan song" of the Q people.[124] The last movement of their symphony may have been the *Gospel of the Hebrews*, which almost made its way into the New Testament canon.

---

[122] Q presumes Jesus' death and vindication (Q 13:35) but does not provide any salvific interpretation of Jesus' death. See Kloppenborg Verbin 2000, 369–379.

[123] Q obviously depicts Jesus in line with Deuteronomistic prophets. However, I agree with Kloppenborg (against Sato and Horsley) that the genre of Q is more that of a wisdom collection. See Kloppenborg Verbin 2000, 196–213, 379–385.

[124] Cf. Robinson 2007, 80.

CHAPTER FOUR

PASSION TRADITIONS REINTERPRETED

Some of the surviving fragments of Jewish-Christian gospels include passion and resurrection traditions that differ from the canonical gospels in important respects. All the references are quite short and as such they do not allow any secure reconstructions of larger passion narratives from which they might have been taken. However, it is possible to delineate some general tendencies in these narratives and to sketch their ideological and social-historical background by comparing them with their canonical counterparts and reflecting on their contents in the light of other information we have about early Jewish Christians.

I shall mainly deal with four passages in this main chapter. First (Chapter 4.1), I deal with a fragment that Epiphanius quotes in his *Medicine Chest* (*Panarion* 30.22.3–5). This passage from the gospel that was used by the Ebionites concerns the preparations of Jesus' last Passover meal. Second, (Chapter 4.2) I deal with two fragments that are in Jerome's *Commentary on Matthew* (*Comm. Matt.* 27.16; 27.51). Finally, Chapter 4.3 examines Jerome's *On Illustrious Men* where he tells about Jesus' appearance to the James the Just (*Vir. ill.* 2).

4.1. The Last Supper in the
Gospel of the Ebionites and Luke (Codex Bezae)

4.1.1. *Introduction*

Luke's description of Jesus' Last Supper with his disciples has sometimes been characterized as "a scholar's paradise and a beginner's nightmare."[1] A glance at a synopsis soon reveals the reason: when compared to Matthew and Mark, Luke's passage has several distinctive features which catch the attention of a scholar interested in the early phases of Jesus traditions. Although the differences and the similarities are obvious, they are not very easy to explain.

---

[1] Caird 1965, 237.

146   CHAPTER FOUR

The first interesting difference is that Luke has prefixed a passage from his own tradition that does not appear in Matthew or Mark to the institution of the Eucharist. Jesus announces, before the institution of the bread and cup, that he has been looking forward to eating Passover with his disciples before his suffering because after this, he will not eat (Passover) before the arrival of the kingdom of God. Jesus also passes on the cup, exhorts the disciples to share it with each other and says that he will not drink wine before the arrival of the kingdom of God (Luke 22:15–18). Matthew and Mark do not have exact parallels to this passage although they have Jesus say, after the institution, that Jesus will not drink wine until he will drink that new in the Kingdom of God/Father (Mark 14:25 par. Matt 26:29). Second, Luke's wording in the description of the institution of the bread and cup also differs from Matthew and Mark but largely agrees with the tradition Paul is quoting in 1. Cor 11:23–26.

These differences are clearly observable in the Greek text of Nestle-Aland's latest editions (from the 26th onwards) and in most of the modern translations. However, there is also a third interesting difference in some of the manuscripts. Codex Bezae (D), Old Latin and Old Syriac manuscripts have a shorter version of the institution of the Eucharist which ends in the middle of verse 22:19:

Longer Text (RSV, modified)	Shorter text (RSV, modified)
15: And he said to them, "I have earnestly desired to eat this passover with you before I suffer;	15: And he said to them, "I have earnestly desired to eat this passover with you before I suffer;
16: for I tell you I shall not eat it until it is fulfilled in the kingdom of God."	16: for I tell you I shall not eat it until it is fulfilled in the kingdom of God."
17: And he took a cup, and when he had given thanks he said, "Take this, and divide it among yourselves;	17: And he took a cup, and when he had given thanks he said, "Take this, and divide it among yourselves;
18: for I tell you that from now on I shall not drink of the fruit of the vine until the kingdom of God comes."	18: for I tell you that from now on I shall not drink of the fruit of the vine until the kingdom of God comes."
19: And he took bread, and when he had given thanks he broke it and gave it to them, saying, "This is my body which is given for you. Do this in remembrance of me."	19: And he took bread, and when he had given thanks he broke it and gave it to them, saying, "This is my body."
20: And likewise the cup after supper, saying, "This cup is the new covenant in my blood, that is shed for you."	

As the synopsis indicates, the shorter text has no reference to Jesus' blood or the atoning character of Jesus' death. The text seems to reflect an ideology where Jesus death was not interpreted in terms of sacrifice and atonement. The significance of Luke's shorter text has often been debated but scholars have been mainly interested in the question whether the shorter text should be regarded as the original one. Although these considerations cannot be avoided here, I will mainly focus on an aspect which has received less attention but which may open a new viewpoint in the discussion about the tradition-historical setting of the shorter reading.[2] I will compare the shorter reading with the fragments derived from the *Gospel of the Ebionites*. This gospel provides an interesting point of comparison for the shorter reading because of its fierce criticism of sacrifices.

4.1.2. *Arguments for and against the Shorter Reading*

Westcott and Hort argued that, when the Old Latin and the Old Syriac versions agreed with Codex Bezae, they represented an older, non-interpolated text. This is precisely the case in Luke 22:19b–20. However, after the publication of the second edition of the Greek New Testament, where the so-called "Western non-interpolations" were abandoned, the Greek New Testament and Nestle–Aland editions have agreed on the longer Lukan text as the original reading.[3]

Although textual critics may still have to discuss the significance of the Old Latin and the Old Syriac versions agreeing with each other against B and its allies,[4] I do not venture here to launch a new defense of the Western non-interpolations, regardless of how tempting that might be in light of the hypothesis to be developed in the following. The manuscript evidence for the longer reading is overwhelming (provided one does not accept Westcott and Hort's principle) and I consider the longer reading older. Nevertheless, the defenders of the shorter reading have also presented theological arguments in favor of their solution. Because this theological discussion has bearing on the topic of this chapter, I will take it up here.

---

[2] I am indebted to Matti Myllykoski for originally bringing to my attention the significance of the Codex Bezae in the study of Jewish Christianity and especially in the discussion about the tradition history of Luke 22:15–20.

[3] For the overview of the different editions, see Fitzmyer 1985, 1388.

[4] Cf. Petersen 1994, 21–22.

The defenders of the shorter reading have tried to show that the omission of the idea of Jesus' blood of atonement would be related to Luke's tendency to avoid the idea of the atoning effect of Jesus' blood.[5] Theological arguments easily start to run in a circle because the institution of the Eucharist is the best example of Jesus' blood of atonement in Matthew and Mark, as well. There are not many instances in Mark which might have given Luke a reason to refer to the idea of atoning elsewhere in his gospel unless he wanted to put special emphasis on it.

One such occasion would certainly have been Mark 10:45: "... the Son of Man came not to be served but to serve, and to give his life a ransom for many." Luke does not have this verse, which the defenders of the shorter reading interpret as a sign of Luke's tendency to avoid the idea of atonement.[6] However, it is unfortunate for the defenders of the shorter reading that Luke seems to have deleted here the whole section Mark 10:35-45 where the sons of Zebedee would like places next to Jesus in the future glory. Had Luke decided to follow Mark's narrative, he would have told about the sons of Zebedee after Luke 18:34. Later on, Luke has introduced a passage which deals with the same theme but the wording differs considerably from Mark 10:35-45 (and Matthew 20:20-28), showing that Luke either derived this section from his own source or composed it freely. Had Luke only wanted to avoid referring to Jesus' atoning death, he could have deleted only a part of Mark 10:45. However, he obviously had some other reason for removing the whole passage that was dealing with the question of the sons of Zebedee.

On the other hand, the defenders of the longer reading have been able to point out places in Luke's writings, particularly in Acts (most prominently Acts 20:28, but see also 2:23; 3:18; 8:32-35; 26:22), sufficient to show that Luke is not the most likely editor to have swept the idea of Jesus' atoning death totally under the rug.[7]

---

[5] Parker 1997, 154-157.

[6] Thus, for instance, Ehrman 1993, 200. Ehrman also tries to show that, in Mark 15:39, there is another "deletion." However, his argumentation is tied with a specific interpretation of Mark's description of the tearing of the curtain of the Temple which he himself admits to be subtle (1993, 200-201). Only two pages later, this subtle reference has become an example of Luke blatantly eliminating any notion of Jesus' death as an atoning sacrifice (p. 203).

[7] Ehrman 1993, 202, defending the short reading, argues that the idea of atoning can be seen in Acts 20:28 only if read as a remnant of Pauline theology. However, Acts 20:28 is a part of Paul's speech and Luke seems to have known at least some of Paul's letters and used them as his sources (see Aejmelaeus 1987, 266). This speaks for Luke's conscious adoption of these "Pauline" ideas.

Finally, if Luke had been the original composer of the shorter text, would he have ended verse 19a as abruptly as it is now in D and others? Is it not more probable that the abrupt ending in verse 19 is due to a later deletion where the narrative has not been reworked to the extent that Luke did when he edited Mark's gospel?

The longer reading (Luke 22:15–20) as it now stands in Sinaiticus, Vaticanus and others, is perfectly understandable as a balanced composition where Luke has first (inspired by Mark 14:25?), in verses 22:15–18, presented two identically formulated sayings about Jesus' abstaining from eating (οὐ μὴ φάγω) and drinking (οὐ μὴ πίω) before the arrival of the kingdom of God. After this, Luke has presented the institution of the Eucharistic bread and cup, both phrased mainly according to Pauline tradition but slightly adjusted to fit in the Markan narrative. Notably, even the beginning of the last verse of the shorter reading, the institution of the bread in Luke 22:19, echoes the Pauline tradition.[8] The shorter reading leaves the institution of the Eucharistic cup orphaned, with no parallel to its key phrase of institution "this is" (τοῦτό ἐστιν). The reader of the shorter reading is tempted to look for the "institution" of the cup in the preceding verses where Jesus—in conjunction with his words about abstaining from wine—passes on the cup to his disciples. However, this forms a poor pair with the institution of the bread since nothing of the parallelism typical of all other liturgical traditions of the institution of the Eucharist appears.[9] There is no "this is" sentence in connection with the first cup because this section is actually phrased to pair with Jesus' words about refraining from eating. The clumsy construction of the shorter reading is unlikely to have served any liturgical purpose. It is understandable only as a scribal correction which has not had any direct bearing on liturgical practice.

However, it has not been very easy for the defenders of the longer reading of Luke 22:15–20 to find an explanation for the omission of verses 22:19b–20. A scribe's attempt to avoid unnecessary repetition with the description of the cups is not convincing as an explanation because repetition could have been avoided much more eloquently by removing the first cup. Furthermore, assuming the deletion aims at avoiding repetition, there seems to be no reason whatsoever to remove

---

[8] εὐχαριστήσας instead of εὐλογήσας, and λάβετε omitted.
[9] Notably, even *Didache* 9:1–5, which represents a totally different theological interpretation of the Eucharist (more on this below), uses many identical phrases in the institution of its cup and bread.

the second half of verse 19.[10] A suggestion by Jeremias, according to whom the rest may have been deleted since it was a liturgical tradition known to everyone, is more desperate than convincing.[11] Overall, the inability of the defenders of the longer reading to provide a satisfactory reason for the shortening of the text is still considered to be the best argument for the shorter reading.[12]

In my view, the simplest explanation would be that the text was shortened by a copyist[13] who was offended by the idea of Jesus' sacrificial death and atonement. The copyist simply skipped the part where these ideas were expressed. What kind of theological tradition would a copyist like that come from? Obviously, the copyist did not represent any of the theologies that were acknowledged in the formative Catholic tradition. Therefore, our chances finding appropriate comparative material for the shorter reading increase if we direct our attention outside the "mainstream," to the writings and theology of the Ebionites.

4.1.3. *Reconstructing the Passion Narrative in the* Gospel of the Ebionites

The Ebionite literature Epiphanius quoted (see Chapter 2.1.4) was probably derived from the Ebionites he met in Cyprus where he was bishop (*Pan.* 30.2.7–8; 30.18.1). Epiphanius knew passages from a gospel that was used by the Ebionites, the Ebionites' *Acts of the Apostles* (different from the canonical one) and from *Pseudo-Clementine* sources that are presumed to precede the present *Pseudo-Clementine Recognitions* and *Homilies*. At some points, Epiphanius also quoted the *Book of Elchasai*. In the following discussion, I will especially draw on the *Gospel of the Ebionites* and Pseudo-Clementine *Recognitions* 1:27–71 while illuminating the central features of Ebionite theology.

Rec. 1:27–71 is generally considered to be one of the Pseudo-Clementine sources that was available to Epiphanius.[14] In any case, it has

---

[10] Cf. Jeremias 1977, 157–158; Ehrman 1993, 207.

[11] Nevertheless, it is still cited approvingly as the best possible one by Nolland 1993, 1041. For criticism, see also Ehrman 1993, 208.

[12] See Fitzmyer 1985, 1388; Nolland 1993, 1041.

[13] By "copyist," I simply refer to the person who originally shortened the text. This was not necessarily the one who prepared the D text of Luke. D has not found the idea of sacrifice problematic in Matthew and Mark. If these were not prepared by different copyists, then the short text must already have been in the exemplar that was used as the basis for the D text of Luke.

[14] See Chapter 2.1.4.

such close connections to the ideas of the *Gospel of the Ebionites* and to Epiphanius' own observations about the practices of the Ebionites that it can be used to illustrate the Ebionites' views. Theologically, the most significant similarity is the abandoning of the prophets and Christ's rejection of the sacrificial cult. Epiphanius' Ebionites and *Rec.* 1.27–71 also share marked anti-Paulinism. The idea that Jesus came to abolish sacrifices and the Temple was destroyed because people were reluctant to cease sacrificing is so unique within the early Christian tradition that its appearance both in *Rec.* 1.27–71 and the *Gospel of the Ebionites* cannot be coincidental.[15]

Epiphanius presents eight quotations from the *Gospel of the Ebionites*.[16] He quotes the gospel mainly in order to show its inconsistencies or in order to show how the Ebionites have twisted the wording of the canonical gospels. What interests us here is that he also finds examples of the Ebionites' rejection of meat in their gospel. They have changed John the Baptist's diet from locusts to honey cakes (*Pan.* 30.13.4–5) and they have made Jesus say that he does "not earnestly desire to eat meat" with the disciples at Passover (*Pan.* 30.22.4–5). The latter passage is especially important for the present discussion and deserves closer examination.

Panarion has the following description of Jesus' conversation with his disciples before the Last Supper where Epiphanius criticizes the wording of the *Gospel of the Ebionites*.

> Next the Lord himself says: "I earnestly desired to eat this Passover with you." And he did not say Passover alone but this Passover lest somebody should adapt this saying to his own purpose by tricks. The Passover consists, as I said, of meat roasted in fire and the other things. They, however, destroyed the true order and changed the passage; that is clear to everyone because of the words that belong together, and they made the disciples to say: "Where do you wish that we prepare the Passover to eat for you?" And they made him answer: "I do not earnestly desire to eat meat with you this Passover." But how then will this deceit not be brought to light, since—the order of words being clear—the "mu" and the "eta" have been added? For instead of saying: "I earnestly desired" (ἐπιθυμίᾳ ἐπεθύμησα) they added the word "not" (μή). Actually he said: "I earnestly desired to eat this Passover with you." They, however, added "meat" and deceived

---

[15] Bauckham 2003, 168.
[16] For the quotations and commentary, see Klijn 1992, 65–76.

themselves recklessly speaking the words: "I did not desire earnestly to eat meat with you this Passover." It is clearly demonstrated that he both celebrated Passover and ate meat, as I said before.

(*Panarion* 30.22.3–5; trans. Klijn & Reinink 1973, modified).

Epiphanius first makes his own case by paraphrasing Luke's description about preparations for the Last Supper. The preparations culminate in Jesus' exclamation: "With desire I have desired to eat this Passover with you." Epiphanius points out that Jesus explicitly refers to "this Passover" and not just to a Passover in general. In Epiphanius' view, this makes it clear that the Jewish Passover, which involved eating meat, is meant. Epiphanius complains, however, that the Ebionites have changed the wording of the passage and added "mu" and "eta" and have also added the word "meat" to Jesus' words. Thus, in the Ebionites' gospel, Jesus says: "I did not earnestly desire to eat meat with you this Passover."

The disciples' question—as it is quoted by Epiphanius and as it appears to have been in the *Gospel of the Ebionites*—is paralleled only in Mark and Matthew (Mark 14:12; Matt 26:17). The wording of the *Gospel of the Ebionites* is closer to Matthew, the only difference being a slightly different word order. On the other hand, Jesus' answer is paralleled only in Luke (cf. Luke 22:15–18) because there is no parallel for this section in Mark or Matthew. Thus, in this section, the *Gospel of the Ebionites* seems to have used at least Matthew and Luke. It also seems obvious that there was some sort of passion narrative in the *Gospel of the Ebionites* and that it was composed, somewhat creatively, using Matthew and Luke, at least.

Unfortunately, Epiphanius does not present any other quotations from the *Gospel of the Ebionites* that could be located in the passion narrative. However, it is possible to draw some conclusions about the passion narrative on the basis of this passage and other passages Epiphanius quotes from the *Gospel of the Ebionites*, especially if we also make use of other information about the Ebionites' practices and theology.[17] In the

---

[17] It is clear that this kind of argumentation remains hypothetical since the logic is to try to figure out what there must have been or what there cannot have been in the Ebionites' passion narrative. However, the argumentation is not too precarious since we have some examples of cases where the contents of the *Gospel of the Ebionites* fit with other information about the Ebionites. For example, Epiphanius seems to know about the Ebionites' practice of not eating meat from his own experience—he probably met Ebionites in Cyprus where he was acting as bishop (*Pan.* 30.15.3–4). On the other hand, he presents two examples from the *Gospel of the Ebionites* where the Ebionites have changed the synoptic wording in order to support their own practice. For a discussion of what Epiphanius knew from his own experience and what he derived from his sources, see above 2.1.4.

following, I intend to show that—given there was some coherence in the passion narrative and the ideology of the Ebionites—the wording of their gospel must have been, at some points, quite close to what we can now see in manuscript D in Luke.

Epiphanius' quotations from the *Gospel of the Ebionites* give the impression that Jesus has expressed his unwillingness to eat meat with his disciples as an answer to the disciples' question where Jesus wants them to prepare the Passover meal. This suggests that the *Gospel of the Ebionites* did not include Jesus' instructions to the disciples on how to find a location for the Passover meal. This is natural enough: if Jesus was not willing to eat the Paschal Lamb with his disciples, there was no need for him to give special instructions on how to arrange such a meal.

How did the story continue after Jesus' "touched-up" answer quoted by Epiphanius? Could there have been similar words of institution as we can find in the synoptic gospels? A bit earlier, Epiphanius has quoted another passage of the gospel which may shed some light on this. In *Panarion* 30.16.5, he writes: "As the writing that they call a gospel has: 'I have come to abolish the sacrifices and if you do not stop sacrificing the wrath will not cease from you.'" Could a gospel that explicitly denies sacrifices have included a description of the institution of the Eucharist where Jesus' blood would have been interpreted as blood shed for the disciples (Mark 14:24; Luke 22:20) or for the forgiveness of sins (Matt 26:28)?

At this juncture, it is worth noting that, in the Ebionites' theology, Jesus was really understood as having come to abolish sacrifices, not to replace them. The Ebionites did not believe that the sacrifices could be abolished by replacing them with Jesus' own once-and-for-all sacrifice. In this regard, the Ebionites' theology clearly differed from the theology expressed in the Letter to the Hebrews. The Ebionites and Hebrews agree that the OT sacrificial cult was only a temporary arrangement (Heb 9:9–10; *Rec.* 1.36.1). However, while according to Hebrews, the old sacrificial cult anticipated Christ's perfect sacrifice (Heb 7:26–27; 9:11–28; 10:11–12; 13:10–13), the Ebionites thought that Christ came to finish the abolition that was already started by Moses. Because the passion for sacrificing was so ingrained in people, Moses knew that he could not make them give up sacrificing all at once. He was only able to set up regulations for the sacrifices and announce that, after him, will come a true prophet who will finish the task (*Rec.* 1.36.1–37.2). For the Ebionites, Jesus was this prophet. Thus, in the Ebionites' view, there was nothing good in sacrifice. They found proofs for this view even in the history of God's people. People always prospered when they obeyed the law without sacrificing but when they started sacrificing, they immediately faced disasters. (*Rec.* 1.37.4) Finally, their temple will be destroyed because they did not stop sacrificing (*Rec.* 1.64.1–2).

The above considerations are also supported by what we otherwise know about the Ebionites' Eucharistic practices. In the part where Epiphanius describes the doctrines of the Ebionites, before he actually starts to refute them, he says that "they celebrate mysteries year after year, if you please, in imitation of the sacred mysteries of the church, using unleavened bread—and the other part of the mystery with water only" (*Pan.* 30.16.1). Before Epiphanius, Irenaeus had also mentioned the Ebionites' practice of using only water in their Eucharistic meals. Irenaeus discusses the Ebionites' Christology but the metaphor he uses suggests that, behind it, there has to be the Ebionites' true practice of using only water instead of the mixture of wine and water (Irenaeus, *Haer.* 5.1.3).[18] Thus, the Ebionites were known for using water and unleavened bread in their Eucharistic ceremony. Because Irenaeus' information was recorded at the end of the second century, it suggests that the Ebionites must already by then have had some texts that they used to support their own Eucharistic practices.

Against this background, it seems clear that the Ebionites' gospel cannot have included a passage where Jesus instituted the Eucharistic cup of blood. The idea that Jesus would have given his body for atonement or for ransom would have been equally strange to the Ebionites.

To summarize the conclusions of the reconstruction: Epiphanius' quotation from the *Gospel of the Ebionites* indicates that there was a description of preparations for the Last Supper where Jesus says that he does not want to eat meat. Because another quotation from the *Gospel of the Ebionites* reveals that the Ebionites opposed sacrifices, it is unlikely that they would have granted a sacrificial value to Jesus' blood. Thus, it is also unlikely that the *Gospel of the Ebionites* would have included the institution of the Eucharistic cup of blood. Epiphanius' remark a bit earlier in Panarion about the Ebionites' practice of celebrating Passover year after

---

[18] Origen, for his part, referred to the Ebionites' practice of using unleavened bread in the Passover meals that they celebrated in the manner of the Jews (*Comm. ser. Matt.* 79). Origen possibly refers here to the Quartodecimanians, a group of Asian Christian communities that wanted to continue celebrating Passover on the 14th of Nisan instead of postponing the celebration to the following Day of the Lord, as was the custom in other communities (Eusebius, *Hist. eccl.* 5.23–24).

year with unleavened bread and water confirms the assumption that there could not have been any institution of the Eucharistic cup of blood in the *Gospel of the Ebionites*.

4.1.4. *The Gospel of the Ebionites and Luke (D, Old Latin and Old Syriac)*

There are two notable features that draw attention to Luke's version of the Last Supper if one tries to trace the closest possible point of comparison for the wording of the *Gospel of the Ebionites*: the wording of Jesus' answer in the *Gospel of the Ebionites* is paralleled only in Luke, and Jesus' vows not to eat the Passover meal and not to drink wine are most vehement in Luke.

All the synoptic gospels have, in the passage on the Last Supper, Jesus' words that he will not be drinking wine until in the kingdom of God (Mark 14:25; Matt 26:29; Luke 22:18). However, this vow is the most outspoken in Luke since it is presented before the institution of the Eucharist and it is coupled with the words about not eating the Passover meal—in the canonical Luke, Jesus yearns to eat Passover with his disciples but only this last time before his passion. The next time will be in the kingdom of God.

If one takes Luke's description of the Last Supper (Luke 22:15–20) as the starting point—assuming that the opening verse was formulated the way Epiphanius describes—would the story have been acceptable to the Ebionites? Jesus words about not eating Passover and not drinking wine before the Kingdom of God arrives (Luke 22:15–18) would fit very well with the Ebionites' diet and their Eucharistic practice, which did not include meat or wine. It is even quite possible to interpret Luke 22:17–18 as an institution of a Eucharistic cup that contained water only. Verse 19 would also still be acceptable and even necessary as an institution of the Eucharistic bread although the words about the body "given for you" might have some suspiciously sacrificial overtones. The problems begin with the second cup in verse 20 where Jesus' blood is assigned a sacrificial role.

As it happens, manuscript D, the Old Latin and Old Syriac translations have a shorter version of the Last Supper in Luke, which conveniently ends precisely at the point where the story begins to be problematic from the Ebionite point of view, the last words being "this is my body."

In the case of the Last Supper, the relation of the *Gospel of the Ebionites* to D, the Old Latin and Old Syriac translations remains hypothetical but there are two other instances where the wording of the *Gospel of the Ebionites* demonstrably agrees with the same group of manuscripts. This supports the view that the match between the presumed contents of the *Gospel of the Ebionites* and these manuscripts of Luke is not coincidental.

First, in the description of Jesus' baptism (*Pan.* 30.13.7–8), the *Gospel of the Ebionites* agrees with this same group of manuscripts against others by including Ps 2:7 at the end of the words sounding from the Heaven: "Today I have begotten you." The same reading can also be found in Justin's *Dialogue with Trypho* (See *Dial.* 88.8, 88.3) which demonstrates that it was already known in the middle of the second century. Second, even more significant is the observation that both the *Gospel of the Ebionites* and the Codex Bezae read—in accordance with Mark—that the Spirit in the form of the dove descended *into* Jesus. The wording of the *Gospel of the Ebionites*, in particular, indicates that the reading is not randomly picked up from Mark because the preposition is also prefixed to the main verb: εἰςελθούσης εἰς αὐτὸν (*Pan.* 30.13.7–8). This reading accords with the Ebionites' view that Christ went *into* Jesus at (or after) his baptism (*Pan.* 30.2.4–6; see also *Pan.* 30.16.4).[19]

Although there was significant development in the Ebionite movement from the mid-second century, when Irenaeus first refers to the Ebionites, to the end of the fourth century (Epiphanius), all the theological ideas that have come up during the preceding discussion are likely to have been part of the Ebionites' symbolic universe from very early on.[20] Yet, there is no basis for using these Ebionite connections to support the

---

[19] M. Goulder, in particular, has argued that the Ebionites' *possessionist* Christology was already known to Mark. See Goulder 1994, 128–142. See also Häkkinen 2005, 266–269. Since the Gospel of the Ebionites presumes that the Spirit entered Jesus when he was baptized by John, the question arises whether the Spirit might have flown away at the time of his death. If the Gospel of the Ebionites was consistent with the Christology of the Ebionites as it is described by Epiphanius (cf. *Pan.* 30.3.1–6, 30.14.4, 30.16.1), then there probably was also a description of the departure of the Spirit/Christ. The *Gospel of Peter* indicates that such beliefs were also expressed in the gospel narratives. In the *Gospel of Peter* 19, the Lord cries: "My power, power, you have forsaken me." Whether the *Gospel of the Ebionites* referred to Power, Christ or Spirit remains uncertain but on the basis of the key features of the Ebionite Christology, it is seems very likely that there was some sort of separation of the man Jesus and his heavenly occupant at the end of the gospel.

[20] The Ebionites' practice of using water in the Eucharist is attested by both Irenaeus and Epiphanius (cf. above). The idea of Christ/Spirit entering Jesus is more explicit in Epiphanius' description but also seems to be presupposed by Irenaeus when he compares the Ebionites' Christology with the Christology of Cerinthus (*Haer.* 1.26.2; I agree with scholars who read here, on the basis Hippolytus' parallel "similiter" pro "non similiter."

view that D's reading should be taken as the original one in Luke's Last Supper or that the *Gospel of the Ebionites* was one of Luke's sources.[21] Nevertheless, the Ebionite connections cast light on the theological motives behind the shortened Lukan text. The scribe who changed Luke's text here and in some other places (see above) was, at least partly, influenced by Ebionite ideas. As such, the shorter reading also approximates the wording of the institution of the Eucharist as it must have stood in the *Gospel of the Ebionites*.

Further examples of communal meals that differ from the synoptic-Pauline type can be found in the *Didache*. *Didache* 9–10 describes a meal where there first comes a cup, just like in Luke's shortened text,[22] and there is no reference at all to Jesus' blood. Instead, the prayers accompanying the meal express the anticipation of the kingdom of God where the church will be gathered from all over the world. The character of the meal described in the *Didache* differs so markedly from the synoptic-Pauline type that it is sometimes assumed that it only deals with the Agape-meal, but this is an unnecessary attempt to harmonize the *Didache's* practice with the synoptic-Pauline type of Eucharistic meals. Bernd Kollmann has argued convincingly against this kind of harmonization.[23]

4.1.5. *The Dating of the Shorter Reading and the* Gospel of the Ebionites

It is clear that the *Gospel of the Ebionites*, in the form that Epiphanius knew it, was composed after the synoptic gospels. It is usually dated to the first half of the second century[24] and the place of origin may have been Syria or the regions east of the Jordan where the Ebionites were located by Eusebius and Epiphanius (Eusebius, *Onom.* ed. Lagarde 1966 [1887], p. 172,1–3; *Hist. eccl.* 3.5.3; Epiphanius, *Pan.* 29.7.7–8; 30.2.7–9).

The Ebionites Christology was similar to the Christology of Cerinthus who separated Christ and Jesus). The critical attitude towards the sacrificial cult agrees with using water in the Eucharist, but it may also be rooted in the theology of the Hellenists in the early Jerusalem church—if the Ebionites' history can be traced back to them. See Chapters 2.1 and 4.1.7.

[21] In contrast to Edwards 2002.

[22] Although it seems clear that Luke's shortened text has not directly served any liturgical purposes, the shortening would be more understandable if the copyist was familiar with Eucharistic practices where the cup preceded the bread.

[23] Kollman 1990, 91–98.

[24] Klijn 1992, 29; Vielhauer & Strecker 1991² (1963¹), 169.

158   CHAPTER FOUR

F. Stanley Jones dates the Pseudo-Clementine source of *Rec.* 1:27–71, which is clearly connected to the *Gospel of the Ebionites* (see above Chapter 2.1.4), to around 200 CE and locates it "quite possibly" in Judaea or Jerusalem because of its interest in the land of Israel.[25] However, Richard Bauckham has correctly noted that such an interest might also be characteristic of people who were exiled from the land.[26]

As regards the textual history of the Codex Bezae, it is interesting to note that David C. Parker locates the genesis of the manuscript in Berytus. According to Parker, the Codex Bezae, which has both the Greek and Latin text, would have been copied by a Latin-speaking scribe, possibly a lawyer, shortly before the year 400. The codex was produced so as to be used by the Latin-speaking Christians that were drawn to Berytus by its famous law school.[27] Because the manuscript was copied from exemplars already themselves bilingual, Parker suggests that its traditions were formed in the early part of the third century when the law school—founded in the late second century[28]—had already gained a footing in the region.[29]

Parker's reconstruction places the Codex Bezae approximately in the same geographical area where the *Gospel of the Ebionites* and *Rec.* 1.27–71 were composed. The time of composition could also be estimated as approximately the second century in all cases. Thus, it seems that, at some point in the second century or at the beginning of the third century, Luke's description of the Last Supper was abbreviated in the circles that found its references to Jesus' blood of atonement offensive. Because the part that was removed from Luke exemplifies a Pauline understanding of the Eucharist, it is most probable that the theologian who was responsible for the deletion was closely connected to the Jewish Christians who the church fathers labelled the Ebionites. Their gospel could not have contained that kind of description and they were also already known in the second century as a group that repudiated Paul (Irenaeus, *Haer.* 1.26.2; Eusebius *Hist. eccl.* 3.27.4; Jerome *Comm. Matt.* 12.2).

---

[25] Jones 1995, 166–167.
[26] Bauckham 2003, 166.
[27] Parker 1992, 277. The Alands suggest that the text was written in either Egypt or elsewhere in North Africa. See Aland & Aland 1989, 109.
[28] Parker 1992, 270.
[29] Parker 1992, 119, 277–278, 280–281.

4.1.6. Eucharistic Tradition Preceding Luke?

Is it possible to trace the tradition about the Last Supper in the *Gospel of the Ebionites* back even earlier, to the time preceding the composition of the Gospel of Luke? Although it is clear that the wording of the *Gospel of the Ebionites* depends on the Gospel of Luke in its final form, it is still possible that Luke used an earlier Eucharistic tradition when he composed verses 22:15–20. Heinz Schürmann and Joachim Jeremias, for instance, have argued in their detailed linguistic studies on the Eucharistic tradition that, although Luke is clearly responsible for the details of the description, he nevertheless based his description on a preexisting Eucharistic tradition which was characterized by abstinence from wine and meat until the coming of the kingdom of God.[30] Jeremias even thinks that the first Christians could only have derived the practice from the historical Jesus who actually abstained from eating meat and drinking wine at his Last Supper with the disciples.

Nevertheless, it seems to me that Luke's hand is so clear in verses 22:15–18 that, on linguistic grounds, it is not possible to reconstruct a tradition that Luke might have used. If one adds Luke's characteristic diction together with the liturgical language he could have taken from the Pauline tradition, nothing else is needed to explain the wording of Luke 22:15–18.

In verse 15, the phrase "with desire I have desired" (ἐπιθυμίᾳ ἐπεθύμησα) seems to be from Luke's pen. The structure of the phrase is Semitic in flavor but it can be understood as a Septuagintism typical of Luke. The word ἐπιθυμέω appears six times in the canonical gospels, twice in Matthew and four times in Luke. Luke's first usage is in the story of the Prodigal Son where the son desires to eat the food of pigs (15:16). The second is in the story of Lazarus and the rich man where Lazarus desires to eat what fell from the rich man's table (16:21). Both these parables can be found only in Luke's gospel. The third occurrence can be found in the introduction to the words about the coming of the Son of Man (17:22). Luke has taken this eschatological section from Q and most likely penned the introduction to it.

The idea of the necessity of Jesus' suffering (22:15) is emphasized by Luke in 17:25, in a section based on Q, as well as at the end of the gospel, on the road to Emmaus (Luke 24:26,46).

---

[30] Schürmann 1953, 1–74, 123; Jeremias 1977, 160–164.

The verb δέχομαι at the beginning of the verse 17, which differs from the verb used in Matthew, Mark and 1 Cor (λαμβάνω), appears in Luke much more often than in Mark and Matthew (Matt 10, Mark 6 and Luke 16 occurrences). Four of the occurrences are in unparalleled material, but there are also a couple of places were the word is clearly editorial (8:13, 9:53). The expression εὐχαριστήσας εἶπεν reflects the liturgical language of 1 Cor 11:23–26. The verb διαμερίζω in verse 17 is perhaps the most obvious part of the whole section which certainly comes from Luke's pen. The verb occurs 11 time in the New Testament of which 7 are in Lukan writings while, in Mark and in Matthew, there is only one occurrence in each. (Luke's redaction in 11:17,18; from Q or redactional in 12:52,53; from Luke's special tradition in 12:17; from the LXX in 23:34). As a matter of fact, verse 17 on the whole seems to be from Luke's pen. This accords with the observation that, in contrast to Matthew and Mark, Luke seems to have transposed Jesus' words about not drinking wine from the end of the section to its beginning (cf. Matt 26:26–29 and Mark 14:22–25). After the transposition, Luke was compelled to create words where Jesus takes the cup in his hands. Matthew and Mark do not need this detail in their narratives because Jesus already holds the cup. When Luke composed verse 17, he used his favorite diction combined with familiar liturgical phrases he knew from the Pauline tradition.[31]

On the whole it seems that if Luke used traditional material in verses 22:15–19a, he either did not know the tradition in a written form or did not want to quote it in its original wording. Therefore, if we want to trace the tradition to the time preceding Luke's editorial work, the arguments have to be based on non-linguistic grounds.

In practice, we are left with Jesus' prediction that he will not drink wine until he will drink it in the kingdom of God, recorded in Mark 14:25 and with the Q tradition concerning a banquet with Abraham, Isaac and Jacob in the future kingdom of God (Matt 8:11–12 par. Luke 13:28–29; Matt 19:28 par. Luke 22:30). Whether or not these might reflect a memory of Jesus' Last Supper where he might have anticipated the dawning of the kingdom of God and would have abstained from eating and drinking until its full coming, is surely an interesting question but goes beyond the scope of the present volume. Nevertheless, even though

---

[31] For a more detailed analysis of Luke's use of the Pauline Eucharistic tradition, see Leppä 2005. Leppä has also argued for Luke's knowledge and (critical) use of Galatians. See Leppä 2002.

we may not be able to reach back to the historical Jesus, it may be possible to say something about the prehistory of the Ebionite interpretation of the Last Supper.

4.1.7. Ebionites—An Offshoot of the Hellenists?

It is clear that Jesus' statement in the *Gospel of the Ebionites*, according to which he has come to abolish the sacrifices, finds its canonical cousin in the story about Jesus' cleansing of the temple.[32] Although it is unclear just how critical an attitude towards the Temple on the part of the historical Jesus this incident demonstrates, the assumption that the incident worked as a catalyst in the events leading to Jesus' execution is well grounded.[33] Thus, the memory of Jesus having been involved in a conflict with the Temple belongs to the earliest layers of Jesus traditions and it is also likely to have received various interpretations, in particular if (as it seems likely) Jesus' attitude towards the law and the Temple was not clearly articulated.[34]

The critical attitude towards the temple characterizes the traditions connected to Stephen and the so-called "Hellenists" of the earliest Jerusalem community. Luke's account of Stephen's speech in Acts 6:8–8:1 certainly avoids making Stephen explicitly guilty of the "false" charges leveled against him. Stephen does not clearly deny the validity of the law but the reader gets the impression that he has something against the temple although it is not easy to determine exactly what it is that he criticizes in the Temple.[35] The speech seems to set Moses' tent of witness against the Temple of Jerusalem and it suggests that the peoples' rage was partly caused by Stephen's words stating that God does not live in the handmade temple in Jerusalem. From a historical point of view, it also seems clear that Stephen must have said something against the temple

---

[32] Of course, the story may also have been in the *Gospel of the Ebionites* but we cannot be sure about this.
[33] Sanders 1985, 301–306.
[34] Cf. Sanders 1985, 267–269.
[35] Thus, Salo 1991, 180–185. Luke also reduced the significance of Jesus' criticism of the Temple as the reason for his execution by moving the "false accusations" from Jesus' trial (Mark 14:57–58) to the story about Stephen in Acts. Accordingly, Luke's version of the cleansing of the Temple is more peaceful than Mark's (and Matthew's; cf. Luke 19:45–46 parr.). Overall, Luke's lesson is that if anyone can be accused of criticizing Moses and the Temple, it was Stephen and in his case, the accusation was based on "false witnesses." Nevertheless, Stephen's speech, which focuses on Moses and the Temple, seems to be the immediate cause of his execution.

which caused his execution and the flight or the other Hellenists from Jerusalem but did not result in the persecution of the whole Jerusalem community.[36]

Heikki Räisänen has also suggested—following S.K. Williams—that Paul adopted the idea of Jesus' death as a salvific event (Rom 3:25–26) not from Stephen himself but from the Hellenists in Antioch who had developed the idea from Jewish martyr theology as it is expressed in *4 Maccabees*.[37] Although Räisänen does not explicitly assume several groups of Hellenists, in the last analysis, his interpretation—which postulates distinctive Antiochene Hellenistic ideas about the significance of Jesus' death—leaves the door open for the possibility that there were at least two kinds of Hellenistic Jewish Christians: the Antiochenes and the circle around Stephen.[38] If the latter carried with them the true memory of Stephen's criticism of the temple but did not adopt the Antiochenes' interpretation of Jesus' death as a salvific event, their theology would certainly have taken a different course of development when compared to the Antiochenes' Hellenistic theology and its further development by Paul. If we combine criticism of the temple with the idea that Jesus' death had no special value for salvation, are we not approaching the kind of theology that was developed by the Ebionites and in *Rec.* 1:27–71?

The above-sketched hypothesis is certainly possible—as hypotheses usually are—but do we have any evidence which would make it reasonable to review the history of early Jewish Christianity in the light of this hypothesis? A thorough analysis of this subject is not possible in this context but there are some loose ends—both in the history of the earliest Jerusalem community and in the history of the Ebionites—which suggest that the hypothesis about the Ebionites' roots in the circle around Stephen deserves further consideration.[39]

---

[36] Räisänen 1992, 166–180, argues convincingly that although Stephen's criticism of the temple is rather veiled in Luke's narrative, the speech may still have preserved a true memory of the reasons for Stephen's execution. However, Räisänen's analysis also points out that it is hard to find explicit criticism of the law in Stephen's speech. Thus, it seems that Stephen must have said something against the temple but not necessarily against the law in general. If this is correct, then Stephen's position would come quite close to the Ebionites' criticism of the temple which did not lead to a total rejection of the law (see below).

[37] Räisänen 1992, 184–185.

[38] Cf. Räisänen 1992, 151–155. The hypothesis about several groups of Hellenists is also supported by the observation that the names in Acts 6:5 do not have anything in common with the clearly Antiochene list of names in 13:1. Cf. also Theissen 2000, 345–347.

[39] Van Voorst 1989, 170,180, has suggested that the *Ascents of James* (as he calls *Rec.*

It is interesting to note that several key issues from Stephen's speech and martyrdom in Acts reappear in *Rec.* 1:27–28. Promises given to Abraham and especially Moses' announcement of the future prophet who will be like him, play a central role both in Stephen's speech and in the account of the history in *Rec.* 1:27–71. It is also clear that the martyrdom of James in *Rec.* 1:27–71 has made use of elements of Stephen's martyrdom as it is described in Acts. The most notable similarity is that both descriptions of the executions assume the presence of Paul (in *Rec.* he even instigates the attack) and describe Paul's further actions against Christians in Damascus. Furthermore, criticism of the temple cult is one of the key issues and one of the reasons for the execution in both narratives.

Undoubtedly, *Rec.* 1:27–71 has here made creative use of Acts. Thus, it is clear that we have at least some evidence of the reception of Stephen traditions in the Ebionites' literature. We also know that these traditions were central building blocks in the Ebionites' interpretation of history, since the prophet announced by Moses, his criticism of the temple cult and anti-Paulinism are the main characteristics of the theology of the Ebionites.

As regards Epiphanius' Ebionites, their prehistory before Epiphanius meets them in Cyprus is unknown. We know that these Ebionites were a Greek-speaking community that gathered in synagogues (*Pan.* 30.18.2–3) and made use of a Greek gospel that was a harmony prepared from the canonical gospels. Thus, if they had their origins among the Hebrews of the early Jerusalem community, we have to assume that at some point they switched their language or—as would be more probable—Hebrew missionaries would have been received by Hellenistic Jews who then had prepared for themselves a gospel on the basis of the canonical Greek gospels. Even in this case, we would have to explain how the Greek Ebionites, as the followers of the "Hebrews," might have ended up adopting a critical attitude towards the sacrificial cult. As far as we

---

1:33–71) is connected to Stephen: "While there is not enough evidence to conclude that the community of the *AJ* is the lineal *physical* descendant of the Hellenist Jewish Christians of Acts, it is certainly a *spiritual* descendant of Stephen and his circle." However, van Voorst does not provide any discussion of the Hellenists in Acts or of Stephen's speech, which he simply reads as radical criticism of sacrifices. Furthermore, Van Voorst does not regard the *Ascents of James* as an Ebionite writing (pp. 179–180). Stephen has also been connected to the Ebionites in earlier research. Cf. Schoeps 1949, 222, 440–441. For further references, see Räisänen 1995, 1470 n. 17.

know, the Hebrews of the early Jerusalem community, with James as their leader, had relatively peaceful relations with the temple and its cult.[40]

There is one peculiar feature in Epiphanius' discussion of the Ebionites which has perhaps not received enough attention. According to Epiphanius, the Ebionites accepted only the Pentateuch.[41] It is difficult to imagine that Epiphanius would have invented this idea because it does not quite accord with the earlier reports about the Ebionites. Epiphanius also relates the Ebionites critical attitude towards the prophets in a form which indicates that he conversed with them personally (*Pan.* 30.15.4; 30.18.7–9). Because the Ebionites accept only the Pentateuch, Epiphanius concludes that their founder Ebion—in reality, a fictitious person but Epiphanius probably believed that he existed—must have been a Samaritan (*Pan.* 30.1.5). It is clear that the assumption about the Ebionites' Samaritan background is based on Epiphanius' own reasoning but that does not necessarily mean that his suggestion is so wide of the mark (see above Chapter 2.1.4).

We can also approach the problem of the Samaritan Christians from the viewpoint of another loose end. What happened to the Samaritans who became Christians thanks to the Hellenists' missionary work among them?[42] According to Acts, the execution of Stephen resulted in the dispersion of the Hellenists ("all others except the Apostles") all around Judea and Samaria (Acts 8:1–3).[43] Philip, who was first in rank among the Hellenists after Stephen's execution, headed first to the Samaritans and had success among them.[44] Undoubtedly, the criticism of the temple

---

[40] It is sometimes assumed that the destruction of Jerusalem would have caused the Jewish Christians to change their attitude to the worship in the Temple. Thus, for instance, Lüdemann 1983, 245. There is no doubt that the events of 70 CE and 135 CE had their effect on Jewish and Christian opinions about the temple. Yet it seems (likely) that those who had a positive attitude towards the worship usually ended up reinterpreting its significance, instead of starting to think that the whole thing was misconstrued from the very beginning.

[41] *Pan.* 30.15.2; 30.18.4–5. The Ebionites even rejected parts of the Pentateuch (*Pan.* 30.18.7–9).

[42] According to Justin, *1 Apol.* 26, almost all the Samaritans followed Simon. However, this comment seems simply to repeat Acts 8:9–11 and is hardly historically accurate. Theissen 2000, 345–347, 351 esp. n. 14, 15, links Philip's mission in Samaria to Johannine Christianity.

[43] Those who were "dispersed" are usually thought to have been the Hellenists. See, Pesch 1986, 265, 272.

[44] According to Pesch 1986, 270–271, Luke probably found a story about Philip's mission among the Samaritans in his sources because it does not cohere with his overall view of the mission.

cult in Jerusalem would have been well received among Samaritans. Acts also refers to Cyprus, where we meet Epiphanius' Ebionites, as the target of the missionary work that followed Stephen's execution (Acts 11:19–20).

Notably, these earliest stages of missionary work launched by Stephen's execution did not receive Luke's unreserved acceptance because the work needed to be checked out and completed by more qualified apostles. In Luke's view, the religiosity of both Samaria and Cyprus are characterized by false prophets and magicians. Peter and John followed Philip to Samaria, delivered the Holy Spirit to the Samaritans and confronted Simon with whom Philip had had no problems (Acts 8:4–25). Paul, Barnabas and John went to Cyprus where they met a Jewish false prophet, Bar-Jesus, whom Paul accused of "perverting" the ways of the Lord (Acts 13:4–12).

Do we have here reminiscences of the early missionary activity of the circle around Stephen? Did some of the Hellenists find refuge among the Samaritans or closely related groups after the execution of Stephen? In any case, it seems clear that Epiphanius' Ebionites and *Rec.* 1.27–71 found something to build on in the traditions connected to Stephen. Stephen's "proclamation," as it is described in Acts, found acceptance among Hellenistic Jewish Christians who criticized the temple and sacrifices and saw in Jesus mainly a prophet predicted by Moses.

4.2. Passion Fragments in Jerome's *Commentary on Matthew*

The collection of anti-rabbinic passages that Jerome received from the Nazarenes (see Chapter 3.3.) includes two sections that are related to passion and resurrection. Jerome's *Commentary on Matthew* (398 CE) contains an alternative interpretation of the name Barabbas in Matt 27:16:

> The name of this man is interpreted in the Gospel which is written according to the Hebrews as son of their master ...[45]

In this passage, Jerome appears to claim that in the gospel according to the Hebrews, the name Barabbas (בר אבא) which means son of the/his father in Hebrew, was followed by an interpretation that the name

---

[45] Translation from Klijn 1992, 91.

means "son of their master." However, as Lagrange has pointed out—in this context the "interpretation" does not refer to a translation but to spelling/reading the name in such a way that it comes to mean the "son of *our* master" instead of the "son of (our) father."[46] If placed back in Matthew's narrative, the form "son of *our* master/rabbi" is perfect in the mouth of the crowds. Jerome's "interpretation," for its part, expresses the same thing from his own, Christian point of view: the crowds wanted to free the "son of *their* master/rabbi."

When Jerome is explaining the death of Jesus in the Gospel of Matthew, he refers to the following difference he found in the gospel used by the Nazarenes:

> The veil of the temple has been rent and all the mysteries of the law which were formerly covered have been made public and have come over to the people of the gentiles. In the Gospel which we have already often mentioned we read that a lintel of an enormous size was broken and split. Josephus also tells that the angelic powers, once the overseers of the temple, at the same moment proclaimed: Let us go away from these places.
> (*Comm. Matt.* 27:51; trans. Klijn 1992).

Jerome also refers to the same incident in one of his letters (*Epist.* 120.8, a letter to Hedibia), with slightly different words: "a lintel of wonderful size of the temple collapsed."[47] Minor differences in the key words of the passage indicate that Jerome was not providing literal translations from the original but quoted the passage freely from his memory. Jerome had already discussed the "lifted" lintel of the temple in Isa 6:4 in his letter to Damasus some twenty years earlier (*Epist.* 18; *sublatum est superliminare*). According to Jerome, a Greek scholar interprets the "lifting" of the lintel as a sign of the coming destruction of the Jerusalem temple although many others think that, in Isaiah, the reference is to the moment when the veil of the temple will be rent.[48]

---

[46] Lagrange 1922, 329, followed by Klijn 1992, 92. See above Chapter 3.3.

[47] The Latin runs: *Epist.* 120,8: *superliminare templi mirae magnitudinis conruisse*; *Comm. Matt.* 27,51: *superliminare templi infinitae magnitudinis fractum esse*. For the Latin text and translations, see Klijn 1992, 93–94.

[48] Klijn 1992, 96. The lifting of the lintel corresponds to the Greek text of Isa 6:4. This confirms that the idea about the lifted lintel of the temple as a sign of the future destruction was derived from commentators writing in Greek. The fact that Jerome does not refer to actual collapsing or breaking when he is writing to Damasus suggests that at that time, he did not yet know about the wording in the gospel used by the Nazarenes.

Because the lifting or moving of the lintel of the temple is especially connected by Greek commentators to the temple's future destruction, it is probable that the reference to the breaking of the lintel was already in the Greek version of Matthew from which the Nazarenes' Aramaic translation was prepared.[49] While the renting of the veil is open to several interpretations,[50] the broken lintel is more clearly a sign of the future destruction of the temple.

The Nazarenes themselves were pro-Pauline and had nothing against the mission to the gentiles.[51] Nevertheless, they were extremely critical of early rabbis. In their exposition of Isaiah, they indicated that the Savior had become to them a "destruction and shame." (Jerome, *Comm. Isa.* 8,11–15). Thus, the interpretation which takes the broken lintel as a sign of the future destruction of the temple suits their thinking very well, although they probably were not responsible for the original phrasing in Matthew.

The surviving fragments do not reveal much about how the Nazarenes interpreted Jesus' death. Because they admired Paul as the missionary of the gospel of Christ (see above, Chapter 2.2.4, the Nazarenes' interpretation of Isa 9:1), it is probable that they also understood Jesus' passion and death roughly the same way as Paul did.

The only relatively certain thing we know about their interpretation of Jesus' death is that they went even further than Matthew when putting blame for Jesus' death on the people of Israel. While Matthew said that the "people as a whole" (Matt 27:25) were ready to take Jesus' blood on them and their children, the Nazarenes also claimed that this was because the people wanted to have "the son of their rabbi" released. Although it is regrettable on the viewpoint of modern research that we have only some fragments of early Jewish-Christian gospels available, in this case it is perhaps better that the Nazarenes' interpretation and anti-rabbinic collection did not get wider publicity. The effective history of the Matthean version is sad enough.

---

[49] Notably, the interpretation of the name Barrabban in the Nazarenes' version of Matthew (see above) also seems to presuppose the Greek accusative form (βαραββᾶν) which has inspired the twisted Aramaic reinterpretation of the name as "Son of our Master." Thus, there are traces in both fragments of an earlier Greek version from which the Nazarenes' gospel was translated.

[50] For different possibilities, see Luz 2002, 357–364.

[51] This becomes clear from the Nazarenes' exposition of Isaiah that Jerome quotes in his own Commentary on Isaiah (*Comm. Isa.* 9,1).

4.3. Jesus' Appearance to James the Just

In *On Illustrious Men*, Jerome describes how Jesus appeared to his brother, James the Just:

> ... also the Gospel which is called according to the Hebrews and which I have recently translated into Greek and Latin of which also Origen often makes use, says after the account of the resurrection of the Lord: But the Lord after he had given linen cloth to the servant of the priest, went to James and appeared to him (for James had sworn that he would not eat bread from the hour in which he drank the cup of the Lord until he had seen him rising again from those who sleep), and again, a little later, it says: Bring the table and bread, said the Lord. And immediately it is added: He brought bread and blessed and brake it and gave it to James the Just and said to him: My brother, eat thy bread for the Son of Man is risen from those who sleep. (Jerome, *Vir. ill.* 2; trans. Klijn 1992).

Since Jerome refers to Greek as the target language of the translation and also refers to Origen, it is obvious the fragment represents a case where Jerome is relying on a Greek source, probably Origen (see above Chapter 3.3). This means that the passage is likely to date from the second or early third century. The 3GH attributes it to the *Gospel of the Hebrews*. The hypothesis that has been developed in this book also takes the *Gospel of the Hebrews* as a possible origin of the fragment, although it understands the character of the *Gospel of the Hebrews* somewhat differently, in a closer relationship to the synoptic gospels.

The canonical gospels do not mention Jesus' appearance to James. On the contrary, in Mark, James appears in a critical light since he is listed together with Jesus' relatives (Mark 6:3) who go after Jesus because they think he is out of his mind (Mark 3:20–21, 31). Paul lists James among the many witnesses of Jesus' resurrection (1 Cor 15:7) but by no means as the first one, as appears to be the case in Jerome's passage. According to Paul, Christ first appeared to Peter and then to the twelve. After that, he appeared to more than five hundred brothers and sisters before it was James' turn. Obviously, one of the central concerns of this fragment is to write James into the gospel narrative, attributing to him the role of being among the first witness of the resurrection. This would better fit with the high esteem in which James was held among early Christians, but this was hardly the only motive for the addition. There also have to be some other motives which are more directly connected to the oath of James. I will discuss these in more detail after having sketched the context of the passage in the *Gospel of the Hebrews* and its tradition-historical parallels.

As such, the passage suggests that the gospel from which it was taken included a passion narrative akin to the narratives in the synoptic gospels. It must have included at least the Last Supper, (most likely) a description of Jesus' death, and a story about his burial. The fragment suggests a setting where there are several witnesses to the resurrection, among them a servant of the (high?) priest, to whom Jesus gives the linen cloth that has been used for burial, presumably as evidence of resurrection.[52]

The witnesses to the resurrection bring to mind the *Gospel of Peter* (38-42) where Roman solders are keeping watch at the tomb with a centurion and the elders of the people. They testify how three men with their heads reaching to heaven come out of the tomb, followed by a cross. A voice from heaven asks: "Have you preached to those who sleep?" A voice from the cross replies: "Yes." The *Gospel of the Hebrews* obvious shares with the *Gospel of Peter* the multiple witnesses and a reference to those who sleep. In the *Gospel of the Hebrews*, Jesus "is risen from those who sleep."

Within the synoptic tradition there is a parallel in Matthew's story about the guards at the tomb. It also contains elements that seem to resemble the setting we have in the *Gospel of the Hebrews*. In Matthew (27:62-66; 28:4, 11-15), the outside witnesses are Roman soldiers but they are there under the commission of the "high priests and the Pharisees" who managed to convince Pilate that it is necessary to keep an eye on Jesus' tomb. Interestingly, when the soldiers go to give their report after the resurrection, they go to the high priests. Pharisees are no longer mentioned. Thus, the soldiers are not exactly the servants of the high priest as in the *Gospel of the Hebrews*, but not very far from it either.

Finally, there is a parallel in the minuscule 1424 which includes in its margin a quotation from a Jewish gospel: "The Jewish gospel: And he gave them armed men that they sat opposite the tomb and kept watch over him days and nights."[53]

Thus, we have a total of three references to soldiers watching the tomb, in the *Gospel of Peter*, in Matthew and in a Jewish gospel, A priest or priests are connected to the appearance story both in Matthew and in the *Gospel of the Hebrews*. Although there are thematic connections, there are no clear verbal parallels between these passages. This shows that the idea about the soldiers and Jewish leaders, either high priests or elders, testifying to the resurrection became relatively widespread after the composition of the Gospel of Matthew.

---

[52] Thus, Klauck 2003, 42-43, following Waitz 1924d, 49.
[53] See, Klijn 1992, 115.

In addition to giving James a role among the first witnesses, the fragment also exhibits other concerns. Why is the appearance connected to James' oath of not eating bread before he has seen the Son of Man risen? James the Just was known for his virtue and ascetic lifestyle (Eusebius, *Hist. eccl.* 2.23). Eusebius presents a long quotation from Hegesippus' *Memoirs* where Hegesippus describes James' virtues:

> He drank no wine or liquor and ate no meat. No razor came near his head, he did not anoint himself with oil, and took no baths. He alone was permitted to enter the sanctum, for he wore not wool but linen. He used to enter the temple alone and was often found kneeling and imploring forgiveness for the people, so that his knees became hard like a camel's from his continual kneeling in worship...
> (Eusebius, *Hist. Eccl.* 2.23; trans. Maier 1999).

However, this type of ascetic fame does not explain the passage. The point is not James' ascetic lifestyle in general but a specific vow which actually involves only a short-term abstinence. What could be the reason for James' quite limited asceticism in the *Gospel of the Hebrews*?

Hans-Josef Klauck sees here an apologetic argument: if James, a just man, deviates from his vow of not eating bread, the resurrection "has indeed taken place and the risen Lord has encouraged his brother to resume eating."[54]

I find it hard to see in the fragment the kind of apologetics for resurrection that Klauck suggests. In my view, the apologetics seems to be channeled more directly through the group of witnesses to the resurrection. In the *Gospel of the Hebrews*, there seem to have been quite many of them: the servant of the priest to whom Jesus gives his burial linen, James to whom he appears thereafter and some unnamed persons, possibly disciples, whom Jesus tells to prepare the table and the bread. However, Klauck may be on the right track when he notes that the fragment makes a point of the fact that James resumes eating.

The fragment includes obvious traces of a Eucharistic setting: There are some persons around who serve Jesus, and the table and the bread are prepared according to Jesus' instruction. After the preparations, Jesus breaks the bread, blesses it and gives it to James the Just saying: "Eat your bread since the Son of Man is risen from those who sleep." Thus, it seems that the fragment intends to combine James with the practice of fasting that ends with the Eucharist, celebrated on the day of the resurrection.

---

[54] Klauck 2003, 43.

One possible context where there would have been a need for such a legitimization is the so-called "Easter controversy" that arose towards the end of the second century between Asian and other dioceses (Eusebius, *Hist. eccl.* 5.23–25). When Victor became the bishop of Rome, he tried to excommunicate all the Asian churches who followed the Jewish practice and always celebrated Easter on the fourteenth of Nisan which could be any day of the week. In the Jewish calendar, the fourteenth of Nisan was the day when fasting ended and the lambs were slaughtered. According to Eusebius (*Hist. eccl.* 5.23), several conferences and synods were held because of the controversy. The bishops Theophilus of Caesarea and Narcissus of Jerusalem presided over one of these conferences in Palestine. They defended the majority view according to which the Easter fast should always end on the day of the Savior's resurrection (i.e., Sunday), not on the fourteenth of Nisan. According to Eusebius, Irenaeus urged Victor to be tolerant and pointed out that the dispute was not only about the date of the Paschal festival but also about the correct practice of fasting (*Hist. eccl.* 5.24). Thus, we can be quite sure that the Quartodeciman controversy was also about fasting. But is there something that would make James the Just especially important in this debate?

Notably, Eusebius states (5.25) that the Palestinian bishops, Narcissus and Theophilus, wrote a long defense of their practice, claiming that they had received it from the apostolic succession. Since Narcissus was the bishop of Jerusalem, in his case, the apostolic succession would naturally go back to James, the brother of Lord, who was regarded as the first bishop of Jerusalem. Thus, Narcissus would have had a good reason to legitimate his non-Quartodeciman practice by referring to James the Just. Moreover, Eusebius quotes a passage from Narcissus and Theophilus where they point out that dioceses in Palestine and Alexandria exchange letters in order to insure that Easter is celebrated at the same time in both places. This shows that the congregations in Palestine and in Alexandria had coordinated their calendars.

Eusebius' information is significant for the interpretation of the present passage in two respects. First, it presents a natural context for a story about James the Just who did not end his "Paschal fast" on the fourteenth of Nisan when the Paschal lambs were slaughtered but waited, as he had vowed, until the day of the resurrection. Second, it shows how the story about Jerusalem's first bishop could have easily ended up in Alexandria and with Origen. Although Narcissus and Theophilus worked in Palestine, they were defending the "Christian" timing of Easter and the Alexandrian dioceses belonged to the same faction. Since Origen lived first in Alexandria and then in Palestine, he naturally belonged to the Palestinian-Alexandrian faction in this controversy. We even have Origen's own testimony that such was the case. In his *Commentary on Matthew* (*Comm. ser. Matt.* 79), Origen notes it is an Ebionite heresy to celebrate Easter/Passover the Jewish way. Origen's comment makes it clear that his main target is not Jews or Ebionites but other "Christians" who are in danger of falling prey to the Ebionite heresy if they do some investigating and start to celebrate Easter/Passover the way Jews do (see above Chapter 2.1.2).

If the above reconstruction of the setting of Jesus' appearance to James the Just has been on the right track, would that not suggest that the passage was not really from the *Gospel of the Hebrews*? Should we not expect the Hebrews rather to side with the Quartodeciman practice instead of transmitting the tradition about James the Just who seems to legitimize the non-Quartodeciman position?

If the passage was composed in the heat of the Easter dispute, which I find very likely, then it cannot represent the oldest stratum of the *Gospel of the Hebrews* because the first references to this gospel are by Papias and Hegesippus, from the beginning of the second century.[55] However, theoretically—even if it was later added to the *Gospel of the Hebrews*—it may well have been in the version that was quoted by the Alexandrian writers, Origen and Clement, at the beginning of the third century.[56]

Should we perhaps assume that the circles who used the *Gospel of the Hebrews* in Alexandria sided with other local Christians and followed the non-Quartodeciman timing of Easter? It may well have been so, and it is also possible that the version of the *Gospel of the Hebrews* that remained in use in those Asian communities where Papias first found it, did not include this passage. In my view, this is the most likely scenario; if the passage really was in the *Gospel of the Hebrews*, it must have been a later addition.

In any case, it should be noted that this particular passage fits better with the character of the *Gospel of the Hebrews* as it is reconstructed in this book than with the gnostisizing *Gospel of the Hebrews* of the 3GH. Even though the strong reminiscences of synoptic tradition in this passage would cohere better with my hypothesis, I am well aware of the speculative nature of the attribution. I have included the passage in my reconstruction of the *Gospel of the Hebrews* but with hesitation. We may

---

[55] Quoted in Eusebius, *Hist. eccl.* 3.39.17 and 4.22.8. See above Chapter 3.4.2.
[56] For the date of the first Alexandrian references, see Klijn 1992, 47–52.

very well be dealing here with a case where the half-canonical status of the *Gospel of the Hebrews* and its reputation of representing the old traditions of the Hebrews were used by the mainstream bishops as the setting of a passage which linked the Easter practices of Palestinian and Alexandrian communities to Jerusalem's first bishop, James the Just.

4.4. Conclusion:
Passion Traditions in Jewish-Christian Gospels

The fragments connected to Jesus' passion and resurrection in the Jewish-Christian gospels discussed in this chapter come from three different gospels, two of which can be characterized as apocryphal: the *Gospel of the Ebionites* and the *Gospel of the Hebrews*. The third one, the Nazarenes' Aramaic gospel, seems to have been simply a slightly altered version of the canonical Matthew.

Epiphanius quotes the *Gospel of the Ebionites* in order to show how the Ebionites have twisted the wording of the true gospel to support their abstinence from meat. The reference is short, but if combined with other information about the Ebionites' practices, the fragment opens a window on the Ebionites' interpretation of passion narratives which may also have affected the manuscripts of the canonical gospels (Luke's D, Old Latin and Old Syriac versions). In this tradition, Jesus' death is not given any sacrificial meaning. It exemplifies the interpretative tradition of the Ebionites who were critical of the sacrificial cult in general.

The Nazarenes' anti-rabbinic collection shows how key elements in Matthew's passion narrative were reinterpreted and "updated" by Jewish Christians who had a similar, close love-hate relationship with their Jewish compatriots as the original editor(s) of the gospel.[57] If a full translation of this gospel were available, scholars would probably find it equally difficult to place it on the axis between Judaism and Christianity as they do the present canonical version of the Gospel of Matthew.

The fragment from the *Gospel of the Hebrews* gives James the Just a role in the passion narrative which corresponds to the high esteem in which he was held, especially among early Jewish Christians. Although James the Just was originally the spokesman of conservative Jewish Christians,

---

[57] Although Matthean scholars disagree on whether Matthew should be placed intra muros or extra muros in relation to Judaism, it is largely acknowledged that Matthew struggles to make sense of his Jewish heritage in the light of the new commitment to Jesus. For an overview of the recent discussion, see Carter 2007.

his person was later embraced equally by proto-orthodox Christians, Jewish Christians of the *Pseudo-Clementines* as well as Gnostic circles.[58] In the heat of the Easter dispute his person was used to support the non-Quartodeciman timing of Easter/Passover.

---

[58] For an overview of the development of James traditions, see Painter 2001.

CHAPTER FIVE

JEWISH-CHRISTIAN GOSPELS AND SYRIAC GOSPEL TRADITIONS

5.1. Three Rich Men in the *Gospel of the Hebrews* and the *Diatessaron*

5.1.1. *Introduction*

The Latin translation of Origen's commentary on Matthew's gospel contains a story about a rich man (cf. Mark 10:17–22; Matt 19:16–22, Luke 18:18–23).[1]

> It is written in a certain gospel which is called according to the Hebrews (if, however, it pleases somebody to accept it, not as authority but in order to bring to light the question that has been put): Another rich man,[2] it says, said to him: "Master what good must I do in order to live?" He said to him: "Man, do[3] the law and the prophets." He answered him: "I have done." He said to him: "Go, sell all that you possess and divide it among the poor and come, follow me." But the rich man begun to scratch his head and it did not please him. The Lord said to him: "How can you say: I have done the law and the prophets?[4] For it is written in the law: love your neighbor as yourself. See, many of your brothers, sons of Abraham, are covered with

---

[1] Origen, *Comm. Matt.* 15.14. The translation draws on Klijn & Reinink 1973, 128–129 and Vielhauer & Strecker 1991² (1963¹), 161.

[2] Klijn & Reinink 1973 translate "Another of the rich men," and the English edition of Vielhauer & Strecker 1991² (1963¹) "The other of the two rich men." Both translations are possible on the basis of the Latin original (*alter divitum*) but because it is not clear from the context how many men there were, I prefer the simple translation "another rich man."

[3] The English edition of Vielhauer & Strecker 1991² (1963¹) reads: "fulfil the law and the prophets." "Fulfill" would be a strict translation of the Latin *impleo* or Greek πληρόω. Since different versions of this story do not use the same verbs, I have preferred here a literal translation: 'do' for Latin *facio*. The synoptic stories about the rich man have φυλάσσω (observe, obey). There may also be a difference in meaning between "doing the law" (refers more to individual commandments; cf. ποιέω in LXX Deut 27:26; Gal 3:10,12; 5:3) and "fulfilling the law" (following the central principles; cf. πληρόω in Matt 5:20; Rom 13:8; Gal 5:14).

[4] Due to a printing error, the first part of the question is missing from Klijn and Reinink's reprinted translation in Klijn 1992, 56. The original runs "And the Lord said to him: Why do you say: I did the law and the prophets? Is it not written ..." The Latin

> dung, dying from hunger and your house is full of many good things, and nothing at all comes out of it for them." He turned and said to Simon, his disciple that was sitting by him: "Simon, Son of Jonah, it is easier for a camel to go through the eye of a needle than for a rich man to enter the kingdom of heaven."

Scholars generally agree that the passage was not a part of the original commentary but was added by the Latin translator.[5] The translator and the exact time of the translation are unknown. We only have a very general dating between the fifth and ninth centuries.[6]

According to the quotation, the text is from the "Gospel According to the Hebrews." However, the passage is usually regarded either as a part of the "Gospel of the Nazarenes" or the *Gospel of the Hebrews*, depending on how the number and content of the ancient Jewish-Christian gospels is reconstructed.

The following literary- and source-critical analysis will also show—in contrast to Klijn's view—that the passage added to the Latin translation is clearly later than the canonical Gospel of Matthew. It also draws on Lukan tradition to the extent that it can hardly be taken as a Nazarene edition of Matthew's gospel or of pre-Matthean traditions. Thus, it does not reflect an independent pre-canonical tradition closely resembling the Gospel of Matthew and originating from a small group of *fratres*.[7] Instead, a concluding discussion of *indicators of a Jewish-Christian profile*[8] will show that the quotation testifies to a continuous reinterpretation and rewriting of gospel traditions within a Syriac-speaking, Jewish-Christian community. Although the community uses the Christian gospel tradition, it also presumes the knowledge of Jewish law, lives as a part of the larger Jewish community, and still has a clearly Jewish self-understanding. Therefore, in the framework of the N2GH that has been developed above, the most

---

text of the later edition should also read on line ten: "Et dixit..." (pro "Et dicit..."). There is also a very unfortunate error in the last paragraph of p. 59 where the Greek citations from Matthew and Mark/Luke have traded places. Due to this error, the citations appear to support Klijn's conclusion that the passage in Origen's commentary cannot depend on Matthew.

[5] Schmidtke 1911, 90–94. The passage is also regarded as a later addition by Klijn 1966, 149, and Klijn 1992, 24. However, H.J. Vogt includes the passage in his translation, assuming that it is original. See, Vogt 1990, 109–110, 146 n. 30.

[6] Schmidtke 1911, 94; Klijn 1988, 4020; Klijn 1992, 24.

[7] Klijn 1992, 58–60. See, however, also Klijn 1966, 153–155, where he is inclined to think that the *Gospel of the Hebrews* was based on the Gospel of Matthew, and the *Diatessaron* on the *Gospel of the Hebrews*.

[8] For the outline of the approach, see Chapter 1.3.

likely source for this passage is the *Gospel of the Hebrews* which was originally composed in Greek but later on translated into Syriac.

5.1.2. *The Rich Man in Origen's* Commentary on Matthew

The Latin text of Origen's commentary on Matthew often differs from the Greek one. Although the translation may include some original readings,[9] the story about the rich man proves to be a later addition.

In the context preceding the passage, Origen reasons that since the love commandment is missing in the parallel passages of Mark and Luke, and because Jesus would surely have objected had the man really claimed to have kept the love commandment, it must be a later addition in Matthew's gospel.[10] Origen himself also gave another interpretation—which now follows the added passage—for those who do not agree that the love commandment is a later addition. According to Origen, one can also think that the Lord wanted to gently show the man that he had not fulfilled the commandment. Therefore, the Lord said that if the man wants to be perfect he must go and sell everything he has and give to the poor. By doing this, he would then fulfill the love commandment in reality. Obviously, the added passage where Jesus openly reprimands the man for neglecting his neighbors does not fit with Origen's "gentle" Jesus. However, this contradiction did not bother the translator who added the story, probably because it showed so well how difficult it is for a rich man to be generous and thus love one's neighbor.[11]

---

[9] E. Klostermann found the Latin translation a useful tool for reconstructing the original text of the commentary. See Vogt 1990, vii–xi. Other scholars have not been so optimistic. See, for instance, Vogt 1980, 207–212.

[10] Obviously, modern redaction critics would agree with Origen: The love commandment is added by Matthew, the editor of the gospel!

[11] Klijn 1992, 24–25, thinks that the translator took offence at the way in which the Greek original superficially implied that a passage in the New Testament could be deleted. Therefore, the translator quoted the *Gospel of the Hebrews* in order to show that the love commandment was recorded there, too. In Klijn's view, this shows that the translator attached some importance to the *Gospel of the Hebrews*. It is difficult to agree with this explanation because the Latin text still includes Origen's clear arguments for the secondary character of the love commandment and because, according to the Latin text, it is up to the readers to assess Origen's reasoning: *iudicent autem qui possunt, utrum vera sint quae tractamus an falsa*. The introduction to the quotation also leaves it for the readers to take it or leave it: *si tamen placet alicui suscipere illud, non ad auctoritatem, sed ad manifestationem propositae quaestiones*. Klijn may have been influenced by Schmidtke 1911, 92, who believes that the Latin translator totally undermines Origen's original criticism. I do not think so. In my view, the translator only says in the first part of his addition that, in the New Testament, Origen did not dare to set forth the parameters for

The way in which the *Gospel of the Hebrews* is introduced in the Latin translation resembles Origen's own introductions to a passage from the "Gospel According to the Hebrews" in the commentary on John and in the homily on Jeremiah (*Comm. Jo.* 2.12; *Hom. Jer.* 15.4)[12] The introductory note also shows the translator's acquaintance with Jerome's references to the *Gospel of the Hebrews*.[13] Since the Latin translator seems to imitate both Origen and Jerome, he must have worked after them.

5.1.3. *Comparison with Parallel Passages*

A.F.J. Klijn provides a comparison of the passage with its synoptic parallels and with Diatessaronic traditions. He points out several features that Origen's passage shares with the canonical versions of the story, Diatessaronic traditions and variant readings in the manuscripts. In Klijn's view, the passage is based on an independent tradition that was also known to the author of Matthew's gospel. He also suggests ("we cannot exclude the possibility ...") that similarities between Origen's passage and the variant readings are to be understood as a result of the influence of the same independent tradition on the manuscript tradition.[14] The following analysis will make a different case, which—it is to be hoped—gives a more satisfactory explanation.

In the first two parts, the comparison will concentrate only on the "original" forms of the synoptic stories as they are reconstructed in Nestle—Aland.[15] If it can be shown that Origen's passage contains words or expressions that were created either by Matthew or Luke when they edited their writings, I take this as a strong indication of the dependence of Origen's passage on the canonical gospels. If the passage depends on both Matthew and Luke, this makes the case even stronger.

The subsequent parts of the comparison examine the variants in the manuscripts and Diatessaronic witnesses. Since copyists tended to harmonize the wordings of parallel synoptic stories, later writers did not necessarily get their "Matthean" or "Lukan" readings from the "originals" but from the copy (or copies) that they used. The study of the variants in the

---

solving the origin of the reading through critical signs (obelisks and asterisks) but felt obliged to set forth his reasons more in detail.

[12] Already noted by Resch 1906, 216–218.
[13] Schmidtke 1911, 94. For instance, Jerome, *Vir. ill.* 2; *Comm. Matt.* 6.11; 27.16.
[14] Klijn 1992, 59–60.
[15] Nestle & Aland 1993.

manuscripts helps to reconstruct the factual sources that were available to the composer of Origen's story.

In contrast to many earlier discussions about the *Gospel of the Hebrews*, I will not speculate about independent traditions if parallel expressions can be explained on the basis the Two Document Hypothesis. If a believable trajectory from the "original" canonical gospels to Origen's story can be demonstrated through existing variant readings, versions and Diatessaronic witnesses, then there should be no reason to assume a separate, independent tradition that would have effected the development of textual tradition at several stages.

Matthew
There are four notable features that Origen's passage shares with the Gospel of Matthew.

First, in contrast to Mark and Luke, who relate that a person "asked" Jesus, both Matthew and Origen's Latin quotation use the verb "say."

Second, in Matthew, as well as in Origen's passage, the teacher is not "good." Instead, the man asks "what good" or "good things" (τί ἀγαθόν, *quid bonum*) he should do in order to live.

On the basis of the Two Document Hypothesis, it was the editor of Matthew's gospel who made the man ask "Teacher, what good ..." instead of "Good teacher, what ..." Consequently, in Matthew, Jesus responds "Why do you ask me about good ...?" instead of "Why do you call me good ...? The above expressions are also clearly Matthean elsewhere. The phrase "came and said" (προσελθών ... εἶπεν) and the address "teacher" (διδάσκαλε)—without the word "good"—are Matthean expressions in passages where outsiders pose questions to Jesus.[16] On the basis of the similarities in the introduction, there seems to be no doubt that the present quotation from the *Gospel of the Hebrews* was written after the canonical Gospel of Matthew.

Third, both Matthew and Origen's passage refer to the love commandment. The commandment is Matthew's addition at the end of verse 19:19 and it is the only commandment that is mentioned explicitly in Origen's passage.

Fourth, Origen's quotation does not list the individual commandments as the synoptic versions of the story do. Instead, Jesus only tells the

---

[16] See, for instance, U. Luz's list of Matthew's favorite expressions: Luz 1989, 35–53. A fuller discussion of the above expressions and of the usability of word statistics in the study of Matthew's gospel in general is to be found in Luomanen 1998, 63–66, 291, 298.

man "to do the law and the prophets," and Jesus' subsequent reply to the man makes it clear that the law and the prophets also include the commandment of love.

None of the synoptic gospels mentions the law and the prophets in this connection but the phrase has a central position in the symbolic world of Matthew's gospel where it is closely connected to the love commandment. The editorial verse Matt 7:12 closes the middle section of the Sermon on the Mount: "In everything do to others as you would have them do to you; for this is the *law and the prophets*." Furthermore, the same expression appears as the editor's addition in Jesus' answer in the Lawyer's Question, Matt 22:34–40 (cf. Mark 12:28–34; Luke 10:25–28): "He said to him, 'You shall love the Lord your God with all your heart, and with all your soul, and with all your mind.' This is the greatest and first commandment. And a second is like it: 'You shall love your neighbor as yourself.' On these two commandments hang all *the law and the prophets*" (trans. NRSV). Matthew makes it very clear that the concept of the law and the prophets is tied to the love commandment. Because Origen's passage makes the same connection, it is possible that its author was familiar with one of the key convictions of Matthew's symbolic world.

To be sure, although the term "the law and the prophets" has a more central role in Matthew's theology than in the other synoptics, Matthew is not the only one who uses it. The phrase is also in Luke (and originally in Q; cf. Luke 16:16 and Matt 11:13), although not so closely tied with the love commandment. As a matter of fact, the convergence of Matthean and Lukan usages of the term "the law and the prophets" in the *Diatessaron* offers the best explanation for its appearance in Origen's passage. Understandably, this assumption will be justified only if it can be proved below that Origen's passage depends not only on Matthew but also on Luke and on Diatessaronic traditions.[17]

Luke

There are two interesting similarities between Luke's version of the story and the one in Origen's commentary.

First, in the beginning of the passage, both Luke's and Origen's passages use a participle form of the verb "do" (ποιήσας in Luke; *faciens* in Origen's quotation). The same participial construction can also be found in the

---

[17] We may also note that in contrast to Mark and Luke and in accordance with Origen's passage, the proper name "Jesus" is not mentioned in the introduction to Jesus' answer in the beginning of the verse Matt 19:17, but very little can be built on this.

Lawyer's Question in Luke 10:25–28 (cf. Matt 22:34–40; Mark 12:28–34) that contains a similar opening phrase (cf. Luke 10:25 and 18:18): "Teacher, what must I do to inherit eternal life?" (Luke 10:25 omits only the adjective "good"). In both instances, Luke's phrasing differs from that of Mark. Since the Rich Man's Question and the Lawyer's Question deal with the same theme and, in Luke, have similar phrases, it is easy to understand that a scribe may have used these passages together. This hypothesis also finds support in Eusebius' canon tables that give both Luke 10:25–28 and 18:18–21 as parallels for the story about the rich man (cf. Matt 19:16–20 and Mark 10:17–20).[18]

Second, Jesus' exhortation to sell everything and divide it among the poor is phrased similarly in Luke and in Origen's passage. Both exhort the rich man to sell "everything" that he has (πάντα ὅσα ἔχεις; *omnia quae possides* in the *Gospel of the Hebrews*) against Matthew's "your possessions" and Mark's "what you own." Luke's διάδος is also a bit closer to the Latin "divide" in Origen's commentary than the plain "give" of Matthew and Mark. The fact that there are only four occurrences of the verb διαδίδωμι in the New Testament and three of them are to be found in Lukan writings (Luke 11:22; 18:22; Acts 4:35; John 6:11) speaks for Luke's editing.

On the basis of the Two Document Hypothesis, all the above characteristics of Luke are to be regarded as the result of Luke's editing of the story about the rich man. In addition, Origen's passage uses Lukan phrases that are editorial elsewhere in the gospel.

The words that Jesus uses when he reminds the man of what there is written in the law resemble Luke's wording in the Lawyer's Question (Luke 10:25–28). Origen's passage reads: "*dixit ad eum dominus: quomodo dicis . . . quoniam scriptum est in lege*." The phrasing comes notably close to Luke 10:26 in the Vulgate: "*dixit ad eum: in lege quid scriptum est quomodo legis*"[19] Luke's wording differs from Mark and Matthew, and is to be regarded as editorial.[20]

---

[18] For the Eusebian canon tables, see, for instance, Nestle–Aland, 84–89.

[19] For the sake of comparison, I have given here the Latin text where the word order is similar to Origen's passage. The Greek reads: ὁ δὲ εἶπεν πρὸς αὐτόν. ἐν τῷ νόμῳ τί γέγραπται; πῶς ἀναγινώσκεις; It is hard to say whether the difference between the word order of the Greek and Latin is purely language related or indicates a possible variant reading behind Origen's passage and Luke 10:26. Greek editions that were available to me did not give any variants for the position of ἐν τῷ νόμῳ in Luke 10:26. Syriac translations that otherwise share many readings with Origen's passage (see the discussion below) here follow the Greek word order.

[20] Clearly, Luke 10:25–28 is a bit problematic for the Two Document Hypothesis,

The address *homo* and the participle *conversus* are also typical of Luke. In the synoptic gospels, the vocative ἄνθρωπε is to be found only in Luke: 5:20 (Luke replaces Mark's τέκνον); 12:14 (Luke's special tradition); 22:58, 61 (Luke rewrites Mark?). Mark does not use the word στρέφω at all, and in Matthew, Jesus "turns to" his disciples or supplicants twice: Matt 9:22 and 16:23. In Luke this happens seven times: 7:9, 44; 9:55; 10:23; 14:25; 22:61; 23:28. None of the occurrences is in Markan material which would make them clearly editorial, but they are distributed between Q passages and Luke's special material, which makes Luke's editing most probable, at least in some of the occurrences. It should also to be noted that one of the occurrences (10:23) of στρέφω precedes the Lawyer's Question which seems to share several phrases with Origen's passage. Furthermore, ἄνθρωπε is also to be found in the section (Luke 12:13–21; a warning against avarice and the Parable of the Rich Fool) that preceded the story about the rich man in the *Diatessaron*.

The observations about typically Lukan language in Origen's passage are telling as such but the evidence will become even more forceful below when we see how the Lawyer's Question and the Parable of the Rich Fool (with a preceding warning) were used by the author of Origen's passage when he put the story together.

There is certainly some room left for those who want to speculate about the possibility that the writer of the *Gospel of the Hebrews* knew only Matthew's gospel. Two of the features that have been labeled Lukan in the passage about the rich man can also be found in some Matthean manuscripts.[21] However, these variants should be understood as later

---

since it includes several *minor agreements*. Thus, some scholars assume that Luke did not here follow Mark but used another source, possibly Q. See, for instance, Bovon 1996, 84. However, J. Kiilunen's detailed study of the passage shows that the similarities are to be understood as a result of Matthew's and Luke's independent editorial work. See, Kiilunen 1989, 57–60, 93–94. Kiilunen's arguments are summarized approvingly by Salo 1991, 105–109, who also notes that in the whole double work, Luke avoids the question of the greatest commandment. This observation also supports the view that the question of the lawyer in Luke 10:25 stems from Luke's pen. Overall, recent Q studies seldom include Luke 10:25–28 in Q, and it was also excluded by The International Q Project. See Robinson, et al. 2000, 200–205; Kloppenborg Verbin 2000, 93, 152 n. 76.

[21] Sinaiticus and some other manuscripts use a participial form of the verb "do." Nestle–Aland gives the following witnesses: ℵ L 33. (579). 892. *l* 2211 *pc* (sy s.c.hmg) (sa^ms bo) *txt* B Ξ Δ Θ 700*. Furthermore, the phrase "everything that you have" (πάντα ὅσα ἔχεις) is to be found, according to Huck & Greeven 1981 in Pseudo-Athanasius, Old Latin, the Vulgate, Cyprianus, Irenaeus and Syriac translations. As a matter of fact, the Old Syriac translations even have the same order of words as Origen's passage (cf. below).

harmonizations where Luke's gospel has influenced Matthew's text. Thus, they do not contradict the conclusion that Origen's passage contains features of Matthew's and Luke's editorial work and depends on the canonical gospels.

Origen's passage has no notable similarities with Mark's gospel if compared with the critical text of the 27th edition of Nestle–Aland, but there are some agreements with Mark's textual variants as will become evident in the next section.

5.1.4. *Comparison with Variant Readings and Diatessaronic Witnesses*

According to Klijn, Origen's passage agrees with variant readings that can be found particularly in Caesarean manuscripts like f^1 and f^{13}, and in the Syriac tradition represented by the *Diatessaron*, Old Syriac translations, as well as Aphrahat and Ephrem.[22] Connections between these manuscript traditions and Origen's passage are remarkable, indeed. Nevertheless, more than with anything else, Origen's passage agrees with the Old Syriac translations. Together with the features that the passage shares with Diatessaronic witnesses, the agreement suggests that Origen's passage was composed in a context where the Old Syriac translations and the *Diatessaron* were available.

The relation of Tatian's *Diatessaron* to the Old Syriac translations continues to be debated but today most scholars seem to think that Tatian's Syriac *Diatessaron* preceded the Old Syriac translations.[23] Theoretically, if Origen's passage agrees with the Old Syriac translations, this may be due to the dependance of Origen's passage on the *Diatessaron* (or on its traditions) or due to the dependance on the finished Syriac translations (or on their other sources besides the *Diatessaron*). For each individual variant there are, of course, many possible explanations but in my opinion the force of the cumulative evidence is compelling: no other sources in addition to the *Diatessaron* and the Old Syriac translations need to be assumed. Because the reconstruction of the original wording of the *Diatessaron* is a subject of its own and an extremely demanding one, I have treated the Old Syriac translations and other Diatessaronic witnesses as one group that comes close to the sphere of tradition where

---

[22] Klijn 1992, 60.
[23] See, Metzger 1977, 45–48. Petersen 1994, 426–438, 490. For Syriac as the original language of the *Diatessaron*, see also Petersen 1986, 325–343.

Origen's passage was composed without trying to decide which expressions were in the original *Diatessaron*.

In the following, the agreement with the **Old Syriac translations**[24] is indicated with **bold** and agreement with <u>Diatessaronic witnesses</u> with <u>double underlining</u>.[25] *Italics* indicate a variant reading *not present in the "original" synoptics*. Other witnesses for the variants can be found in standard text critical editions.[26]

At this juncture, the analysis will concentrate solely on the parts that have a synoptic parallel, leaving out the middle section that is peculiar to Origen's story. The middle section is influenced by the context of the *Diatessaron* and it will be discussed later in this chapter.

> **Dixit**, inquit, **ad eum** <u>alter divitum</u>: "**magister, quid bonum** faciens <u>vivam</u>? **dixit ei:** "**homo, legem et prophetas** fac." *respondit* **ad eum**: "<u>*feci*</u>." **dixit ei:** "**vade**, *vende* **omnia quae possides et** divide **pauperibus et veni sequere me.**"

> coepit autem dives scalpere caput suum et non placuit ei. et dixit ad eum dominus: "quomodo dicis: feci legem et prophetas? quoniam scriptum est in lege: diliges proximum tuum sicut te ipsum, et ecce multi fratres tui filii Abrahae amicti sunt stercore, morientes prae fame, et domus tua plena est multis bonis, et non egreditur omnino aliquid ex ea ad eos." et conversus dixit Simoni discipulo suo sedenti apud se:

> "Simon, fili Ionae, **facilius est camelum** *intrare* **per foramen acus quam divitem in** *regnum coelorum*."

Dixit ... ad eum. Matthew, Mark and Luke all have this reading in Sy[s,c,p]. As was noted earlier the expression "say" instead of "ask" was originally Matthew's contribution and not present in Mark and Luke.

<u>alter divitum</u>. In the Liège Harmony and in the Arabic version of the *Diatessaron*, there is a sequence of three stories about rich men: 1) the Parable of the Rich Fool (Luke 12:13–21), 2) The Rich Young Man (Mark 10:17–22; Matthew 19:16–22; Luke 18:18–23), 3) The Parable of the Rich Man and Lazarus with the introductory note about the Pharisees' love of wealth (Luke 16:14–15, 19–31).[27] Since the Liège Harmony and

---

[24] A useful tool for comparison is Kiraz 1996. The standard edition for Syrus Sinaiticus is Lewis 1910.

[25] In addition to Klijn's listing of the Diatessaronic witnesses, in Klijn 1992, 57–60 (see esp. fn. 26–27), I have consulted the following editions and translations: Hogg 1965; Leloir 1954; Pierre 1989.

[26] However, note that the 27th edition of Nestle–Aland, *Novum Testamentum Graece*, does not give all the pertinent variants for the present passage. In addition, I have used the synopsis of Huck & Greeven 1981.

[27] See, Klijn 1992, 57; Petersen 1994, 258–259. Petersen provides a helpful summary

the Arabic version of the *Diatessaron* belong to different branches of Diatessaronic tradition, their agreement should be regarded as a reliable witness to the original composition of the *Diatessaron*.[28] Therefore, it seems that there were three stories about rich men in Tatian's *Diatessaron* of which the story about the rich young man was the second one. Dependance on the *Diatessaron* makes understandable the expression "another" which is inexplicable in the synoptic narratives.

Both Ephrem and Aphrahat say, like Origen's passage, that the man was rich. None of the synoptic gospels states this explicitly.[29]

magister, quid bonum. Matthew changed the location of the word "good." The Old Syriac translation of Matthew (Sy^s) retains the original Matthean position for the word but also harmonizes with the majority of manuscripts by adopting the Markan/Lukan position, too: "Good teacher, what good..." Since Origen's passage completely omits the short monotheistic discussion launched by the address, it is no wonder that the adjective "good" is missing before the word "teacher."

<u>vivam</u>. In contrast to the synoptic gospels, according to which the man asks what he must do in order to inherit/enter eternal life, both Ephrem and Origen's passage mention only life. Ephrem's commentary reads, according to the Latin translation (of the Armenian version), "*quid faciam ut vivam*" and Origen's Latin passage *quid bonum faciens vivam*.

dixit ei: Origen's passage uses this phrase twice as an introduction to Jesus' words. For the first occurrence, there is a parallel in Matthew's gospel where the proper name "Jesus" is omitted. Matthew's Old Syriac translation (sy^s) follows suit. Mark and Luke both read—in Greek as well as in Syriac—"Jesus said to him." There is no exact parallel for the second occurrence since both Greek and Syriac versions refer to Jesus by name. Nevertheless, all versions use some form of the verb "say."

respondit **ad eum**: The Old Syriac version (Sy^s) of Mark reads here (with Peshitta and the majority of Greek manuscripts) "answered (ܥܢܐ) and said (ܘܐܡܪ) to him" in contrast to the "original" synoptic gospels where "answered" is omitted.

"*feci*." Mark's Old Syriac translation (Sy^s) uses here the verb "do" (ܥܒܕܬ) in contrast to other Old Syriac versions that translate the Greek

---

of the observations of C.A. Phillips who was the first one to note the connection between the *Diatessaron* and "another Rich Man" in the *Gospel of the Hebrews*.

[28] See, Petersen 1994, 373–377, 490.

[29] It can also be found in a marginal note of Mark's Harclean Syriac version. See, Klijn 1992, 57.

ἐφυλαξάμην with (ܢܛܪܬ) (both in Matthew and in Luke). Ephrem's commentary on the *Diatessaron* also uses the verb "do" (*facio*) in the same context. Ephrem's Latin translation runs "*factum a mea est.*" Aphrahat also uses the verb "do."

vade, *vende* **omnia quae possides** ... It was Luke who originally added the word "all." The Old Syriac versions have the same "Lukan" reading in Matthew (Sy^s) and Mark (Sy^s) as well. In contrast to the synoptic gospels, they have the same word order ("sell" precedes "all that you possess") like Origen's passage.

pauperibus et veni sequere me. The Old Syriac versions follow here the "original" synoptic text that accords with Origen's passage. Aphrahat omits here the promise "and you will have treasure in heaven," that precedes the exhortation to follow Jesus in the synoptic gospels, and so agrees with the shorter reading of Origen's passage.[30]

facilius est camelum *intrare* **per foramen acus**. The Old Syriac versions of Matthew (Sy^s), Mark (Sy^s) and Luke (Sy^{s,c}) have the same word order as Origen's passage where *intrare* precedes *foramen acus* in contrast to the (Greek) word order of the original synoptics that place the verb εἰςηλθεῖν after the "eye of needle."

quam divitem in *regnum coelorum*. The Old Syriac translations of Matthew (Sy^{s,c}) and Mark (Sy^s) refer here to the "kingdom of heaven" in contrast to "the kingdom of God" of the "original" synoptics (and the Old Syriac of Luke).

In addition, we may also note that the address *Simon, fili Ionae*, is used more often in the Syriac translations than in the synoptic gospels. The phrase is missing in the synoptic versions of the Rich Man's Question; its is found only in Matt 16:17. Syriac translations and some other manuscripts (notably including f^1, and f^{13}) also have this name in John 1:42; 21:15, 16, 17 while the majority of the manuscripts read "Son of John."

The above analysis indicates that almost every expression in the story of Origen that can be compared with the synoptic versions finds a corresponding expression in the Old Syriac translations and (other) Diatessaronic witnesses. Of course, there are also other manuscripts

---

[30] According to Klijn 1992, 58, both the Old Syriac translation of Matthew (Sy^s) and Aphrahat omit here the promise "and you will have treasure in heaven." This, however, must be a mistake since the phrase is in Lewis' edition of the Syrus Sinaiticus (Sy^s) and, as far as one can tell from A. Hjelt's faximile copy, Hjelt 1930, fol. 14a, the line beginning with the word "treasure" is there. Nevertheless, Aphrahat does seem to omit the phrase and he also agrees with Sy^c by adding "take your cross" (cf. Mark 8:34).

that share some of the readings with the Old Syriac and Diatessaronic witnesses but no single manuscript or family of manuscripts comes as close to the wording of Origen's passage as do the Old Syriac translations. In fact, there are only two synoptic expressions in Origen's story for which there are no parallels in the Syriac tradition. The Lukan participle *faciens* is not paralleled in the Old Syriac translations but this is only natural since, due to the different character of the language, Greek participial constructions are usually expressed in Syriac with a parataxis of two finite verbs.[31] Origen's *divide* is another expression not paralleled in the Old Syriac translations. Notably, parallels for that expression are listed only in the Old Latin versions a (*distribute*) and k (*divide*) and in the Greek group of f[13]. Thus, it is clear that if *divide* is not from the pen of the Latin translator, it is only attested in versions that are usually regarded as close relatives of the Old Syriac translations.

5.1.5. *The Influence of the Diatessaronic Context*

Despite all the similarities between Origen's quotation and the Diatessaronic witnesses, it is clear that the actual story about the rich man in the *Diatessaron* was not the same as that of Origen. The analyzed Diatessaronic witnesses show no sign that the beginning of the story would not have included the list of individual commandments in the *Diatessaron*. Furthermore, in the Diatessaronic witnesses, there are no traces of the second, enlarged discussion between the rich man and Jesus that forms the main point in Origen's quotation.

There are two main possibilities for explaining both the differences and the similarities. We may assume that Origen's quotation is rooted in an earlier harmony of synoptic gospels which was used by Tatian when he composed his *Diatessaron* or we may date the tradition in Origen's quotation after Tatian and take it as a later representative of traditions rooted in Tatian's *Diatessaron*. As was seen above, the second option explains the final wording of Origen's passage very well. Nevertheless, the influence of a pre-Diatessaronic composition in the earlier stages of the transmission also seems probable as will become clear in the following.

In the *Diatessaron*, the story about the rich man was placed between two Lukan passages: the Rich Fool from Luke 12:13–21, and the Rich Man and Lazarus from Luke 16:14–15, 19–31. As discussed before, there are notable similarities between Origen's quotation and these two

---

[31] For this, see Brock 1977, 91–92.

passages of Luke's gospel. In the following, the phrases that are echoed in the immediate **context of the Diatessaron** are indicated with **bold**. Comparison with the synoptics also showed that Origen's passage shares some expressions with the Lawyer's Question (Luke 10:25–28). The phrases that are paralleled <u>in the Lawyer's Question</u> and its immediate context are indicated with <u>double underlining</u>.

> Dixit, inquit, ad eum alter divitum: "magister, quid bonum faciens vivam?" dixit ei: "**homo.** <u>legem et prophetas</u> fac." respondit ad eum: "feci." dixit ei: "vade, vende omnia quae possides et divide pauperibus et veni sequere me."
>
> coepit autem dives scalpere caput suum et non placuit ei. et dixit ad eum dominus: "<u>quomodo dicis:</u> feci <u>legem et prophetas?</u> <u>quoniam scriptum est in lege:</u> diliges proximum tuum sicut te ipsum, et ecce multi **fratres tui filii Abrahae** amicti sunt stercore, morientes prae fame, et **domus tua plena est multis bonis** et non egreditur omnino aliquid ex ea ad eos." et <u>conversus dixit</u> Simoni discipulo suo sedenti apud se:
>
> "Simon, fili Ionae, facilius est camelum intrare per foramen acus, quam divitem in regnum coelorum."

1. According to the passage in Origen's commentary, the house of the rich man is full of many good things (*domus tua plena est multis bonis*). The situation is similar to the one that the rich fool finds problematic in Luke 12:13–21. The storage rooms of the fool had become too small for his crop. Therefore, he plans to build bigger ones and "store there all his grain and **good things**" (Greek: τὰ ἀγαθά μου).[32] Then he will say: "Soul, you have **many good things** (Greek: πολλὰ ἀγαθά; Sy[s,c]: ܛܒܬܐ ܣܓܝܐܬܐ) stored for many years." Furthermore, in the same context, there is also a parallel for the Lukan address **homo** in Luke 12:14 (ἄνθρωπε). This section preceded the story about the rich man in the *Diatessaron*.[33]

2. Origen's passage also refers to **the brothers** of the rich man and to **Abraham** who are in a central position in Rich Man and Lazarus (Luke 16:19–31). This story followed the story about the rich man in the *Diatessaron*.

3. Comparison with the synoptics also showed that Origen's passages shares some expressions with the Lawyer's Question: Luke

---

[32] The Old Syriac translations do not refer here to "good things" but the wording is in the Peshitta.

[33] The *Gospel of Thomas* (l. 72) also has the expressions "man" and "turned to." For Quispel 1966, 378–379, this was one indication of the dependance of the *Gospel of Thomas* on the *Gospel of the Hebrews*. For the discussion of this theory see below Chapter 5.2.

10:26 reads in the Vulgate: <u>dixit ad eum: in lege</u> quid <u>scriptum est quomodo legis</u>, which comes notably close to the phrasing of Origen's passage. Assuming that the author of Origen's passage also used the Lawyer's Question, it is quite possible that he also picked up the Lukan <u>conversus dixit</u> that was available only a few verses above (10:23).

4. Once the connection between the Lawyer's Question and Origen's story has been established, we may also note that, in the *Diatessaron*, the Lawyer's Question follows Matthew's gospel by saying "On these two commandments, then, are hung the *law and the prophets*" (34, 25–36, cf. Matt 22:40). Thus, the term "the law and the prophets" that was found common to both Matthew's gospel and Origen's Latin passage (see above) had a central role in the very same Diatessaronic passage that seems to have made its mark on the Rich Man's Question in Origen's Commentary. Furthermore, in the *Diatessaron*, the Lawyer's Question concludes with the Lukan phrase "Do this and you shall live." (cf. Luke 10:28).[34] The phrasing corresponds to the question of the rich man in Origen's Latin passage (*quid bonum faciens vivam*) and in Ephrem's Commentary on the *Diatessaron* (*quid faciam ut vivam*).[35]

However, the Lawyer's Question in the *Diatessaron* mainly follows Matthew and Mark. The phrases that in Origen's passage resemble Luke's version (*quomodo dicis, quoniam scriptum est en lege*)[36] cannot be found in the Diatessaronic witnesses. The Diatessaronic version of the story provides parallels only for the expressions "the law and the prophets," "live," and "do." This suggests that the writer must have been familiar with both

---

[34] The above quotations are based on the English translation of the Arabic *Diatessaron*. For the purposes of the present study, I did not find it necessary—and there was no access to editions needed—to discuss the "original" phrasing of the *Diatessaron*. The presence of these phrases in the Arabic version is enough to show how easily these expressions were fused together in Diatessaronic witnesses or in a tradition influenced by the *Diatessaron* as is the case with Origen's Latin passage.

[35] The author of Origen's passage may also have been influenced by another occurrence of the term "law and the Prophets" in the *Diatessaron*. A central lesson in Rich Man and Lazarus is that had the man given ear to *Moses and the prophets*, he would not have found himself in Hades. Although the story refers to "Moses and the prophets," in Luke's gospel the term <u>the law and the prophets</u> is to be found only a few verses above (Luke 16:16–17): "The law and the Prophets were in effect until John came ..." According to the Arabic version, the section (Luke 16:14–15) that preceded these verses functioned as an introduction to Rich Man and Lazarus in the *Diatessaron*.

[36] The Old Syriac versions translate Luke 10:26: ܐܝܟܢܐ ܟܬܝܒ ܒܢܡܘܣܐ ܩܪܐ ܐܢܬ. Thus the wording could be based on the Old Syriac translations but also on Greek since there is no great difference.

the Diatessaronic version of the story and the separate Syriac gospels. The fact that Origen's passage follows Matthew by saying "Master, *what good must I do . . .*" also indicates this familiarity. The phrase cannot be found in the Diatessaronic witnesses with which Origen's passage agrees, but it is in the Old Syriac translations (see above).

5.1.6. Summary and Conclusions of the Text- and Source Critical Analysis

1. Origen's passage contains several expressions that are typical of both the editor of Matthew's gospel and the editor of Luke's gospel. Therefore, it clearly represents a tradition that depends on the canonical gospels of Matthew and Luke.
2. Origen's passage is closely connected to the Syriac gospel tradition as it is illustrated in the Old Syriac gospels and (other) Diatessaronic witnesses.
3. The passage in Origen's commentary is based on a text that has had the same sequence of passages as the *Diatessaron*. The thematic and terminological connections between the *Diatessaron* and Origen's passage are not restricted only to the passage about the rich man. They are also to be found in the stories that *surrounded* the story about the rich man in the *Diatessaron*.
4. Despite the common sequence of passages and similar phrases, the the Rich Man's Question in Origen's passage is clearly different from the one in the *Diatessaron*. It makes a different point and nothing that is peculiar to Origen's story (e.g., the rich man scratching his head) can be found in the *Diatessaron*.
5. Origen's passage clearly shares some features with the Lawyer's Question in the Gospel of Luke. However, in the *Diatessaron*, the Rich Man's Question was not fused together with the Lawyer's Question to the same extent as in Origen's passage.
6. Origen's passage also shares features with the Old Syriac translation of Matthew's gospel—in contrast to the *Diatessaron*'s reading. Furthermore, the wording of the Lawyer's Question in Origen's passage is closer to the Old Syriac translations than the *Diatessaron*.

These facts allow the following conclusions:

1. The Latin passage in Origen's commentary must be based on an earlier Syriac version.
2. Origen's passage cannot be linked with Syriac gospel tradition only through the *Diatessaron* or only through the Old Syriac translations. It is connected to both of them.

3. Because Origen's story draws on the phrases and topics that were available in the stories surrounding it (in the Diatessaronic sequence), it represents a secondary stage of tradition which reinterprets an earlier version of the Rich Man's Question, which was already placed between two other stories.
4. Because the connection to the surrounding stories and to the Lawyer's Question both concentrate on the middle section of the passage that is peculiar to Origen's story, the Lawyer's Question was also consulted at a secondary stage of reinterpretation.

A crucial question is where the reinterpreter found the sequence of the three stories. Was it in the *Diatessaron*? In that case, the reinterpreter would have had to consult not only the surrounding stories in the *Diatessaron* but also their (later) separate versions in the Old Syriac translations as well as the separate version of the Lawyer's Question. This is not impossible but presumes a relatively complicated process or, alternatively, a series of "redactions." Why would a reinterpreter want to consult the separate gospels if everything needed was available in the *Diatessaron*? Furthermore, if the re-interpreter was a Jewish Christian who was reediting the *Diatessaron* as a whole and wanted to avoid quoting the Gospel of John—as did the editor of the *Gospel of the Ebionites*—he would have had to delete the Johannine parts of the *Diatessaron*.

What kind of a person would be the most likely candidate for consulting separate Syriac gospels when writing a Syriac harmony? Would not that be someone who was translating a harmony of gospels into Syriac with the help of separate Syriac gospels? And how did he locate the passages to be consulted in the separate gospels? Perhaps with a list of parallel passages similar to Eusebius' canon tables which would, in this case, also draw attention to the Lawyer's Question.

These considerations lead to the following hypothesis: *Origen's passage derives from a gospel harmony that had the same sequence of passages as the Diatessaron. The harmony was translated into Syriac with the help of separate Old Syriac translations of the synoptic gospels by a Jewish Christian who wanted to avoid using the Diatessaron itself, perhaps due to its dependance on the Gospel of John.*

This hypothesis not only explains the similarities and the differences in Origen's passage in respect to the Diatessaronic witnesses, but also accords with other information concerning pre-Diatessaronic traditions and Jewish-Christian gospels.

First, in several studies on the *Diatessaron*, it has been suggested that Tatian's harmony was based on Justin's earlier Greek harmony which did not include Johannine parts. This theory has been convincingly defended by William L. Petersen.[37] Thus, the compositional agreements between Origen's passage and the *Diatessaron* may very well be based on a common Greek harmonistic tradition that Tatian and the composer of Origen's passage were using independently.[38] Tatian was using Justin but in the case of the composer of Origen's passage, a dependence on harmonizing traditions that preceded Justin is more likely, as will become clear below (Chapter 5.2)

Second, two detailed observations made in the course of the above analysis can now be explained in the light of Justin's harmony and harmonizing traditions that preceded it. In another context, Petersen has argued that the wording of Jesus' reply in the Lawyer's Question in the *Diatessaron* was similar to that in Justin's harmony.[39] If this is correct, then it is easy to understand why allusions to the Lawyer's Question in Origen's passage can agree with both the Old Syriac translations (consulted by the Syriac translator of the Jewish-Christian harmony) and with the Diatessaronic version (which would go back to Justin's harmony and the traditions he used). It was also noted above that there are only two synoptic expressions for which there are no parallels in the Diatessaronic witnesses. The first one was the Lukan participle *faciens* which could not be expressed in Syriac, and the second one was the verb *divide*, for which there were parallels in the Old Latin manuscripts *a* (*distribute*) and *k* (*divide*), and in the Greek group of f^{13}. Notably, it is precisely in *k* where Petersen finds, in the case of Lawyer's Question, a Diatessaronic reading that goes back to Justin's harmony. Thus, it is quite possible that also *divide*, found in both *k* and Origen's passage, is based on an early harmonistic tradition related to Justin's harmony.

---

[37] Petersen 1994, 426–438, 490.

[38] The *Gospel of the Ebionites* also contains Diatessaronic readings and shares some traditions with Justin. For instance, the story about Jesus' baptism that Epiphanius cites from the *Gospel of the Ebionites* (*Pan.* 30.13.6–8) includes a reference to a great light that was seen around the place of Jesus' baptism. Justin already knew this reading (*Dial.* 88.3) and it was also in Tatian's *Diatessaron*. For the tradition history of the reading, see Petersen 1994, 14–20. Petersen takes this as an evidence that Jewish-Christian gospel fragments would ultimately go back to only one Jewish-Christian gospel. In my view differences in the accounts of Jesus baptism do not allow such conclusion; there were at least two different gospels. Nevertheless, we do not have to go as far as H.-J. Klauck who argues that the baptismal accounts presume three different gospels. See above Chapter 3.4.2.

[39] Petersen 1994, 420–424.

Third, the hypothesis also accords with the fact that Epiphanius once equated the *Diatessaron* with the *Gospel of the Hebrews* (Epiphanius, *Pan.* 46.1.9). In the light of the present passage, it seems that he was on the right track: by the time of Epiphanius, the Syriac-speaking Jewish Christians used a gospel that included traditions that were also available in Tatian's *Diatessaron*.

Tatian's *Diatessaron*, which is thought to precede the Old Syriac translations, was probably composed around 165–180, most likely between 172 and 175. On the other hand, the Peshitta, with which Origen's passage seldom agrees, started to replace the separate gospels during the 5th century,[40] and that has also been considered as the first possible timing for the Latin translation of Origen's commentary. Thus, the passage in Origen's commentary was probably translated into Syriac during the third or fourth centuries. However, if it is connected to the earlier Greek harmonistic tradition, as suggested above, then its earlier versions are rooted in the second century.

I agree with Petersen that the harmonistic readings that can be found in both the "Gospel of the Nazarenes" of the 3GH and in the *Gospel of the Ebionites*, raise the question whether the quotations have been assigned correctly.[41] However, instead of supporting a theory of only one Jewish-Christian gospel preceding the *Diatessaron*, as suggested by Petersen, or a theory of a fifth, Jewish-Christian, source that Tatian used in his *Diatessaron*, as suggested in earlier Diatessaronic studies,[42] I support an alternative explanation for the similarities: the composers of Jewish-Christian gospels were drawing on pre-Diatessaronic harmonizing traditions, and Origen's passage is derived from the *Gospel of the Hebrews* that was composed before Justin's harmony (cf. Appendix 3).

5.1.7. *Mapping Jewish-Christian Profiles*

Although Klijn's analysis of the Jewish-Christian gospels mostly deals with tradition historical and literary historical questions, he also briefly summarizes the theology and historical setting of the gospels he has reconstructed. In his view, the "Gospel of the Nazarenes," which shares

---

[40] Metzger 1977, 56–63; Petersen 1994, 432. According to Black 1972, 132–133, the archetype of the Old Syriac translations (Sy^s and Sy^c) dates from the middle of the fourth century.

[41] Petersen 1994, 29–31, 39–41.

[42] Tatian's possible use of a fifth, Jewish-Christian, source has been discussed since the beginning of Diatessaronic studies (Petersen 1994, 427).

pre-canonical traditions with Matthew, must have originated within a small group of people with a Jewish background. The members of the community were expected to live with each other as brothers and they apparently lived in poor conditions. In Klijn's view, the gospel is preoccupied with Jewish law. The Jews are considered "the children of Abraham who are not following and are unable to follow the law." The community is critical of the Temple and is in constant debate with Jewish leaders. Although Klijn's reconstruction is based on all the passages that he considers part of the "Gospel of the Nazarenes," many details of the reconstruction are derived from the Latin Origen: preoccupation with the law, a community of a small group of brothers, a critical attitude towards "the children of Abraham."[43]

Klijn's "tentative"[44] reconstruction is problematic. First of all, on the basis of the tradition historical analysis, the Latin story about the rich man does not meet the criteria on which Klijn based his reconstruction of the "Gospel of the Nazarenes" (cf. Chapter 3.1). Second, a closer look at the way characters in the text are used for the reconstruction of the social reality behind it reveals some inconsistencies and presuppositions that deserve closer examination.

For instance, Klijn refers to the fact that the rich man refuses to divide his possessions among his "brothers, sons of Abraham" both in order to reconstruct the inner character of the community (a small group of brothers) as well as in order to exemplify the brotherhood that should unite all Jews. He cannot have I both ways: the word "brothers" cannot denote a small group of poor people and at the same time work as a traditional Jewish identity marker on the basis of which the rich man should understand his responsibility for his poorer compatriots. If the rich man and the poor people are "brothers"—as the text obviously presumes—then the word "brothers" cannot be taken as a self-designation of a small group of poor people for whom the rich man is a hostile Jewish outsider.

Klijn's reconstruction also raises the question of on what grounds certain characterizations in the text can be labeled either Jewish or Christian. For Klijn, the discussion of whether or not the rich man

---

[43] Klijn 1992, 37, 39–41, 58, 60.
[44] Klijn himself emphasizes that his attempt to summarize the background of the gospels is bound to remain "tentative" because of the limited number of passages. He thinks that 22 fragments are from the "Gospel of the Nazarenes" but notes that many of these say very little about the theological contents of the gospel. See Klijn 1992, 39–40.

fulfilled the law and the prophets that include the love commandment, seems to mean "preoccupation with the Jewish law."[45] This may be the case—as a matter of fact, I argue below that the passage presumes a Jewish understanding of the law—but how can one come to a conclusion like this? Origen was haunted by the same problem, and for him, the problem was created by one first century Christian gospel editor, namely Matthew, who had added the love commandment to the story about a rich man (see above).[46] What makes the discussion in Origen's Latin passage Jewish? In the following, I will approach these questions by drawing attention to the Jewish-Christian profile of the passage.[47]

5.1.8. *The Jewish-Christian Profile of Origen's Story*

The Role of Jewish Law

It was noted above that it is difficult to label the discussion about the love commandment as either Christian or Jewish. The commandment is found in Leviticus 19:18: "You shall not take vengeance or bear a grudge against any of your people, but you shall love your neighbor as yourself: I am the Lord."[48] There is no doubt about the Jewish origin of the commandment. Nevertheless, by the time of the writing of the passage, it obviously also was an integral part of Christian interpretation of the law, too.

A notable feature in Origen's passage, if compared with its synoptic counterparts, is that it does not list the individual commandments and concentrates only on the love commandment. Is this an indication of the Jewish context of the writer? Does the passage take the obedience to ten commandments and Jewish law in general for granted, and, in practice, "doing the law and the prophets" means following traditional

---

[45] Klijn 1992, 40.

[46] Whether or not Matthew and his community were still Jewish is a question that has often occupied Matthean scholars. I have suggested that Matthew's community is best understood as a (Christian) cult movement that is moving away from Judaism. For this, see Luomanen 2002b.

[47] For the analysis of indicators of Jewish Christianity and Jewish-Christian profiles, see Chapter 1.3.

[48] When we are discussing the social background of the passage, we should also keep in mind that the Jewishness of the rich man does not necessarily prove that the authors or editors of the passage were also Jews, as Klijn (1992, 60) seems to imply. Nevertheless, there are other features in the passage, e.g., the particularistic use of the love commandment as well as the phrase "Simon Son of Jonah" that reveal the Jewish viewpoint of the editor.

Jewish law with all its regulations? Then the love commandment would be just one commandment—important though—among others. Or are the commandments ignored because of a Christian point of view? Had the love commandment become a magic key, a divine justification for loosening the bonds of Jewish law?[49]

We may also note here a possible difference in meaning between the expressions "doing the law (and the prophets)" and "fulfilling the law (and the prophets)." Because the verb "do" (LXX: ποιέω) is used, for instance, in Deut 27:26 where anyone who does not "do" the law is cursed, it is possible that the verb "do" connotes the "doing" of individual OT commandments, whereas "fulfill" is preferred by Christian writers in contexts where general principles of the law are discussed.[50] This may indicate that the writer of Origen's passage takes the love commandment more as one of the Old Testament commandments than as a "Christian" summary of the ethical core of OT teaching.

A closer look at the context of the discussion also reveals a clear "Christian" point of view in the synoptic versions of the story which is missing in Origen's story. The synoptic versions seem to serve two functions. First, the listing of the individual commandments probably serves the prebaptismal teaching of pagan converts. Every Jew surely knew the commandments and there would be no reason to cite them word-for-word in a purely Jewish context. Second, the listing probably also serves the building of the self-identity of the group and legitimation of its teaching over and against the Jews. In the synoptic gospels, this is the only place where Jesus shows that his teaching includes the ten commandments. If they were missing here in the *Gospel of the Hebrews*, are we to assume that they were listed in another passage? Or is it more likely that everyone knew them from the Torah?

With or without the commandments, none of the tradition historical variants of the story about the rich man explicitly discusses the points of

---

[49] This is the way in which, for instance, Paul and Matthew use the love commandment. In Romans, Paul makes a connection between the love commandment and individual commandments: All the commandments "are summed up in this word, 'Love your neighbor as yourself'" (Romans 13:9). In Galatians (5:13–15), the application of the love commandment is more liberal. It sets aside the individual commandments and emphasizes the necessity to obey the love commandment. For the role of the love commandment in Paul's understanding of the law in Gal and in Romans, see Räisänen 1986, 62–65. For Matthew's use, see above.

[50] For the discussion of Paul's possible distinction between "doing" and "fulfilling," see Räisänen 1986, 63–64 n. 104. According to Räisänen it is not possible to find an intentional terminological distinction by Paul.

Jewish law that were a watershed between Jewish and Christian communities: circumcision, the Sabbath, purity laws. The ten commandments and the love commandment should be regarded as part of the common stock of Jewish-Christian tradition and therefore the fact that they are discussed (or ignored) does not make the passage more Christian or Jewish. Only the rhetoric of the discussion, which seems to take the teachings of the Torah for granted, may tell us something about the degree of Jewishness of the community.

Jesus' Role and the Borders of the Community
Another "deletion" in the *Gospel of the Hebrews* is also revealing. The Christological/Monotheistic implications of the synoptic version are plain: Jesus singles out the address "Good teacher" in order to make a short, monotheistic point that only God is good. Notably, the monotheistic note ("only One is good") is still present in Matthew, although at the beginning of the discussion Matthew did not want to contrast God's goodness with that of Jesus as clearly as Mark and Luke. As we have seen, Matthew changed Mark's "Good teacher, what ...?" into "Teacher, what good ...?" and the passage in Origen's commentary follows Matthew. However, in contrast to Matthew, Origen's passage totally bypasses the opportunity for a short lesson on monotheism. Together with other Jewish features of the text, this suggests that the writer of the passage and his audience took monotheism for granted.[51]

In the story, Jesus is addressed as a teacher. The same address is always used by outsiders who fail to understand Jesus' true identity as Kyrios in Matthew's gospel.[52] For Matthew, the address is one means of showing that the man comes to Jesus with the wrong expectations. He pays a visit to a teacher in order to get some additional tips on how enter eternal life but is suddenly challenged by an exhortation to sell everything and to follow Jesus. Although the other synoptics do not use the terms "teacher"

---

[51] As for Matthew, the fact that his Jesus does not explicitly deny his own "goodness" may indicate that in his community, Jesus was gradually gaining divine status. It is should be noted that, in contrast to Mark, but in accordance with Luke, Matthew omits Israel's traditional creed in Matt 22:37 (cf. Mark 12:29). A more detailed discussion in Luomanen 1998, 282–283.

[52] The occurrences of the address "teacher" in Mark 4:38; 9:17; 10:20, 35 and 13:1, that are on the lips of Jesus' followers or supplicants, are either omitted by Matthew or replaced with another word. The correct address for the disciples and supplicants in Matthew is Kyrios.

and "Kyrios" like Matthew, they have the same challenge embedded in the structure of the story. Their lesson to the man is that, although it is a good thing to obey the commandments, what one really should do is to sell everything and follow Jesus. Selling and following are required in addition to traditional Jewish piety (Matthew makes this very clear by referring to perfectness). Jesus' exhortation is the thing that gives the story its Christian edge and lends it something of the character of a conflict story that points out where the border between Jesus' followers and traditional Judaism lies. But in Origen's passage—although Jesus first advises the man to sell everything just as the synoptics do—the latter part of the story is more concerned with the question of showing mercy. The man is not really criticized for not selling everything he has but for not giving something to his ailing brothers. In the synoptic versions of the story, poverty is an ideal but in Origen's version it is a plague that the people with means should try to alleviate.

The Genealogy of the Group
It has often been noted that Jesus' words to the rich man imply a particularistic understanding of brotherhood: The rich man should show mercy to his fellow Jews, "sons of Abraham." Overall, if compared with the synoptic parallel stories, Origen's passage does not make any effort to use the story for the education of possible pagan members of the community nor does it appear to legitimate its teaching against hostile Jews. It seems to focus only on the parenesis within a Jewish community. Although an exhortation to obey the love commandment would also be possible within a Christian community, other features in the text suggest a Jewish context. One indication of this is that Peter is addressed only as Simon, which suggests a Semitic background.

Summary: The Jewish-Christian Profile of the Community
In terms of the indicators of Jewish-Christian profiles, the passage does not touch any of the questions that would clearly mark the borderline between Judaism and Christianity. It focuses on the commandment of love which has a role in Jewish as well as in Christian interpretation of the law. Synoptic versions of the story deal with the commandments and the question of monotheism in order to show that Jesus agrees with these parts of Jewish tradition but represent following Jesus as something that surpasses the traditional modes of Jewish piety. Origen's version of the story seems to presuppose that the readers/hearers of the story know the contents of Jewish law and the love commandment as a part of it. It

also discusses the application of the commandment from a clearly Jewish point of view. The questions as such cannot be labeled either Christian or Jewish but the way they are discussed reveals the Jewish viewpoint of the editor.

The passage profiles a community with a clearly Jewish self-understanding, living as a part of a larger Jewish community or on relatively peaceful terms with it. Nothing suggests that the group might be small and that the members themselves might all be poor. It draws on Jewish tradition and represents Jesus as a teacher who discusses the application of Jewish law.

5.1.9. Conclusion: Where Did the Men Come From?

On the whole, the tradition history of the passage testifies to a sort of re-judaization of gospel traditions in the eastern parts of Christendom. It shows that some time after Tatian there was a community of Jewish Christians who continued to use and reinterpret gospel traditions for their own purposes. In the light of this study, the early gospel traditions about Jesus appear as a common stock of stories from which different Jewish-Christian/Christian writers took material and to which they contributed. This reminds us to keep our eyes open for the variety of ways the traditions and communities evolved during the first centuries CE. Jewish Christians did not live in a vacuum. There was probably more interaction among Jewish, Christian and Jewish-Christian communities during the first centuries than is often assumed.

Careful study of the literary history of Origen's Latin passage shows that a Jewish point of view in a passage is not necessarily an indication of its early date. However, this observation should not lend Jewish Christianity the character of a secondary development or a series of unfortunate lapses into uncritical interest in Jewish traditions and praxis by Christian communities. Jewish-Christian groups of the first centuries were different from the early Jerusalem community, but their genetic, social and ideological distance from those early days in Jerusalem was hardly any greater than that of any other Christian groups.

5.2. The *Gospel of Thomas* and Jewish-Christian Gospel Fragments

5.2.1. *Introduction:* Thomas *and Jewish Christians*

Soon after the *Gospel of Thomas* was available for scholars, Gilles Quispel presented a hypothesis that a significant amount of *Thomas'* logia were based on a Jewish-Christian gospel.[53] As such, the hypothesis has not found many supporters but it is acknowledged that Quispel's studies include important observations about similarities between the *Gospel of Thomas* and Jewish-Christian gospel tradition.[54] At least the following similarities are obvious: (1) Some of the logia of the *Gospel of Thomas* are paralleled in Jewish-Christian gospel fragments. (2) Both the *Gospel of Thomas* and the Jewish-Christian gospel fragments include readings paralleled in the Western and Syrian textual traditions as well as in Diatessaronic witnesses. (3) Some of the logia in the *Gospel of Thomas* are thought to be based on Semitic originals, which suggests connections to Jewish-Christian gospel traditions (4) James the Just has a central role in both the *Gospel of Thomas* (logion 12) and in Jewish Christianity. (5) Both criticize riches and business. (6) Jewish religious practices are explicitly discussed in the *Gospel of Thomas*, which suggests a connection—at least a polemical one—between the Thomasine Christians and a Jewish/Jewish-Christian community.

In addition to Quispel's hypothesis, it is possible to discern four other scholarly stances on the relation between *Thomas* and Jewish-Christian gospels: 1) *Agnosticism.* Because so little is known about Jewish-Christian

---

[53] Quispel attributed about 60% of *Thomas'* logia to a Jewish-Christian gospel. See Quispel 1967, 75. First (see Quispel 1967, 75–111, esp. p. 106) Quispel assumed that the author of the *Gospel of Thomas* had used two sources: a Jewish-Christian gospel of the Nazarenes/Hebrews and an encritite gospel of the Egyptians. Later on, a third, Hermetic source was added. For the summary of Quispel's hypothesis, see Fallon & Cameron 1988, 4216–4219.

[54] Recently, A.D. DeConick has presented the hypothesis that *Thomas* was a "rolling corpus" and suggested that its earliest kernel could be related to the Jewish-Christian gospel postulated by Quispel. See DeConick 2002, 197. Some scholars also assume a Jewish-Christian *collection of sayings* behind the *Gospel of Thomas*. Thus, Cullmann 1960, 321–334. Frend 1967, 13–26; Grobel 1961/62, 370, 373. Grobel supports his view with Semitisms he finds in some of the logia of the *Gospel of Thomas*, and locates the *Gospel of Thomas* in Egypt. Several scholars also assume a connection between *Thomas* and Q's earliest layers. H. Koester, in particular, has emphasized the independence of the traditions of the *Gospel of Thomas* and its connection to the earliest layer of Q's wisdom sayings, prophetic sayings, proverbs and community rules. See Koester 1990, 86–89.

gospels, it is impossible to draw definite conclusions.[55] 2) *Pure coincidence.* A "free-floating" saying may have ended up in several gospels that do not necessarily have any genetic connection with each other.[56] 3) *Common independent tradition.* Helmut Koester has defended the independence of *Thomas*' traditions from the canonical gospels. If this is correct and Jewish-Christian gospel fragments also partly draw on the same independent gospel/sayings tradition, this may explain some of the similarities.[57] 4) *Common post-Diatessaronic tradition.* Han J.W. Drijvers, for instance, has argued that both the *Gospel of Thomas* and the *Gospel of the Ebionites* must depend on Tatian's *Diatessaron*.[58]

This chapter focuses on discussing the logia and fragments which are similar enough to suggest a literary dependence between the *Gospel of Thomas* and Jewish-Christian gospel traditions. The passages to be discussed are: (1) *Gos. Thom.* 2 (P.Oxy. 654.5–9) / Clement, *Strom.* II IX 45.5; V XIV 96.3, (2) *Gos. Thom.* 99 / Epiphanius, *Pan.* 30.14.5, (3) *Gos. Thom.* 39 (P.Oxy. 655) / A "Jewish" marginal reading[59] in Matt 10:16 ("To Ioudaikon;" Codex Novi Testamenti 1424, ad Matth. 10:16) and *Ps.-Clem. Rec.* 1.54.6–7; *Hom.* 3.18.2–3. (4) *Gos. Thom.* 72 / Origen, *Comm. Matt.* 15.14. In addition to the linguistic comparison of these passages, I also discuss two aspects of Wisdom and Spirit traditions that connect the Jewish–Christian fragments to Thomasine writings: The idea of the Spirit as Jesus' mother and Jesus himself as Wisdom incarnate.

---

[55] See, for instance, Baarda 1983, 137.

[56] Thus, Cameron 1984, 334 and Fieger 1991, 22. In fact, this explanation partly overlaps with the third one. Sometimes it is difficult to discern whether scholars are thinking about independent sayings collections to which Thomas would have a genetic connection or only referring to traditions that were freely floating around. Cameron and Fieger offer clear examples of the latter, coincidental explanation. See also Vielhauer & Strecker 1991² (1963¹), 136, and Klijn 1992, 36–37, who emphasizes that the traditions in the *Gospel of the Hebrews* (including the parallel to *Thomas*' logion 2) must have been "circulating in the Christian community."

[57] See, Koester 1989, 38–39. Patterson 1993, 68.

[58] Drijvers & Reinink 1988, 92, 104; repr. in Drijvers 1994, IV. This hypothesis has been defended by Perrin 2002.

[59] In this volume, I have excluded the "Jewish" marginal readings from my reconstruction of Jewish-Christian gospels (see above Chapter 3.1). This is mainly because these readings are probably derived from a variety of sources. Nevertheless, it is possible to discuss individual readings, their tradition history and Jewish-Christian profile without any specific theory about the origin of all the marginal readings.

5.2.2. *The Provenance of the* Gospel of the Hebrews *and the* Gospel of Thomas

Before the actual analysis of the points of contact, it is necessary to briefly discuss the current commonly accepted views of the *Gospel of the Hebrews* and the *Gospel of Thomas*. The assumptions about the geographical locations of these gospels have their effect on what kinds of contacts between them are deemed possible and probable.

The provenance of the *Gospel of Thomas* is generally located in Syria because the apostle Thomas and especially the name Didymos Judas Thomas (*Gos. Thom.* Prol.) are closely connected to Christianity in Syria and because there are similarities between the *Gospel of Thomas* and Syrian literature, in particular the *Acts of Thomas*.[60]

For purposes of comparison with the *Gospel of Thomas*, it is noteworthy that in the traditional Three Gospel Hypothesis (the 3GH), the *Gospel of the Hebrews* is located in Egypt and regarded as the most "Gnostic" of the three Jewish-Christian gospels. It is precisely this hypothesized gospel which has clear connections to Thomasine traditions. It is supposed to include a saying that is similar to *Gos. Thom.* 2 and P.Oxy. 654. 5–9 (Clement, *Strom.* II IX 45.5; V XIV 96.3) and a saying that talks about the Holy Spirit as Jesus' mother (Origen, *Comm. Jo.* 2.12)—a theme characteristic of Syrian Christianity and the *Acts of Thomas* (cc. 7, 27, 39, 50) in particular. In addition, a couple of Jerome's quotations that deal with the Spirit (Jerome, *Comm. Isa.* 11.1–3; Jerome, *Comm. Ezech.* 18.5–9) and James the Just (Jerome, *Vir. ill.* 2) are also attributed to this gospel. Consequently, according to Philipp Vielhauer and Georg Strecker, the Jewish Christianity of the *Gospel of the Hebrews* "contains syncretistic-gnostic elements," and its Christology of the baptism pericopae belongs "to the circle of such gnostic speculations" as can be found in the "Jewish-Christian-gnostic *Kerygmata Petrou*" (see *Ps.-Clem. Hom.* 3.20.2).[61]

Notably, Klijn emphasizes that the *Gospel of the Hebrews* was composed in the first half of the second century and "known in Egypt only." In his view, the *Gospel of the Hebrews* "reflects material that was current during a pre-canonical period" and the "Gospel was composed without

---

[60] See Fallon & Cameron 1988, 4227; Koester 1989, 38–40; Fieger 1991, 4–5.
[61] Vielhauer & Strecker 1991² (1963¹), 173–174.

the help of canonical traditions." Thus, the 3GH postulates an independent, pre-canonical gospel tradition and locates it in Egypt although it represents the same kind of Wisdom and Spirit traditions that appear in the Thomasine writings composed in Syria.[62]

The contradictory views concerning the provenance of the *Gospel of Thomas* and the provenance of the *Gospel of the Hebrews* justifies the question whether scholarship has correctly located these gospels. As I have noted in Chapters 3.1 and 3.4, it is the reconstruction of the *Gospel of the Hebrews* and its Egyptian origin that are most subject to criticism.

The New Two Gospel Hypothesis advanced in this book assumes that the *Gospel of the Hebrews* was originally composed in the Syro-Palestinian area and that it became only secondarily known in Egypt. The new reconstruction agrees with the 3GH about the wisdom character of the *Gospel of the Hebrews* (see Chapter 3.4.3) but sees a closer relationship between the *Gospel of the Hebrews* and the synoptic gospels which makes its comparison with the *Gospel of Thomas* even more interesting.

The fragments to be discussed below also have connections to the *Gospel of the Ebionites*. A detailed analysis of these features shows that the *Gospel of the Ebionites* and the *Gospel of Thomas* share pre-Diatessaronic harmonizing gospel traditions and that they also have connections to 2 Clement and Pseudo-Clementine traditions.

There are only a handful of points of contact and even among these there are some cases where we have only indirect evidence of agreement. Thus, it is clear that all explanations will remain hypothetical to some extent. However, although the observations are few and inconclusive as single cases, when they are viewed together, a remarkably coherent picture emerges which justifies the following conclusion: the *Gospel of Thomas* and Jewish-Christian gospel fragments are partly drawing on the same harmonizing pre-Diatessaronic gospel tradition but interpreting it freely in their own theological frameworks (cf. Appendix 3).

---

[62] Klijn 1992, 33, 36–37. However, a few pages earlier (p. 12, 30) Klijn notes that the *Gospel of the Hebrews* was said to be known to the Palestinian Christian Hegesippus (Eusebius, *Hist. eccl.* 4.25.1). Elsewhere Klijn has also argued that the *Gospel of the Hebrews* was a product of one of the Egyptian wisdom schools. See Klijn 1992, 40; Klijn 1986, 161–175. Vielhauer and Strecker also emphasize that the *Gospel of the Hebrews* differs "considerably from the canonical Gospels" and that "Its stories and sayings scarcely permit of their being understood as developments of synoptic or Johannine texts" (Vielhauer & Strecker 1991^2 (1963^1), 172).

5.2.3. Let Him Who Seeks Continue Seeking

Gos. Thom. 2 / P.Oxy. 654. 5-9 / Clement, Strom. II IX 45.5; V XIV 96.3[63]

Gos. Thom. 2	Clement, Strom. II IX 45.5 (N2GH: The *Gospel of the Hebrews*)[64]
Jesus said, "Let him who seeks continue seeking until he finds. When he finds, he will become troubled. When he becomes troubled, he will be astonished, and he will rule over the all."	"He who has become astonished will become king and he who has become king will rest."

P.Oxy. 654. 5-9	Strom. V XIV 96.3
[Jesus said], "Let him who seeks continue seeking until he finds. When he finds, he will be amazed. And when he becomes amazed, he will rule. And [once he has ruled], he will [attain rest]."	"He who seeks will not cease until he finds and having found he will marvel and having marvelled he will become king and having become king, he will rest."

The Jewish-Christian version of the saying has to be reconstructed from two quotations presented by Clement in his *Stromata* (II IX 45.5; V IX 96.3). Clement's first quotation seems to be an abbreviated version which is presented as a parallel to Plato's thought according to which the beginning of all knowledge is wondering (*Theaetetus* 155d).[65]

---

[63] If not otherwise indicated, the translations of the *Gospel of Thomas* are from Layton 1989. Translations from the Coptic are by B. Layton (pp. 53-93) and from the Greek (P.Oxy.) by H. Attridge (pp. 126-128). The translations of the Jewish-Christian fragments are—if not otherwise indicated—from Klijn 1992, 47-48, 74, 109-110. A remote synoptic parallel for the admonition "to seek" is to be found in Matt 7:8/Luke 11:9 (Q) but there are so many differences between logion 2 and the synoptic passage that there is no need to assume any literary dependance. Logia 38, 92 and 94 are much closer parallels for the Q-saying, but their analysis would go beyond the scope of this discussion.

[64] The attributions presented in connection with the translations are according to the new reconstruction (N2GH) which, however, in this chapter often agrees with the attributions of the 3GH. In case the 3GH has a different attribution, that is indicated in the footnote.

[65] Connection to Plato's wondering (θαυμάζω) also explains why the first quotation uses the verb θαυμάζω while the second one has θαμβέω. The second quotation should be regarded as original. Thus, Klijn 1992, 48-49. The first quotation also uses the verb ἀναπαύω while the second one has ἐπαναπαύομαι. Because there is no difference in meaning between these words, there is no need to try to decide which one was in the Jewish-Christian gospel.

It is often noted that the second, more complete, quotation agrees better with the Greek P.Oxy. version of the saying than with the Coptic Nag Hammadi version. The sequence in the Coptic version is: seeking, finding, being troubled, being astonished, ruling over the all, while the Greek Jewish-Christian/P.Oxy. version has: seeking, finding, being astonished, ruling, resting. Thus, the Coptic version has one more step in the middle of the sequence: being troubled[66] and at the end, it refers to "ruling over the all" while the Greek version refers to rest. Rest and reigning often appear as parallel expressions in Wisdom traditions describing the last stage(s) in the process of "salvation" (*Acts Thom.* c. 136; *Thom. Cont.* 145,8–15; *2 Apoc. Jas.* 56.2–5.).[67] Although the theme of resting is prominent in the Coptic *Gospel of Thomas* elsewhere (50, 51, 60), it is omitted in logion 2. These changes are obviously linked together: "rest" has been removed, "trouble" added and at the end, it is emphasized that the persistent seeker will "rule over the all." The changes suggest that the Coptic version of the saying—or a Greek "2nd edition" preceding it—was written in a more polemical context than the Greek Jewish-Christian/P.Oxy. version. The troubles the author has in mind could be connected to the fight against one's "corpse" (56, 60), i.e.,

---

[66] The addition is correctly noted by Fieger 1991, 20–21. However, Attridge 1989, 100—followed by Fallon and Cameron (Fallon & Cameron 1988, 4203) and Klijn (1992, 49)—note that in contrast to the Coptic text, the Greek P.Oxy. version of logion 2 does not have the expression "he will be astonished, and" (ϥⲛⲁⲣ̄ ϣⲡⲏⲣⲉ ⲁⲩⲱ). This remark implies that the verb θαμβέω in the Greek fragment would correspond to ϣⲧⲟⲣⲧⲣ̄ of the Coptic text. If this is correct, then the Coptic text did not add the expression "being troubled" but "being astonished." However, although θαμβέω may sometimes include an element of being "astounded" or "shocked" in amazement, it is not so clearly connected to the idea of being "disturbed," "upset" or "troubled" as the Coptic ϣⲧⲟⲣⲧⲣ̄, and if one has to choose which one of the Coptic expressions (ϣⲧⲟⲣⲧⲣ̄ or ⲣ̄ ϣⲡⲏⲣⲉ) is the one that stands for θαμβέω, ⲣ̄ ϣⲡⲏⲣⲉ would seem to be a more natural choice. See Liddell & Scott 1973, θαμβέω and Crum 1939, 581, 597–598, ϣⲡⲏⲣⲉ, ϣⲧⲟⲣⲧⲣ̄. Notably, Attridge also translates the Greek θαμβέω in logion 2 "being amazed," and in the same edition, T.O. Lambdin translates the Coptic ϣⲧⲟⲣⲧⲣ̄ "become troubled." For the use of ⲣ̄ ϣⲡⲏⲣⲉ elsewhere in *Gos. Thom*, see logion 29. Unfortunately, due to a misprint in Klijn's book (there is the same translation for *Thomas* and P.Oxy. version; Klijn 1992, 47–48) it is impossible to say for sure which translation he follows.

[67] For instance, Fieger 1991, 21, thinks that the P.Oxy. version, which contains both "rest and reigning," corresponds better with Gnostic theology and must therefore be original. In Fieger's view, the Coptic translator may have misread ἀνὰ πάντα in the place of ἀναπαήσεται. This conjecture is unlikely to be correct because in that case, the translator should also have skipped καὶ βασιλεύσας. Below, it will be argued that the differences between the Coptic and Greek versions probably resulted from conscious reediting.

"persecution within oneself" (69) or even to the actual persecution of Thomasine Christians. As a matter of fact, both these themes are paralleled in the *Book of Thomas the Contender* (142,24–32; 145,8–15). If the *Book of Thomas the Contender* is a later product of the same sphere of tradition as the *Gospel of Thomas*, it is logical to link the editing of the Nag Hammadi version of *Gos. Thom.* 2 to the time when the *Book of Thomas the Contender* was composed or attached to the same Nag Hammadi codex as the *Gospel of Thomas*. In any case, the Coptic version of the saying seems to have reselected and rearranged traditional wisdom topics in the service of a persecuted or more ascetically-oriented community. The Coptic version evidently represents a later stage in the development of the tradition than the Jewish-Christian/P.Oxy. version.[68]

5.2.4. *Your Brothers and Mother Are Standing Outside*

Gos. Thom. 99 / *Epiphanius, Pan.* 30.14.5

Gos. Thom. 99	Epiphanius, *Pan.* 30.14.5. (N2GH: The *Gospel of the Ebionites*).
The disciples said to him, "Your brothers and your mother are standing outside." He said to them, "Those here who do the will of my father are my brothers and my mother. It is they who will enter the kingdom of my father."	Further they deny that he is a man, apparently from the word that the Savior spoke when he was told: "See thy Mother and brothers stand outside," viz. "Who is my mother and who are my brothers?" And he stretched his hand over the disciples and said: "Those are my brothers and my mother and my sisters who do the will of my Father."

2 Clem. 9.11: For the Lord also said: "My brothers are those who do the will of my Father."[69]

The Jewish-Christian Fragment
Epiphanius quotes the *Gospel of the Ebionites* in order to show that the Ebionites deny Jesus' being a man. The synoptic parallels for the

---

[68] Scholars usually ascribe the differences between the P.Oxy. version and the Coptic version to the (Coptic) editor of the *Gospel of Thomas*. See Klijn 1992, 51; Fitzmyer 1971, 416; Fieger 1991, 20–23.

[69] The translation is from Holmes 1999, 115.

quotation are in Matt 12:46–50/Mark 3:31–35/Luke 8:19–21. The *Gospel of the Ebionites* is generally known as a harmonizing gospel which contains readings from all synoptic gospels. The phenomenon is also observable here.

SYNOPSIS:

Matthew 12.47	Mark 3.32	Luke 8.20
[εἶπεν δέ τις αὐτῷ· ἰδοὺ ἡ μήτηρ σου καὶ οἱ ἀδελφοί σου ἔξω ἑστήκασιν ζητοῦντές σοι λαλῆσαι.] 12.48 ὁ δὲ ἀποκριθεὶς εἶπεν τῷ λέγοντι αὐτῷ, τίς ἐστιν ἡ μήτηρ μου καὶ τίνες εἰσὶν οἱ ἀδελφοί μου; 12.49 καὶ ἐκτείνας τὴν χεῖρα αὐτοῦ ἐπὶ τοὺς μαθητὰς αὐτοῦ εἶπεν, ἰδοὺ ἡ μήτηρ μου καὶ οἱ ἀδελφοί μου. 12.50 ὅστις γὰρ ἂν ποιήσῃ τὸ θέλημα τοῦ πατρός μου τοῦ ἐν οὐρανοῖς αὐτός μου ἀδελφὸς καὶ ἀδελφὴ καὶ μήτηρ ἐστίν.	καὶ ἐκάθητο περὶ αὐτὸν ὄχλος, καὶ λέγουσιν αὐτῷ, ἰδοὺ ἡ μήτηρ σου καὶ οἱ ἀδελφοί σου καὶ αἱ ἀδελφαί σου ἔξω ζητοῦσίν σε. 3.33 καὶ ἀποκριθεὶς αὐτοῖς λέγει, τίς ἐστιν ἡ μήτηρ μου καὶ οἱ ἀδελφοί μου; 3.34 καὶ περιβλεψάμενος τοὺς περὶ αὐτὸν κύκλῳ καθημένους λέγει, ἴδε ἡ μήτηρ μου καὶ οἱ ἀδελφοί μου. 3.35 ὃς γὰρ ἂν ποιήσῃ τὸ θέλημα τοῦ θεοῦ, οὗτος ἀδελφός μου καὶ ἀδελφὴ καὶ μήτηρ ἐστίν.	ἀπηγγέλη δὲ αὐτῷ, ἡ μήτηρ σου καὶ οἱ ἀδελφοί σου ἑστήκασιν ἔξω ἰδεῖν θέλοντές σε. 8.21 ὁ δὲ ἀποκριθεὶς εἶπεν πρὸς αὐτούς, μήτηρ μου καὶ ἀδελφοί μου οὗτοί εἰσιν οἱ τὸν λόγον τοῦ θεοῦ ἀκούοντες καὶ ποιοῦντες.

The *Gospel of the Ebionites*

Πάλιν δὲ ἀρνοῦνται εἶναι αὐτὸν ἄνθρωπον, δῆθεν ἀπὸ τοῦ λόγου οὗ εἴρηκεν ὁ σωτὴρ ἐν τῷ ἀναγγελῆναι αὐτῷ ὅτι ἰδοὺ ἡ μήτηρ σου καὶ οἱ ἀδελφοί σου ἔξω ἑστήκασιν, ὅτι τίς μού ἐστι μήτηρ καὶ ἀδελφοί; καὶ ἐκτείνας τὴν χεῖρα ἐπὶ τοὺς μαθητὰς ἔφη· οὗτοί εἰσιν οἱ ἀδελφοί μου καὶ ἡ μήτηρ καὶ ἀδελφαὶ οἱ ποιοῦντες τὰ θελήματα τοῦ πατρός μου.

The *Gospel of Thomas*

ⲠⲈϪⲈ ⲘⲘⲀⲐⲎⲦⲎⲤ ⲚⲀϤ ϪⲈ
ⲚⲈⲔ ⲤⲚⲎⲨ ⲘⲚ ⲦⲈⲔⲘⲀⲀⲨ
ⲤⲈⲀϨⲈⲢⲀⲦⲞⲨ ϨⲒⲠⲤⲀ ⲚⲂⲞⲖ

ⲠⲈϪⲀϤ ⲚⲀⲨ ϪⲈ ⲚⲈⲦⲚⲚⲈⲈⲒⲘⲀ ⲈⲦⲢⲈ
ⲘⲠⲞⲨⲰϢ ⲘⲠⲀⲈⲒⲰⲦ ⲚⲀⲈⲒⲚⲈ ⲚⲀⲤⲚⲎⲨ
ⲘⲚ ⲦⲀⲘⲀⲀⲨ
ⲚⲦⲞⲞⲨ ⲠⲈ ⲈⲦⲚⲀⲂⲰⲔ ⲈϨⲞⲨⲚ
ⲈⲦⲘⲚⲦⲈⲢⲞ ⲘⲠⲀⲈⲒⲰⲦ

2 *Clem.* 9.11 καὶ γὰρ εἶπεν ὁ κύριος· ἀδελφοί μου <u>οὗτοί εἰσιν οἱ ποιοῦντες τὸ θέλημα τοῦ πατρός μου</u>.

The exact extent of Epiphanius' direct quotation is not perfectly clear because he seems to fill in the setting of the saying with his own words. The verb ἀναγγελῆναι is likely to be a reminiscence from Luke 8:20 (ἀπηγγέλη). The *Gospel of the Ebionites* also shares with Luke the expression οὗτοί εἰσιν in contrast to ὅστις / ὃς γὰρ ἄν of Matthew and Mark. Epiphanius himself may have added the verb ἀναγγελῆναι but less likely the expression οὗτοί εἰσιν. Most of the other synoptic expressions in the quotation are paralleled in the Gospel of Matthew. ἰδοὺ ἡ μήτηρ σου καὶ οἱ ἀδελφοί σου ἔξω ἑστήκασιν is directly from Matt 12:47.[70] The word order of Jesus' rhetorical question τίς μού ἐστι μήτηρ καὶ ἀδελφοί; differs from both Matthew and Mark (Luke omitted the question), but the wording is a bit closer to Mark because Matthew has added in the plural subject and predicate (τίνες εἰσίν). Nevertheless, καὶ ἐκτείνας τὴν χεῖρα ἐπὶ τοὺς μαθητὰς follows Matthew again and at the end of the quotation, the *Gospel of the Ebionites* refers to the will of "my father" (τὰ θελήματα / τὸ θέλημα τοῦ πατρός μου), which is paralleled only in Matthew. Thus, Epiphanius' quotation has connections to all the synoptic gospels, most clearly to Matthew. It also repeats words that are without doubt editorial in Matthew's gospel: καὶ ἐκτείνας τὴν χεῖρα ἐπὶ τοὺς μαθητὰς, τὸ θέλημα τοῦ πατρός μου (τοῦ ἐν οὐρανοῖς).

The Gospel of Thomas

In *Thomas'* logion 99, the disciples address Jesus as they do in several other logia. Thus, the introduction of logion 99 is typical of the *Gospel of Thomas* in general.[71] The *Gospel of Thomas* agrees with the synoptic version of the story by saying that Jesus' relatives are "standing outside" (ⲥⲉⲁϩⲉⲣⲁⲧⲟⲩ ϩⲓⲡⲥⲁ ⲛⲃⲟⲗ). The expression is most natural in the synoptic narrative context but it comes out of the blue in the introduction of logion 99. It is not a precise "brief situational introduction" as in logia 22 and 100.[72] Rather, it *presupposes* a situation which is not described in the

---

[70] The verse is in the majority of Greek manuscripts but is omitted in: ℵ*, B, L, Γ, *pc*, ff¹, k, sy^{s,c}, sa. Obviously, the verse was in the copy on which the *Gospel of the Ebionites* is based although it may not have been in Matthew's "original" manuscript.

[71] However, it can be noted that some manuscripts of Matthew's gospel (according to Nestle-Aland, ℵ¹, (892), *pc*, (bo)) explicate that it was "someone of the disciples" who notified Jesus about his relatives who were "standing outside."

[72] Patterson 1993, 67–68, contends that both *Thomas* and Mark have "a brief situational introduction (*Gos. Thom.* 99a; Mark 3:31 f.)." Similarly, Koester 1990, 110. In con-

actual saying. This suggests that the saying is based on a tradition that was at some point transmitted within a wider narrative framework.

In contrast to Mark, Matthew and the *Gospel of the Ebionites*, the *Gospel of Thomas* skips Jesus' rhetorical question and gives only his answer. In this respect, *Thomas* resembles Luke who also omits Jesus' rhetorical question. However, the wording of Jesus' answer goes its own way in Luke—for which there are no parallels in Matthew, Mark, the *Gospel of the Ebionites* or *Thomas*—when its refers to the "word" of God which one has to hear in order to be regarded as Jesus' true relative.

In the *Gospel of Thomas*, there is an additional remark which cannot be found in the parallel passages: "It is they who will enter the kingdom of my father." However, the same idea is expressed in Matt 7:21: "Not everyone who says to me, 'Lord, Lord' will enter the kingdom of heaven but the one who does the will of my father in heaven." According to Schrage, this clearly shows that *Thomas* must depend on the Gospel of Matthew.[73] Since there is no parallel for the clause in the *Gospel of the Ebionites*, the question will be left open here.

Agreement between Thomas and the Jewish-Christian Fragments

It is more important that there are three points where the *Gospel of Thomas* and the *Gospel of the Ebionites* agree against synoptic parallels. Two of these common phrases are also paralleled in *2 Clem.* 9.11:[74] (1) Matthew and Mark begin Jesus' answer with an exclamation: "See, my mother and my brothers" which is followed by a generalizing statement "Whoever does ..." In the *Gospel of Thomas* and in the *Gospel of the Ebionites*, Jesus' answer is directed only to the people around him and it *begins* with the Lukan "These/those here (οὗτοι/ⲚⲈⲦⲚ̄ⲚⲈⲈⲒⲘⲀ) ... Originally Luke had placed this phrase after "mother and brother." Lukan οὗτοί εἰσιν οἱ ποιοῦντες can also be found in *2 Clem.* 9.11. (2) The *Gospel of the Ebionites*, *Thomas* and *2 Clem.* refer to the "will of the

---

trast to logia 22 ("Jesus saw infants being suckled.") and 100 ("They showed Jesus a gold coin.") saying 99 *presupposes* a situation—which if described—would read: "Jesus was teaching in a house." In Mark, the situation is already described in 3:20–21.

[73] Schrage 1964, 187. Even Patterson 1993, 68 and Koester 1990, 110, who argue for the independence of *Thomas*' traditions, take the final clause as sign of the secondary influence of the synoptic gospels on *Thomas*.

[74] Clement of Alexandria also seems to have known one version of the same saying. *Ecl.* 20.3: ἀδελφοὶ γάρ, φησὶν ὁ κύριος, καὶ συγκληρονόμοι οἱ ποιοῦντες τὸ θέλημα τοῦ πατρός μου. Although Clement's version comes quite close to *2 Clem.* 9.11, it does not have οὗτοί εἰσιν making its parallelism with *Thomas* and the *Gospel of the Ebionites* less significant.

Father." Notably, the *Gospel of the Ebionites*, which in this passage mostly follows Matthew, has shortened the Matthean "my Father in heaven" and refers only to "my Father." (3) Only *Thomas* and the *Gospel of the Ebionites* have the sequence "brothers and mother" (followed by sisters in the *Gospel of the Ebionites*) in the final clause. In the synoptic gospels, the order is "brothers, sisters, mother" (Mark and Matthew)[75] or "mother and brothers" (Luke).

These similarities show that the *Gospel of Thomas* and the *Gospel of the Ebionites* are drawing on a non-canonical tradition. As regards the character of this tradition, two hypotheses have been presented: (1) The *Gospel of Thomas* and the *Gospel of the Ebionites* both draw on an independent sayings tradition.[76] (2) The *Gospel of Thomas* and the *Gospel of the Ebionites* depend on a gospel harmony or harmonizing gospel tradition.[77]

Patterson, who has argued for the first option, ascribes to the independent, "less embellished," tradition the phrases πατρός μου and οὗτοί εἰσιν, which are common to *2 Clem.* 9.11, the *Gospel of the Ebionites* and *Thomas*, as well as the absence of Jesus' rhetorical question and gesture (Mark 3:33–34/Matt 12:48–49), omitted by *Thomas* and Luke. In practice, Patterson's hypothesis means that the independent tradition would have had a multiple impact on the formation of the passage in the *Gospel of the Ebionites*. In the first stage, it would have been available to the editor of Luke's gospel (omission of the question and the gesture, οὗτοί εἰσιν) and to the editor of Matthew's gospel (πατρός μου). In addition, the same independent tradition should have been still available to the editor of the *Gospel of the Ebionites*, who at least used canonical Matthew for this passage but took from the independent tradition the form of the

---

[75] However, the majority of Greek manuscripts read in Mark 3:31 "brothers and mother" (Nestle–Aland: (A al), f[13], M, sy[(s).h]). In addition, the Old Latin manuscript *b* has the same reading in Luke 8:21. Notably, Mark 3:31 forms the beginning of the present synoptic passage but it is not explicitly quoted in the *Gospel of the Ebionites* or in the *Gospel of Thomas*. Therefore, if one wishes to see the influence of Mark's variant in the *Gospel of the Ebionites* and *Thomas*, one must also assume that their passages were originally part of a larger narrative. Even so, the dependance of *Thomas* and the *Gospel of the Ebionites* on the common harmonizing tradition is indicated by the combination of this secondary Markan reading with the elements paralleled in Luke and Matthew, which characterizes only *Gos. Thom.* and the "*Gospel of the Ebionites*," (with the exception of Old Latin *b* that is also probably influenced by Mark's secondary reading).

[76] Patterson 1993, 68. Sieber 1965, 152.

[77] Schrage 1964, 187; Fieger 1991, 252.

final clause (οὗτοί εἰσιν), the sequence "brothers and mother,"[78] and on the basis of the "original," decided to drop Matthew's "in heaven" after the "Father." The *Gospel of Thomas*, for its part, would have stuck quite close to the original form of the tradition. Although a process like this is not totally impossible, it has to be asked if it is really believable that, in the synoptic/Jewish-Christian trajectory, the independent tradition would have been hanging around and conveniently available for so many editors who used only parts of it whereas in *Thomas*' trajectory, the tradition would have remained almost intact from pre-synoptic times until the composition of the Coptic edition of the *Gospel of Thomas*.

The hypothesis about harmonizing traditions provides an easier explanation. The final clause in the *Gospel of the Ebionites* is understandable as a combination of Lukan οὗτοί εἰσιν ... οἱ ποιοῦντες with Matthean τὸ θέλημα τοῦ πατρός μου. These two phrases are also conflated in *2 Clem.* 9.11 (see above). Although *2 Clem.* 9.11 is sometimes taken as an indication of the independent character of the tradition,[79] it speaks more for the hypothesis of harmonizing tradition. As Helmut Koester has shown, several citations in *2 Clem.* are harmonizations of Matthew and Luke. According to him, the above conflation of the "Matthean and Lukan redactional changes of Mark's text" in *2 Clem.* 9.11 are one example of this secondary harmonization.[80] Consequently, the combination of "those here who do" with "the will of my Father" in the *Gospel of Thomas* should also suggest the existence of the same harmonizing tradition in the *Gospel of Thomas*.[81] Because *Thomas* and the *Gospel of the Ebionites* also share the same order "brothers and mother," it is difficult to explain the similarities between *Thomas* and the *Gospel of the Ebionites* as the result of two independent harmonizations that would agree only incidentally. Thus, the dependence of these gospels on the same harmonized

---

[78] Patterson himself has not noted the same order of "brothers and mother" in the *Gospel of the Ebionites* and *Thomas*.

[79] Patterson 1993, 68.

[80] See Koester 1957, 77–78, 109–111; Koester 1990, 351, 360.

[81] However, Koester does not draw this conclusion. In *Synoptische Überlieferung* (Koester 1957, 77–79), (when *Thomas* was not yet available to him?) he argues that *2 Clem.* 9.11 and the parallel in the *Gospel of the Ebionites* combine Matthean and Lukan editorial elements. In *Ancient Christian Gospels* (Koester 1990, 351), he summarizes his earlier arguments, referring to his "more detailed documentation" in *Synoptische Überlieferung*. Nevertheless, when in the *Ancient Christian Gospels* he discusses *Gos. Thom.* 99 (p. 110), he does not deal with the existence of the "Matthean" and "Lukan" elements in logion 99 or with its connections to *2 Clem.* and "the *Gospel of the Ebionites*."

tradition is the easiest solution. Notably, there are no parallels for the above harmonized readings that *Thomas* and the *Gospel of the Ebionites* share in the Old Latin, Old Syriac or other Diatessaronic witnesses.[82] This shows that, at least in this case, the common denominator of *Thomas* and the *Gospel of the Ebionites* does not depend on Diatessaronic traditions. Instead, it probably is pre-Diatessaronic because it agrees with *2 Clement*.

This assumption is confirmed by the fact that the connections between *2 Clement*, *Thomas* and the Jewish-Christian gospel(s) are not restricted to this passage. It is well known that logion 22 ("When you make the two one ...") is paralleled in *2 Clem.* 12.2,6.[83] On the other hand, *2 Clem.* 4.5a ("If you were ... in my bosom ...") finds a parallel in a "Jewish gospel," i.e., in the marginal reading of the minuscule 1424 ("To Ioudaikon;" Codex Novi Testamenti 1424, ad. Matth. 7:5).[84] Because *2 Clem.* 12.2,6/ *Gos. Thom.* 22 is a non-canonical saying, it does not reveal anything about possible harmonization. However, *2 Clem.* 4.5a—although a non-canonical saying itself—is in the middle of a collection of sayings which otherwise harmonize with canonical Matthew and Luke.[85] This confirms that the author of *2 Clement* had access to pre-Diatessaronic harmonizing traditions that also ended up in the *Gospel of Thomas* and in the Jewish-Christian gospel fragments.[86]

---

[82] See Baarda 1983, 46.

[83] See for instance, Koester 1990, 358.

[84] The Three Gospel Hypothesis ascribes this fragment to the "Gospel of the Nazarenes."

[85] See Koester 1990, 355–357. Koester argues that the saying in *2 Clement* 4.5.a cannot be from the "Gospel of the Nazarenes" because there are no traces of Matthean language. It is true that the Matthean "will of my father in heaven" is missing in *2 Clem.* 4.5a and that this shows that *2 Clem.* 4.5a cannot be directly dependant on the "Jewish Gospel" ("To Ioudaikon;" Cod. NT 1424, ad. Matth. 7:5). Nevertheless, it does not prove that the saying quoted in *2 Clem.* 4.5 must have been in a "free tradition." Moreover, *2 Clem.* 4.5 uses the verb ἀποβάλλω which fits well with the (ἐκ)βάλλω repeated several times in verses Matt 7:4–6.

[86] It should be noted that *Thomas* and the *Gospel of the Ebionites* did not get their common readings directly from *2 Clement* or from a collection that would have included only the "Sayings of Lord" (cf. *2 Clem.* 9.11) because they have one additional expression in common and they also both presuppose a larger narrative framework when they refer to Jesus' relatives that are "standing outside."

5.2.5. *Wise As Serpents*

Gos. Thom. 39/ P.Oxy. 655/ Codex Novi Testamenti 1424, ad. Matth. 10:16/ *Ps.-Clem. Rec.* 1.54.6–7; *Hom.* 3.18.2–3

According to a marginal note in manuscript 1424, a "Jewish Gospel" ("To Ioudaikon") reads for Matthew 10:16: "more than serpents" (ὑπερ ὄφεις).[87] Thus the whole verse must have read in the "Jewish Gospel":

> See, I am sending you like sheep into the midst of wolves; so be *wiser than serpents* and innocent as doves.

As indicated above, although it is not possible to trace all the "Jewish" readings to one and the same Jewish-Christian gospel, it is meaningful to discuss the tradition history of individual readings (cf. Chapter 3.1). In this case, the "Jewish" reading is paralleled at the end of *Gos. Thom.* 39/ P.Oxy. 655. However, the reconstructed Greek version of the Thomasine saying in P.Oxy. 655 is different from the "Jewish" reading. In practice, the latter part of the Greek version of *Thomas*' saying is the same as verse 10:16b in the canonical Matthew. Nevertheless, there is an indirect connection to the *Gospel of the Ebionites* as will become clear below.

> *Gos. Thom.* 39 (Coptic)
>
> The pharisees and the scribes have taken the keys of knowledge (gnosis) and hidden them. They themselves have not entered, nor have they allowed to enter those who wish to. You, however, be as wise as serpents and as innocent as doves.

The beginning of *Thomas*' logion 39 is paralleled in the Q woe against Jewish authorities (lawyers/scribes and Pharisees in Luke 11:52/Matt 23:13). Although there is no direct parallel for the first part of *Thomas*' saying in the Jewish-Christian gospel fragments, it is relevant for the present theme because there are Jewish-Christian parallels in *Pseudo-Clementine Recognitions* and *Homilies*.

> *Ps.-Clem. Rec.* 1.54.6–7 (Latin)
>
> Both the scribes and the Pharisees are drawn away into another schism. They were baptized by John, and holding on to the word of truth received from Moses' tradition as being the key to the kingdom of heaven, they hid it from the ears of the people.[88]

---

[87] The Three Gospel Hypothesis ascribes all "To Ioudaikon" variants to the "Gospel of the Nazarenes." See Klijn 1992, 25, 31–32.

[88] Translation is from Jones 1995, 88. Jones provides a useful translation of Syriac and Latin *Rec.* in parallel columns.

Ps.-Clem. Hom. 3.18.2–3

The scribes and the Pharisees sit in Moses' seat; all things whatsoever they say to you, hear them. Hear *them*, He said, as entrusted with the key of the kingdom, which is knowledge, which alone can open the gate of life, through which alone is the entrance to eternal life. But truly, He says, they possess the key, but those wishing to enter they do not suffer to do so.

SYNOPSIS:

Matt 23:13
Οὐαὶ δὲ ὑμῖν, γραμματεῖς καὶ Φαρισαῖοι ὑποκριταί, ὅτι κλείετε τὴν βασιλείαν τῶν οὐρανῶν ἔμπροσθεν τῶν ἀνθρώπων· ὑμεῖς γὰρ οὐκ εἰσέρχεσθε οὐδὲ τοὺς εἰσερχομένους ἀφίετε εἰσελθεῖν.
Matt 10:16b
γίνεσθε οὖν φρόνιμοι ὡς οἱ ὄφεις καὶ ἀκέραιοι ὡς αἱ περιστεραί.
"To Ioudaikon" in Matt 10:16b (reconstruction)
γίνεσθε οὖν φρόνιμοι ὑπὲρ ὄφεις καὶ ἀκέραιοι ὡς αἱ περιστεραί.

Luke 11:52
οὐαὶ ὑμῖν τοῖς νομικοῖς, ὅτι ἤρατε τὴν κλεῖδα τῆς γνώσεως· αὐτοὶ οὐκ εἰσήλθατε καὶ τοὺς εἰσερχομένους ἐκωλύσατε.

P. Oxy. 655
λέγει Ἰησοῦς· οἱ φαρισαῖοι καὶ οἱ γραμματεῖς ἔλαβον τὰς κλεῖδας τῆς γνώσεως. αὐτοὶ ἔκρυψαν αὐτάς. οὔτε εἰσῆλθον, οὔτε τοὺς εἰσερχομένους ἀφῆκαν εἰσελθεῖν. ὑμεῖς δὲ γείνεσθε φρόνιμοι ὡς ὄφεις καὶ ἀκέραιοι ὡς περιστεραί.[89]

Gos. Thom. 39
ⲡⲉϫⲉ ⲓ̅ⲥ̅ ϫⲉ ⲙ̅ⲫⲁⲣⲓⲥⲁⲓⲟⲥ ⲙⲛ̅ ⲛ̅ⲅⲣⲁⲙⲙⲁⲧⲉⲩⲥ ⲁⲩϫⲓ ⲛ̅ϣⲁϣⲧ ⲛ̅ⲧⲅⲛⲱⲥⲓⲥ ⲁⲩϩⲟⲡⲟⲩ ⲟⲩⲧⲉ ⲙ̅ⲡⲟⲩⲃⲱⲕ ⲉϩⲟⲩⲛ ⲁⲩⲱ ⲛⲉⲧⲟⲩⲱϣ ⲉⲃⲱⲕ ⲉϩⲟⲩⲛ ⲙ̅ⲡⲟⲩⲕⲁⲁⲩ ⲛ̅ⲧⲱⲧⲛ̅ ⲇⲉ
ϣⲱⲡⲉ ⲙ̅ⲫⲣⲟⲛⲓⲙⲟⲥ ⲛ̅ⲑⲉ ⲛ̅ⲛ̅ϩⲟϥ ⲁⲩⲱ ⲛ̅ⲁⲕⲉⲣⲁⲓⲟⲥ ⲛ̅ⲑⲉ ⲛ̅ⲛ̅ϭⲣⲟⲙⲡⲉ.

---

[89] The Greek is translated: [Jesus said: "The pharisees and the scribes have taken the keys] of [knowledge (gnosis) and] hidden [them. They themselves have not] entered, [nor have they allowed to enter those who were about to] come in. [You], however, [be as wise as serpents and as] innocent [as doves]."

Ps.-Clem. Rec. 1.54.6–7
Scribae quoque et Pharisaei in aliud schisma deducuntur. sed hi baptizati ab Iohanne, et velut clavem regni caelorum verbum veritatis tenentes ex Moysei traditione susceptum, occultarunt ab auribus populi.

Ps.-Clem. Hom. 3.18.3
αὐτῶν δὲ εἶπεν ὡς τὴν κλεῖδα τῆς βασιλείας πεπιστευμένων, ἥτις ἐστὶν γνῶσις, ἣ μόνη τὴν πύλην τῆς ζωῆς ἀνοῖξαι δύναται, δι' ἧς μόνης εἰς τὴν αἰωνίαν ζωὴν εἰσελθεῖν ἔστιν. ἀλλὰ ναί (φησίν), κρατοῦσι μὲν τὴν κλεῖν, τοῖς δὲ βουλομένοις εἰσελθεῖν οὐ παρέχουσιν.

Thomas' Relation to the Synoptic Gospels
The original wording of Q in Luke 11:52/Matt 23:13 is not easy to reconstruct but no matter how it is done, it is clear that in this case, *Thomas* follows at least the canonical Matthew and Luke/Q. First of all, *Thomas* agrees with Matthew's "scribes and Pharisees," and it is generally accepted that this is Matthew's editorial formulation.[90] It is possible to argue that, in other parts of the saying, Thomas is following the original Q although there is no consensus about this: *Thomas* agrees with Luke's "key(s) of knowledge" against Matthew's "locking people out of the kingdom of heaven," and here Luke may have followed the original wording of Q.[91] Furthermore, *Thomas* and Matthew use the verb ἀφίημι while Luke has κωλύω which is often used in Lukan writings (NT 23; Luke-Acts 12). Thus, *Thomas* and Matthew's ἀφίημι may also be closer to the Q-wording. Nevertheless, it is clear that *Thomas*' saying combines at least Matthean and Lukan/Q elements with each other and connects the unit with a saying to be found elsewhere in Matthew's gospel. The same phenomenon was observed in logion 99.

It is likely that the author/editor of the *Gospel of Thomas* was responsible for the combination of the keys of knowledge saying with the wise as serpents saying. Concerning the wise as serpents saying, we may note that the first part of the verse Matt 10:16 is from Q (Luke 10:3/Matt 10:16a)

---

[90] See Luz 1997, 318–319. Patterson (1993, 36), who argues for the independence of *Thomas*, also acknowledges the connection to Matthew but characterizes it as a relatively late harmonization, a text critical problem.

[91] See, for instance, Luz 1997, 320.

but the second half (Matt 10:16b) is regarded as a Matthean addition.[92] If this is correct, then also the latter part of *Thomas'* saying shows knowledge of Matthew's redaction.

Thomas' Relation to the Diatessaron and Pseudo-Clementine Recognitions

No Jewish-Christian gospel parallel has survived for the first part of *Thomas'* saying but, as was noted above, Quispel has pointed out a Jewish-Christian parallel in the *Pseudo-Clementine Recognitions*.[93] The parallel shares with *Thomas* the expressions "scribes and Pharisees," "receiving," "keys" and "hiding." A closer look at *Thomas'* relation to Luke also reveals that *Thomas'* readings agree especially with the variants in Old Latin, Old Syriac and Diatessaronic textual traditions. Thus, we are dealing here with a classic example of *Thomas'* relationship to Tatian's *Diatessaron*.[94] Quispel has explained the similarities by assuming that both *Thomas* and the *Diatessaron* depend on a Jewish-Christian gospel.

Thomas and *Ps.-Clem. Hom.* (3.18.3) refer to the "those who wish to"[95] enter in contrast to "those who were entering" (τοὺς εἰσερχομένους) of Matthew and Luke.[96] The reading is also to be found in some Diatessaronic witnesses (Persian, Tuscan and Venetian harmonies). *Thomas'* plural "keys" is also attested in Diatessaronic witnesses (Persian harmony, Ephrem and Aphrahat). However, the plural is used by Justin as well (*Dial*.17.4).

The reading "have hidden" instead of Luke's canonical "have taken away" is attested in D and several Old Latin (*a b c d e q r²*) and Old Syriac (Sy^s.c) manuscripts as well as in Ephrem's commentary on the *Diatessaron* and in the Arabic version of the *Diatessaron*.[97] As such, the agreement of these Eastern and Western witnesses to the *Diatessaron* does indicate

---

[92] See Robinson, et al. 2000, 162–163; Uro 1987, 75–76. Luz 1990, 105 assumes an addition in Q^Mt.

[93] Quispel 1975, 24–25. For the summary and assessment of Quispel's arguments, see Petersen 1994, 273–300.

[94] See Baarda 1983, 41.

[95] For an overview of the connections of logion 39 to *Homilies* and *Recognitions*, see Baarda 1983, 41. The connections were already pointed out by Quispel 1975, 24.

[96] The Greek reconstruction of logion 39 here follows the wording of Matthew and Luke but because the fragment is so badly damaged, the reconstruction remains hypothetical.

[97] See Petersen 1994, 275.

that Tatian's original used the verb "hide."[98] But where did the authors of the *Recognitions* and *Thomas* get the same verb? Do they depend on the *Diatessaron* or are they perhaps both using a pre-Diatessaronic Jewish-Christian gospel?

The wording of the Arabic *Diatessaron* suggests (but does not prove) that Tatian did not conflate Matthew 23:13 with Luke 11:52, as *Thomas* and *Recognitions* did, but presented them separately and successively.

> *Diatessaron* XL 42–44 (Arabic)
>
> 43 Woe unto you, scribes and Pharisees, hypocrites! because ye have shut the kingdom of God before men. 44 Woe unto you that know the law! for ye concealed the keys of knowledge: ye enter not, and those that are entering ye suffer not to enter.

This shows that harmonization in *Thomas* and *Rec.* goes further than in the (Arabic) *Diatessaron*. Moreover, both *Thomas* and *Recognitions* refer to the "receiving"[99] of the keys which is not present in synoptic parallels or in Diatessaronic witnesses.

All the above similarities show that both *Thomas* and *Pseudo-Clementines* have used the same harmonizing gospel tradition that has some connections to Diatessaronic traditions but it has clearly been a harmony of its own. Is it possible that we are dealing here with the same tradition that surfaced in logion 99 which is paralleled in the *Gospel of the Ebionites*? The existence of the same tradition in Epiphanius' *Gospel of the Ebionites* and in *Pseudo-Clementines* would not be surprising because it is often assumed that Epiphanius was creating his picture of the Ebionites on the basis of Pseudo-Clementine writings (or their sources; see Chapter 2.1.4). Moreover, F. Stanley Jones, in his monograph on *Rec.* 1.27–71, concludes that the source of *Rec.* 1 was using the *Gospel of the Ebionites*. According to Jones: "The most remarkable common element is the explicit statement that the Pharisees were baptized by John (*Pan.* 30.13.4.; *Rec.* 1.54.6–7)."[100] In *Recognitions*, this is stated in the same verses that we are dealing with here. Because it is never stated in the

---

[98] For the criteria to be used in the reconstruction of the *Diatessaron's* readings, see Petersen 1994, 373–377, 490.

[99] Notably, both the Coptic ⲭⲓ as well as the Greek λαμβάνω in logion 39 can be translated "to take" or "to receive." In Layton's edition, Lambin (Coptic) and Attridge (Greek) have translated "have taken the keys." However, "have received the keys" would also be an acceptable translation. The Greek especially might even read better if the meaning is 'to receive' because the lacuna in the manuscript seems to presuppose a full stop after the "keys of knowledge." For the reconstruction, see Attridge 1989, 123.

[100] Jones 1995, 148–149.

218   CHAPTER FIVE

canonical gospels that the Pharisees really were baptized by John,[101] it is highly probable that the writer of *Rec.* 1 derived the information from the *Gospel of the Ebionites* or its source. Consequently, the harmonizing source from which *Thomas* received the expressions that it shares with *Recognitions* (and perhaps also *Hom.*) was presumably the *Gospel of the Ebionites*—or more probably its source, as was the case with logion 99.

To summarize, although there is no direct parallel for the "Jewish" marginal reading in *Gos. Thom.* 39, the first part of the logion is paralleled in *Pseudo-Clementine Recognitions* (1.54.6–7) which has most likely used the *Gospel of the Ebionites*. Thus, the writer of the *Gospel of Thomas* is either using the *Gospel of the Ebionites* or—more probably—sharing some pre-Diatessaronic sources with it.

Does this also indicate that the "Jewish" marginal reading in Matt 10:16 of Cod. 1424 is from the *Gospel of the Ebionites*? That is possible but not sure, for two reasons. First, the analysis indicated that the editor of *Thom.* 39 was probably responsible for combining the tradition about the keys of knowledge with the saying "wise as serpents and innocent as doves" (i.e., combined 30a with 30b). Second, *Gos. Thom.* 39b does not agree with the marginal reading. Thus, the "Jewish" marginal reading in Matt 10.16 may come from another gospel although the *Gospel of the Ebionites* is a good candidate.

5.2.6. "O Man" and "He Turned To"

Gos. Thom. 72 / Origen, *Comm. Matt.* 15.14

One of the arguments which Quispel has presented to support his view that *Thomas* must have used the *Gospel of the Hebrews* is a stylistic affinity between logion 72 and a fragment that is quoted in Origen's *Commentary on Matthew* (*Comm. Matt.* 15.14).[102] Both these passages include the expressions "man" and "he turned to."

---

[101] In Matt 3:7 they have just come to John in order to be baptized when John starts to reprimand them.
[102] Quispel 1966, 378–379. Another instance where some scholars have seen stylistic affinity is the question "what sin have I committed" that is found in logion 104 and Jerome, *Pelag.* 3.2. However, although both passages discuss practices that the synoptic gospels connect with John the Baptist, there seems to no other points of contact between these passages, making it impossible to draw any conclusions about their literary relationship.

Saying 72

[A man said] to him, "Tell my brothers to divide my father's possessions with me." He said to him, "*O man*, who has made me a divider?" *He turned to* his *disciples* and said to them, "I am not a divider, am I?"

Origen, *Comm. Matt.* 15.14[103]
(*The Gospel of the Hebrews*)[104]

It is written in a certain gospel which is called according to the Hebrews (if, however, it pleases somebody to accept it, not as authority but in order to bring to light the question that has been put): Another rich man, it says, said to him: "Master what good must I do in order to live?" He said to him: "*Man*, do the Law and the prophets." He answered him: "I have done." He said to him: "Go, sell all that you possess and divide it among the poor and come, follow me." But the rich man begun to scratch his head and it did not please him. The Lord said to him: "How can you say: 'I have done the Law and the Prophets?' For it is written in the Law: love your neighbor as yourself. See, many of your brothers, sons of Abraham, are covered with dung, dying from hunger and your house is full of many good things, and nothing at all comes out of it for them." *He turned* and said *to* Simon, *his disciple* that was sitting by him: "Simon, Son of Jonah, it is easier for a camel to go through the eye of a needle than for a rich man to enter the kingdom of heaven."

Stylistic Similarity

Quispel notes that the expression στραφεὶς πρὸς τοὺς μαθητάς is found in the NT only in Luke 10:23 but he thinks that "Thomas and H. Ev., however, show that this stylistic device is not exclusively Lukan."[105] For Quispel, the rarity of the expression seems to indicate that there must be a connection between the fragment in Origen's passage and the *Gospel of Thomas*, but in his view, the connection is not related to Luke.

Quispel's stylistic argument has not received much attention. However, he may have been on the right track although the hypothesis about the independence of *Gos. Thom.* and the *Gospel of the Ebionites* from Luke is difficult to prove. First of all, the only unique feature in the expression στραφεὶς πρὸς τοὺς μαθητάς is an explicit use of the noun μαθητής. Second, both ἄνθρωπε and στραφεὶς πρὸς τοὺς … are clearly compatible with Luke's style and are used several times in his gospel.

---

[103] The translation draws on Klijn & Reinink 1973, 128–129, and Vielhauer & Strecker 1991² (1963¹), 161.
[104] The 3GH attributes this to "the Gospel of the Nazarenes". For analysis, see Chapter 5.1.
[105] Quispel 1966, 378–379.

Luke is the only synoptic writer that uses the address "man" (ἄνθρωπε) and it is also typical of Luke to describe Jesus' "turning to" people.[106] Thus, it seems clear that the phrases were originally created by Luke. Nevertheless, there is evidence which indicates that both *Thomas* and the *Gospel of the Hebrews* did not get these expressions directly from the Gospel of Luke but from a harmonistic gospel that is somehow related to the *Diatessaron*.

Three Rich Men in the Diatessaron
The synoptic parallel for logion 72 is in Luke 12:13-15. Because these verses are only found in Luke, the discussion about the tradition history of logion 72 has usually focused on the question of whether or not it is possible to see traces of Luke's editorial work in *Thomas'* saying, and it has often escaped the notice of scholars that the same verses were also in the *Diatessaron*. It is known that, in the *Diatessaron*, Luke 12:13-15 functioned as an introduction to the Parable of the Rich Fool (Luke 12:16-21) which was the first story in the sequence of three stories about rich men. The second one in the series was the Rich Man's Question (Mark 10:17-22; Matthew 19:16-22; Luke 18:18-23). That is precisely the same story of which a Jewish-Christian version is quoted in Origen's *Commentary on Matthew*. The third story in the *Diatessaron* was the Parable of the Rich Man and Lazarus (Luke 16:14-15, 19-31).[107] Thus, when Quispel pointed out a stylistic similarity between logion 72 and the fragment in Origen's *Commentary*, he was in fact referring to two passages that followed each other in the *Diatessaron*. Because these passages are not linked together in the synoptic gospels, the observation that they followed each other in the *Diatessaron* increases the probability that their stylistic similarities are not coincidental. However, the *Diatessaron's* sequence of passages cannot prove anything unless there is further evidence which shows that the writers of logion 72 and the Jewish-Christian fragment knew the same sequence.

---

[106] ἄνθρωπε occurs three times in Luke: in 5:20 it replaces Mark's τέκνον, 12:14 is in Luke's own tradition, and in 22:58 Luke probably rewrites Mark 14:70. Mark does not use στρέφω at all, and, in Matthew, Jesus "turns to" his disciples (Peter) or supplicants twice: Matt 9:22 and 16:23. In Luke this happens seven times: 7:9, 44; 9:55; 10:23; 14:25; 22:61; 23:28.
[107] The first one to notice this Diatessaronic sequence of passages was C.A. Phillips in 1931. For the summary of Phillips' observations, see Petersen 1994, 257-259.

Because I have dealt with Origen's passage in detail above (Chapter 5.1), I will only summarize the points that explain how the expressions ἄνθρωπε and στραφεὶς πρός ended up in both Origen's fragment and the *Gospel of Thomas*.

Three Rich Men in Origen's Fragment
In the case of Origen's fragment, the knowledge of the Diatessaronic sequence is generally acknowledged. One indicator of the sequence is the expression "another rich man" which shows that the passage presupposes a sequence of at least two stories about rich men. In addition, several readings common to the fragment and Diatessaronic witnesses have been discovered.[108] However, what is not usually noticed is the infusion of ideas and phrases from the two surrounding stories into the fragment preserved in Origen's commentary. As in the Parable of the Rich Fool (Luke 12:16–21; the first story), the rich man in Origen's fragment is a man whose house is "full of many good things" (*domus tua plena est multis bonis*; cf. Luke 12:19 ψυχή, ἔχεις πολλὰ ἀγαθά). Furthermore, he is addressed as "man" (*homo*) like in Luke 12:14 (ἄνθρωπε). The third story, for its part, is reflected in the idea that the rich man should know, on the basis of the *law and the prophets*, to take care of his *brothers, the sons of Abraham*, just like the rich man and his *brothers, the "sons of Abraham"* (the rich man addresses Abraham as "father") should know merely on the basis of *Moses and the prophets* how to take care of poor people like Lazarus.

The above observations about the impact of the surrounding stories make clear the route along which the Lukan address ἄνθρωπε traveled to end up in the *Gospel of the Hebrews*: It was adopted from the "first" story about the rich man (Luke 12:13–15), from verses that are also paralleled in logion 72. But where did the expression "he turned to" come from?

In Luke's gospel, the Lawyer's Question is in many respects a twin to the story about the rich man. Both stories open with a similar question "(Good) teacher, what must I do to inherit eternal life," and both deal with obeying the Jewish law. Eusebius's canon tables, for instance, give both Luke 10:25–28 and 18:18–21 as parallels for the story about the rich man.[109] The Lawyer's Question shares several features with the passage in Origen's commentary.[110] All these similarities show that the framer of the

---

[108] See, for instance, Klijn 1992, 56–60.
[109] For Eusebius' canon tables, see Nestle & Aland 1993, 84–89.
[110] In addition to the participle *faciens*, which Luke 18:18 and 20:25 share with Origen's

second story about a rich man in the *Gospel of the Hebrews* consulted both the story about the rich man and the Lawyer's Question. When he consulted the Lawyer's Question in Luke 10:25–28, he probably also found the expression "he turned to" in Luke 10:23. This is the same verse where Quispel saw the "unique" stylistic similarity for logion 72 and the *Gospel of the Hebrews.*

All the above observations indicate that the fragment in Origen's commentary is not presynoptic and it is clearly from a harmonizing gospel. Consequently, the New Two Gospel Hypothesis which this volume proposes, attributes the passage to the *Gospel of the Hebrews.*

Three Rich Men in Thomas' Source?
There is no conclusive evidence which would make it absolutely clear that the people who passed on *Thomas'* traditions must have known the same collection of passages as the *Gospel of the Hebrews* but there are several observations which speak for this hypothesis.

First, the parallel to the story about the Rich Fool is to be found in logion 63. This means that, in the *Gospel of Thomas* (in logia 72 and 63), there is parallel material for the whole Diatessaronic story about the "first" rich man. Second, both these logia include Diatessaronic readings. Especially logion 63—*Thomas'* Rich Fool—is a classic example of a case where *Thomas'* readings crop up in several Old Latin and Old Syriac translations and Diatessaronic witnesses.[111] Third, in the *Gospel of Thomas*, the Rich Fool also opens a cluster of logia where rich people, "businessmen and merchants" are criticized. We might note in passing that "marked animosity against business" was one of the features that indicated to Quispel a close connection between the *Gospel of Thomas* and the *Gospel of the Hebrews.*[112] Fourth, the other two Diatessaronic stories—the Rich Man's Question and the Rich Man and Lazarus—are so clearly connected to Jewish tradition and observance of the Jewish law that their absence in the *Gospel of Thomas* is no surprise (cf. logia 6, 14,

---

passage in contrast to Matthew and Mark, the phrasing of Jesus' rhetorical question is similar. Origen's passage reads: "**dixit ad eum dominus: quomodo dicis ... quoniam scriptum est in lege.**" Luke 10:26 reads in the Vulgate: "**Dixit ad eum: in lege quid scriptum est quomodo legis.**" Interestingly, the parallel passages in Matthew and Mark do not mention at all "what is written in the law." Furthermore, Origen's passage and the Lawyer's Question do not discuss individual commandments as all the synoptic gospels in the Rich Man's Question do. Instead, they concentrate only on the (double) love commandment.

[111] See Baarda 1983, 44.
[112] Quispel 1966, 379.

27, 53, 89, 104).[113] Finally, Origen's version of the Rich Man's Question made clear the infusion of expressions from the surrounding Diatessaronic stories and from the Lawyer's Question into the second story about a rich man. Therefore, the appearance of the same phenomenon in the first story of the same cluster would be natural. In this case, the emergence of the Lukan "he turned to" in logion 72 would reveal the hand of the same editor who, at some point, implanted the same expression in the second story.

We may also consider whether it is possible that all the above similarities are purely coincidental: Is it only a coincidence that both the *Gospel of Thomas* and the fragment in Origen's commentary have independently—in contrast to known synoptic parallels—added the (Lukan) "he turned to" to a story where one can also find another Lukan expression, the address "(O) man." Is it only a coincidence that, in these passages, both these gospels have Diatessaronic readings? Is it only a coincidence that these stories happened to follow each other in the *Diatessaron*? Of course, all this is possible, but as the list of coincidences grows, the probability of a more simple explanation also grows: the *Gospel of Thomas* and Origen's fragment have made use of the same harmonizing gospel tradition that is related to the *Diatessaron*. On the basis of my earlier analysis of Origen's passage, it seems probable that the cluster of three stories about rich men already existed in the pre-Diatessaronic tradition. The Latin passage in Origen's commentary is most likely based on an earlier Syriac version which is clearly later than the *Diatessaron* but there are some features in Origen's story which support the assumption that there was an even earlier Greek version of the story that was connected to Justin's harmony. Thus, the above connections to the Diatessaronic composition do not mean that *Thomas* must depend on the *Diatessaron* itself, but instead they suggest a link on the pre-Diatessaronic level (cf. Appendix 3)

5.2.7. *Jewish-Christian Gospel Fragments and the* Gospel of Thomas: *A Summary of Literary Relationships*

The *Gospel of Thomas* and the Jewish-Christian gospel fragments have one non-canonical saying in common. The wording of the Jewish-Christian version of this saying is closer to *Thomas*' Greek logion. The

---

[113] For *Thomas*' relation to Jewish religious practices, see Marjanen 1998a, 163–182. Marjanen convincingly argues that *Thomas*' negative attitude towards Jewish practices reflects the position of the author in an ongoing debate about Thomasine Christians' relation to Judaism (pp. 180–182).

paleographical dating of the Greek fragments (between 200 and 250 CE)[114] and the date of Clement's quotation (202/215 CE) cohere, showing that the similarities already existed in the beginning of the third century.

Logion 99 and a quotation from the *Gospel of the Ebionites* share three variant readings and two of them can also be found in *2 Clement* (9:11). Notably, the author of *2 Clement* has received the variants as part of a tradition that had harmonized canonical Matthew and Luke. Assuming that *2 Clem.* was written between 100–150 CE, it is evident that, at least in this case, the common denominator of the *Gospel of Thomas* and the *Gospel of the Ebionites* is independent of the *Diatessaron*. No Diatessaronic witnesses for the variants have been found.

Logion 39 and the manuscript 1424 (in Matt 10:16) indicate that both The *Gospel of Thomas* and a Jewish-Christian gospel had a parallel to Matt 10:16. Their wording is different but the beginning of *Thomas*' logion harmonizes canonical Matthew and Luke/Q. Logion 39 also agrees with some expressions in *Ps-Clem. Rec.* 1.54.6–7 that are not attested in the synoptic gospels or in the Diatessaronic tradition. It is highly likely these were derived from the *Gospel of the Ebionites* or its source. In addition, there are some connections to Diatessaronic traditions.

Logion 72 (with 63) shares two stylistic features with the Rich Man's Question in Origen's *Commentary on Matthew*. This stylistic similarity is easiest to explain by assuming that both depend on the same harmonistic tradition which is somehow related to the *Diatessaron*. The cluster of three stories about rich men already existed in the pre-Diatessaronic tradition.

Some more general conclusions can be drawn. First, the three cases for which there is synoptic parallel material available show a close connection of both *Thomas* and Jewish-Christian fragments to a harmonizing gospel tradition. Second, although *Thomas* and the Jewish-Christian fragments are generally known for their connections to Diatessaronic readings, the harmonizing features that they share in the analyzed passages have only indirect connections to the *Diatessaron*. Their connections to *2 Clement* and Justin also indicate that the common readings are probably pre-Diatessaronic. Therefore, Drijvers' suggestion, that the *Gospel of Thomas* and the *Gospel of the Ebionites* are dependent on the *Diatessaron*, is problematic.[115] It is also clear that Quispel's hypothesis

---

[114] Attridge 1989, 96–98.
[115] The same applies to N. Perrin's theses. According to Perrin, the catchword connec-

concerning a pre-synoptic Jewish-Christian gospel behind the *Gospel of Thomas* and the *Diatessaron* does not find any support in the above observations.

However, it is theoretically possible that the harmonizing features shared by *Thomas* and the Jewish-Christian fragments were in fact derived from a *harmonizing* Jewish-Christian gospel. As a matter of fact, if one is to draw conclusions only on the basis of the fragments analyzed in this chapter, Ockham's razor would cut through all the hypotheses which speculate about an unknown harmony behind *Thomas* and the Jewish-Christian fragments because it is quite possible that *Thomas*' logia 39, 99 and 72 derived their harmonizing readings from the same gospel(s) from which the Jewish-Christian fragments come. Nevertheless, the number of passages common to the *Gospel of Thomas* and the Jewish-Christian fragments is too small to allow any firm conclusions from this perspective and analyses in other chapters of this volume have shown that the *Gospel of the Ebionites* and the *Gospel of the Hebrews* were two different compositions, although they both were harmonizing pre-Diatessaronic gospel traditions. It is also possible to hypothesize about "floating" harmonistic collections available to Thomasine Christians and Jewish Christians. It has to be noted that this explanation also works better if *Thomas* and the Jewish-Christian fragments are placed in the same cultural and geographical setting, as will be discussed in the following section.

5.2.8. *Jesus As Wisdom Incarnate and the Spirit As Jesus' Mother*

In the course of the above discussion, a hypothesis has been developed that the *Gospel of Thomas* and the Jewish-Christian gospel fragments have used the same harmonizing gospel traditions. Alongside the similarities, a significant number of disagreements were also recorded. This

---

tions he finds in his Syriac retroversion of the *Gospel of Thomas* indicate that the *Gospel of Thomas* must have been written in Syriac. Because the *Diatessaron* was the first gospel record in Syriac, it must have been among *Thomas*' sources. Perrin also finds support for his thesis in the fact that at some points, *Thomas*' logia follow the order of Diatessaronic tradition (See Perrin 2002, 183–188). Although the study includes several valuable observations about *Thomas*' connections to Syriac (or Semitic) gospel traditions, I do not find Perrin's arguments for Syriac as the original language of *Thomas* convincing, mainly because the definition of the catchword connection is too broad—Perrin accepts semantic, phonological and even etymological (!) associations as catchword connections (p. 50). The observations about the Diatessaronic order of some of the logia of *Thomas* are more promising but in the light of the present analysis, I would suggest that the same order is derived from a common, pre-Diatessaronic tradition.

shows that Thomasine Christians and Jewish Christians had made use of the products of the same scribal culture but they had also freely reinterpreted their common stock material. In the following section, attention will be turned to possible contacts on the ideological level. If both trajectories deal with similar theological topics—whether agreeing or disagreeing with each other—this shows that the writings in question also shared an ideological milieu and were probably created by two distinct communities living in the same cultural context.

The *Gospel of Thomas* takes a critical stance towards Jewish practices and Jews and so it must also have done with the Jewish Christians who were using the Jewish-Christian gospels because these "heretics" were known precisely for adhering to Jewish practices. Therefore, it is to be expected that there are opposing views, and, as far there is agreement, it is likely to be found in the marginal ideas rather than in the central ideas of these trajectories.

Jesus As a Ruler and Wisdom's Rest

Thomas' logion 2 (its P.Oxy. version in particular, see above) should be understood as an exhortation to a seeker of Wisdom to continue seeking until he/she finds rest. The description of Jesus' baptism in a fragment preserved by Jerome seems to illustrate the same objectives from the viewpoint of Wisdom which has finally found rest in Jesus:

> But according to the Gospel that was written in Hebrew language and read by the Nazoreans: "The whole fountain of the Holy Spirit came upon him." ... Further in the gospel ...: "It happened then when the Lord ascended from the water, that the whole fountain of the Holy Spirit descended and rested upon him and said to him: My son, I expected you among all the prophets that you should come and that I should rest upon you. For you are my rest, you are my first-born son, who shall reign in eternity."
> (Jerome, *Comm. Isa.* 11.1–3; N2GH: the *Gospel of the Hebrews*).

Notably, the description of the baptism characterizes Jesus both as "rest" and as a "ruler." Thus, the passage depicts Jesus as a person in whom the ideal state of every seeker of Wisdom—as described in logion 2 and its parallels—has already been realized.

There is no description of baptism in the *Gospel of Thomas* but there is a logion where Jesus—obviously speaking as personified Wisdom—promises rest to his followers:

> Jesus said, "Come unto me, for my yoke is easy and my lordship is mild and you find repose for yourselves." (*Gos. Thom.* 90).

The synoptic parallel for this saying is in Matt 11:28–30 (Matthew's special tradition). On the whole, Matt 11:25–30 is the section within the synoptic gospels where Jesus most clearly speaks as personified Wisdom. Although it remains open whether Matt 11:28–30, paralleled in *Gos. Thom.* 90, was in a Jewish-Christian gospel,[116] it is clear that the tenor of *Thomas*' logia 2 and 90 accords well with the surviving fragment about Jesus' baptism in the *Gospel of the Hebrews*.[117]

The Spirit—The Mother of Jesus and Her Relation to Men
In contrast to synoptic accounts, where a voice is heard "from heaven(s)" (Mark 1:11; Matt 3:17; Luke 3:22), in the fragment about Jesus' baptism, the Holy Spirit claims to have given birth to Jesus. This accords with another fragment—usually ascribed to the same gospel—which explicitly describes the Holy Spirit as Jesus' mother.

> A moment ago my Mother the Holy Spirit, took me by one of my hairs and brought me to the great hill, the Tabor.
> (Origen, *Comm. Jo.* 2.12; N2GH: the *Gospel of the Hebrews*).

It is often noted that the idea of the Spirit as mother seems to presuppose a Semitic original where the gender of the word would have been correct, feminine.[118] It was also noted above that the Holy Spirit is often characterized as "mother" in the *Acts of Thomas* (c. 7, c. 27, c. 39, c. 50) which is usually regarded as a product of the same Syrian sphere of tradition as the *Gospel of Thomas*. *Thomas* does not explicitly refer to the Spirit as mother but it makes a distinction between Jesus' earthly mother and his true one:[119]

---

[116] A marginal reading in Matt 11:25 ("To Ioudaikon;" Codex Novi Testamenti 1424, ad. Matth. 11:25) indicates that at least the preceding verses, Matt 11:25–27, were also in a "Jewish" gospel. However, it is impossible to be sure whether this "Jewish" gospel was the *Gospel of the Ebionites*, the *Gospel of the Hebrews*, or some other gospel that the scribes regarded "Jewish" enough (cf. the discussion in Chapter 3.1 and 5.2.7). Nevertheless, given the strong influence of Wisdom traditions on the *Gospel of the Hebrews* and the fact that *Gospel of the Hebrews* used synoptic traditions, I would be surprised if Matt 11:25–27/Luke 10:21–22 and Matt 11:28–30 had not found their way into the *Gospel of the Hebrews*.

[117] In contrast to the 3GH which assumes that the Jewish variant readings were all derived from the "Gospel of the Nazarenes."

[118] This was already noticed by Jerome in one of the places where he quoted this saying (*Comm. Isa.* 40.9–11).

[119] In *Pelag.* 3.2. (written in 415 CE, five years after the *Commentary on Isaiah*), Jerome quotes a passage where Jesus' mother and brothers ask him to be baptized by John. The Three Gospel Hypothesis ascribes this passage to the "Gospel of the Nazarenes." However, the argument of the hypothesis is circular and there is no compelling reason to assume

228 CHAPTER FIVE

⟨Jesus said⟩ "Whoever does not hate his [father] and his mother as I do cannot become a [disciple] to me. And whoever does [not] love his [father and] his mother as I do cannot become a [disciple to] me. For my mother [...], but [my] true [mother] gave me life." (Gos. Thom. 101).

The beginning of logion 101 is verbatim that of logion 55. These two logia form one of the doublets which some scholars have used as a basis for trying reconstruct *Thomas'* sources.[120] Quispel, for instance, originally argued, on the basis of the doublets, that the *Gospel of Thomas* must be based on two written sources: The *Gospel of the Hebrews* and an encratite *Gospel of the Egyptians*.[121] However, other scholars have instead taken the doublets as evidence of different layers in the *Gospel of Thomas*.[122] Jon Ma. Asgeirsson, for instance, has identified five real doublets in *Thomas* of which four have their second, more elaborated part towards the end of the gospel.[123] Thus, the doublets reveal more about the development of traditions within the Thomasine community than about the sources used for the gospel. If this is correct, then the reference to the "true mother" would have been added to the saying at a secondary stage of interpretation because it is missing in logion 55.[124] If the "true mother" can be identified with the Holy Spirit,[125] as in the Jewish-Christian fragments and in the *Acts of Thomas*, logion 101 would indicate the beginnings of the development of a Spirit theology which is more clearly observable in the *Acts of Thomas*. It is interesting to note that the part that is common to logia 101 and 55 seems to harmonize Matthean and Lukan/Q expressions[126]—a phenomenon that was also observed in the above analyzed passages. Thus, we have in logia 101

---

that the quotation in *Pelag.* would not be from the same gospel as that in the *Commentary on Isaiah*.

[120] For an overview of the role of the doublets in reconstructing Thomas' sources and layers, see Asgeirsson 1997, 59–65.

[121] Quispel 1967, 93–96.

[122] For a summary and assessment of recent theories about Thomas' redactional layers, see Uro 2003.

[123] Asgeirsson 1997, 75. Asgeirsson's doublets are in logia 21b/103; 22c/106; 55/101; 56/80; 87/112.

[124] Irrespective of their overall theories, scholars usually ascribe logion 101 to a later layer in *Thomas*. Thus, Arnal 1995, 479, n. 32: (secondary Gnostic stratum). Asgeirsson 1997, 75, 77 (a chria elaboration). DeConick 2002, 191–194 (secondary encratite saying).

[125] Thus, for instance, Meyer 1992, 104–105 n. 101. W.E. Arnal assumes that the "true mother" refers to Sophia. See Arnal 1995, 478 n. 18.

[126] The expression "worthy of me" in logion 55 is typical of Matthew (Matt 10:37). See, for instance, Luz 1990, 134. Otherwise *Thomas* is closer to the Lukan/Q version. Thus, Uro 2003.

and 55 two Thomasine applications of the same harmonizing saying. That fits with the hypothesis according to which harmonizing gospel traditions would have been further developed in Thomas' scriptural-oral culture.

Be that as may, it is clear that the *Gospel of Thomas* does not (yet?) explicitly identify the "true mother" with the Spirit as do the Jewish-Christian gospel fragments. In the *Gospel of Thomas*, the "living father" overshadows the role of the "true mother" (see *Gos. Thom.* 3, 37, 50). She is referred to in logion 101 but the theme is not developed further in other logia. This is probably connected to the fact that women appear in a negative light in the *Gospel of Thomas*; they can be saved only through becoming male. In logion 114, Jesus promises to lead Mary "in order to make her male so that she too may become a 'living spirit' resembling you males."[127] Furthermore, in the Coptic version of the *Gospel of Thomas*, the Greek word τὸ πνεῦμα gets a masculine article (as do the Greek neuter words in general). Thus, in logion 44, where the blasphemy against the Holy Spirit is declared unforgivable, at least the Coptic editor/author probably had in mind the male "living spirit" of the "living father," which made its home "in this poverty" (29, 3) and which one has to find within oneself in order to enter the kingdom of heaven. The saying that clearly connects the "living spirit" with male disciples is the last one in the collection. This, too, may indicate that the problem of female spirits—heavenly and earthly—started to occupy *Thomas*' transmitters only during the composition of the final layers of the gospel.[128]

In any case, the Spirit that is given to men (Jewish-Christian fragments) or is to be found within men (*Thomas*) is something that must not be offended (logion 44; Jerome, *Comm. Ezech.* 18,5–9):

> Jesus said, "Whoever blasphemes against the father will be forgiven, and whoever blasphemes against the son will be forgiven, but whoever blasphemes against the holy spirit will not be forgiven either on earth or in heaven." (*Gos. Thom.* 47).

---

[127] Marjanen argues that logion 114 does not exclusively refer to the return to prelapsarian androgynous state (thus A.D. DeConick) or to a movement from physical and earthly to heavenly and spiritual (thus M. Meyer) but also implies a devaluation of the feminine. See Marjanen 1998b, 99–104, in contrast to DeConick 1996, 18, and Meyer 1985, 567.

[128] Marjanen 1998b, 103, argues—following S.L. Davies—that logion 114 was added to the gospel relatively late in the second century. He points to connections that logion 114 has to third century apocryphal acts and late second century Valentinian and Nasseene texts.

> Jesus said to them, "If you fast you will give rise to sin for yourselves, and if you pray, you will be condemned; and if you give alms, you will do harm to your spirits ..." (Gos. Thom. 14).
>
> Jesus said, "If the flesh came into being because of spirit it is a wonder, but if spirit came into being because of the body it is a wonder of wonders. Indeed, I am amazed how this great wealth has made its home in this poverty." (Gos. Thom. 29).
>
> "And in the Gospel which is according to the Hebrews which the Nazarenes are accustomed to read, among the worst crimes is set he who has distressed the spirit of his brother."
> (Jerome, *Comm. Ezech*.18,5–9; N2GH: the *Gospel of the Hebrews*).
>
> And in the same volume: "If your brother, he said, sinned to you with a word and makes amends to you, accept him seven times a day. Simon, his disciple said to him: Seven times a day? The Lord answered and said to him: And I say to you until seventy times seven. For even among the prophets after they were anointed with the Holy Spirit there was found a word of sin." (Jerome, *Pelag*. 3.2; N2GH: the *Gospel of the Hebrews*).[129]

Although both *Thomas* and the Jewish-Christian fragments contain admonitions not to harm the spirit, their understanding of the origin of the spirit is different. The Jewish-Christian fragments presuppose an endowment of the Holy Spirit during baptism or anointing while in *Thomas*, the spirit is used as a term to describe that part in men which has its origins above, in the light of the living father (*Gos. Thom.* 50), and which one has to find within oneself in order to enter the kingdom of heaven.[130]

Thomas and the Jewish-Christian fragments both use topics of traditional Jewish Wisdom theology in their description of Jesus (logion 90, Jesus' baptism) and his message to the "seekers of Wisdom" (logion 2 parr.). They also share the idea about the spirit living in men although they understand differently its origin and "gender." The idea about the Holy Spirit as Jesus' mother—assuming it can be seen in logion 101—is marginal in Thomas and possibly attested only in its later layers, but more clearly stated in the *Acts of Thomas*. Interestingly, the *Acts of Thomas* also seems to accept the traditional forms of Jewish piety: fasting, prayer and

---

[129] The 3GH attributes this to the "Gospel of the Nazarenes."
[130] Some sayings also presuppose a distinction between "flesh" (or "body") and "soul." (*Gos. Thom.* 87, 112). Whether this indicates a knowledge of the "classic" Gnostic tripartite anthropology spirit-soul-flesh or just shows that, in Thomas' terminology "soul" and "spirit" have overlapping meanings, must be left open in this connection.

almsgiving, which are explicitly rejected in the *Gospel of Thomas*. Thus, in some respects the Jewish-Christian fragments are ideologically closer to later Thomasine writings than to the *Gospel of Thomas* itself.

5.2.9. Conclusion: Common Roots in Harmonized Synoptic Tradition

The observations about the literary and ideological connections between *Thomas* and the Jewish-Christian fragments are compatible with the hypothesis that *Thomas* and the Jewish-Christian fragments were composed in the same Syro-Palestinian milieu but, due to the writers' different ideological orientation, they cultivated different parts of their common scriptural tradition. If the reconstruction of the Diatessaronic sequence of three rich men, of which *Thomas* used the first one and the *Gospel of the Hebrews* the second one, is on the right track then it is a prime example of the "pick and choose" that was going on: *Thomas* further developed the discussion about the "divider" that was closely connected to its ideology and used the Rich Fool as one example in its own criticism of the "businessmen." The framers of the *Gospel of Thomas* had no interest in the Jewish story about a rich man but that story inspired the editors of a Jewish-Christian gospel who used it in their own inner-Jewish polemics against the rich who did not show mercy to their Jewish compatriots, "sons of Abraham."

The material analyzed in this chapter is too restricted to allow any firm conclusions about *Thomas*' relation to the *Diatessaron*, but it suggests that it might be profitable to look for the answer in harmonizing traditions that preceded the *Diatessaron* rather than trying to show that *Thomas* depended directly on the *Diatessaron* or vice versa. A hypothesis that suggests pre-Diatessaronic harmonizing gospel traditions to be the source of sayings that were further developed in a context where "scribal and oral cultures were intertwined"[131] would provide a fruitful starting point for future discussion about *Thomas*' origins.

Although it is often presented in defense of *Thomas*' independence that there is no editorial coherence in the way in which snippets of synoptic expressions from different gospels and from different parts of the same gospel are found together in *Thomas*,[132] the same phenomenon is

---

[131] Thus Uro 2003 who provides a useful summary and assessment of the discussion about the role of oral tradition in the formation of the *Gospel of Thomas*.

[132] In the case of *Gos. Thom.* 36 Patterson (1993, 36) argues that "If Thomas were

observable in harmonizing collections of Jesus sayings. This is clearly demonstrated in several studies.[133] Harmonizing collections focused on certain topics rather than on following the narrative setting of the synoptic gospels or on a coherent repetition of the style and favorite expressions of individual synoptic editors. Therefore, their impact on gospel traditions cannot be traced with conventional redaction-critical tools. For the study of the *Gospel of Thomas*, this means that if the hypothesis of the influence of harmonistic tradition on *Thomas* is taken seriously—and many observations suggest that this is what should be done—then the discussion about *Thomas*' dependence should make more room for comparison with harmonizing collections and less room for assessing *Thomas* merely on the basis of what is known about the work of the editors of the synoptic gospels.

intentionally borrowing this *topos* ["scribes and pharisees"] from Matthew one would expect to see it incorporated into Thomas' text more frequently."

[133] See, Bellinzoni 1967, 140–142; Koester 1957, 109–111; Kline 1975, 81–84. Kline makes a helpful distinction (p. 13) between "harmonized readings" (from different gospels) and "conflated readings" (from different parts of the same gospel).

CHAPTER SIX

CONCLUSION: TOWARDS THE
HISTORY OF EARLY JEWISH CHRISTIANITY

6.1. THE EBIONITES AND THE NAZARENES

Historians are always faced with the challenge of bridging the gap between present and ancient realities. This cannot be reasonably accomplished without using concepts that are—at least provisionally—understandable to modern readers. In this regard, the concept of Jewish Christianity fares relatively well since many people today have some sort of idea what "Judaism" and "Christianity" are about and what the "mixture" of these categories might involve. Things become problematic only if these kinds of provisional ideas—whether of a scholarly nature or common sense—are not adjusted and refined according to the object of study.

In the this book, the category of Jewish Christianity is qualified by drawing attention to the *indicators of Jewish Christianity*. The discussion in the second main chapter of this volume revealed a variety of Jewish Christianities, of which the following ones played key roles.

The Jewish Christianity of *Irenaeus' Ebionites* involved obedience to Jewish law (including circumcision), anti-Paulinism, rejection of Jesus' virgin birth, reverence for Jerusalem (direction of prayer), use of Matthew's Gospel, Eucharist with water, and possibly the idea that Christ/Spirit entered Jesus at his baptism. Irenaeus' Ebionites are not easy to locate because Irenaeus wrote in the West (Lyons) and was unlikely to have had personal contacts with the Ebionites. Although this characterization partly reflects an educated, Western view of the Ebionites at the end of the second century, it has clear connections to what we know about the early Jerusalem community. This justifies the assumption that the Ebionites, as they were known to Irenaeus, were an offshoot of the earliest Jerusalem community and probably closer to its Hebrew faction.

Although Origen's literary production mostly dates from the time he was active in Caesarea, his references to the Ebionites are sparse and the historical value of his discussion of the Ebionites is questionable. This is partly because, for him, the Ebionites were not so much a contemporary sectarian group as an example of a theologically questionable "Jewish" position. He takes the name of the Ebionites to mean their "poor" intellect which is exemplified in their literal understanding of the law. Origen also labels the Quartodeciman timing of Easter as Ebionite. Although this probably characterizes the Ebionites' practice correctly, it is clear that Origen's main point is to criticize his contemporaries who are in danger of falling prey to this "heresy."

Although Origen's description of the Ebionites depends on the work of his predecessors, it is usually thought that his distinction between the two types of Ebionites, the ones that accepted the virgin birth and the ones who denied it, is historically reliable. However, a closer look at Origen's sources and his characterization of these two branches of the Ebionites reveals that Origen has created the picture on the basis of the writings of his predecessors. The distinction can actually be traced back to Irenaeus' description, of which there were two textual variants: the original according to which the Ebionites' Christology was "similar" to Cerinthus (did not believe in the virgin birth) and the corrupted one, according to which it was "not similar" to Cerinthus (believed in the virgin birth).

Eusebius provides some additional information about the geographical location of the Ebionites and their practice of observing both the Sabbath and the Lord's Day. However, he does not seem to have any significant first hand information about the Ebionites.

Some two hundred years after Irenaeus, the Jewish Christianity of *Epiphanius' Ebionites* was characterized by similar basic ideas and practices as Irenaeus' Ebionites: obedience to Jewish law, anti-Paulinism, reverence for Jerusalem, Eucharist with water and distinction between Jesus and the Spirit/Christ who entered him at baptism. These similarities suggest a connection between Irenaeus' and Epiphanius' Ebionites. However, the explicit rejection of the temple and its cult, the idea of the True Prophet and the (selective) acceptance of the Pentateuch only, show that Epiphanius' Ebionites were not direct successors of Irenaeus' Ebionites. Because it is not easy to picture a linear development from Irenaeus' Ebionites to Epiphanius' Ebionites and because the Samaritans seem to link Epiphanius' Ebionites with the Hellenists of the early Jerusalem community, I am inclined to suggest that Epiphanius' Ebionites were in fact successors of the Hellenistic "poor" of the early Jerusalem community. The connection to the Jerusalem community would explain the features they shared with Irenaeus' Ebionites (who were closer to the Hebrews of the early Jerusalem community).

The Jewish-Christian profile of the *Elchasaite missionaries* as they were described by Origen and Hippolytus would fit with the assumption that the missionaries were originally "ordinary" Ebionites of the Irenaean and/or the Hellenistic-Samaritan type who had adopted a Jewish apocalyptic book and interpreted its "Great Power" as the Christian Christ. Both types of Ebionites were open to the message of the book because of their interest in water rites and the distinction they made between Christ and Jesus.

The religious profile of *Epiphanius' Nazarenes* was ingeniously developed by Epiphanius himself because he also needed a pure category of "Jewish Christianity" in his *Panarion*. The Ebionites of his day had too many peculiar beliefs and practices to serve as the only example of a "heresy" that tried to combine Judaism with Christianity.

Jerome had probably learned from Epiphanius that Christians who were "too Jewish" can also be called Nazarenes. Nevertheless, the profile of *Jerome's own Nazarenes* remained fuzzy. On the one hand, he used the term interchangeably with the term Ebionites, referring to "Jewish Christians" in general. On the other hand, he had met Syriac Christians who were called "Nazarenes" and had acquired from them two anti-rabbinic collections: explanations of some chapters of Isaiah and a hand-picked collection of anti-rabbinic passages from the Gospel of Matthew. Judging from the basis of these collections, the religious profile of Jerome's Nazarenes includes mainly Christian elements. The Nazarenes had a clear Christian self-understanding and were pro-Pauline. Thus, they differed considerably from both branches of the Ebionites. Since the Nazarenes used Hebrew/Aramaic gospels and their commentaries involved word plays with Hebrew/Aramaic script, it is probable that they were of Jewish pedigree. In the light of their pro-Pauline statements, it seems unlikely that their Jewishness would have gone much beyond that.

6.2. Jewish-Christian Gospels (cf. Appendix 3)

The third main chapter of this book approached the history of early Jewish Christians from the view point of their surviving gospel fragments. It is clear that when the *Gospel of Thomas* was found, the foundations on which the categorizations of the Three Gospel Hypothesis (the 3GH) were built had actually collapsed but it was not realized. The categorizations of the 3GH have been based on a false assumption about pure synoptic and "Gnostic" gospel genres. In the present volume, I have sought more neutral criteria for the reconstruction by placing the fragments in Jerome's biography and using as my key criteria (1) the time when Jerome presented the fragments and (2) the information about the language of the fragments as it is described in their introductions.

The application of these criteria led to the recovery of an anti-rabbinic collection of gospel fragments that Jerome derived from the version of the Gospel of Matthew that was used by the Nazarenes. Thus, just like the "sect" of the Nazarenes turned out to be a product of Epiphanius' "scholarly" imagination, so also the assumption about an independent "Gospel of the Nazarenes" has only reflected the imagination of modern scholars. An examination of the evidence that is transmitted by Eusebius confirmed that the earliest references to the *Gospel of the Hebrews* suggest a Syro-Palestinian milieu, not Egyptian, as the most probable place of origin for the *Gospel of the Hebrews*.

Chapters 4 and 5 presented case studies on two themes. Chapter 4 discussed Jewish-Christian passion traditions and Chapter 5 the relation of some of the fragments to the *Diatessaron* and to the *Gospel of Thomas*. There has been much discussion about the relationships between Jewish-Christian gospels, the *Diatessaron* and the *Gospel of Thomas*. The analyses in Chapters 4 and 5 indicate that the points of contact must be located at the post-synoptic/pre-Diatessaronic stage in the development of Jewish-Christian gospel traditions. In the light of the analyzed passages, none of the three traditions depends directly on the others. Instead, they all show traces of post-synoptic/pre-Diatessaronic harmonizing traditions. This confirms the hypothesis that the *Gospel of the Hebrews* was a post-synoptic composition which has clear connections to harmonizing gospel traditions. In this regard, it is similar to the *Gospel of the Ebionites* which is also clearly a post-synoptic harmonizing gospel.

The fragment from the *Gospel of the Hebrews* analyzed in Chapter 4.2 gives James the Just a role in the passion narrative which corresponds to the high esteem in which he was held. Although James the Just was originally the spokesman of conservative Jewish Christians, his person was later embraced equally by proto-orthodox Christians, Jewish Christians of the *Pseudo-Clementines* as well as Gnostic circles. Therefore, it is also difficult to give only one possible Sitz im Leben for the fragment that Jerome quotes in his *On Illustrious Men*. Although the fragment possibly was in the *Gospel of the Hebrews*, it may also have served the needs of mainstream bishops in their dispute over the correct Easter practice. On the whole, the hypothesis about the *Gospel of the Hebrews* that has been developed in this volume, because it locates both synoptic and strong

Wisdom traditions in the *Gospel of the Hebrews*, might make it more understandable why traditions about James were embraced in so many early Christian circles.

The analysis of the Last Supper in the *Gospel of the Ebionites* revealed notable literary and theological connections to Pseudo-Clementine sources, especially to one of the oldest sections in *Rec.* 1.27–71, and also to Luke's account of the Last Supper in the manuscript D. When these observations are combined with the line of development of the Ebionite movement as sketched in Chapter 2, it is possible to see a cluster of religious ideas and practices shared by the Hellenists of the early Jerusalem community, the *Gospel of the Ebionites* (and *Pseudo-Clementines*) and Epiphanius' Ebionites in Cyprus. One of the constitutive collective memories of this branch of Jewish Christianity is Jesus' and Stephen's criticism of the Temple and its sacrificial cult. The Ebionites' poverty, their non-sacrificial interpretation of Jesus' death and their understanding of Jesus as (the True) prophet also resonates with Q.

However, the comparison between the *Gospel of the Hebrews* (as it is reconstructed in this volume) and Q revealed even more points of contact in their traditions (Chapter 3.4.3). The evidence available does not betray any criticism of the Temple or sacrifices in the *Gospel of the Hebrews* and there is strong emphasis on Wisdom tradition and spirit possession which shows a closer relationship between the *Gospel of the Hebrews* and the genre and central themes of Q than there is between the *Gospel of the Ebionites* and Q.

If the *Gospel of the Ebionites* is to be connected with the Hellenistic-Samaritan branch of the successors of the earliest Jewish-Christians in Jerusalem, could the *Gospel of the Hebrews* represent the Hebrew branch of the Jerusalem community?

Although the lack of Temple criticism makes it easier to link the *Gospel of the Hebrews* with the Hebrews of the early Jerusalem community, there is still the problem of language. Both the *Gospel of the Ebionites* and the *Gospel of the Hebrews* were originally composed in Greek. There is also some time lag between the early Jerusalem community and the *Gospel of the Hebrews* which was composed after the synoptic gospels (which is true of the *Gospel of the Ebionites* as well). Thus, if there is a connection between the *Gospel of the Hebrews* and the early Jerusalem community, it is clear that the *Gospel of the Hebrews* is not exactly the "Gospel of the Hebrews of the early Jerusalem community."

Nevertheless, if we take Irenaeus' Ebionites as an example of a sort of baseline Ebionism from which the Epiphanian Ebionites differed because of their closer affinity with early Hellenistic-Samaritan traditions, it is possible to wonder whether *the Gospel of the Hebrews* would have been acceptable to Irenaeus' Ebionites. There is nothing that would clearly contradict this, and there is also some theological affinity. The account of baptism in the *Gospel of the Hebrews* (see Appendix 1) would fit with the idea that the adoption of Jesus by his mother, the Holy Spirit, happened at baptism. Thus, the gospel would probably have been acceptable to Ebionites of the Irenaean type who did not accept the virgin birth. However, in the baptism account of the *Gospel of the Ebionites*, the idea of adoption and the announcement of sonship are even more pronounced. There is also a minor difference in the Christology of the baptism accounts. Although the *Gospel of the Hebrews* emphasizes the influence of the Spirit, this is more like an anointing where the Spirit rests upon Jesus (see also fragments 7 and 9 in the Appendix) than a clear possession as believed by the Irenaean Ebionites (assuming they agreed with Cerinthus). In the *Gospel of the Ebionites*, the Holy Spirit infiltrates Jesus which is closer to the Christology of Irenaean Ebionites who—just like Cerinthus and the *Pseudo-Clementines*—thought it was Christ who entered Jesus, an ordinary man, in the process of baptism.

In the final analysis, it seems that the religious profile of *the Gospel of the Hebrews* is not exactly the same as the Hebrews of the early Jerusalem church or Irenaeus' baseline Ebionites. However, there are so many common elements that it is natural to see the *Gospel of the Hebrews* as the product of one type of Ebionites, perhaps a post-synoptic manifestation of Jewish Christianity that also lurks in the margins of canonical New Testament writings. As far as it is possible to draw conclusions from the surviving fragments, the closest relatives of the *Gospel of the Hebrews*, within the gospel tradition and in terms of central ideas and themes, are Q and the Gospel of Matthew. Furthermore, if we follow Patrick Hartin and John Kloppenborg, who have argued for the use of Q in the Letter of James,[1] we may have come close to having detected the family of early Christian writings within which the *Gospel of the Hebrews* finds its home. Notably, the *Gospel of the Hebrews* shares with James the critical attitude towards the rich and an appropriation of Wisdom traditions. If

---

[1] Kloppenborg 2008, 98–121; Hartin 1991. Understandably, there has not been any discussion about the relationship between the *Gospel of the Hebrews* and James because of the way in which the *Gospel of the Hebrews* was reconstructed in the 3GH. If the new reconstruction I am proposing here becomes accepted, this is one area which would deserve closer examination.

the composers of the *Gospel of the Hebrews* were some type of Ebionites who opposed Paul, they would probably also have agreed with James' understanding of righteousness, which is totally different from that of Paul.

Nevertheless, even we do see some family resemblance between Q, the Gospel of Matthew, James and the *Gospel of the Hebrews* it is not sure if speak in terms of traditions connected to a history of one specific community (or communities). Since Wisdom traditions are so apparent in the *Gospel of the Hebrews*, the case might actually be the same as with the *Gospel of Thomas* and "Gnosticism." It is not so much a question about clearly definable "religion" or communities as about a philosophy and wisdom that can be cultivated in different but like-minded communities. The results of the last analytical chapter of this volume, where the *Gospel of Thomas* was compared with Jewish-Christian fragments, would fit this kind of overall picture.

As the above discussion shows, it is difficult to find a home for the *Gospel of the Hebrews* (and its branch of Ebionism) in the early heresiological accounts. There are probably two reasons for this. First, the heresiologists were mostly interested in those groups that caused trouble within Christian communities and especially so in the West. This is exemplified in the fact that we do not have any description of the heresy of "Thomasites" in the heresiological accounts. However, had there been a teacher in Rome who had based his/her proclamation mainly on the *Gospel of Thomas*, we would probably have this heresy also listed. The criteria for "heresies" were different in the East and in the West. Tatian, for instance, appeared heretical in the eyes of the Western writers but was fully accepted in the East.[2] In the previous chapters, I have argued that the *Gospel of Thomas* and the *Gospel of the Hebrews* are best understood if placed in the approximately same geographical and literary setting: the Syro-Palestinian geographical area and post-synoptic harmonizing gospel traditions. Thus, it is understandable that there are no "heresies" connected to these gospels although the gospels themselves were known to the church fathers.

The second reason is that the framers of the *Gospel of the Hebrews* were probably living mainly within Jewish communities, first in the Hellenistic diaspora and later also among Syriac speaking Jews. The analysis of the Rich Man's Question in the Latin translation of Origen's *Commentary*

---

[2] Luomanen & Marjanen 2005; Petersen 2005.

on Matthew showed how the synoptic story had been re-judaized in the *Gospel of the Hebrews*. The rewritten story clearly presumes a Jewish group identity and intra Jewish setting for its moral exhortations. The assumption that the "Hebrews" of the *Gospel of the Hebrews* were mostly living as part of Jewish communities also accords with the way in which Eusebius introduces the *Gospel of the Hebrews* in Theophania Syriaca (see Chapter 3.4.1)

It is clear that by the time the *Gospel of the Hebrews* was composed (first half of the second century), heresiological discourse was not yet developed. This can be observed, for instance, in Justin's *Dialogue with Trypho*. Justin approves of the law observant Jewish Christians if they live in peace with other Christians and if they do not demand that gentile Christians be circumcised and keep the Sabbath and other ordinances (*Dial.* 46–47). Justin even allows Jewish Christ believers—whom he counts as part of "your race", i.e., Jews like Trypho—not to accept his proofs of Jesus' divine origin if they admit that he was chosen by God and anointed as Christ (*Dial.* 48).

There is a tendency among scholars to "correct" the text in *Dial.* 48 so that it does not refer to "your race" (Jews) but to "our race" (Christians) because earlier scholarship presumed a split between Jews and Christians and thought that Christ believers must, of course, be living among Christians. During the past decades, this whole paradigm has been proven wrong by Daniel Boyarin and others (see Chapter 1.2). There is no need to correct Justin's text. The Christ believers in *Dial.* 48 were obviously living among other Jews and this was perfectly natural by the first half of the second century, and even later on.

On the whole, the *indicators approach* that has been applied in this volume has revealed a variety of Jewish Christianities. The overall picture emerging from these studies challenges the Baurian idea of two main trajectories. In the second century, when both the *Gospel of the Ebionites* and the *Gospel of the Hebrews* were composed, there were still many different Jewish-Christian groups using both written and oral traditions—the latter also being based to a large extent on secondary orality.

The results also show that scholars should give up attempts to reconstruct a pre-synoptic gospel from information that has survived from the early Jewish-Christian gospels. All the available evidence points to the direction that the *Gospel of the Hebrews*, the *Gospel of the Ebionites* (and the "Gospel of the Nazarenes") were post-synoptic productions. This is not to say that the canonical gospels as we have them would be the most secure lead to the roots of early Christianity. Rather, it seems that the writing of gospels was first the undertaking of the more liberal Hellenistic wing of earliest Christianity because this section was more in need of legitimating its position in relation to Jewish traditions.

Those Christ believers for whom their new faith did not mean a break with their earlier Jewish identity or practices, were not so much in need of these foundation stories. The Hebrew Bible, the Septuagint and some collections of Jesus' teachings were enough for them.[3] However, once the Greek gospels were out, it became apparent that the "Hebrews" and the "Ebionites" should also write gospel stories of their own from the materials available. It is perfectly possible that in this process they included some "original" Jesus traditions from their own stock. If these gospels someday surface from excavations, a hidden cave or an ancient dumping ground, we will have more opportunities to discuss the history of their individual passages. The evidence we have today indicates that these gospels, as full compositions, were clearly post-synoptic.

6.3. Summary and Conclusion

To summarize, in this volume I have sketched six early Jewish-Christian profiles:

1. *Irenaeus' Ebionites* seem to have been related to the Hebrew (non-Samaritan) section of the early Jerusalem community and were openly anti-Pauline. The composers of the *Gospel of the Hebrews* were related to this type of Ebionism (see below).
2. *Elchasaites* combined the basic notions of Irenaeus' Ebionites (the base line) with the religious practices and eschatological ideas adopted from the *Book of Elchasai*.
3. *Epiphanius' Ebionites/Hellenistic-Samaritan Ebionites* probably were an offspring of the missionary activity of the Hellenists of the early Jerusalem community among the Samaritans. Later on, they also adopted some Elchasaite ideas. Epiphanius found the *Gospel of the Ebionites* among them.
4. *Epiphanius' Nazarenes* (and to some extent also Jerome's Nazarenes) were an imaginary, stereotyped picture of a "pure" Jewish-Christian heresy that Epiphanius had (re)constructed on the basis of Acts and Eusebius' *Ecclesiastical History*, for the purpose of his own

---

[3] Cf. Kloppenborg's analysis of the (possible) use of Q in *1 Clement, Didache* and James. Kloppenborg 2008, 98–106, 111–121.

heresiological discourse in the *Panarion*. The "heresy" of the Nazarenes (as described by Epiphanius) never existed. Consequently, there was no heretical "Gospel of the Nazarenes."
5. The real, *historical Nazarenes* were Syriac-speaking Christians with Jewish background. There must have been influential Jewish converts in this group because their literature shows the mastery of Semitic languages and knowledge of early rabbinical traditions. However, these Nazarenes clearly had a Christian identity and they were openly pro-Pauline.
6. *The Hebrews* of the *Gospel of the Hebrews* were Christ believing Jews living among Greek and Syriac-speaking diaspora communities in the Syro-Palestinian area. They were related to the Irenaean type of Ebionites although there were differences in their Christological speculations. They are, in many respects, the opposite of the historical Nazarenes. The Nazarenes were Jewish converts who had adopted a clear Christian identity and belonged to a Christian religious community but were engaged in fierce polemics with the representatives of their ancestral religious traditions. The Hebrews of the *Gospel of the Hebrews* had become Christ believers but had not abandoned their Jewish identity or religious practice and were therefore able to continue living within Jewish religious communities.

The fact there are no manuscripts of early Jewish-Christian gospels currently available tells more about the preferences and power policy of the developing orthodoxy than about the relative importance of these gospels among Christ followers during the first centuries CE As a matter of fact, as Jörg Frey notes, there are more quotations from these gospels and references to their contents in the writings of the fathers than from any other apocryphal gospels.[4] The character of the references also shows that the fathers did not simply disagree with some of the contents of these gospels but even valued them, and hoped to find in them information about some early Hebrew followers of Jesus.

Because of the scantiness of the evidence, discussion about Jewish-Christian gospel traditions is bound to remain hypothetical. Although it is impossible to draw absolutely certain conclusions, I hope I have succeeded in pointing out some interesting variations in the traditions of early Jewish-Christian gospels, some of their characteristic features not

---

[4] Thus, Frey 2010.

known elsewhere, but also some examples of their close relationship with the canonical gospels. Obviously, there was not just one Jewish-Christian interpretation of Jesus, his teaching and his story, just like there was not just one Jewish Christianity but many, of which we would know even more if we had the entirety of the Jewish-Christian gospels available.

ABBREVIATIONS AND APPENDICES

Abbreviations

For ancient sources I have used the abbreviations as provided in Alexander, Patrick H. et al. (ed.), 1999, *The SBL Handbook of Style: For Ancient Near Eastern, Biblical, and Early Christian Studies*. (Peabody, Mass.: Hendrickson). In addition, I have used the following abbreviations:

3GH	Three Gospel Hypothesis (see Introduction)
ANF	Ante-Nicene Fathers
BDB	Brown, et al. 1979
DA	*Didascalia Apostolorum*
GEb	the *Gospel of the Ebionites*
GHeb	the *Gospel of the Hebrews*
GNaz	the "Gospel of the Nazarenes" (for quotation marks, see Introduction)
GThom	the *Gospel of Thomas*
LkS	Luke's special tradition
MtS	Matthew's special tradition
N2GH	New Two Gospel Hypothesis (see Introduction)
NIV	New International Version
NRSV	New Revised Standard Version
RSV	Revised Standard Version

Appendix 1: The New Two Gospel Hypothesis

Translations (if not indicated otherwise) according to A.F.J. Klijn, *Jewish-Christian Gospel Tradition*. Leiden: Brill, 1992.

Gospel of the Hebrews

1. The baptism of Jesus

1a. [… but according to the Gospel which was written in the Hebrew language and read by the Nazarenes:]

The whole fountain of the Holy Spirit came upon him.

[Further in the Gospel which we mentioned above we find that the following is written:]

It happened when the Lord ascended from the water, that the whole fountain of the Holy Spirit descended and rested upon him and said to him: My son, I expected you among all the prophets that you should come and that I should rest upon you. For you are my rest, you are my first-born son who shall reign in eternity. (Jerome, *Comm. Isa.* 11.1–3).

1.b. [In the Gospel according to the Hebrews which was written in the Chaldaic and Syriac language but with Hebrew letters, and is used up to the present day by the Nazarenes, I mean that according to the Apostles, or, as many maintain, according to Matthew, which Gospel is also available in the Library of Caesarea, the story runs:]

See, the mother of the Lord and his brothers said him: John the Baptist baptizes for the remission of the sins, let us go to be baptized by him. He said to them, however: What sin have I committed that I should go and be baptized by him? Unless perhaps something which I said is ignorance. (Jerome, *Pelag.* 3.2; trans. Klijn 1992, modified).

2. The Holy Spirit takes Jesus to Tabor

[If somebody accepts the Gospel according to the Hebrews, where the Saviour himself says:]

A moment ago my Mother, the Holy Spirit, took me by one of my hairs and brought me to the great hill, the Tabor. (Origen, *Comm. Jo.* 2.12, *Hom. Jer.* 15.4; Jerome, *Comm. Mich.* 7.5–7, *Comm. Isa.* 40.9–11, *Comm. Ezech.* 16.13).

3. Matthias and Levi are the same

It seems that Matthew is named Levi in the Gospel according to Luke. But they are not the same, but Matthias who replaced Judas and Levi are the same with a double name. This appears from the Gospel according to the Hebrews. (Didymus, *Comm. Ps.* ed. M. Groenewald p. 184,9–10).

4. Jesus chooses the good ones

[Then he taught about the divisions of the souls which will come about in the houses, as we have found somewhere in the Gospel which exists among the Jews in the Hebrew language, in which it is said:]

I choose for myself the good ones, the good ones whom my Father in heaven has given to me. (Eusebius, *Theoph. Syr.* 4.12).

5. Attaining rest

[For similar to these the following is possible:]

He who seeks will not cease until he finds and having found he will marvel and having marvelled he will become king and having become king, he will rest. (Clement of Alexandria, Strom. V XIV 96.3; Strom. II IX 45.5; cf. Gos. Thom. 2).

6. Mason's prayer

[In the Gospel which the Nazarenes and the Ebionites use which we translated recently from Hebrew to Greek and which is called the authentic text of Matthew by a good many, it is written that the man with the withered hand is a mason, praying for help with words of this kind:]

I was a mason earning my living with my hands, I pray for you, Jesus, to restore my health lest I must beg shamefully for my food. (Jerome, Comm. Matt. 12.13)

7. Distressing one's brother

And in the Gospel which is according to the Hebrews which the Nazarenes are accustomed to read, among the worst crimes is set he who has distressed the spirit of his brother. (Jerome, Comm. Ezech. 18.5–9).

8. How to look at one's brother

[... as we read in the Hebrew Gospel that the Lord said to the disciples:]

And never rejoice, he said, unless when you look at your brother in love. (Jerome, Comm. Eph. 5.4).

9. Woman accused of many sins

Version A, Eusebius

Papias also used evidence from 1 John and from 1 Peter and provides another story of a woman falsely accused before the Lord of many sins, which is contained in the Gospel of the Hebrews. (Eusebius, *Hist. Eccl.* 3.39; trans. Maier 1999).

Version B, Didymus the Blind

We find in certain Gospel. A woman, it says, was condemned by the Jews for a sin and was being sent to be stoned in a place where that was customary to happen. The Saviour, it says, when he saw her and observed that they were ready to stone her said to those who were about to cast stones: He who has not sinned let him take a stone and cast it. If anyone is conscious in himself of not having sinned, let him take a stone and smite her. And no one dared. Since they knew in themselves and perceived that they themselves were guilty in some things, they did not dare to strike her. (Didymus the Blind, *Comm. Eccl.* 4.233,7–13).

Version C, NIV

3 The teachers of the law and the Pharisees brought in a woman caught in adultery. They made her stand before the group 4 and said to Jesus, "Teacher, this woman was caught in the act of adultery. 5 In the Law Moses commanded us to stone such women. Now what do you say?" 6 They were using this question as a trap, in order to have a basis for accusing him. But Jesus bent down and started to write on the ground with his finger. 7 When they kept on questioning him, he straightened up and said to them, "Let any one of you who is without sin be the first to throw a stone at her." 8 Again he stooped down and wrote on the ground. 9 At this, those who heard began to go away one at a time, the older ones first, until only Jesus was left, with the woman still standing there. 10 Jesus straightened up and asked her, "Woman, where are they? Has no one condemned you?" 11 "No one, sir," she said. "Then neither do I condemn you," Jesus declared. "Go now and leave your life of sin."

10. Even anointed prophets sinned

[And in the same volume [In the Gospel according to the Hebrews which was written in the Chaldaic and Syriac language but with Hebrew letters, and is used up to present day by the Nazarenes, I mean that according to the Apostles, or, as many maintain, according to Matthew, which Gospel is also available in the Library of Caesarea]]:

If your brother, he said, sinned to you with a word and makes amends to you, accept him seven times a day. Simon his disciple said him: Seven times a day? The Lord answered and said to him: And I say to you until seventy times seven. For even among the prophets after they were anointed with the Holy Spirit there was found a word of sin. (Jerome, *Pelag.* 3.2; Parallels in Cod. 566 and 899.)

11. The rich man

[It is written in a certain gospel which is called according to the Hebrews (if, however, it pleases somebody to accept it, not as authority but in order to bring to light the question that has been put):]

Another rich man, it says, said to him: "Master what good must I do in order to live?" He said to him: "Man, do the Law and the Prophets." He answered him: "I have done." He said to him: "Go, sell all that you possess and divide it among the poor and come, follow me." But the rich man begun to scratch his head and it did not please him. The Lord said to him: "How can you say: I have done the Law and the Prophets? For it is written in the Law: love your neighbor as yourself. See, many of your brothers, sons of Abraham, are covered with dung, dying from hunger and your house is full of many good things, and nothing at all comes out of it for them." He turned and said to Simon, his disciple that was sitting by him: "Simon, Son of Jonah, it is easier for a camel to go through the eye of a needle than for a rich man to enter the kingdom of heaven." (Origen, *Comm. Matt.* 15.14; trans. PL).

12. The parable of the talents

However, the Gospel which has come to us in Hebrew letters, does not direct its threat against the one who had hidden [the talent] but against the one who lived in extravagance. For he had three slaves, one who spend the fortune of the master with harlots and flute-girls, the second who multiplied his trade and the third who hid his talent. One of the servants was accepted, the second one only rebuked, but the third one sent into prison. I wonder whether the threat in Matthew which, according to the letter was spoken against the one who did nothing, applies no to him but to the first one who was eating and drinking with those who were drunken, by way of resumption. (Eusebius, *Theoph.* ed. Migne pp. 685–688; trans. Klijn 1992, modified). Cf. Matt 25:14–30.

13. Jesus breaks bread for James the Just

[… and also the Gospel which is called according to the Hebrews and which I have recently translated into Greek and Latin of which also Origen often makes use, says after the account of the resurrection of the Lord:]

But the Lord after he had given the linen cloth to the servant of the priest, went to James and appeared to him (for James had sworn that he would not eat bread from the hour in which he drank the cup of the Lord until he had seem him rising again from those who sleep) and again, a little later, it says: Bring the table and bread, said the Lord. And immediately it is added: He brought bread and blessed and brake it and gave it to James the Just and said to him: My brother, eat thy bread for the Son of Man is risen from those who sleep. (Jerome, *Vir. ill.* 2).

The Nazarenes' Anti-Rabbinic Collection

1. In Bethlehem of Judea

And they said to him: In Bethlehem of Judea. Here there is an error on the part of the copyists; for we believe that the evangelist in his first edition wrote, as we read in the original Hebrew: *Juda* and not Judea. (Jerome, *Comm. Matt.* 2.5)

2. Bread for tomorrow.

In the Gospel which is called according to the Hebrews, I found *MAAR* in place of "which is necessary to support life" which means "for tomorrow …" (Jerome, *Comm. Matt.* 6.11; *Tract. Ps.* 135).

3. Zacharia son of Jojada

In the Gospel which the Nazarenes use, we find that there is written son of *Jojada* instead of son of Barachia. (Jerome, *Comm. Matt.* 23.35.)

4. Son of their master

The name of the man is interpreted in the Gospel which is written according to the Hebrews as *son of their master*. (Jerome, *Comm. Matt.* 27.16).

5. The lintel of the temple.

In the Gospel which we have already often mentioned we read that a lintel of an enormous size was broken and split. (Jerome, *Comm. Matt.* 27.51; *Epist.* 120.8).

The Gospel of the Ebionites

1. The beginning of the *Gospel of the Ebionites*

[The beginning of the gospel among them reads:]

It happened in the days of Herod the king of Judea that John came, baptizing with the baptism of conversion in the river Jordan. Of him it is said that he was from the family of Aaron the priest, the son of Zacharias and Elisabeth. And all went out to him. (Epiphanius, *Pan.* 30.13.6; 30.14.3).

2. John's diet

[And:]

It happened that John baptized and the Pharisees went out to him and were baptized and all Jerusalem. And John was dressed in a mantle of camel's hair and a leather belt was round his waist. And his food was, it said, wild honey, of which the taste was that of manna, like cakes in olive oil. (Epiphanius, *Pan.* 30.13.4–5).

3. The Baptism of Jesus

[And after much is said in the Gospel it continues:]

After the people had been baptized Jesus also came and was baptized by John. And when he ascended from the water the heavens opened and he saw the Holy Spirit in the form of a dove descending and entering into him. And a voice from heaven said: "You are my beloved son, in you I am pleased." And next: "Today I have begotten you." And suddenly a great light shone around that place. When John saw it, they say, he said to him: "Who are you, Lord?" And again a voice from came from heaven which said to him: "This is my beloved Son, in whom I am well pleased." After this, it says, John fell down before him and said: "I pray you, Lord, baptize me." But he withstood him and said: "Let it be, it is appropriate that everything is fulfilled this way." (Epiphanius, *Pan.* 30.13.7–8; trans. Klijn 1992, modified).

4. The Savior's true brothers and mother

[Further they deny that he is a man, apparently from the word that the Saviour spoke when he was told:] "*See, your mother and your brothers stand outside.*" "*Who is my mother and who are my brothers?*" *And he* stretched his hand over the disciples and said: *"Those are my brothers and my mother and my sisters who do the will of my Father."* (Epiphanius, *Pan.* 30.14.5).

5. Jesus abolishes sacrifices

[As the writing that they call a gospel has:]

I have come to abolish the sacrifices and if you do not stop sacrificing the wrath will not cease from you. (Epiphanius, *Pan.* 30.16.5; trans. Klijn 1992, modified).

6. Did Jesus eat Passover?

[They, however, destroyed the true order and changed the passage; that is clear to everyone because of the words that belong together, and they made the disciples to say:] *"Where do you wish that we prepare the Passover to eat for you?"*

[And they made him answer:]

"I do not earnestly desired to eat meat with you this Passover." (Epiphanius, *Pan.* 30.22.4).

7. The call of disciples (= Epilogue of the gospel or an introduction to the Ebionite Acts of Apostles?).

[The Gospel which is called with them according to Matthew which is not complete but falsified and distorted, they call it the Hebrew Gospel and in it can be found:]

There was a man called Jesus, about thirty years old, who chose us. And came to Caphernaum, he entered the house of Simon, also called Peter, and opened his mouth and said: When I went by the sea of Tiberias I chose John and James, the sons of Zebedee, and Simon and Andrew and Thaddeus and Simon the Zealot and Judas the Iskariot and you Matthew, who was sitting at the custom-house; I called you and you followed me. I wish you to be twelve apostles for the testimony to Israel. (Epiphanius, *Pan.* 30.13.2–3).

ABBREVIATIONS AND APPENDICES 253

Appendix 2:
Parallel Sayings and Common Harmonizing Readings in Jewish-Christian Gospel Fragments and the *Gospel of Thomas*

Symbols: Crd = common reading, Diat = the *Diatessaron*, Lk = typical of Luke, Mt/Lk = combination of Matthean and Lukan elements, Syn = Synoptic gospels.

Lines connect parallel passages, **dotted lines** the passages that freely use the same tradition

Circles list the common readings in the passages

Example: Pan. 30.14.5 and GThom 99 are parallels that have 1Crd, ≠ Syn, that is, one common reading that is different from the synoptic gospels ("my brothers and mother").

1. *Let Him Who Seeks Continue Seeking*

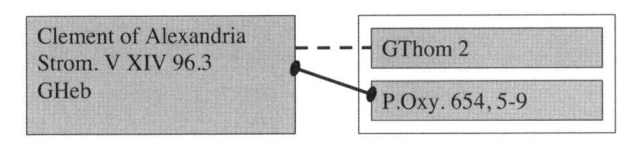

Clement of Alexandria Strom. V XIV 96.3 GHeb	- - -	GThom 2
		P.Oxy. 654, 5-9

2. *Your Brothers and Mother Are Standing Outside*

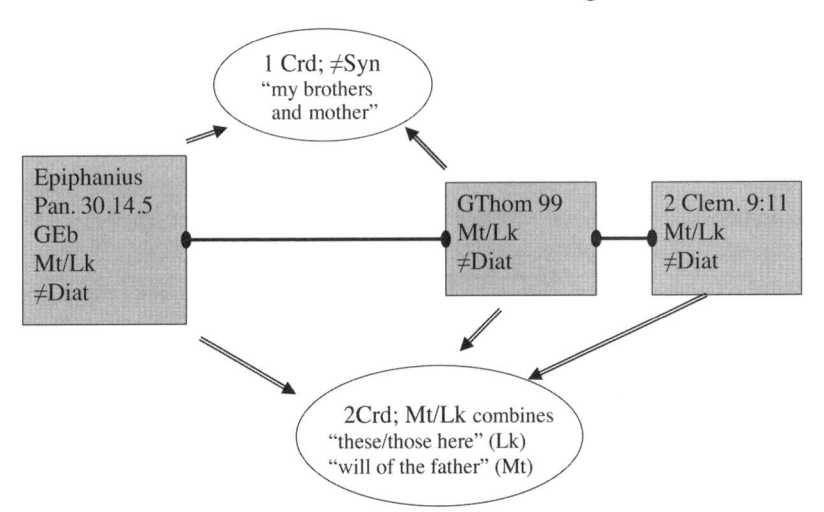

(1 Crd; ≠Syn "my brothers and mother")

| Epiphanius Pan. 30.14.5 GEb Mt/Lk ≠Diat | GThom 99 Mt/Lk ≠Diat | 2 Clem. 9:11 Mt/Lk ≠Diat |

(2Crd; Mt/Lk combines "these/those here" (Lk) "will of the father" (Mt))

3. Wise as Serpents

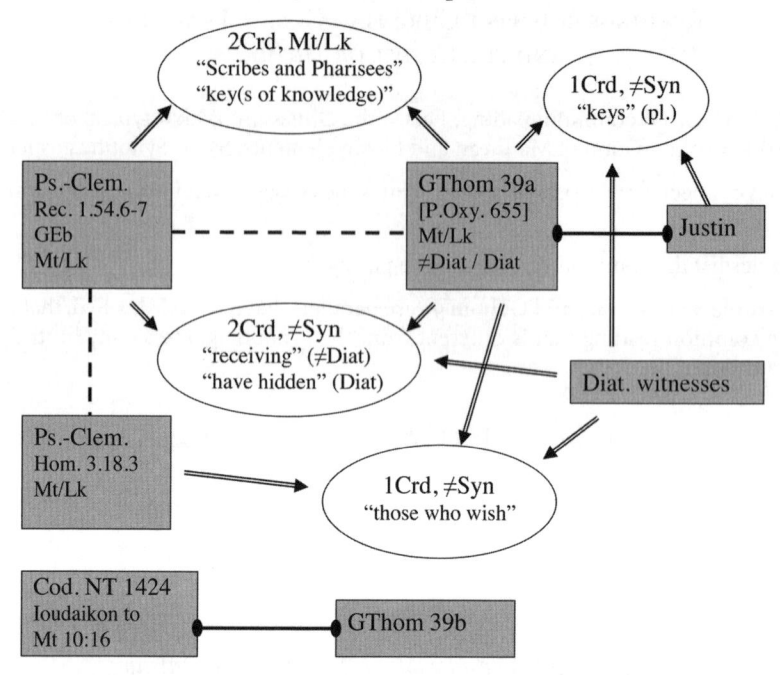

2Crd, Mt/Lk
"Scribes and Pharisees"
"key(s of knowledge)"

1Crd, ≠Syn
"keys" (pl.)

Ps.-Clem.
Rec. 1.54.6-7
GEb
Mt/Lk

GThom 39a
[P.Oxy. 655]
Mt/Lk
≠Diat / Diat

Justin

2Crd, ≠Syn
"receiving" (≠Diat)
"have hidden" (Diat)

Diat. witnesses

Ps.-Clem.
Hom. 3.18.3
Mt/Lk

1Crd, ≠Syn
"those who wish"

Cod. NT 1424
Ioudaikon to
Mt 10:16

GThom 39b

4. "O Man" and "He Turned To"

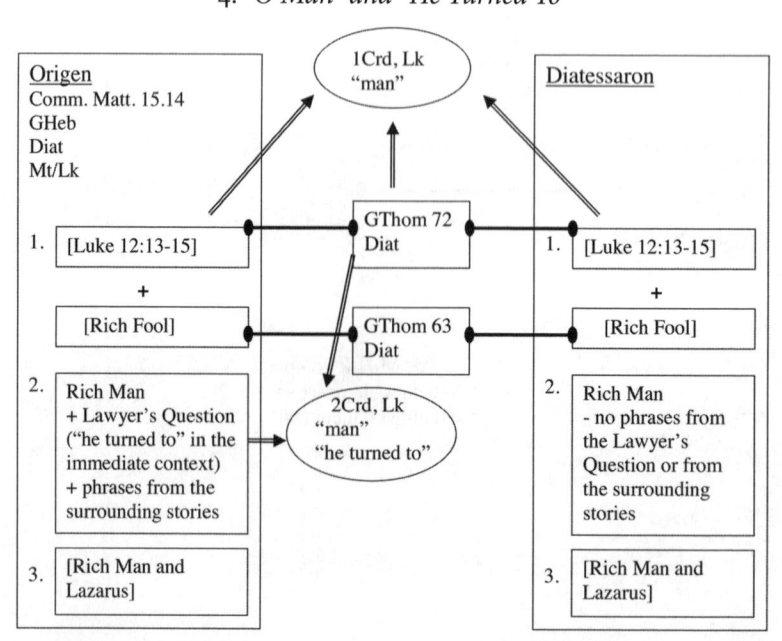

Origen
Comm. Matt. 15.14
GHeb
Diat
Mt/Lk

1Crd, Lk
"man"

Diatessaron

1. [Luke 12:13-15]

GThom 72
Diat

1. [Luke 12:13-15]

+

[Rich Fool]

GThom 63
Diat

+

[Rich Fool]

2. Rich Man
+ Lawyer's Question
("he turned to" in the
immediate context)
+ phrases from the
surrounding stories

2Crd, Lk
"man"
"he turned to"

2. Rich Man
- no phrases from
the Lawyer's
Question or from
the surrounding
stories

3. [Rich Man and Lazarus]

3. [Rich Man and Lazarus]

ABBREVIATIONS AND APPENDICES   255

APPENDIX 3.
DEVELOPMENT AND TESTIMONIES
OF JEWISH-CHRISTIAN GOSPEL TRADITIONS

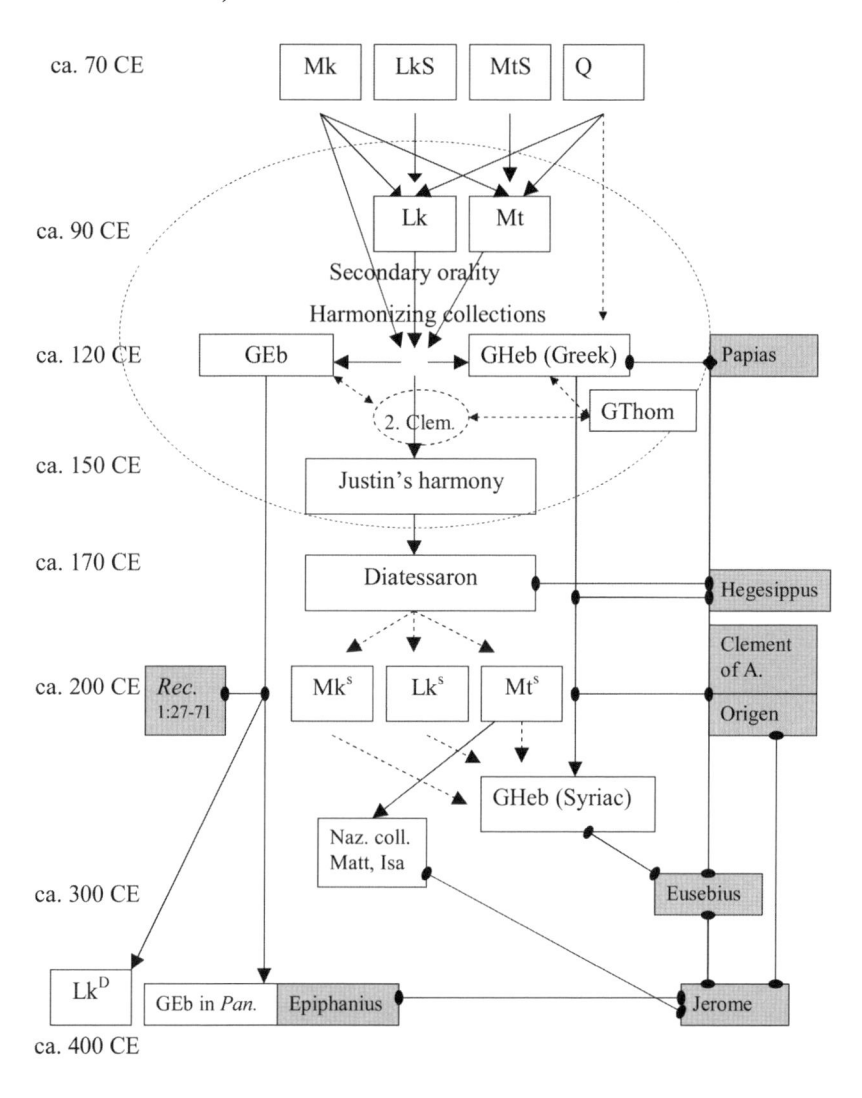

ca. 70 CE — Mk, LkS, MtS, Q

ca. 90 CE — Lk, Mt

Secondary orality
Harmonizing collections

ca. 120 CE — GEb, GHeb (Greek), Papias

2. Clem., GThom

ca. 150 CE — Justin's harmony

ca. 170 CE — Diatessaron, Hegesippus

ca. 200 CE — *Rec.* 1:27-71, Mk^s, Lk^s, Mt^s, Clement of A., Origen

GHeb (Syriac)

Naz. coll. Matt, Isa

ca. 300 CE — Eusebius

Lk^D, GEb in *Pan.*, Epiphanius, Jerome

ca. 400 CE

REFERENCES

Aejmelaeus, Lars
1987 *Die Rezeption der Paulusbriefe in der Miletrede (Apg 20:18–35)*. Annales Academiae Scientiarum Fennicae B232. Helsinki: Academia Scientiarum Fennica.

Aland, Kurt & Barbara Aland
1989 *The Text of the New Testament: An Introduction to the Critical Editions and to the Theory and Practice of Modern Textual Criticism*. Trans. Erroll F. Rhodes. Leiden: Brill.

Arnal, William E.
1995 "The Rhetoric of Marginality: Apocalypticism, Gnosticism, and Sayings Gospels." *Harvard Theological Review* 88, 471–494.

Asgeirsson, Jon Ma.
1997 "Arguments and Audience(s) in the Gospel of Thomas (Part I)." *Society of Biblical Literature Seminar Papers*, 47–85.

Attridge, Harold W.
1989 "Appendix: The Greek Translations." *Nag Hammadi Codex II, 2–7. Together with XIII, 2*, Brit. Lib. Or. 4926(1), and POxy 1, 654, 655: Gospel According to Thomas, Gospel According to Philip, Hypostasis of the Archons, and Indexes*. Ed. Bentley Layton. Nag Hammadi Studies 20. Leiden: Brill, 95–128.

Baarda, Tjitze
1983 *Early Transmission of Words of Jesus: Thomas, Tatian and the Text of the New Testament*. Amsterdam: VU Boekhandel/Uitgeverij.

Barth, Fredrik
1994 "Enduring and Emerging Issues in the Analysis of Ethnicity." *The Anthropology of Ethnicity: Beyond "Ethnic Groups and Boundaries"*. Ed. Hans Vermeulen & Cora Govers. Amsterdam: Het Spinhuis, 11–32.

Bauckham, Richard
2003 "The Origin of the Ebionites." *The Image of the Judaeo-Christians in Ancient Jewish and Christian Literature*. Ed. Peter J. Tomson & Doris Lambers-Petry. Wissenschaftliche Untersuchungen zum Neuen Testament 158. Tübingen: Mohr Siebeck, 162–181.

Baur, Ferdinand C.
1966 (1860) *Das Christentum und die christliche Kirche der drei ersten Jahrhunderte*. Ausgewählte Werke in Einzelausgaben Vol. 3. Hrsg. Klaus Scholder mit einer Einführung von Ulrich Wickert. Stuttgart-Bad Cannstatt: Friedrich Fromann Verlag (Günther Holzboog).

Becker, Adam H. & Annette Yoshiko Reed (ed.)
2007 *The Ways That Never Parted: Jews and Christians in Late Antiquity and Early Middle Ages*. Minneapolis: Fortress Press.

Becker, Ulrich
1963 *Jesus und die Ehebrecherin: Untersuchungen zur Text- und Überlieferungsgeschichte von Joh. 7:73–8:11*. Beihefte zur Zeitschrift für die neutestamentliche Wissenschaft 28. Berlin: Alfred Töpelmann.

Bellinzoni, Arthur J.
1967 *The Sayings of Jesus in the Writings of Justin Martyr*. Novum Testamentum Supplements XVII. Leiden: Brill.

Black, Matthew
1972 "The Syriac Versional Tradition." *Die Alten Übersetzungen des Neuen Testaments, Die Kirchenväterzitate und Lektionare*. Ed. Kurt Aland. Arbeiten zur neutestamentlichen Textforschung 5. Berlin / New York: de Gruyter.

Blanchetière, François
2001 *Enquête sur les racines juives du mouvement chrétien (30–135)*. Initiations. Paris: Cerf.

Bless, Herbert, Klaus Fiedler & Fritz Strack
2004 *Social Cognition: How Individuals Construct Social Reality*. Hove: Psychology Press.

Bovon, François
1996 *Das Evangelium nach Lukas, Lk 9,51–14,35. 2. Evangelisch-katholischer Kommentar zum Neuen Testament III/2*. Zürich / Neukirchen—Vluyn: Benzinger / Neukirchener.

Boyarin, Daniel
1999 *Dying for God: Martyrdom and the Making of Christianity and Judaism*. Stanford: Stanford University Press.
2003 "Semantic Differences; or, 'Judaism'/'Christianity.'" *The Ways that Never Parted: Jews and Christians in Late Antiquity and the Early Middle Ages*. Ed. Adam H. Becker & Annette Yoshiko Reed. Texte und Studien zum antiken Judentum 95. Tübingen: Mohr Siebeck.
2004 *Border Lines: The partition of Judaeo-Christianity*. Philadelphia: The University of Pennsylvania Press.

Brewer, Marilynn B.
1988 "A Dual Process Model of Impression Formation." *Dual Model of Impression Formation: Advances in Social Cognition, Volume I*. Ed. Thomas K. Strull & Robert S. Wyer. Hillside, NJ: Lawrence Erlbaum Associates, 1–36.

Brock, S.P.
1977 "The Limitations of Syriac in Representing Greek." *The Early Versions of the New Testament: Their Origin, Transmission, and Limitations*. Ed. Bruce M. Metzger. Oxford: Clarendon Press, 82–98.

Brockelmann, Carl
1928 *Lexicon Syriacum*. Halle: Niemeyer.

Brown, Raymond E.
1983 "Not Jewish Christianity and Gentile Christianity but Types of Jewish/Gentile Christianity." *Catholic Biblical Quarterly* 45, 74–79.

Brown, Francis, S.R. Driver & Charles A. Briggs
1979 *The New Brown—Driver—Briggs—Gesenius Hebrew English Lexicon. With an Appendix Containing the Biblical Aramaic*. Peabody, Mass.: Hendrickson.

Caird, G.B.
1965 *The Gospel of St Luke*. The Pelican New Testament Commentaries. Harmondsworth: Penquin Books.

Cameron, Ron
1982 *The Other Gospels: Non-Canonical Gospel Texts*. Louisville; London: Westminster John Knox Press.
1984 "The Gospel of the Hebrews." *The Other Bible*. Ed. Willis Barnstone. San Francisco: HarperCollins, 333–335.

Carter, Warren
2007 "Matthew's Gospel: Jewish Christianity, Christian Judaism, or Neither?" *Jewish Christianity Reconsidered: Rethinking Ancient Groups and Texts*. Ed. Matt Jackson-McCabe. Minneapolis: Fortress Press, 155–179.

Cohen, Shaye J.
1999 *The Beginnings of Jewishness: Boundaries, Varieties, Uncertainties*. Berkeley; Los Angeles; London: University of California Press.

Crum, Walter E.
1939 *A Coptic Dictionary*. Oxford: Oxford University Press.

Cullmann, Oscar
1960 "Das Thomasevengelium und die Frage nach dem Alter in der ihm enthaltenen Tradition." *Theologische Literaturzeitung* 85, 321–334.

de Boer, Martinus C.
1998 "The Nazoreans: Living at the Boundary of Judaism and Christianity." *Tolerance and Intolerance in Early Judaism and Christianity*. Ed. Graham N. Stanton & Guy G. Stroumsa. Cambridge: Cambridge University Press, 239–262.

DeConick, April D.
2002 "The Original Gospel of Thomas." *Vigiliae Christianae* 56, 167–199.
1996 *Seek to See Him: Ascent and Vision Mysticism in the Gospel of Thomas*. Supplements to Vigiliae Christianae 33. Leiden: Brill.

Drijvers, Han J.W.
1994 *History and Religion in Late Antique Syria*. Aldershot, Hampshire: Variorum.

Drijvers, Han J.W. & G.J. Reinink
1988 "Taufe und Licht: Tatian, Ebionäerevangelium und Thomasakten." *Text and Testimony: Essays in Honour of A.F.J. Klijn*. Ed. Tjitze Baarda, et. al. Kampen: J.H. Kok, 91–110.

Dunderberg, Ismo
2008 *Beyond Gnosticism: Myth, Lifestyle, and Society in the School of Valentinus*. New York: Columbia University Press.

Edwards, James R.
2002 "The *Gospel of the Ebionites* and the Gospel of Luke." *New Testament Studies* 48, 568–586.
2009 *The Hebrew Gospel & The Development of the Synoptic Tradition*. Grand Rapids, Mich./Cambridge, U.K.: Eerdmans.

Ehrman, Bart D.
1993 *The Orthodox Corruption of Scripture: The Effect of Early Christological Controversies on the Text of the New Testament*. New York: Oxford University Press.

Esler, Philip F.
1998 *Galatians*. New Testament Readings. London: Routledge.
2003 *Conflict and Identity in Romans: The Social Setting of Paul's Letter*. Minneapolis: Fortress.
2007 "'Remembering My Fetters:' Memorialisation of Paul's Imprisonment." *Explaining Christian Origins and Early Judaism: Contributions from Cognitive and Social Science*. Ed. Petri Luomanen, et al. Biblical Interpretation Series 89. Leiden: Brill, 231–258.

Evans, Craig A
2007 "The Jewish Christian Gospel Tradition." *Jewish Believers in Jesus: The Early Centuries*. Ed. Oskar Skarsaune & Reidar Hvalvik. Peabody, Mass.: Hendrickson, 241–277.

Fallon, Francis T. & Ron Cameron
1988 "The Gospel of Thomas: A Forschungsbericht and Analysis." *Aufstieg und Niedergang der römischen Welt* II 25.6, 4195–4251.

Fieger, Michael
1991 *Das Thomasevangelium: Einleitung, Kommentar und Systematik*. Neutestamentliche Abhandlungen Neue Folge 22. Münster: Aschendorffsche Verlagsbuchhandlung.

Fitzmyer, Joseph A.
1971 "The Oxyrhynchus Logoi of Jesus and the Coptic Gospel According to Thomas." *Essays on the Semitic Background of the New Testament*. London: Geoffrey Chapman, 355–433.
1985 *The Gospel according to Luke (X–XXIV): Introduction, Translation and Notes*. Anchor Bible 28A. New York: Doubleday.

Fonrobert, Carlotte E.
2001 "The *Didascalia Apostolorum*: A Mishnah of the Disciples of Jesus." *Journal of Early Christian Studies* 9, 483–509.

Frend, William H.C.
1967 "The Gospel of Thomas: Is Rehabilitation Possible?" *Journal of Theological Studies* 18, 13–26.

Frey, Jörg
2003a "Die Scholien nach dem 'jüdischen Evangelium' und das sogenannte Nazoräer-evangelium." *Zeitschrift für Neutestamentliche Wissenschaft* 94, 122–137.
2003b "'Et numquam laeti sitis …': Ein apokryphes Jesuswort und die Probleme des Hebräerevangeliums." *Oleum Laetitiae: Festgabe für P. Benedict Schwank OSB*. Ed. Gunda Brüske & Anke Haendler-Kläsener. Jerusalemer Theologisches Forum 5. Münster: Aschendorff, 187–212.
2010 "Zur Vielgestaltigkeit judenchristlicher Evangelienüberlieferungen." *Jesus in apokryphen Evangelienüberlieferungen: Beiträge zu ausserkanonischen Jesusüberlieferungen aus verschiedenen Sprach- und Kulturtraditionen*. Ed. Jörg Frey, et al. Wissenschaftliche Untersuchungen zum Neuen Testament 254. Tübingen: Mohr Siebeck.

Funk, Robert W. (ed.)
1985 *New Gospel Parallels. Volume 2, John and the other Gospels*. Foundations and Facets, New Testament 6. Philadelphia: Fortress Press.

Goranson, Stephen
1994 "Nazarenes." *Anchor Bible Dictionary* 4. Ed. David N. Freedman. New York: Doubleday, 1049–1050.

Goulder, Michael D.
1994 *A Tale of Two Missions.* London: SCM Press.

Gregory, Andrew
2006 "Hindrance or Help: Does the Modern Category of 'Jewish-Christian Gospel' Distort our Understanding of the Texts to which it Refers?" *Journal for the Study of the New Testament*, 387–413.

Grobel, Kendrick
1961/62 "How Gnostic is the Gospel of Thomas?" *New Testament Studies* 8, 367–373.

Grützmacher, Georg
1901–1908 *Hieronymus: Eine Biographische Studie zur alten Kirchengeschichte.* Studien zur Geschichte der Theologie und der Kirche 6.3. Leipzig: Dietrich'sche Verlags-Buchhandllung.

Häkkinen, Sakari
2005 "Ebionites." *A Companion to Second-Century Christian "Heretics".* Ed. Antti Marjanen & Petri Luomanen. Supplements to Vigiliae Christianae 76. Leiden: Brill, 247–278.

Hakola, Raimo
2007 "Social Identities and Group Phenomena in Second Temple Judaism." *Explaining Christian Origins and Early Judaism: Contributions from Cognitive and Social Science.* Ed. Petri Luomanen, et al. Biblical Interpretation Series 89. Leiden: Brill, 259–276.

Halton, Thomas P. (trans.)
1999 *Jerome, On Illustrious Men.* The Fathers of the Church: A New Translation, Vol. 100. Washington, DC: Catholic University of America.

Handmann, Rudolf
1888 *Hebräer-Evangelium: Ein Beitrag zur Geschichte und Kritik des Hebräischen Matthäus.* Texte und Untersuchungen zur Geschichte der altchristlichen Literatur, Bd. 5,3. Leipzig: J.C. Hinrichs'sche Buchhandlung.

Harnack, Adolf von
1893 *Geschichte der Altchristlichen Litteratur bis Eusebius. Erster Teil: Die Überlieferung und der Bestand.* Leipzig: J.C. Hinrichs'sche Buchhandlung.

Hartin, Patrick J.
1991   *James and the "Q" Sayings of Jesus.* Journal of the Study of New Testament Supplements 47. Sheffield: Sheffield Academic Press.

Hennecke, Edgar & Wilhelm Schneemelcher (ed.)
1959³ (1904¹)   *Neutestamentliche Apokryphen in deutscher Übersetzung: Evangelien.* Tübingen: J.C.B. Mohr.

Hennings, Ralph
1994   *Die Briefwechsel zwischen Augustinus und Hieronymus und ihr Streit um den Kanon des Alten Testaments und die Auslegung von Gal. 2,11–14.* Supplements to Vigiliae Christianae 21. Leiden: Brill.

Hjelt, Arthur (ed.)
1930   *Syrus Sinaiticus.* Helsingfors.

Hogg, Hope W. (trans.)
1965   "The Diatessaron of Tatian." *The Ante-Nicene Fathers, Vol. 10.* Ed. Allan Menzies. Grand Rapids, Mich.: Eerdmans.

Hogg, Michael A. & Dominic Abrams
1999   "Social Identity and Social Cognition: Historical Background and Current Trends." *Social Identity and Social Cognition.* Ed. Dominic Abrams & Michael A. Hogg. Malden, Mass.: Blackwell Publishers, 1–25.

Hogg, Michael A. & Dominic Abrams (ed.)
1988   *Social Identifications: A Social Psychology of Intergroup Relations and Group Processes.* London: Routledge.

Holmes, Michael W. (ed.)
1999   *The Apostolic Fathers: Greek Texts and English Translations.* Translated by J.B. Lightfoot and J.R. Harmer, 2nd updated edition edited and revised by Michael W. Holmes. Grand Rapids, Mich.: Baker.

Horbury, William
1982   "The Benediction of the Minim and Early Jewish Christian Controversy." *Journal of Theological Studies* 33, 19–61.

Howard, George
1995   *Hebrew Gospel of Matthew.* Macon, Ga.: Mercer University Press.

Huck, Albert & Heinrich Greeven (ed.)
1981   *Synopsis of the First Three Gospels: With the Addition of the Johannine Parallels.* 13th ed. Tübingen: J.C.B. Mohr.

Jackson-McCabe, Matt
2007 "What's in a Name? The Problem of 'Jewish Christianity.'" *Jewish Christianity Reconsidered: Rethinking Ancient Groups and Texts*. Ed. Matt Jackson-McCabe. Minneapolis, Minn.: Fortress, 7–38.

Jeremias, Joachim
1977 *The Eucharistic Words of Jesus*. Trans. Norman Perrin. Die Abendmahlsworte Jesu, 3rd. ed., with the author's revisions to July, 1964. Philadelphia: Fortress.

Jokiranta, Jutta
2007 "Social Identity in the Qumran Movement: The Case of the Penal Code." *Explaining Christian Origins and Early Judaism: Contributions from Cognitive and Social Science*. Ed. Petri Luomanen, et al. Biblical Interpretation Series 89. Leiden: Brill, 277–298.

Jones, F. Stanley
1995 *An Ancient Jewish-Christian Source on the History of Christianity: Pseudo-Clementine Recognitiones 1.27–7*. Society of Biblical Literature Texts and Translations 37, Christian Apocrypha Series 2. Atlanta, Ga.: Scholars Press.
1996 "The Genre of the Book of Elchasai: A Primitive Church Order, Not an Apocalypse." *Historische Wahrheit und theologische Wissenschaft: Gerd Lüdemann zum 50. Geburtstag*. Ed. Alf Özen. Franfurt am Main: Peter Lang, 87–104.
2005 "Jewish Christianity of the *Pseudo-Clementines*." *A Companion to Second-Century Christian "Heretics"*. Ed. Antti Marjanen & Petri Luomanen. Supplements to Vigiliae Christianae 76. Leiden: Brill, 315–334.

Joosten, Jan
2002 "The 'Gospel of Barnabas' and the Diatessaron." *Harvard Theological Review* 95, 73–96.

Kartveit, Magnar
2009 *The Origin of the Samaritans*. Supplements to Vetus Testamentum 128. Leiden: Brill.

Kee, Howard C.
1997 "The Formation of the Christian Community." *The Cambridge Companion to the Bible*. Ed. Howard C. Kee et al. Cambridge: Cambridge University Press, 441–583.

Kelly, J.N.D.
1975 *Jerome: His Life, Writings, and Controversies*. New York: Harper & Row.

Kiilunen, Jarmo
1989 *Doppelgebot der Liebe in Synoptischer Sicht: Ein Redationkritischer Versuch*. Annales Academiae Scientiarum Fennicae B 250. Helsinki: Academia Scientiarum Fennica.

Kimelman, Reuven
1975 "Birkat ha-Minim and the Lack of Evidence for Anti-Christian Jewish Prayer in Late Antiquity." *Jewish and Christian Self-Definition, Vol. 2: Aspects of Judaism in the Greco-Roman Period*. Ed. E.P. Sanders, et al. London: SCM Press.

Kiraz, Georg A.
1996 *Comparative Edition of the Syriac Gospels Aligning the Sinaiticus, Curetonianus, Peshîtta & Harklean Versions*. Vol. I–III. Leiden: Brill.

Klauck, Hans-Josef
2003 *Apocryphal Gospels: An Introduction*. London: T&T Clark International.

Klijn, A.F.J.
1966 "The Question of the Rich Young Man in a Jewish-Christian Gospel." *Novum Testamentum* 8, 149–155.
1972 "Jerome's Quotations from a Nazorean Interpretation of Isaiah." *Judéo-Christianisme: Recherches historiques et théologiques offertes en hommage au Cardinal Jean Daniélou; Recherches de science religieuse* 60, 241–255.
1974 "The Study of Jewish Christianity." *New Testament Studies* 30, 419–431.
1986 "Jewish-Christianity in Egypt." *The Roots of Egyptian Jewish Christianity*. Ed. Birger A. Pearson & James E. Goehring. Philadelphia: Fortress Press.
1988 "Das Hebräer- und das Nazoräerevangelium."*Aufstieg und Niedergang der römischen Welt* 25.5, 3997–4033.
1992 *Jewish-Christian Gospel Tradition*. Supplements to Vigiliae Christianae 17. Leiden: Brill.

Klijn, A.F.J. & G.J. Reinink
1973 *Patristic Evidence for Jewish-Christian Sects*. Novum Testamentum Supplements 36. Leiden: E.J. Brill.

Kline, Leslie L.
1975 *The Sayings of Jesus in the Pseudo-Clementine Homilies*. Society of Biblical Literature Dissertation Series 14. Missoula, Mo.: Scholars' Press.

Kloppenborg, John
2008 *Q the Earliest Gospel: An Introduction to the Original Stories and Sayings of Jesus*. Louisville; London: Westminster Knox Press.

Kloppenborg Verbin, John
2000 *Excavating Q: The History and Setting of the Sayings Gospel*. Minneapolis, Minn.: Fortress.

Koester, Helmut
1957   *Synoptische Überlieferung bei den apostolischen Vätern*. Texte und Untersuchungen 65. Berlin: Akademie-Verlag.
1989   "Introduction [to the Gospel According to Thomas]." *Nag Hammadi Codex II, 2–7. Together with XIII, 2*, Brit. Lib. Or. 4926(1), and POxy 1, 654, 655. Vol. 1: Gospel According to Thomas, Gospel According to Philip, Hypostasis of the Archons, and Indexes*. Ed. Bentley Layton. Nag Hammadi Studies XX. Leiden: Brill.
1990   *Ancient Christian Gospels: Their History and Development*. Harrisburg: Trinity Press International.

Kollman, Bernd
1990   *Ursprung und Gestalten der frühchristlichen Mahlfeier*. Göttinger Theologische Arbeiten 43. Göttingen: Vandenhoeck & Ruprecht.

Kraft, Robert A.
1972   "In Search of 'Jewish Christianity' and its 'Theology': Problems of Definition and Methodology." *Rescherches de science religieuse* 60, 82–92.

Kraus, Thomas J. & Tobias Nicklas (ed.)
2004   *Das Petrusevangelium und die Petrusapokalypse: Die griechischen Fragmente mit deutscher und englischer Übersetzung*. Die Griechischen Christlichen Schriftsteller der ersten Jahrhunderte. Neue Folge 11. Neutestamentliche Abhandlungen I. Berlin: Walter de Gruyter.

Lagarde, Paul de (ed.)
1911 [1854]   *Didascalia Apostolorum syriace*. Göttingen: Dietrich.
1966 [1887]   *Onomastica sacra*. Nachdr. der 2. Aufl. Göttingen 1887. Hildesheim: Olm.

Lagrange, R.P.
1922   "L' Evangile selon les Hébreux." *Revue Biblique* 31, 2:161–181 and 3:321–149.

Layton, Bentley (ed.)
1989   *Nag Hammadi Codex II, 2–7. Together with XIII, 2*, Brit. Lib. Or. 4926(1), and POxy 1, 654, 655. Vol. 1: Gospel According to Thomas, Gospel According to Philip, Hypostasis of the Archons, and Indexes* Leiden: Brill.

Leloir, Lois (ed.)
1954   *Éphrem de Nisibe, Commentaire de L'Évangile concordant, version arménienne [Latin translation]*. Corpus Scriptorum Christianorum Orientalium 145. Louvain: L. Durbecq.

Leppä, Heikki
2002   *Luke's Critical Use of Galatians*. Doctoral thesis. University of Helsinki, Helsinki.

2005   "Luke's Account of the Lord's Supper." *Lux humana, Lux Aeterna: Essays on Biblical and Related Themes in Honour of Lars Aejemelaeus.* Ed. Antti Mustakallio, et al. Publications of the Finnish Exegetical Society 89. Helsinki: Finnish Exegetical Society, 364–373.

Lewis, Agnes Smith (ed.)
1910   *The Old Syriac Gospels or Evangelion Da-mepharreshê: being the text of the Sinai or Syro-Antiochene Palimpsest, including the latest additions and emendations, with the variants of the curetonian text, corroborations from many other mss., and a list of quotations from ancient authors.* London: Williams & Norgate.

Liddell, Henry G. & Robert Scott
1973   *Greek-English Lexicon.* London: Clarendon Press.

Lüdemann, Gerd
1980   "The Successors of Pre-70 Jerusalem Christianity: A Critical Evaluation of the Pella-Tradition." *Jewish and Christian Self-Definition, Vol. 1: The Shaping of Christianity in the Second and Third Centuries.* Ed. E.P. Sanders. London: SCM Press, 161–254.
1983   *Paulus, der Heidenapostel, Band II: Antipaulinismus im frühen Christentum.* Forschungen zur Religion und Literatur des Alten und Neuen Testaments 130. Göttingen: Vandenhoeck & Ruprecht.
1996   *Heretics: The Other Side of Early Christianity.* Trans. John Bowden. Louisville, Ky.: Westminster John Knox.

Lührmann, Dieter
2004   *Die apokryph gewordenen Evangelien: Studien zur neuen Texten und zu neuen Fragen.* Supplements to Novum Testamentum 112. Leiden: Brill.

Luomanen, Petri
1998   *Entering the Kingdom of Heaven: A Study on the Structure of Matthew's View of Salvation.* Wissenschafliche Untersuchunen zum Neuen Testament 2/101. Tübingen: Mohr Siebeck.
2002a   "Nasaretilaisten historia." *Teologinen Aikakauskirja (Finnish Journal of Theology)* 107, 508–520.
2002b   "The 'Sociology of Sectarianism' in Matthew: Modeling the Genesis of Early Jewish and Christian Communities." *Fair Play: Diversity and Conflicts in Early Christianity: Essays in Honour of Heikki Räisänen.* Ed. Ismo Dunderberg, et al. Leiden: Brill, 107–130.
2003   "Where Did Another Rich Man Come From?: The Jewish-Christian Profile of the Story About a Rich Man in the 'Gospel of the Hebrews' (Origen, Comm. in Matth. 15.14)." *Vigiliae Christianae* 57, 243–275.
2005a   "Sacrifices Abolished: The Last Supper in Luke (Codex Bezae) and in the Gospel of the Ebionites." *Lux Humana, Lux Aeterna: Essays on Biblical and Related Themes in Honour of Lars Aejemelaeus.* Ed. Antti Mustakallio in collaboration with Heikki Leppä and Heikki Räisänen. Publications of

Finnish Exegetical Society 89. Helsinki/Göttingen: Finnish Exegetical Society/Vandenhoeck & Ruprecht, 186–208.

2005b "Nazarenes." *A Companion to Second-Century Christian "Heretics"*. Ed. Antti Marjanen & Petri Luomanen. Supplements to Vigiliae Christianae 76. Leiden: Brill, 279–314.

2005c "On the Fringes of Canon: Eusebius' View of the 'Gospel of the Hebrews.'" *The Formation of the Early Church*. Ed. Jostein Ådna. Wissenschaftliche Untersuchungen zum Neuen Testament 183. Tübingen: Mohr Siebeck, 265–281.

2006 "'Let Him Who Seeks Continue Seeking': The Relationship Between Jewish-Christian Gospels and the *Gospel of Thomas*." *Thomasine Traditions in Antiquity: The Social and Cultural World of the Gospel of Thomas*. Ed. Jon Ma. Asgeirsson, et al. Nag Hammadi and Manichean Studies 59. Leiden: Brill, 119–153.

2007a "Ebionites and Nazarenes." *Jewish Christianity Reconsidered: Rethinking Ancient Groups and Texts*. Ed. Matt Jackson-McCabe. Minneapolis, Minn.: Fortress Press, 81–118.

2007b "The Sociology of Knowledge, the Social Identity Approach and the Cognitive Study of Religion." *Explaining Christian Origins and Early Judaism: Contributions from Cognitive and Social Science*. Ed. Petri Luomanen, et al. Biblical Interpretation Series 89. Leiden: E.J. Brill, 199–229.

2010 "Passion and Resurrection Traditions in Early Jewish-Christian Gospels." *Gelitten, Gestorben, Auferstanden: Passions- und Ostertraditionen im antiken Christentum*. Ed. Tobias Nicklas, et al. Wissenschaftliche Untersuchungen zum Neuen Testament II/273. Tübingen: Mohr Siebeck, 187–208.

Luomanen, Petri & Antti Marjanen
2005 "Introduction." *A Companion to Second-Century Christian Heretics*. Ed. Antti Marjanen & Petri Luomanen. Supplements to Vigiliae Christianae 76. Leiden: Brill, ix–xiii.

Luttikhuizen, Gerard P.
1985 *The Revelation of Elchasai: Investigations into the Evidence for a Mesopotamian Jewish Apocalypse of the Second Century and its Reception by Judaeo-Christian Propagandists*. Texte und Studien zum antiken Judentum 8. Tübingen: J.C.B. Mohr (Paul Siebeck).
2005 "Elchasaites and Their Book." *A Companion to Second-Century Christian "Heretics"*. Ed. Antti Marjanen & Petri Luomanen. Supplements to Vigiliae Christianae 76. Leiden: Brill, 335–164.

Luz, Ulrich
1989 *Das Evangelium nach Matthäus, Mt 1–7*. Evangelisch-katholischer Kommentar zum Neuen Testament I/1. Zürich; Braunschweig/Neukirchen-Vluyn: Benzinger Verlag/Neukirchener Verlag.

1990 *Das Evangelium nach Matthäus, Mt 8–17*. Evangelisch-katholischer Kommentar zum Neuen Testament 1/2. Zürich; Braunschweig / Neukirchen-Vluyn: Benziger Verlag / Neukirchener Verlag.
1997 *Das Evangelium nach Matthäus, Mt 18–25*. Evangelisch-katholischer Kommentar zum Neuen Testament 1/3. Zürich; Düsseldorf / Neukirchen-Vluyn: Benziger Verlag / Neukirchener Verlag.
2002 *Das Evangelium Nach Matthäus, Mt 26–28*. Evangelisch-katholischer Kommentar zum Neuen Testament 1/4. Düsseldorf; Zürich / Neukirchen-Vluyn: Benziger Verlag / Neukirchener Verlag.

Maier, Paul M. (trans.)
1999 *Eusebius, The Church History: A New Translation with Commentary.* Trans. Paul M. Maier. Grand Rapids, Mich.: Kregel Publications.

Malina, Bruce J.
1976 "Jewish Christianity or Christian Judaism: Toward a Hypothetical Definition." *Journal for the Study of Judaism* 7, 46–57.

Malina, Bruce J. & Richard L. Rohrbaugh
1992 *Social Science Commentary on the Synoptic Gospels.* Minneapolis, Minn.: Fortress Press.

Marjanen, Antti
1998a "Thomas and Jewish Religious Practices." *Thomas at the Crossroads: Essays on the Gospel of Thomas* Ed. Risto Uro. Edinburgh: T&T Clark, 163–182.
1998b "Women Disciples in the Gospel of Thomas." *Thomas at the Crossroads: Essays on the Gospel of Thomas.* Ed. Risto Uro. Edinburgh: T&T Clark, 99–104.
2005a "What is Gnosticism? From the Pastorals to Rudolph." *Was There a Gnostic Religion?* Ed. Antti Marjanen. Publications of the Finnish Exegetical Society 87. Helsinki / Göttingen: Finnish Exegetical Society / Vandenhoeck & Ruprecht, 1–54.
2005b "Montanism and the Formation of the New Testament Canon." *The Formation of the Early Church.* Ed. Jostein Ådna. Wissenschafliche Untersuchungen zum Neuen Testament 183. Tübingen: Mohr Siebeck, 239–263.
2008 "Gnosticism." *The Oxford handbook of early Christian studies.* Ed. S.A. Harvey & D.G. Hunter. Oxford handbooks in religion and theology. Oxford: Oxford University Press, 203–220.

Markschies, Christoph & Jens Schröter (ed.)
Forthcoming. *Antike Christliche Apokryphen I: Evangelien.* Tübingen.

Medin, Douglas L.
1989 "Concepts and Conceptual Structure." *American Psychologist* 44, 1469–1481.

Metzger, Bruce M.
1977   *The Early Versions of the New Testament: Their Origin, Transmission and Limitations.* Oxford: Clarendon Press.
1988   *The Canon of the New Testament: Its Origin, Development and Significance.* Oxford: Clarendon Press.

Meyer, A.
1904a   "Ebionitenevangelium." *Neutestamentliche Apokryphen.* Ed. Edgar Hennecke. Tübingen: J.C.B. Mohr (Paul Siebeck), 24–27.
1904b   "Hebräerevangelium." *Neutestamentliche Apokryphen.* Ed. Edgar Hennecke. Tübingen; Liepzig: J.C.B. Mohr (Paul Siebeck), 11–21.

Meyer, Marvin
1985   "Making Mary Male: The Categories 'Male' and 'Female' in the Gospel of Thomas." *New Testament Studies* 31, 554–570.
1992   *The Gospel of Thomas: The Hidden Sayings of Jesus.* San Francisco: Harper.

Mimouni, Simon C.
1998   *Le judéo-christianisme ancien: Essais historiques.* Paris: Cerf.

Morgan, Robert
1994   "Tübingen school." *A Dictionary of Biblical Interpretation.* Ed. R.J. Coggins & J.L. Houlden. London: SCM Press, 710–713.

Murray, Robert
1974   "Defining Judaeo-Christianity." *Heythrop Journal* 15, 303–310.
1982   "Jews, Hebrews and Christians: Some Needed Distinctions." *Novum Testamentum* 24, 194–208.

Myllykoski, Matti
2005   "Cerinthus." *A Companion to Second-Century Christian "Heretics".* Ed. Antti Marjanen & Petri Luomanen. Supplements to Vigiliae Christianae 76. Leiden: Brill, 279–314.

Myllykoski, Matti & Petri Luomanen
1999   "Varhaisen juutalaiskristillisyyden jäljillä." *Teologinen Aikakauskirja (Finnish Journal of Theology)* 104, 327–348.

Nautin, Pierre
1983   "Le premier échange épistolaire entre Jérôme et Damase: Lettres réelles ou fictives?" *Freiburger Zeitschrift für Philosophie und Theologie* 30, 331–344.
1986   "Hieronymus." *Theologische Realenzyklopädie* 15, 304–315.

Nestle & Aland (ed.)
1993   *Novum Testamentum Graece.* 27. revidierte Auflage. Stuttgart: Deutsche Bibelgesellschaft.

Niclós, José Vicente
1999 "L'Évangile en hébreu de Shem Tob Ibn Shaprut: Une traduction d'origine judéo-catalane replacée dans son Sitz im Leben." *Revue Biblique* 106, 358–407.

Nolland, John
1993 *Luke 18:35–24:53*. Word Biblical Commentary 35C. Dallas, Tex.: Word Books.

Oakes, Penelope, S. Alexander Haslam & John C. Turner
1998 "The Role of Prototypicality in Group Influence and Cohesion: Contextual Variation in the Graded Structure of Social Categories." *Social Identity: International Perspectives*. Ed. Stephen Worchel et al. London: Sage Publications, 75–92.

Paget, James Carleton
2007 "The Definition of the Term Jewish Christian and Jewish Christianity in the History of Research." *Jewish Believers in Jesus: The Early Centuries*. Ed. Oskar Skarsaune & Reidar Hvalvik. Peabody, Mass.: Hendrickson, 22–52.

Painter, John
2001 "Who Was James? Footprints as a Means of Identification." *The Brother of Jesus: James the Just and His Mission*. Ed. Bruce Chilton & Jacob Neusner. Louisville, Ky.; London: Westminster John Knox Press, 10–65.

Parker, David C.
1992 *Codex Bezae: An early Christian Manuscript and Its Text*. Cambridge: Cambridge University Press.
1997 *The Living Text of the Gospels*. Cambridge: Cambridge University Press.

Patterson, Stephen J.
1993 *The Gospel of Thomas and Jesus*. Sonoma, Calif.: Polebridge Press.

Perrin, Nicholas
2002 *Thomas and Tatian: The Relationship Between the Gospel of Thomas and the Diatessaron*. Academia Biblica 5. Atlanta, Ga.: Society of Biblical Literature.

Pesch, Rudolph
1986 *Die Apostelgeschichte (Apg 1–12)*. Evangelish-katholischer Kommentar zum Neuen Testament 5.1. Zürich; Einsiedeln; Köln / Neukirchen–Vluyn: Benziger Verlag / Neukirchener Verlag.

Petersen, William L.
1986 "New Evidence for the Question of the Original Language of the Diatessaron." *Studien zum Text und zur Ethik des Neuen Testaments: Festschrift*

zum 80. Geburtsdag von Heinrich Greeven. Ed. Wolfgang Schrage. Beihefte zur Zeitschrift für die neutestamentliche Wissenschaft 47. Berlin; New York: de Gruyter.

1989 "Review of G. Howard, *The Gospel of Matthew according to a Primitive Hebrew Text*." *Journal of Biblical Literature* 108, 722–726.

1992 "Zion Gospel Edition." *Achor Bible Dictionary* 6, 1097–1098.

1994 *Tatian's Diatessaron: Its Creation, Dissemination, Significance and History in Scholarship*. Supplements to Vigiliae Christianae 25. Leiden: Brill.

1998 "The Vorlage of Shem-Tob's 'Hebrew Matthew.'" *New Testament Studies* 44, 490–512.

2005 "Tatian the Assyrian." *Second Century Christian "Heretics"*. Ed. Antti Marjanen & Petri Luomanen. Supplements to Vigiliae Christianae 76. Leiden: Brill, 125–158.

Pierre, Marie-Joseph (ed.)

1989 *Aphraate le sage Persan, Les exposés II: Exposés XI–XXIII*. Sources chrétiennes 359. Paris: Cerf.

Pritz, Ray A.

1988 *Nazarene Jewish Christianity: From the End of the New Testament Period Until Its Disappearance in the Fourth Century*. Studia Post-Biblica 37. Leiden: Brill.

Quispel, Gilles

1975 "L'Evangile selon Thomas et les Clementines." *Gnostic Studies II*. Uitgaven van het Nederlands historisch-archaeologisch instituut te İstanbul 34. Istanbul: Nederlands Historisch-Archaeologisch Instituut, 17–29.

1966 "'The Gospel of Thomas' and the 'Gospel of Hebrews.'" *New Testament Studies* 12, 371–382.

1967 *Makarius, das Thomasevangelium und das Lied von der Perle*. Supplements to Novum Testamentum 15. Leiden: Brill.

Räisänen, Heikki

1986 *Paul and the Law*. Philadelphia: Fortress Press.

1992 *Jesus, Paul and Torah: Collected Essays*. Journal for the Study of New Testament Supplement Series 43. Sheffield: JSOT Press.

1995 "Die 'Hellenisten' der Urgemeinde." *Aufstieg und Niedergang der römishen Welt II* 26.2. Berlin: de Gruyter, 1468–1514.

Resch, Alfred

1906 *Agrapha: Aussercanonische Schriftfragmente*. Texte und Untersuchungen 15.3/4. Leipzig: Hinrisch'sche Buchhandlung.

Riegel, Stanley K.

1978 "Jewish Christianity: Definitions and Terminology." *New Testament Studies* 24, 410–415.

Ritschl, Albrect
1857 Die Entstehung der altkatholischen Kirche: Eine kirchen- und dogmengeschichtliche Monographie. Bonn: Adolph Marcus.

Robinson, James M.
2007 Jesus According to the Earliest Witness. Minneapolis, Minn.: Fortress Press.

Robinson, James M., Paul Hoffmann & John S. Kloppenborg (ed.)
2000 *The Critical Edition of Q: Synopsis Including the Gospels of Matthew and Luke, Mark and Thomas with English, German and French Translations of Q and Thomas*. Managing editor Milton C. Moreland. Leuven: Peeters.

Rosch, Eleanor
1975 "Cognitive Representations of Semantic Categories." *Journal of Experimental Psychology* 104, 192–233.

Salo, Kalervo
1991 *Luke's Treatment of the Law: A Redaction Critical Investigation*. Annales Academiae Scientiarum Fennicae. Dissertationes Humanarum Litterarum 57. Helsinki: Academia Scientiarum Fennica.

Sanders, E.P.
1985 *Jesus and Judaism*. London: SCM Press.

Schaeder, H.H.
1967 "Ναζαρηνός, Ναζωραῖος." *Theological Dictionary of the New Testament* 4, 874–879.

Schäfer, Peter
1975 "Die sogenannte Synode von Jabne: Zur Trennung von Juden und Christen im ersten/zweiten Jh. n. Chr." *Judaica* 31, 54–64, 116–124.

Schenke, Hans-Martin (ed.)
2001 *Coptic Papyri I: Das Matthäus-Evangelium im mittelägyptischen Dialekt des Koptischen (Codex Schøyen)*. Manuscripts in the Schøyen Collection. Vol. 2. Ed. Hans-Martin Schenke. Oslo: Hermes.

Schmidt, Peter Lebrecht
1998 "'Und es war geschrieben auf Hebraisch, Griechisch und Lateinisch': Hieronymus, das Hebräer-Evangelium und seine mittelalterliche Rezeption." *Filologia Mediolatina* 5, 49–93.

Schmidtke, Alfred
1911 *Neue Fragmente und Untersuchungen zu den Judenchristlichen Evangelien: Ein Beitrag zur Literatur und Geschichte der Judenchristen*. Texte und Untersuchungen 3.7.1. Leipzig: J.C. Hinrichs'sche Buchhandlung.

Schoeps, Hans J.
1949 *Theologie und Geschichte des Judenchristentums*. Tübingen: J.C.B. Mohr.

Schrage, Wolfgang
1964 *Das Verhältnis des Thomas-evangeliums zur synoptischen Tradition und zu den koptischen Evangelienübersetzungen: Zugleich ein Beitrag zur gnostischen Synoptikerdeutung*. Beihefte zur Zeitschrift für die neutestamentliche Wissenschaft 29. Berlin: Verlag Alfred Töpelmann.

Schürmann, Heinz
1953 *Der Paschamahlbericht, Lk 22, (7–14) 15–18:1. Teil einer quellenkritischen Untersuchung des Lukanischen Abendmahlberichtes Lk 22, 7–38*. Neutestamentliche Abhandlungen 19.5. Münster Westf.: Aschendorff.

Segal, J.B.
2001 [1970] *Edessa: The Blessed City*. Gorgias reprint series 1. Piscataway, N.J.: Gorgias Press.

Sieber, John H.
1965 *A Redactional Analysis of the Synoptic Gospels with regard to the Question of the Sources of the Gospel According to Thomas*. Ph.D. diss. The Claremont Graduate School, Claremont, Calif.

Simon, Marcel
1975 "Réflections sur le Judéo-Christianisme." *Christianity, Judaism and Other Greco-Roman Cults: Studies for Morton Smith at Sixty*. Ed. Jacob Neusner. Studies in Judaism in Late Antiquity 12. Leiden: Brill, 2:53–76.

Skarsaune, Oskar
2007 "The History of Jewish Believers in the Early Centuries: Perspectives and Framework." *The Jewish Believers in Jesus: The Early Centuries*. Ed. Oskar Skarsaune & Reidar Hvalvik. Peabody, Mass.: Hendrickson, 745–781.

Strecker, Georg
1988 "Judenchristentum." *Theologische Realenzyklopädie* 17, 310–325.

Tajfel, Henri
1981 *Human Groups and Social Categories: Studies in Social Psychology*. Cambridge: Cambridge University Press.

Taylor, Joan E.
1990 "The Phenomenon of Early Jewish-Christianity: Reality or Scholarly Invention?" *Vigiliae Christianae* 44, 313–334.
1993 *Christians and the Holy Places: The Myth of Jewish-Christian Origins*. Oxford: Clarendon Press.

Theissen, Gerd
2000   *Die Religion der ersten Christen: Eine Theorie des Urchristentums.* Gütersloh: Kaiser.

Tischendorf, Constantin
1860   *Notitia editionis codicis Bibliorum Sinaitici.* Lipsiae [Leipzig]: F.A. Brockhaus.

Trigg, Joseph
1992   "Origen." *Anchor Bible Dictionary* 5, 42–48.

Uro, Risto
1987   *Sheep Among the Wolves: A Study on the Mission Instructions of Q.* Annales Academiae Scientiarum Fennicae, B Diss 47. Helsinki: Academia Scientiarum Fennica.
2003   *Thomas: Seeking the Historical Context of Thomas.* London; New York: T&T Clark.

Van Voorst, Robert E.
1989   *The Ascents of James: History and Theology of a Jewish-Christian Community.* Society of Biblical Literature Dissertation Series 112. Atlanta, Ga.: Scholars Press.

Verheyden, Joseph
2008   "Jewish Christianity, A State of Affairs: Affinities and Differences with Respect to Matthew, James, and the Didache." *Matthew, James, and Didache: Three Related Documents in Their Jewish and Christian Settings.* Ed. Huub van de Sandt & Jürgen K. Zangenberg. SBL Symposium Series 45. Atlanta, Ga.: Society of Biblical Literature, 123–135.

Vielhauer, Philipp & Georg Strecker
1987   "Judenchristiliche Evangelien." *Neutestamentliche Apokryphen in deutscher Übersetzung.* Ed. Edgar Hennecke & Wilhelm Schneemelcher. 5. Aufl. Tübingen: J.C.B. Mohr (Paul Siebeck), 114–147.
1991^2 (1963^1) "Jewish-Christian Gospels." *New Testament Apocrypha: Vol. 1, Gospels and Related Writings.* Ed. Edgar Hennecke. Revised edition edited by Wilhelm Schneemelcher. English translation edited by R. McL. Wilson. Cambridge: James Clarke & Co., 134–177.

Visotzky, Burton L.
1995   "Prolegomenon to the Study of Jewish-Christianities." *Fathers of the World: Essays in Rabbinic and Patristic Literatures.* Wissenschaftlich Untersuchungen zum Neuen Testament 80. Tübingen: Mohr Siebeck, 129–149.

Vogt, Hermann J.
1980 "Falsche Ergänzungen oder Korrekturen im Mattäus-Kommentar der Origenes." *Theologische Quartalschrift* 160, 207–212.
1990 *Origen, Der Kommentar zum Evangelium nach Matthäus II. Eingeleitet, übersetzt und mit Anmerkungen versehen von Hermann J. Vogt.* Bibliothek der Griechischen Literatur 30. Stuttgart: Anton Hiersemann.

Waitz, Hans
1924a "Die judenchristlichen Evangelien in der altkirchlichen Literatur." *Neutestamentliche Apokryphen*. Ed. Edgar Hennecke. Tübingen: J.C.B. Mohr, 10–17.
1924b "Ebionäerevangelium oder Evangelium der Zwölf." *Neutestamentliche Apokryphen*. Ed. Edgar Hennecke. Tübingen: J.C.B. Mohr, 39–48.
1924c "Das Matthäusevangelium der Nazaräer (Nazaräerevangelium)." *Neutestamentliche Apokryphen*. Ed. Edgar Hennecke. Tübingen: J.C.B. Mohr, 17–32.
1924d "Hebräerevangelium." *Neutestamentliche Apokryphen*. Ed. Edgar Hennecke. Tübingen: J.C.B. Mohr, 48–55.
1937 "Neue Untersuchungen über die sogen. judenchristlichen Evangelien." *Zeitschrift für die Neutestamentliche Wissenschaft* 36, 60–81.

Wilkes, A.L.
1997 *Knowledge in Minds: Individual and Collective Processes in Cognition*. Hove: Psychology Press.

Williams, Francis E.
1985 "The Apocryphon of James." *Nag Hammadi Codex I, vol. 1: Introductions, Texts, Translations, Indices*. Ed. Harold W. Attridge. Nag Hammadi Studies 22. Leiden: Brill, 13–53.

Williams, Frank
1987a "Introduction." *The Panarion of Epiphanius of Salamis: Book I (Sects 1–46)*. Nag Hammadi Studies 35. Leiden: Brill, IX–XXVII.

Williams, Frank (trans.)
1987b *The Panarion of Epiphanius of Salamis: Book I (Sects 1–46)*. Nag Hammadi Studies 35. Leiden: Brill.

Williams, Michael Allen
1995 *Rethinking Gnosticism: An Argument for Dismantling a Dubious Category*. Princeton: Princeton University Press.

Wilson, Stephen G.
1995 *Related Strangers: Jews and Christians 70–170 C.E.* Minneapolis, Minn.: Fortress Press.

INDEX OF ANCIENT AUTHORS AND TEXTS

Abbreviations follow Alexander, Patrick H. et al. (ed.), 1999, *The SBL Handbook of Style: For Ancient Near Eastern, Biblical, and Early Christian Studies.* (Peabody, Mass.: Hendrickson).

1. Hebrew Bible and LXX

Exod
32	76

Deut
23:19–20	131
27:26	175

Isa
6:4	166
8	71
8:11–15	72
8:14	71
8:19	73
8:19–22	74
8:23	72, 74
9	71
9:1	73–74, 167
11:1	52
29:17–21	71, 75
29:21	73
31:6–9	71, 74

Sir.
4.11	86

2. Philo and Josephus

Philo
Ebr.
30	86

Josephus
Bell.
2.458	60

3. Mishnah, Talmud and Other Rabbinic Works

Talmud
b. ʿAbod. Zar.
6a	53

b. Taʿan.
27b	53

b. Yebam.
47a–b	12

Other Rabbinic Works
Gerim
1:1	12

4. New Testament

Q (verse numbers from Luke)
3:21–22	142
4:9–12	144
6:41–42	142
10:3	215
11:9	204
11:9–10	142
11:49–53	142
11:52	213, 215
12:22–34	143
13:35	144
16:16	144
17:3–4	142
17:33–35	142

Matt
2:1–8	111
2:13,16,20	111
2:23	52
3:1–2	116
3:7	218

INDEX OF ANCIENT AUTHORS AND TEXTS

Matt (cont.)

3:17	227
4:5	87
4:15–16	114
6:5–15	114
7:4–6	212
7:5	86
7:8	204
7:21	209
8:11–12	160
9:22	182, 220
10	160
10:16	88, 201, 214–216, 218
10:34–36	133
10:37	228
11:13	180
11:25	227
11:25–30	227
11:28–30	143, 227
12:40	87
12:47–50	37
12:48–49	210
12:47	208
15:14	139, 201, 218
16:17	87, 186
16:23	220
18:21–22	116
18:23–35	143
19:16–22	175, 181
19:17	180
19:21	129
19:28	160
22:34–40	180–181
22:37	197
23:13	213–215
23:29–38	111
23:38	115
24:40–43	133–134
22:40	189
24:45–51	128
25:14–30	128, 249
25:14	129
25:30	128
26:17	152
26:26–29	160
26:28	153
26:29	146, 155
27:15–48	112
27:16	165
27:24	167
27:26	112
27:45–54	112
27:62–66	139
28:4,11–15	169

Mark

1:4	116
1:11	227
2:13	126
3:20–21	168, 209
3:31	168, 208, 210
3:31–35	207
3:32	207
3:33–34	210
4:38	197
6:3	168
8:34	186
9:17	197
10:17–20	181
10:17–22	175, 184, 220
10:20	197
10:25	148
10:35–45	148
10:35	197
12:28–34	180–181
12:29	197
14:12	152
14:22–25	160
14:24	153
14:25	146, 155, 160
14:57–58	161
14:70	220
15:25	149
15:39	148

Luke

3:3	116
3:22	227
5:20	182, 220
7:9	182, 220
7:44	182, 220
7:35	86
8:3	129

8:13	160	17:22	159
8:19–21	207	17:25	159
8:20	207–208	17:33–35	133, 134
8:21	210	18:1–8	132
9	65	18:18	221
9:53	160	18:18–21	181
9:55	182	18:18–23	175, 184, 220
10:3	215		
10:21–22	227	18:22	181
10:23	182, 219–220, 222	18:24	148
		19:45–46	161
10:25	181–182	21:25	125
10:25–28	180–182, 188, 221–222	22:15	159
		22:15–18	146, 152, 155, 159
10:26	188–189, 222	22:15–19a	160
10:28	181	22:15–20	147, 149, 155
11:9	204	22:17	160
11:17	160	22:17–18	155
11:18	160	22:18	155
11:22	181	22:19	149
11:52	213–215, 217	22:19–20	147
12:13–15	220–221	22:20	153
12:13–21	184, 187–188	22:26	159
12:14	181–182, 188, 220–221	22:30	160
		22:46	159
12:16–21	220–221	22:58	182, 220
12:17	160	22:61	182, 220
12:19	221	23:34	160
12:33	129	23:28	182, 220
12:51–53	133	24:26, 46	159
12:52	160		
12:53	160	**John**	
13:28–29	160	1:42	186
14:25	182, 220	6:11	181
15:12	129	7:26	125
15:13	129	7:53–8:11	125, 135
15:16	159–160	8:2	126
15:30	129	17:2	133
16:1–13	132	17:6	133
16:14–15	184, 187–189, 220	17:9	133
		17:24	133
16:16	180	18:19	113
16:16–17	189	21:15	186
16:19–31	184, 188, 197, 220	21:16	186
		21:17	186
16:21	159–160	21:25	125
17:3–4	116		

Acts

2:22	54
2:23	148
2:24	63
2:32	63
2:46	23
3:13	64
3:13–15	65
3:15	63
3:18	148
3:26	64–65
4:10	64
4:24	64–65
4:27	64
4:30	64
4:32–37	33, 35
4:35	181
6:5	162
6:8–8:1	161
7:57–8:1	48
8:1–3	164
8:4–7	47
8:4–25	47, 165
8:13	56
8:18	56
8:32–35	148
11:2–3	55
11.19–20	47, 165
13:4–12	43, 47, 165
15	56
15:19–20	36
15:24	55–56
15:28–29	54, 56
15:29	36
20:28	148
21:17–26	23
24:5	52, 54
24:12–14	54
24:14–15	64
24:20–21	64
26:22	148

Rom

3:25–26	162
13:8	175
15:26	23

1 Cor

11:23–26	146, 160
15:7	168

Gal

2	56, 68
2:10	23
2:11–14	69
3:10	56, 175
3:12	175
5:2	56
5:3	175
5:4	56
5:14	175

Heb

7:26–27	153
9:9–10	153
9:11–28	153
10:11–12	153
13:10–13	153

5. NAG HAMMADI CODICES AND OXYRHYNCHUS PAPYRI

Acts of Thomas
Acts Thom.

7	86, 202, 227
27	86, 202, 227
39	86, 202, 227
50	86, 202, 227
136	205

2 Apocalypse of James
2 Apoc. Jas.

56.2–5	205

Apocryphon of James
Ap. Jas.

6.19–20	86

Book of Thomas the Contender
Thom. Cont.

142,24–32	206
145, 8–15	205–206

Gospel of Thomas
Gos. Thom.

Prol.	202
2	134, 139, 201–202, 204–206, 226, 247, 230
3	229
7	229
12	200
14	230
22	212
29	205, 229–230
36	231
37	229
39	201, 213–214, 216–218, 224–225
44	229
47	229
50	133, 205, 229–230
51	205
55	228
56	205
60	205
60–62	134
61	134
62	132, 134
63	132, 222
64	132
69	206
72	188, 201, 218, 220–223, 225
87	230
90	226–227, 230
99	201, 206, 208, 211, 215, 218, 224–225
101	228–230
104	218
112	230
114	229

Oxyrhynchus papyri
P.Oxy.

654	87
654,5–9	201, 202, 204–206
655	201, 213–214
840	129

6. OTHER EARLY CHRISTIAN TEXTS

Ascents of James
see General Index

Book of Elchasai
see General Index

Circuits of Peter
see General Index

2 Clement
2 Clem.

4.5a	212
9.11	206, 208–212
12.2, 6	212

Didache
Did.

9:1–5	149
9–10	157

Didascalia Apostolorum
(pp. ed. Lagarde 1911)
DA

II/pp. 4–5	76
IV/p.12	76
VII/p. 31	125
XIX/p.79	76
XXI/pp. 91–92	76
XXVI/pp.107–109	76
XXVI/111–112, 115	76
XXVI/pp. 112–115	30

Gospel of the Ebionites
see General Index

Gospel of the Hebrews
see General Index

"Gospel of the Nazarenes"
see General Index

Gospel of Peter
Gos. Pet.
   19   156
   38–42   169

Ignatius of Antioch
Ign. Smyrn.
   3   96, 108

Pseudo-Clementines
Hom.
   1.22.5   39
   3.18.2–3   201, 213–216
   3.20.2   202
   7.8.1   36
   8.10   39
   9.26–27   12
   10.1   12
   11.1   12
   13.4.3–5   39
   13.4–12   12
   13.11.4   39
Rec.
   1.19.5   39
   1.27–28   163
   1.27–44.1   39
   1.27–71   38–41, 45, 48, 150–151, 158, 162–163, 165, 217, 237
   1.32   12
   1.32.4–33.2   39
   1.33–71   162–163
   1.33.5   41
   1.36.1   153
   1.36.1–37.2   153
   1.37.4   154
   1.38.1   40
   1.39.1   40
   1.39.2   39
   1.43.1   45
   1.44.2–53.3   39
   1.45.1–2   39
   1.47.1–4   39
   1.54.6–7   201, 213, 215, 224
   1.58.2–6   36
   1.59.3   40
   1.59.6   40
   1.64.1–2   154
   1.69.1–3   40
   2.42.5   39
   2.71.2   39
   2.72   12
   4.3   12
   4.36.4   36
   4.9   39
   7.29.3–5   39
   7.36.4   39
   8.1   12

7. Greek and Latin Authors

Clement of Alexandria
Strom.
   I 1   138
   II IX 45.5   85–86, 137, 139, 201–202, 204, 247
   V XIV 96.3   85–86, 137, 139, 142, 202, 204, 247
Ecl.
   20.3   209

Didymus the Blind
Comm. Eccl.
   4.223.7–13   125, 248

Epiphanius
Pan.
   18   51
   19   43
   19.2.2   42
   19.3.4   42
   19.3.5   44
   19.7.6   62
   28   31, 56
   29.1.1   54
   29.4.1–4   53

29.5.1–3	53	30.13.7	37
29.5.4	53, 55–56	30.13.7–8	156, 251
29.5.6	54	30.14.5	37, 201, 206, 252
29.5.6–6.1	51	30.15.2	33, 164
29.6.2	54	30.15.3	32
29.6.4	54	30.15.3–4	152
29.6.7	54	30.15.4	35, 164
29.7–8	36	30.16.1	22, 32–33, 154
29.7.2	65	30.16.3	46
29.7.2–8	57–58	30.16.4	33, 46, 156
29.7.3	63–64	30.16.5	33, 38, 251
29.7.5	65	30.16.7	32–33, 38
29.7.7	59	30.16.8–9	32, 34
29.7.7–8	56, 157	30.17.1–3	33, 35
29.7.8	53	30.17.2	60
29.8.1	56, 58	30.17.4	42
29.8.6	54	30.17.4–5	33
29.8.6–7	56	30.17.5–7	33
29.9.1	66, 79	30.18.1	31
29.9.2	57–58, 113	30.18.2	33
29.9.4	57, 59	30.18.2–3	22, 163
30.1.3	32, 36	30.18.4	40
30.1.5	32, 37, 164	30.18.4–5	164
30.2.2	32	30.18.7–9	33, 35, 164
30.2.2–3	36	30.2.4	252
30.2.3	32	30.22.4–5	38, 151
30.2.4	32	30.24.1–6	34
30.2.4–6	156	30.26.1–2	32
30.2.5	32	46.1.9	193
30.2.6	32	51	77
30.2.7–8	31, 150	53	43
30.2.8–9	59	70.10.1–4	76
30.3.1–6	156		
30.3.3	33, 39, 46	Eusebius	
30.3.4–6	33	*Hist. eccl.*	
30.3.4	39, 46	2.13	55
30.3.5	39, 46	2.16	53, 55
30.3.6	33	2.17	53
30.3.7	32, 61	2.23	45, 53, 127, 170
30.13.1	61	2.23.3–18	23
30.13.2	32, 33	2.27.4	60
30.13.2–3	38, 116, 252	3.5	57, 60
30.13.4–5	37, 151, 251	3.5.3	53, 157
30.13.4	217	3.24.6	95
30.13.5	33	3.25	104, 120, 122
30.13.6	61, 116, 251	3.25.3	85
30.13.6–8	192	3.25.5	61

Hist. eccl. (cont.)

3.27	122
3.27.1–3	63
3.27.1–6	32
3.27.4	122, 158
3.28.6	29
3.32	127
3.36–38	123
3.39	123–124, 247
3.39.5–6	124
3.39.16	95
3.39.16–17	61
3.39.17	122, 172
4.2.28	122
4.22	126, 127
4.25.1	202
5.8.2	61, 95
5.23	171
5.23–24	154
5.23–25	171
5.24	171
5.25	171
6.17	32
6.38	28, 42–43

Onom.
ed. Lagarde 1966 [1887]

all	94, 125
p. 301,28–34	30
p. 138,24–25	52
p. 172,1–3	59, 157

Theoph.
pp., ed. Migne, PG 24

4.22, pp.685–688	86, 122, 127–132, 249

Theophania syriaca

4.12	86, 122, 128, 133–135, 240, 246

Hippolytus
Haer.

7.33.1	29
7.34.1	19, 28
7.34.1–2	32
9.14.1	44
10.14.3–15.1	43

Irenaeus
Haer.

1.25.1	29
1.26.1	31
1.26.1–2	65
1.26.2	18, 32, 43, 47, 61, 123, 156, 158
3.1.1	21
3.3.4	34
3.11.7–8	21
3.11.8–9	123
3.21.1	21
5.1.3	22, 46, 154

Jerome
Comm. Am.

1.11–12	53, 68, 113

Comm. Eph.

5.4	92–93, 105, 108, 247

Comm. Ezech.

16.13	94, 99, 105, 107, 139, 246
18.5–9	99, 107, 109, 115, 202, 229–230, 247

Comm. Isa.

Prol. 65	98, 106–107
5.18–19	68
8.11–15	72, 76, 167
8.19–22	74, 114
9.1	73, 114, 118, 167
11.1–3	98, 106, 109, 134, 202, 226, 246
29.17–21	75, 114
31.6–9	72, 75, 115, 119
40.9–11	94, 98, 105, 139, 227, 246
49.7	68
52.4–6	68

Comm. Matt.

2.5	106, 109, 111, 250
6.11	106, 109, 114, 250
12.2	158
12.13	86, 101, 106, 247

23.35	106, 109, 111, 250	Dial.	
27.9–10	68	17.4	216
27.16	106, 109, 112, 145, 250	46–47	240
		46–48	18, 22
27.51	106, 112, 145, 166, 250	48	240
		88.3	156, 192
Comm. Mich.		88.8	156
7.5–7	93–94, 139, 246		
7.6	98, 105	Origen	
Epist.		Cels.	
5.2	103	2.1	25
18	166	5.61	26, 28, 63, 122
20	90–92	5.65	27, 29, 32
20.5	105	Comm. Jo.	
102	97	2.12	86, 94, 105, 137–139, 202, 227, 246
112	63		
112.13	68, 70, 97, 113		
112.16	70	Comm. Matt.	
120.8	166, 250	11.12	25
Pelag.		15.14	6, 86, 103, 139, 175, 201, 218, 249
3.2a	86, 88, 99, 103, 104, 107, 116, 218, 227–228, 230, 246, 248		
		16.12	25
		Comm. ser. Matt	
Ruf.		79	154, 172
2.22	55	Hom. Gen.	
3.6	55	3.5	25, 32
Sit.		Hom. Jer.	
143	68	15.4	94, 105, 139, 246
Tract. Ps.		19.12.2	32
135	106, 250	Princ.	
Vir. ill.		1. praef. 8	96, 106
2	95, 105, 145, 168, 178, 202, 250	4.3.8	25
		Hom. Jer.	
3	68, 95, 102–103, 127	15.4	94, 105, 139, 178, 246
16	95, 98, 106	19.12	25
116	91	19.12.2	32
Justin the Martyr		Plato	
1 Apol.		Thaet.	
26	55, 164	155d	204

GENERAL INDEX

Aaron, 40, 251
Abraham, 33, 35, 39–40, 59, 160, 163, 175, 188, 194, 198, 219, 221, 231, 249
Adam, 33, 39, 44–46
adultery, 124–126, 248
Akiva, 71–72
Alaric, 98
Alchibiades, 42–44
Alexandria, 24–25, 55, 67, 93, 138, 171–173
Alogi, 77
Ambrosius, 25
Ammonius Saccas, 24
Ananias (high priest), 52
Antidicomarians, 77
Antioch, 25, 58–59, 67, 78, 90, 93, 102, 138, 162
  conflict in, 55–56, 68–69
anti-Pauline, anti-Paulinism, 1, 19, 22–23, 25, 29, 32–33, 41, 43, 45, 49–50, 151, 163, 233–234, 241
  see also Paul
anti-rabbinic collections, x, 5, 78, 110, 114–115, 120, 138, 165, 173, 235–236
  reconstruction of, 103–120, 250
Apamea, 42–43
Aphrahat, 183, 185–186, 216
apocalyptic, 42, 235
  see also eschatology
Apollinaris of Laodicea, 71, 88, 90
Apostolic Decree, Council, 36, 54, 56
Aramaic, 42, 48, 78, 83–84, 91, 122, 126–127, 135, 140–141
  translation of Matthew's Gospel, 5, 87, 102, 118, 167, 173, 235
archisynagogue, 33
Aristo of Pella, 60

ascension, 55
Ascents of James (*Anabathmoi Iakobou*), 32, 38–39, 41, 43, 62, 162–163
ascetic, asceticism, 35, 59, 90, 103, 170, 206
Ashtaroth, 59
Asia Minor, 18, 124, 136
Augustine, 27, 63, 68–71, 97, 113

Babylon, 93
baptism
  "Christian", 11–12, 21–22, 30, 33, 39, 42, 45
  rabbinic, 12
  daily baptisms, lustrations, 11, 33, 39, 42
  of Jesus (by John), 20, 28, 37, 46, 61, 98, 109, 115, 137–140, 142, 156, 192, 202, 226–227, 230, 233–234, 238, 245, 251
  of John the Baptist, 61, 116, 138
Barabbas, Barrabban, 112, 114, 165, 167
Bar Kochba war, 50, 60
Bartholomew, 40
Bashan, 57, 59
Basic Writing (Pseudo-Clementine source), 36, 38–39, 41, 45, 77
Beroea, 50, 57, 59, 67, 78, 83, 95, 102, 127
Bethlehem, 93, 99, 106, 111, 250
Book of Elchasai, 28, 32–33, 41–44, 46–47, 49, 62, 150, 241
  see also Elchasai
borders (of community), 12, 21, 78, 197
bread, 42, 114, 168, 170, 249
  Eucharistic, 146–149, 154–155, 157, 168, 249–250
  unleavened, 33, 46, 154, 155

Caesarea, 25, 28–29, 42–44, 60, 95, 99, 102–104, 107, 127, 138, 171, 183, 233
canon, canonical, 3, 4, 6, 32, 52, 85, 89, 104, 120–125, 135–136, 138–139, 143–144, 150, 173, 238
canonical gospels, 3, 5, 13, 21, 37, 52, 85–87, 110, 117, 123, 125, 139–140, 143, 145, 151, 155, 159, 161, 163, 168, 173, 176, 178–179, 183, 190, 201, 203, 210, 212–213, 215–216, 218, 224, 240, 243
   canon tables of Eusebius, 181, 191, 221
   of Jewish scriptures, 36, 44, 47
   Muratorian canon, 121
   non-canonical, 4, 120, 135, 139, 210, 212, 223
   pre-canonical, 176, 194, 203
Carpocrates, 18–20, 29, 46
categorization, 9, 10, 66, 79, 235
Celsus, 28, 95
Cerinthus, Cerinthians, 18–21, 29, 31, 34, 46, 54–56, 62, 65, 69, 79, 156–157, 234, 238
Chalcis, 59, 90, 103
chiliasm, 124
Christ, 14, 19–21, 29, 32–33, 35, 37, 40, 42, 44–47, 52, 57–59, 61–65, 69–71, 73–75, 85, 94–95, 106, 118, 121, 136, 153, 156–157, 167–168, 233, 235–236, 240–242
Christology, 19–22, 45, 154, 202, 234, 238
   possessionist Christology, 20–21, 28, 44, 46, 62, 81, 156–157, 238
church order, 43
Circuits of Peter (*Periodoi Petrou*; Pseudo-Clementine source), 32, 38, 41, 43
circumcision, 11–12, 18–19, 21, 25, 28, 32–34, 36, 41, 44, 55–56, 65, 197, 233

Clement of Alexandria
   life of, 24, 83, 121, 136, 137
   tutors of, 138
   see also Index of Ancient Authors and Texts
Codex Bezae (D), 6, 145–147, 156, 158
Codex Sinaiticus (א), 87, 149, 182
Collyridians, 77
Constantinople, 90
Coptic Matthew, 3
creation (of the world), 40, 58, 63, 65
creed, 27, 70, 197
crucifixion, to crucify, 20, 33, 111–112
cursing, to curse, 53, 58, 68, 70–71, 78, 113–114, 118, 196
Cyprus, 22, 31, 43, 47, 150, 152, 163, 165, 237

Damascus, 30, 59, 163
Damasus (the Pope), 67, 90, 92, 165–166
Daniel, 33
David, 33, 35
Decapolis, 57, 59
Demetrius (the bishop), 24
demiurge, 19, 20, 65
Deuteronomistic (history), 117, 142, 143, 144
deuterosis, deuterotai, 72, 75–76
Diatessaron, 2, 15, 96, 127, 136–137, 175–176, 180–193, 201
   Arabic, 184–185, 216–217
   pre-Diatessaronic, 5, 132, 178, 192–193, 203, 212, 217–218, 223–224, 231, 236
   and the *Gospel of Thomas*, 7, 201, 216–217, 220, 223–225, 231, 236
Diatessaronic witnesses, xii, 2–3, 83, 96, 127, 178–180, 183–187, 189–191, 201, 216–217, 222–225, 231
Didache, 149, 157, 241
   see also Index of Ancient Authors and Texts

Didascalia Apostolorum, 30, 76, 125
  see also Index of Ancient Authors and Texts
Didymos Judas Thomas, 202
Didymus the Blind, 83, 86, 93, 98, 124–125, 246–247

Easter dispute (timing of Easter/Passover), 26, 29, 171–174, 234, 236
Ebion, 23–24, 31–32, 34, 36, 54, 60, 68–69, 80–81, 164
Ebionites, 18–49, 233–243, *passim*.
  Ebionites and the Hellenists, 47–48, 161–165
  see also *Gospel of the Ebionites*
Edessa, 91
Egypt, Egyptian, 30, 53, 55, 57, 83, 86, 93, 125, 136–138, 158, 200, 202, 203, 228, 236
Eighteen Benedictions, 53, 70, 78, 113
ekklesia, 51
Elchasai, Elchasaite, Elchasites (Elxai), 28, 33–34, 41–44, 48–49, 62, 78, 235, 241
  see also *Book of Elchasai*
Eleutheropolis (Beth Guvrin), 59
Elijah, 33, 35, 113
Elisha, 33, 35
Ephrem, 78, 91, 183, 185–186, 189, 216, 264
Epiphanius of Salamis, *passim*
  life of, 30–31
  and Ebionites, 30–49
  and Nazarenes, 49–66
eschatology, end-time, 19, 22–23, 28, 42, 124, 159, 235, 241
Eucharist, Last Supper, vi, 6, 21, 30, 33, 45–46, 145–146, 148–149, 151–161, 169–170, 233–234, 237, 262
Eusebius of Caesarea, *passim*
  life of, 29
  and Ebionites, 29–30
  Eusebius' canon tables, see canon
  and the *Gospel of Hebrews*, 120–137
Evagrius, 90

exemplars (cognitive), 9
Ezekiel, 33, 90
  Jerome's commentary on, 97–99
  see also Index of Ancient Authors and Texts

Farj, 59
fast, fasting, 170–171, 230

gentiles, 1, 11–12, 22–23, 26, 28, 36, 39, 41, 44, 49–51, 69, 74, 76, 114, 141, 166–167, 240
Gnostics, Gnosticism, gnosis ix, xiii, 8, 20, 24–25, 31, 85, 133, 140, 174, 200, 202, 205, 228, 230, 235–236, 239
Gospel of the Apostles, 100, 107, 115–116
Gospel of the Ebionites, 2, 235–243, *passim*
  Epiphanius' quotations from, 37–38
  Last Supper in, 145–161
  in the New Two Gospel Hypothesis, 3–5, 83–84, 235–243
  reconstruction of, 251–252
  in the Three Gospel Hypothesis, 1–3
  see also Index of Ancient Authors and Texts
Gospel of the Hebrews, 1–2, 235–243, *passim*
  in the New Two Gospel Hypothesis (N2GH), 120–139, 235–243
  and Q, 139–144
  reconstruction of, 245–250
  in the Three Gospel Hypothesis (3GH), 1–3, 83–89
  see also Index of Ancient Authors and Texts
"Gospel of the Nazarenes", ix, x, 2, 13, 194, 212, 235–243
  in the New Two Gospel Hypothesis (N2GH), 103–119, 235–243
  in the Three Gospel Hypothesis (3GH), 1–3, 83–103
  see also anti-rabbinic collections

Gospel of Thomas, 5, 7, 132, 133–134, 188, 236, 239
   and Jewish-Christian gospel fragments, 200–232
   and the Three Gospel Hypothesis, 83–89, 235
Greece, 25, 138
Gregory of Nazianzus, 90

Harclean Syriac (translations), 185
harmonizing gospel traditions, v, 5, 14–15, 125, 132, 134, 136, 139, 192–193, 203, 207, 210, 211–212, 217–218, 222–225, 229, 231–232, 236, 239
   gospel harmony, 15, 44, 137, 191, 210
Hebraica veritas, 78, 94, 108
Hebrew Bible, 23, 93, 118, 241
Hebrew gospel, gospel in Hebrew letters/language, 91–94, 98–100, 104–107, 127–128, 133–135, 226, 245–249, 252
Hebrew Matthew, 3
Hebrews, 21, 48, 163–164, 234, 237, 240, 242
Hellenists, Hellenistic, 47–48, 86, 157, 161–165, 234–235, 237–239, 241, 270
heresiology, heresiological, 25, 239–240, 242
   of Epiphanius, see *Panarion*
   of Hippolytus (*Refutatio omnium haeresium*), 19, 28–29; (*Syntagma*), 81
   of Irenaeus (*Adversus haereses*), 17–21, 29, 63, 65, 76, *passim*
   of Justin (*Syntagma*), 18, 56, 76
   see also Index of Ancient Authors and Texts
heresy, 4, 23, 26, 31, 51, 54, 69, 81, 239
   of the Ebionites, 24, 26, 31, 70, 113, 122, 172, 234–235
   of the Nasarenes, 51
   of the Nazarenes, 17, 49, 51, 54–55, 57, 62, 64, 77, 79, 119, 241, 242
Hexapla, 100

Hidden Power (*hayil kesai*), 42, 44
high priest(s), 34, 52, 169
Hillel, 71–73, 114
Hippolytus, 17, 25, 28–29, 31–32, 42–44, 54, 81, 123, 156, 235
   for *Refutatio omnium haeresium*, see heresiology
   see also Index of Ancient Authors and Texts
Hobah, 59
Holy Land, 93, 98–99
Holy Spirit, 37, 98, 106–107, 134, 142, 165, 226, 229–230, 238, 245–246, 248, 251
   as mother (of Jesus), 86, 94, 99, 105, 109, 137, 139, 141, 143, 202, 227–228, 238, 246
honor and shame, 103

identity, 10, 12, 21, 24–25, 51, 76, 79–81, 118–119, 194, 196–197, 240, 241–242
   social, 66, 79, 80
Ignatius of Antioch, 95–96, 106, 108, 123
   see also Index of Ancient Authors and Texts
indicators of Jewish Christianity, 6, 8–15, 19, 41, 117–118, 175, 195, 198, 233, 240
Ioseph Galilaeus, 71
Ioudaikon, 3, 87–88, 201, 212–214, 227
Irenaeus of Lyons, *passim*
   life of, 18
   and Ebionites, 18–24
   see also Index of Ancient Authors and Texts
Isaac, 35, 40, 160
Isaiah, 33, 90, 118
   Jerome's commentary on, 68, 71, 97–99, *passim*
   the Nazarene's commentary on, x, 68, 71–75, 77, 89, *passim*
   see also Index of Ancient Authors and Texts
   see also anti-rabbinic collections

Israel, Israelites, 25, 38, 71, 73–75, 111–112, 114–115, 118–119, 158, 167, 197, 252

James the Just, 23, 33, 39–40, 45, 48, 53, 60, 95, 106, 145, 163–164, 200, 202, 236–237
  Jesus' appearance to, 168–174, 249–250
Jeremiah, 33, 90, 178
Jerome, *passim*
  life and literary production, 67–68, 89–103
  and Nazarenes, 66–81
  see also "Gospel of the Nazarenes"
  see also Index of Ancient Authors and Texts
Jerusalem (Holy City), 18–19, 25, 33, 44–45, 55–56, 71, 75, 90–92, 102, 104, 110, 158, 165, 171, 173, 234
  early Jerusalem community, 1, 4, 11, 23–24, 26, 31, 47–51, 56, 60, 63–65, 79, 81, 157, 161–164, 199, 233–234, 237
  siege and destruction of, 13, 53, 57, 60, 67, 71, 118, 166
Jessaeans, 55–56, 58, 66
Joannes the Son of Zakkai, Yohanan Ben Zakkai, 71, 73
John (the apostle, the Gospel of), 34, 52, 65, 77, 121, 124–126, 133, 165, 191
John the Baptist, 37, 61, 107, 116, 138, 142, 144, 151, 156, 189, 213, 217–218, 227, 246, 251
Joseph, 32
Joshua the Son of Nun, 40
Josua, 71
Judaea, Judaean, Judah, Judea, 106, 111, 158, 250
Julia Mammaea (the empress), 25
Julian, 95
Justin the Martyr, 22, 25, 50, 55–56, 76, 156, 164, 192–193, 216, 223–224, 240

Karnaim, 59
Kingdom of God, 146, 149, 155, 157, 160, 186
Kingdom of Heaven, 176, 186, 209, 213, 215, 219, 229–230, 249
Kyrios, 11, 197

law, the Law (Jewish, Biblical, Mosaic), the Torah, 11, 14, 17–19, 26, 28, 34–37, 40–41, 44, 50, 55–58, 61, 64–65, 69–70, 72, 76, 78–79, 81, 131, 161–162, 166, 175–176, 181, 194, 195–199, 217, 221–222, 248
  the law and the prophets, 40, 76, 175, 180, 189, 195–196, 219, 221, 249
  law-free (mission), 11, 18, 33, 48, 69–70, 76, 117–118
  law observance, 11, 14, 22–23, 29, 32, 57, 69–71, 73, 76, 81, 11–118, 122, 154, 233–234, 240
  purity laws, food laws, 11, 25, 44, 197
law school (in Berytus), 158
Liège Harmony, 184
love commandment, 14, 177, 179–180, 195–198, 222

marriage (to marry), 33, 35, 44, 99
martyr, martyrdom, 95, 162, 163
  see also Justin the Martyr
meat, abstinence from, 33, 35–37, 39, 151–155, 159, 170, 173, 252
Medicine Chest, see *Panarion*
merchants, the critique of, 132, 222
  see also riches
minim, 27, 53, 113
  see also *notsrim*
Mishnah, 75
Moses, 11, 35–36, 40, 45, 47–48, 144, 153, 161, 163, 165, 213–214
  the law of, 11, 76, 189, 221, 248
Mount Gerizim, 36

Nag Hammadi, 205–206
Naphtali, 73, 118

GENERAL INDEX

Narcissus (the bishop), 171
Nasarenes, 51, 52
natsraye, 55, 66
Nazarenes, 49–81, 233–243, *passim*
  and Jerome, 100–103
  see also anti-rabbinic collections
  see also "Gospel of the Nazarenes"
Nazareth, 30, 52
notsrim, 53, 113

Old Latin gospels, 3, 100, 146–147, 155, 173, 187, 192, 210, 212, 216, 222
Old Syriac gospels, 5, 146–147, 155, 173, 182, 183–193, 212, 216, 222
oral tradition, 124, 231, 240
Origen, *passim*
  life of, 24–25
  and Easter dispute (Quartodecimans), see Easter dispute
  and Ebionites, 24–29
  and *the Gospel of the Hebrews*, 137–139
  Origen's *Commentary on Matthew*, 175–199
  see also Index of Ancient Authors and Texts
Oxyrhynchus papyri, 85
  see also Index of Ancient Authors and Texts

Palestine, 18, 25, 30, 43, 59, 68, 78, 93, 99, 108, 138, 171, 172
Panarion (*Medicine Chest*), 17, 26, 31, 53–54, 56–57, 60–61, 64–65, 67–68, 70, 77, 79, 81, 83, 113, 145, 151–154, 235, 242
  composition of, 30–31
  see also Index of Ancient Authors and Texts
Papias, 122–125, 135–136, 138–139, 172, 247
Parthian, 42
Paschal lamb, 153, 171
passion (of Jesus), 5, 7, 14, 144, 236
  traditions in Jewish-Christian gospels, 145–174

Passover, 26, 29, 145–146, 151, 152–155, 172, 174, 252
Paul, Pauline, 1, 11, 14, 18–19, 27, 31, 33, 48, 50, 52, 54, 56, 64, 68–69, 73–74, 76, 79, 93–94, 118–119, 120, 122, 146, 148–149, 157–160, 162–163, 165, 167–168, 196, 235, 239, 242
  see also anti-Pauline
Paula, 91, 93, 97
Paulinus (the bishop), 67, 90
Pelagius, 97, 99, 104
Pella, 57–60, 81
Pentateuch, 33, 35–36, 41, 47–48, 65, 164, 234
  see also Samaritan
Perea, 57
persecution, 24–25, 162, 206
Peshitta, 185, 188, 193
Peter (the apostle), 12, 41, 55, 68–69, 95, 116, 165, 168, 196, 220, 252
Pharisees, 70, 71, 73–75, 111, 113–114, 118, 169, 184, 213–218, 232, 248, 251
Philip (the apostle), 47, 124, 164, 165
Philo of Alexandria, 53, 86
Polycarp, 95–96, 106, 108, 123
polythetic classification, 9
poor, 11, 23, 25, 29, 33, 48, 60, 81, 123, 131, 143–144, 149, 175, 177, 181, 194, 199, 219, 221, 234, 249
prayer, 12, 19, 23, 40, 53, 58, 78, 110–111, 113–114, 157, 230, 233, 247
  see also Eighteen Benedictions
prebaptismal teaching, 196
preexistence, 22, 46
prophet, 11, 22, 111, 165
  Adam as, 39
  the True Prophet, prophet like Moses, 36–38, 40, 45, 47–48, 144, 153, 163, 165, 234, 237
prototypes, prototypicality, 9
Pseudo-Clementines, xi, 12, 32, 35, 38, 41, 45, 74, 140, 174, 217, 236–238

Pseudo-Tertullian, 17, 24, 54
purity (cultic), purifications, to purify, impurity, 11, 32–33, 36, 39, 44–45, 197

Q, Sayings source, xi, 5, 7, 139, 159–160, 180, 182, 204, 213–216, 224, 228
   and the Gospel of the Ebionites, 144, 235–243
   and the *Gospel of the Hebrews*, 139–144, 235–243
   see also Index of Ancient Authors and Texts
Quartodeciman controversy, see Easter dispute

Rabbis, rabbinic, 12, 71–76, 94, 101, 106, 110–112, 114, 117–119, 131, 166, 167, 242
   see also anti-rabbinic collections
Rabbula (the bishop), 78
riches, the critique of, 132, 200
   see also merchants
righteousness, 20, 35, 42, 64, 111
Rome, 22, 25, 42–44, 67–68, 90–93, 97–100, 104, 138, 171, 239
Rufinus, 55, 125

Sabbath, 11, 30, 32, 34, 36, 41, 65, 197, 234, 240
sacrifice, sacrifices, sacrificial death, 35, 45, 147–148, 150, 153–154
   critique and prohibition of, 6, 12, 33, 38–39, 41, 45–46, 48, 147, 151, 153–154, 161, 163, 165, 237, 252
Salamis, 31, 49
Salomon, 33
salvation, 26, 40, 133, 162, 205
Samaria, 47, 164–165
Samaritans, 36, 47, 48, 164, 165, 234, 241
Samson, 33, 35
Samuel, 33, 35

scribes, stenographers (assisting Origen and Jerome), 25, 103, 104
scribes (Jewish), 111, 227
scribes and the Pharisees, 71, 73–75, 111, 114, 118, 213–216, 217, 232
Seleukeia, 43
Semitic
   Christianity, 67
   gospel (traditions), 84, 89, 101, 103, 110, 112–113, 115, 121–122, 129, 137, 143, 198, 200, 225, 227
   language(s), language skills, 55, 67, 77, 96, 113–114, 159, 242
Septimus Severus, 24
Septuagint, 94–95, 101, 159, 241
Shammai, 71–73, 114
Shem Tob, 3
Simon
   the disciple (Peter), 107, 116, 176, 184, 186, 188, 198, 219, 230, 248–249, 252
   Magus, 54, 56, 81, 164–165
   son of Jonah (Peter), 176, 184, 186, 188, 195, 219, 230, 249
sin, to sin, 42, 74, 75, 87, 107, 119, 125, 218, 230, 246–248
Sion, 75
Siricius (the Pope), 92
snakes, 111
   snake bites, 33, 42
social identity approach, 66, 79, 80
   see also identity
Son of God, 70, 74–75, 114–115, 117–119
Son of Man, 148, 159, 168
Sophia, 228
spirit, the Spirit, 99, 106–107, 109, 115, 142, 156, 201–203, 228–230, 237–238, 247, 251
   see also Holy Spirit
Stephen, 47–48, 161–165
stereotypes, 51, 66, 79–80
Stridon, 67
suffering, 146, 159

synagogue, 30, 33, 35, 41, 44, 58, 68–70, 78, 111, 113–114, 118, 163
syncretism, syncretistic, 22, 43, 46, 140, 202
synoptic gospels ix, 5, 15, 38, 87, 115, 126, 129, 135, 137, 139, 141, 143, 153, 155, 157, 168–169, 180, 182, 185, 186–187, 191, 196, 203, 207, 208–210, 215, 218, 220, 222, 224, 227, 232, 237
Syntagma (of Justin Martyr), see heresiology
Syria, 13, 18, 30, 42, 57, 59, 76, 78, 83, 86, 95, 102, 137–138, 157, 202–203

Talmud, Talmudic, 53
Targums, Targumic, 72, 75
Tatian, 2, 15, 127, 137, 183, 185, 187, 192–193, 199, 201, 216–217, 239
  see also *Diatessaron*
Telphon (Tarphon), 71, 72
temple, of Jerusalem, 11, 57, 113, 148, 161, 166, 250
  critique of temple sacrifices, 33, 39–41, 45–46, 48, 151, 154, 162–165, 194, 234, 237
  destruction of, 41, 113, 115, 117, 151, 154, 167
  honored by Jewish Christians, 23, 48, 144, 164, 170
  of Samaritans, see Mount Gerizim
tertium quid, 77

Tertullian, 17, 24, 31, 52, 54
Tertullus, 52
Theodore of Heraclea, 97
Theophilus (the bishop), 171
Therapeutae, 55–56
Torah, see law
Trajan, 42
Transjordan, 42–43
Trypho, 156, 240
Two Document Hypothesis (Two Source Theory), 140, 141, 179, 181

"Urgospel" hypothesis, 140–141

Victorinus of Pettau, 98
virgin birth, 19–22, 25, 26–29, 37, 58, 63, 69–70, 122, 233–234, 238
Vulgate, 72, 73, 181–182, 222

water (Eucharistic), 21–22, 30, 33, 45–46, 154–157, 233–234
wine (Eucharistic), 21, 30, 36, 46, 113, 146, 149, 145, 155, 159–160, 170
Wisdom, 5, 133–134, 136, 139–141, 143–144, 200–203, 206, 226–227, 230, 237–238

yeshuaye, 55, 66
yoke, 73–74, 76, 118, 226

Zebulon, 73, 118
Zion gospel edition, 87

INDEX OF MODERN AUTHORS

Abrams, Dominic, 66, 79
Ådna, Jostein, 6
Aejmelaeus, Lars, 6, 148
Aland, Barbara, 158
    see also Nestle & Aland
Aland, Kurt, 158
    see also Nestle & Aland
Arnal, William E., 228
Asgeirsson, Jon Ma., xi, 7, 228, 255, 266
Attridge, Harold W., 204, 205, 217, 224

Baarda, Tjitze, 201, 212, 216, 222
Barth, Fredrik, 79, 80
Bauckham, Richard, 2, 41, 50, 63, 81, 151, 158
Baur, Ferdinand C., 1, 49–50, 140, 240
Becker, Adam H., 10
Becker, Ulrich, 126
Bellinzoni, Arthur J., 232
Black, Matthew, 193
Blanchetière, François, 1, 50, 55
Bless, Herbert, 47
Bovon, François, 182
Boyarin, Daniel, 9, 10, 240
Brewer, Marilynn B., 9
Brock, S.P., 187
Brockelmann, Carl, 91
Brown, Raymond E., 8

Caird, G.B., 145
Cameron, Ron, 139, 200–202, 205
Carter, Warren, 173
Cohen, Shaye J., 12
Crum, Walter E., 205
Cullmann, Oscar, 200

de Boer, Martinus C., 55, 64, 81, 113
DeConick, April D., 200, 228–229
Drijvers, Han J.W., 201, 224
Dunderberg, Ismo, xiii, 8

Edwards, James R., 87, 141, 157
Ehrman, Bart D., 148, 150
Esler, Philip F., 66, 79–80
Evans, Craig A., 2–3

Fallon, Francis T., 200, 202, 205
Fieger, Michael, 201–202, 205–206, 210
Fitzmyer, Joseph A., 147, 150, 206
Fonrobert, Carlotte E., 76
Frend, William H.C., 200
Frey, Jörg, xii, 2–3, 86–88, 116, 125, 134, 242
Funk, Robert W., 83

Goranson, Stephen, 52
Goulder, Michael D., 1, 50, 156
Greeven, Heinrich, 182, 184
Gregory, Andrew, xii, 13–14, 90, 117–118
Grobel, Kendrick, 200
Grützmacher, Georg, 104

Häkkinen, Sakari, xi, 24, 74, 76, 81, 156
Hakola, Raimo, xiii, 66
Halton, Thomas P., 91, 95, 102
Handmann, Rudolf, 13–14, 83
Harnack, Adolf von, 87
Hartin, Patrick J., 238
Haslam, S. Alexander, 9
Hennecke, Edgar, 2, 84, 87
Hennings, Ralph, 69
Hjelt, Arthur, 186
Hogg, Hope W., 184
Hogg, Michael A., 66, 79
Holmes, Michael W., 206
Horbury, William, 53, 113
Howard, George, 3
Huck, Albert, 182, 184

INDEX OF MODERN AUTHORS

Jackson-McCabe, Matt, xii, 6, 8–9
Jeremias, Joachim, 150, 159
Jokiranta, Jutta, xiii, 66
Jones, F. Stanley, xi, xii, 36, 39, 41, 43, 62, 74, 77, 158, 213, 217
Joosten, Jan, 3

Kartveit, Magnar, 36
Kee, Howard C., 121
Kelly, J.N.D., 59, 67, 69, 90, 93, 97–99, 101, 104, 108
Kiilunen, Jarmo, 182
Kimelman, Reuven, 53, 113
Kiraz, Georg A., 184
Klauck, Hans-Josef, 109, 137, 139–140, 169–170, 192
Klijn, A.F.J., x, 2–3, 8, 22, 26, 42, 52, 57, 59, 66, 70, 72–75, 83–84, 86, 88, 91, 93–96, 98, 99, 104–105, 108–109, 112, 115, 118–119, 124–130, 133–135, 140, 151–153, 157, 165–166, 168–169, 172, 175–178, 183–186, 194–195, 201–202, 204–206, 213, 219, 221, 245, 249
Kline, Leslie L., 232
Kloppenborg, John, 140, 143–144, 182, 238, 241
Koester, Helmut, 200–202, 208–209, 211–212, 232
Kollman, Bernd, 157
Kraft, Robert A., 8

Lagarde, Paul de, 30, 52, 59, 76, 125, 157
Lagrange, R.P., 112, 116, 166
Layton, Bentley, 204
Leloir, Lois, 184
Leppä, Heikki, 6, 160
Lewis, Agnes Smith, 184, 186
Liddell, Henry G., 205
Lüdemann, Gerd, 1, 23, 50, 60, 164
Lührmann, Dieter, 87
Luttikhuizen, Gerard P., xii, 42, 43
Luz, Ulrich, 131–132, 167, 179, 215–216, 228

Maier, Paul M., 120, 170
Malina, Bruce J., 8, 130
MacDonald, Dennis, xi
Marjanen, Antti, xii, 6, 8, 77, 140, 223, 229, 239
Markschies, Christoph, 2
Medin, Douglas L., 9
Metzger, Bruce M., 121–122, 137, 183, 193
Meyer, A., 2, 84
Meyer, Marvin, 228, 229
Mimouni, Simon C., 1, 2, 50, 63, 83–84
Morgan, Robert, 50
Murray, Robert, 8
Mustakallio, Antti, 6
Myllykoski, Matti, x, xi, 6, 20, 31, 147

Nautin, Pierre, 91, 92
Nestle & Aland, 146–147, 178, 181–184, 208, 210, 221, 268
Nicklas, Tobias, xii, 7
Niclós, José Vicente, 3
Nolland, John, 150

Oakes, Penelope, 9

Paget, James Carleton, 8
Painter, John, 24, 174
Parker, David C., 148, 158
Patterson, Stephen J., 201, 208–211, 215, 231
Pehkonen, Nina, xiii
Perrin, Nicholas, 201, 224–225
Pesch, Rudolph, 164
Petersen, William L., xii, 2–3, 83–84, 87, 147, 183–185, 192–193, 216–217, 220, 239
Pierre, Marie-Joseph, 184
Piovanelli, Pierluigi, xii
Pritz, Ray A., 1–2, 26, 50, 52, 63–65, 69, 72–73, 83

Quispel, Gilles, 5, 188, 200, 216, 218–220, 222, 224, 228

Räisänen, Heikki, xi, 6, 55, 162–163, 196
Reed, Annette Yoshiko, 10
Reinink, G.J., 22, 25–26, 42, 52, 57, 59, 66, 70, 72–75, 95, 118–119, 152, 175, 201, 219
Resch, Alfred, 13, 135, 178
Riegel, Stanley K., 8
Ritschl, Albrect, 1, 50
Robinson, James M., xi, 141, 143–144, 182, 216
Robinson, Gesine, xi
Rohrbaugh, Richard L., 130
Rosch, Eleanor, 9

Salo, Kalervo, 161, 182
Sanders, E.P., 161, 163
Schaeder, H.H., 52
Schäfer, Peter, 53, 113
Schenke, Hans-Martin, 3
Schmidt, Peter Lebrecht, 2
Schmidtke, Alfred, 50, 51, 64, 71, 73, 84, 87, 88, 90, 96, 116, 124, 127, 176–178
Schneemelcher, Wilhelm, 2, 84
Schoeps, Hans J., 51, 163
Schrage, Wolfgang, 209–210
Schröter, Jens, 2
Schürmann, Heinz, 159
Scott, Robert, 205
Segal, J.B., 78
Shkul, Minna, xiii
Sieber, John H., 210
Simon, Marcel, 8
Skarsaune, Oskar, 10, 30
Smith, Jonathan Z., 9

Strecker, Georg, x, 2–3, 8, 11, 83–88, 91, 96, 100, 108–109, 115–116, 124–127, 135, 140, 157, 175, 201–203, 219

Tajfel, Henri, 66
Taylor, Joan E., 8, 11, 59, 81
Theissen, Gerd, 162, 164
Tischendorf, Constantin, 87
Torjesen, Karen Jo, xi
Trigg, Joseph, 24
Tuckett, Christopher, xii
Turner, John C., 9

Uro, Risto, xii, xiii, 216, 228, 231

Van Voorst, Robert E., 38, 162–163
Verheyden, Joseph, xii, 8
Vielhauer, Philipp, x, 2–3, 83–88, 91, 96, 100, 108–109, 115–116, 124–127, 140, 157, 175, 201–203, 219
Visotzky, Burton L., 8
Vogt, Hermann J., 176–177

Waitz, Hans, ix, 2, 84–86, 96, 116, 169
Wilkes, A.L., 47
Williams, Francis E., 86
Williams, Frank, 35, 54, 56–58, 65, 77
Williams, Michael Allen, 8
Williams, S.K., 162
Wilson, Stephen G., 63